THE EDITOR'S TOOLBOX

THE EDITOR'S TOOLBOX

A Reference Guide

for Beginners

and Professionals

Buck Ryan and Michael O'Donnell

Iowa State Press
A Blackwell Publishing Company

Leland "Buck" Ryan is an associate professor and the director of the School of Journalism and Telecommunications, University of Kentucky, in Lexington.

Michael J. O'Donnell is an assistant professor of journalism, the University of St. Thomas, St. Paul, Minnesota.

Book design: Justin E. Eccles

© 2001 Iowa State Press
A Blackwell Publishing Company
All rights reserved

Iowa State Press
2121 State Avenue, Ames, Iowa 50014

Orders: 1-800-862-6657

Office: 1-515-292-0140

Fax: 1-515-292-3348

Web site (secure): www.iowastatepress.com

♾ Printed on acid-free paper in the United States of America

First edition, 2001

Library of Congress Cataloging-in-Publication Data
Ryan, Buck
   The editor's toolbox : a reference guide for beginners and
professionals / Buck Ryan and Michael O'Donnell.
      p. cm.
   Includes bibliographical references and index.
   ISBN 0-8138-1129-5
   1. Journalism—Editing—Handbooks, manuals, etc. I. O'Donnell,
Michael J.   II. Title.

PN4778 .R92 2000
070.4'1—dc21   00-029595

The last digit is the print number: 9 8 7 6 5 4 3 2

Dedication

To Anne, Austin and Nina, thanks for the time.
   —BR

To my father, who read the newspaper every night,
To Cindy, who cares deeply about newspapers today, and
To Frances and Dana, who we hope will make headlines tomorrow.
   —MO'D

__Contents

Foreword

Thomas Wolfe once observed that there is probably a genius in every high school class. He could have easily said there is also one kid who loves words and books above all else.

A few of these young wordsmiths migrate to careers working with the language. Most do not, steered away, I suspect, by uninformed counselors, anxious parents or their own suspicions about whether they can make a decent living.

It is a pity. For those who love words and have the temperament for editing, this can be a richly fulfilling and happy life. And yes, it can even be lucrative.

The eminent *New York Times* editor Bill Connolly believes there has never been a better time to become an editor. "That's because in our society," according to Connolly, "for whatever reason, engineers have always been more prolific than poets and artists. As a result our ability to deliver information far outstrips our ability to create and package it to make it understandable and useful and even entertaining—to do what editors do."

He is quite right. We need bright, thinking, competent editors to cut the vast information tangle down to size. Citizens need these editors, too, because Americans are weighted down by so much undigested information.

For those of you contemplating a life of editing or for those already on the trail, Buck Ryan and Mike O'Donnell will help you on your way. There's an old saying about traveling companions: The best ones help you find your way through every town. That's what these guys can do for aspiring editors. They can help you prepare for and handle any imaginable editing problem. They are your experienced traveling companions.

For Ryan and O'Donnell, editing is a lifelong craft built block by block by block. It is by no means some churlish sink-or-swim proposition. They will help you attack language that is sheathed in fatuousness, banality, pomposity and confusion and steer you toward clarity, brevity and accuracy. It is, in other words, a battle against concealment in favor of one based on simplicity and full disclosure.

For me, Ryan is the perfect guide. He lives in twin worlds of professional editing and academic teaching. The business of journalism and the training of journalists would be far better off if there were more Buck Ryans tirelessly building bridges between the two.

I first saw Ryan in action nearly a decade ago at a newspaper convention in Washington, D.C. At the time, I was struck by his common-sense approach to editing and his devotion to collaborative journalism and open communication. I have since worked with him closely on many projects, including one very successful one aimed at empowering and raising the visibility of copy editors at America's newspapers.

Ryan and O'Donnell are first-rate editors and teachers. You will see shortly that they write well, too. I believe you will find their work immensely useful.

After all, an editor's life may be somewhat anonymous, but it can be rewarding and important. Just look to Thomas Wolfe's dedication in *Of Time and the River*: "To Maxwell Evarts Perkins, A great editor and a brave and honest man, who stuck to the writer of this book through times of bitter hopelessness and doubt and would not let him give in to his own despair."

Done right, editing is a high calling indeed.

BOB MONG
Publisher, *Dallas Morning News*

___Preface

Stick close to your desks and never go to sea,
And you all may be Rulers of the Queen's Navee!
—W.S. Gilbert, H.M.S. Pinafore

You are uneasy; you never sailed with me before, I see.
—President Andrew Jackson

"Can you recommend a good editing textbook?"

We can't count the number of times we have been asked that question. The words flow with the trepidation of someone lost at sea. They have come from newspaper reporters promoted to assignment desks; from magazine writers moving to assistant editorships; from newsletter editors wanting to improve their skills; from professionals new to book publishing; from college students preparing to try out for jobs or internships; and from high school teachers and students new to school newspapers or yearbooks.

They have come from beginners eager to learn the basics and from seasoned professionals eager to improve their craft. They have come from people who knew that if they had excellent copy-editing skills, they could work in almost any city of their liking. Copy editing, especially at newspapers, is a land of opportunity.

Our answer was always the same: "We're writing one." And here it is. We have written this book to be a lifeboat for anyone on the high seas of publishing. Many a time we have seen serious errors in books, magazines, newspapers, newsletters and now websites. We aim to save you from those mistakes.

We have benefited from years of working as full-time and freelance editors. We believe that the best way to learn how to edit is through an apprentice-master craftsman relationship. Learning to edit well is a personal, human process. Being a good editor involves not just knowing rules, which you can find in many books, but also understanding human nature. Above all, it involves working closely with a good editor who is willing to help you improve.

What we offer here is a chance for you to sit alongside us and hear us think out loud as we work through copy, or crop photos, or lay out pages. We'll ask you to do work, as any mentor would. Then we'll explain word by word or move by move how we would have handled the same tasks. Precious few supervisors have the time, skill or inclination to teach this way. That's why a book like this is so valuable.

By taking this approach, we will help you develop a skill as important to an aspiring young editor as it is to a senior staff supervisor: the ability to critique a publication constructively. If you want to impress prospective employers with your journalistic skills, the most direct avenue is to show how you could improve their publications. If you are the boss and you want to move your publication forward, the quickest route is through constructive critiques. Whether it be words, sentences, paragraphs or pages, we will show you how best to take their measure, improve them or leave them alone, and explain in simple, convincing ways what is good and what could be better. The ability to critique someone else's work and to explain why something was changed separates the fine editor from the computer jockey. The difference lies not only in the quality of a publication but also in the quality of life in the office that produces it.

No one edits more words a day, or deals more with the challenges of our ever-changing language, than the daily-newspaper copy editor. No one works under more pressure to integrate words, pictures, graphics and design to tell compelling stories. If you can be recognized as an excellent newspaper copy editor, you can adapt those skills to the publications of your choice, from books to websites. Daily newspapers are the best training grounds for editors, and so newspaper work will be our point of departure for helping you learn the craft of editing.

Are you ready to set sail? Good, here's our map.

Chapter 1 presents a tale of a daily newspaper as it works through one of the 20th century's top stories. We can think of no better way to introduce you to the excitement and challenge of copy editing than to show you how a state-of-the-art newsroom handles a historic event. We also can think of no better way to outline the rest of our book. Considerate editors layer information so that busy readers can get the gist of a story by skimming along the top, looking at photos and graphics, and reading headlines and captions. If readers want more information, they can dive into the text and swim to the bottom of the last paragraph. We have designed our book with this approach in mind. You can get the gist of how to edit by reading only the first chapter. "Sidebar" stories provide you with more information on particular points, such as word choice or page design. Everything we discuss in Chapter 1 is explored in detail in the chapters that follow.

In Chapter 2, we take a closer look at the news values that guide editors today and how those values are changing. We discuss how news decisions are made and the importance of location, circulation, design and even page size. Then we go to the micro level and show how editors choose the right word, a decision based on knowledge of the subject matter, the writer's skill and the rules of grammar.

Chapter 3 discusses quotations and their special place in news presentation. Handling quotations requires all the sensitivity and acumen an editor can muster because quotes represent a special relationship between sources and readers.

As we explore language skills in Chapter 4, you will learn how to use a stylebook as your editing guide. Having both a stylebook and a dictionary at hand when you edit is essential. In keeping with our daily-newspaper orientation, we use *The Associated Press Stylebook and Libel Manual* and its recommended companion, *Webster's New World*

College Dictionary, Fourth Edition, published by Macmillan, a division of Simon & Schuster, New York. As the stylebook advises, if this dictionary doesn't address a particular point, we'll turn to *Webster's Third New International Dictionary*, published by G. & C. Merriam Co. of Springfield, Mass. When editing someone else's writing, you can run into disagreements. When the sea gets stormy, it's always important to know where your anchor is. These three books are the journalist's anchor. We'll talk from time to time about how stylebooks and dictionaries differ, so you can get a feel for how editing might be different at various publications.

In Chapter 5, we move from editing words and sentences to editing paragraphs and stories. Obituaries come first because there is no better way to hone your skills as an editor than to deal with writing considered so precious that people will clip it out and put it in the family Bible. In an obituary, every letter of every word has lasting impact. Put another way, make a mistake in an obituary and it will take you a lifetime to live it down.

Chapter 6 focuses on crime stories and other articles that, if mishandled, can prompt law suits against your publication. But rather than presenting legal arguments to win libel cases, we show how to keep your paper from being sued in the first place. We go beyond simply being legally correct and focus on how to apply a fairness test to stories that may accuse a person of wrongdoing.

In Chapter 7, we guide you through handling numbers in stories. Illustrating statistics through graphics presents editors with special problems, particularly when polling is used as a reporting technique. Here we talk about various types of infographics and when to use them. Infographics have moved from newspapers and magazines to web pages, but the concerns about precision remain the same.

Chapter 8 introduces the Maestro Concept. This team-based, story-planning process has captured the attention of journalists everywhere. Whether they work on high school newspapers, college yearbooks, professional trade magazines and newsletters, or major daily newspapers, journalists are using the Maestro Concept to make better publications. Here we explain the basics of maestroing—how to run "idea group" meetings, how to coach writers, how to handle maestro sessions and how to conduct constructive critiques.

Headline-writing skill separates the expert editor from the novice. In Chapter 9, we explain the "condense-and-patch" approach, the "seed" approach and other techniques for developing expert skills. If the page looks ho hum, busy readers may pass it by. In Chapters 10 and 11, we teach picture-editing and page-layout techniques that add spark to the published page. Visit a newsroom today and you'll see editors laying out color pages on the Macintosh, editing and sometimes producing infographics, sizing and cropping photos on the electronic picture desk and even preparing stories for online distribution. Knowing how to create visual impact is important to today's editors.

Finally, in Chapter 12, we turn to editing as a career. Today, with society awash in a sea of information, good editors are in great demand. Professional editors are bolstered by newsletters, magazines, websites, and media institutes. The American Copy Editors Society (ACES)promotes their professional standing. This chapter tells you how to apply for the professional editing job you desire; what to put in an application package is detailed here.

As we said at the outset, reading about editing is not the same as doing it. A unique feature of *The Editor's Toolbox* is the "workout," which we have included in many chapters. After reading about a topic, you can edit practice sentences and paragraphs, then compare your work with how we would have edited those passages. If need be, you can refer back to the discussion to look up an answer before you check our answer. You should have *The Associated Press Stylebook and Libel Manual* at hand as well as *Webster's New World College Dictionary*, current edition. To build your editing skills, a degree of repetition has been built in to these workouts. Consider them your training ship.

A book like this isn't the product of just one or two people. Many others gave of themselves:

For his research on presidential impeachments, thanks to Leland F. Ryan Sr. For their thoughtful suggestions on the manuscript, thanks to Mike Agin, University of Kentucky student media adviser; Bernadette Kinlaw, copy desk chief of the *Virginian-Pilot*, Norfolk, Va.; and Brahm Resnick, business editor of the Rochester (N.Y.) *Democrat and Chronicle*. For their help and hospitality amid history-making, thanks to the staff of the Lexington *Herald-Leader*, particularly Editor Pam Luecke, Managing Editor Tom Eblen, Photo Director Ron Garrison and Presentation Director Steve Dorsey. For their guidance and inspiration, thanks to Don Ranly, Daryl Moen and Brian Brooks, University of Missouri journalism professors; Larry Lowe, former Buffalo *Evening News* copy desk chief; and Mitch Dydo, *Chicago Tribune* metro copy desk chief. For her patience and understanding, thanks to Judi Brown and Linda Ross of Iowa State Press.

Are you ready to set sail? We can't wait to get started. Welcome aboard!

THE EDITOR'S TOOLBOX

1

Inside Editing

——

You can observe a lot just by watching.
—Yogi Berra

PART I: EARLY PLANNING

You are on the fourth floor of the building housing the *Herald-Leader*, a Knight Ridder newspaper in Lexington, Ky. On this Thursday morning, the newsroom's top leadership and select reporters have gathered in a conference room that seats its 26 occupants comfortably (fig. 1.1). Over bakery goods they will discuss President Clinton's fate at his impeachment trial in the U.S. Senate.

Thursday, Feb. 11, 1999

10:04 a.m.: Morning News Meeting Opens

Managing Editor Tom Eblen (fig. 1.2) begins the morning news meeting from the head of the table as his boss, Editor Pam Luecke, sits quietly down the table to his right. The first step is to get a rundown from section or topic editors on what stories look good for tomorrow's paper. City Editor Mary O'Doherty goes first, symbolizing local news as the coin of the *Herald-Leader*'s realm. Government Editor Angie Muhs goes next, representing the flip side of the same coin: public affairs. Regional Editor Liz Petros sees news running hot and cold: It is expected to reach 75 degrees today and snow tomorrow. When she offers a story slugged "Trashgate" about a device that snags trash floating down the

Cumberland River, Eblen quips that this article should not be confused with ones on the schedule, or "budget," for the Clinton impeachment trial.

Eight weeks earlier, on Dec. 19, 1998, the U.S. House of Representatives impeached Clinton on two charges—perjury and obstruction of justice—related to the Paula Jones sexual harassment case against him and to his subsequent grand jury testimony. The *Herald-Leader*'s front-page headline, like many others across the nation, screamed "IMPEACHED," and the news hit the American public with the force of a party balloon. The venerable CBS News network informed citizens of the second impeachment of an American president through a split screen showing the U.S. House of Representatives on one side and the Buffalo Bills football team in action on the other. After all, it was a special NFL Saturday telecast involving the New York Jets.

How could a monumental historical event be met with a yawn by so many Americans? One clue: Jones' suit against Clinton was filed on May 6, 1994. After four and a half years of print, broadcast and world wide web news coverage involving unsavory characters and disgusting details, any such story is bound to deflate, even if it has history written all over it.

How can journalists capture the historical significance of this event and, at the same time, reflect the mood of the country? On this Thursday, it's a question that will be answered in newsrooms around the world. For the *Herald-Leader*, the answer will lie on the first two pages of news coverage. But on what day will the story break?

At the morning news meeting, the roll call for Friday's paper continues with editors highlighting top stories from the state desk and the business section. The sports editor follows with his offerings, as does the features editor. The last to speak are representatives of photo and design. The photo assignment editor notes the probability of fresh or file photos, called "art," for the Trashgate, weather, and other stories, and he checks with the sports editor about the timing of an upcoming event, or photo shoot. The design guru, whose title is "presentation director," says he is focused on the Clinton story.

Fig. 1.1

10 a.m meeting. At the *Lexington Herald-Leader*'s morning news meeting on Thursday, Feb. 11, 1999, two dozen staff members plan for coverage of President Clinton's impeachment trial. (Photo by Ron Garrison)

Fig. 1.2

Daily critique. Managing Editor Tom Eblen leads a news discussion and then conducts a critique of the paper to wrap up the meeting. (Photo by Ron Garrison)

The Pecking Order

In this ritual that is played out day after day in newspaper newsrooms around the country, and in a surprisingly similar way in the rest of the world, an unstated, unofficial hierarchy becomes clear in the order in which staff members are asked to speak. Focusing on local news first is as common as leaving photo and design to last. This can cause problems. In 1994, when the Small Newspapers Committee of the American Society of Newspaper Editors decided on a slogan for the year, it was "Fix Local News—Or Die!" Local news is the fuel, whether the engine be high school and college newspapers, professional nondaily newspapers, or major metropolitan newspapers. The meaning of local changes with the audience, but whatever the publication, when there are great local news stories without great photos or outstanding design, it is often because photo and design are considered last.

10:10 a.m.: Call for Page-One Stories

Eblen calls for page-one stories for the Friday paper. Here is where the rating of previously mentioned stories and the jockeying for position begin. Section editors owe it to their staff members to push their best stories forward. But they do not want to lose credibility with their bosses by offering something they cannot deliver or by overselling something that would land with a thud on doorsteps tomorrow. Eblen puts planning on a toggle switch: one version of tomorrow's front page if the Senate votes tonight at Clinton's trial and a second version if it does not. The impeachment trial raises the stakes, but this is essentially the same game played day after day: contingency planning versus final decision making. The editors try to make as many concrete decisions as early as possible to focus staff members' workdays and move the production of the paper forward, yet they try to stay flexible enough to allow for last-minute changes. Good papers result from a multitude of small, good decisions along the way. At some point, inevitably, any decision will be better than no decision to ensure that the paper makes its various production deadlines and its final closing time before the press starts.

If the Senate votes tonight at Clinton's impeachment trial, tomorrow's front page will be covered with related stories. Unrelated local stories will get bumped off the front page and onto the first page, or "cover," of the local news section. Chances are that the story lengths and the number of related photos will be reduced because of space demands for the Clinton story packages. Assistant Managing Editor Tom Caudill uses the term "squished" to describe this inevitability. He invites discussion on which stories must run in the next day's paper and which could be held a day to ensure enough room to do them justice. If there is no Senate vote tonight, the scenario is reversed: Friday is the day to play up these local stories on the front page.

Planning under the no-vote-Thursday scenario proceeds. The first suggestion for Friday's front page is to give the opening of a University of Kentucky basketball museum big play. The second suggestion focuses on a columnist's discovery that the tradition of a local Kentucky Derby party will end this year. Eblen wonders out loud whether it is a good idea to use a columnist on the front page to break this kind of news. Only silence, not objection, follows. The third suggestion promotes a story about national champion high school cheerleaders from a rural Kentucky county who are boycotting a book tour that has come to town because they feel the author ridiculed them after having gained their trust. At this point, Editor Luecke observes that these stories would make for a "classic" front page in the Bluegrass region of Kentucky. The paper's goal, she says, is to reflect a sense of place.

News judgment is one of a journalist's most valuable skills. As we'll see in Chapter 2, what makes it so difficult to develop, or to teach, is its situational nature. A classic front page in this Kentucky city might be a clunker everywhere else in the world. What is considered a great story or photo in a news meeting may send the phones ringing off the hook with angry readers threatening to cancel their subscriptions. What is riveting to many journalists may be considered callous or sensational by some readers. On those days, life is lonely at the top for senior decision makers like Luecke and Eblen. They will hear many voices, but in the end they must listen to their hearts. It is there that the best news judgment takes place, not by any formula or in any focus group. Years of tough decisions build heart.

10:13 a.m.: Packaging the Clinton Story

The news meeting turns to coverage of President Clinton's impeachment trial and the front-page scenario if senators do vote tonight. Managing Editor Eblen asks staff members to express their ideas in turn. What he gets is how this national story can be turned into local news. "Find the local angle!" his predecessors have shouted for generations. These pros need no such prompting. Government Editor Muhs explains that Gail Gibson, the paper's correspondent in Knight Ridder's Washington, D.C., bureau, is bird-dogging Kentucky's two senators: Mitch McConnell, who might split his vote on acquittal, and Jim Bunning, who apparently cannot wait to nail Clinton on both counts. Gibson also is working on a story about reaction to the vote from Kentucky's members in the House of Representatives. The paper's higher-

Columnists these days rarely come up with "scoops," although celebrated columnists of the past like Walter Winchell regularly broke big stories. A column today is usually a platform for reflection on news and events written by a skilled reporter who has over the years earned the right to be paid for his or her opinions. The *Herald-Leader*'s Tom Eblen says that when he worked at the *Atlanta Journal and Constitution*, the newspaper's policy was to allow no breaking stories in its opinion columns. That led to some odd cases where columnists would write a straight story when they had a scoop, then write a sidebar column with their take on it. The belief was that news belonged in news stories. Beginning journalists often make the mistake of thinking that their first jobs, rather than their last jobs, will be as columnists.

education writer is looking at ways the impeachment trial is being discussed in college classrooms.

Looking ahead, Muhs says a "think piece" for Sunday's paper might involve how the impeachment trial has been very good for Sen. McConnell's visibility nationally. Sen. Bunning has not enjoyed the same media attention.

City Editor O'Doherty mentions the possibility of dueling columnists, something like "yes, people are bored with all this; no, they're not." O'Doherty says education reporters are working on stories about how schoolteachers and schoolchildren are using the trial for educational purposes.

Eblen explores a novel way to get the reaction of local residents in the paper, not the usual uninformed-person-in-the-street interviews or the I-am-a-Republican (Democrat)-and-I-hate (like)-Clinton comments. He and Luecke think the paper is headed toward convening people who had participated in an earlier newspaper poll on the impeachment case into a kind of news-reaction focus group. Unfortunately, the person they thought was handling this was not handling it. Alas, a dime for every time these words have been spoken in a newsroom: "For a communication business, we don't communicate very well." What follows is a gentle readjustment so that the editor in charge now knows she is in charge. No harm done. Eight people will show up for lunch Friday to talk about how the good economy has buoyed Clinton's popularity.

During the readjustment on the news-reaction group, a few comments focused on sampling for public opinion. If you go to a mall, one staff member says, the people you interview will be "self-selecting." How many people should we ask? "Six, it should always be six," someone says with confidence—and everyone laughs. What goes unspoken is that when it comes to doing serious public-opinion polling, many journalists are woefully underprepared and overmatched. Math anxiety may be one of the main reasons many people consider journalism as a career. Amateur researchers are dangerous to journalism. Smart journalists know enough to hire reputable research firms to do their polling. See Chapter 7 for further discussion.

Such is the way daily newspaper newsrooms work. Staff members weave around communication problems, step over cracks where story ideas fall through and climb hills to overcome shortcomings in expertise—and they publish every day. Magazine editorial offices tend to do similar gymnastics; they just operate on different timetables to serve different audiences. Something else is true for both types of publications: For every word heard in a planning meeting, dozens of behind-the-scenes actions have taken place.

The last one to speak in the managing editor's round table is Presentation Editor Steve Dorsey, who oversees graphics and design. He has the courage and persuasive talents to push design considerations to the front of newsroom negotiations when necessary. But this is not the time. When Eblen asks Dorsey for his ideas about tomorrow's paper, Steve replies curtly, "Just preparing for acquittal."

10:20 a.m.: What if . . .

The news meeting turns to a reality check at President Clinton's impeachment trial. For a news-reaction focus group to work tonight, the Senate would have to wrap up its vote by 5 p.m.

The Rush of Opinion

Editorial Page Editor
Vanessa Gallman is
involved in her own
impeachment/acquittal
planning. She has commis-
sioned a perspective piece
from former *Chicago
Tribune* Editor Jim Squires,
who was the *Tribune*'s
Washington bureau chief
during the time of Watergate
and President Nixon's resignation, and later served as
press secretary to Reform
Party presidential candidate
Ross Perot. Squires now has
a home in Kentucky.
Gallman struggles with finding the right balance of letters to the editor to publish.
Letters about Clinton could
easily dominate the editorial
page, drowning out local
and state issues. U.S. Sen.
Mitch McConnell of
Kentucky represents an-
other challenge. His office

The *Herald-Leader* is ready to go with an impeachment-trial front page for Friday's newspaper, thanks to Deputy Managing Editor Mike Johnson's negotiation with George Smith. Smith's job is to "book" the paper, or decide how all the demands for news and advertising space fit with the printing press configuration, especially for color positions. His name is spoken as though he is the newspaper's all great and powerful Wizard of Oz. As negotiations in the Senate on a compromise censure resolution upbraiding the president cooled yesterday, talks at the *Herald-Leader* heated up on the questions of how many more pages would be added to the paper for handling the trial coverage, where those pages would come from, and how they would affect color positions for every part of the paper. Moves in this game of dominoes are made with the grace of flying monkeys.

The first domino fell when Night News Editor Larry Froelich estimated last week that an additional four full pages would be needed to do the coverage justice. That would bring the overall number of pages with impeachment trial stories to 10. His estimate was based on national wire service budgets he had seen regarding stories in progress by Washington, D.C., correspondents and other journalists. The last domino fell like a petition at the feet of wizard Smith. What a newsroom wants is not always what can be done, and power—real or imagined—lies with people like Smith who know what can be done. An aura of power surrounds Smith and his counterparts at other newspapers because they stand at the wicked intersection of news space requests; advertisers' and sales reps' demands for certain pages, particularly color; and production considerations, including what is mechanically possible for presses and humanly possible or acceptable for people.

What does it mean to increase the paper four full pages? Well, for Froelich the goal is to have four more consecutive pages in the front section, or "A" section, to bring continuity and flow to the coverage. To Smith, however, going up four pages means adding two pages to the A section and, because of the way the printing press is configured, having to add two pages to the business section, where more space is not requested, desired or required. Making this kind of change also can throw off color positions on the press aligned with the sale of advertisements well in advance of a given day's newspaper. The four-page puzzle is eventually solved by a newsroom decision to hold coverage of the impeachment trial story in the A section to the front page of Friday's paper, then to devote the second section of the paper (called a "split A section," rather than a "B section") to a full report that will look like a special section of coverage. For one of countless times in the history of journalism, a mechanical limitation has driven an editorial decision: The front page of the paper will become a menu of stories to be read in-depth elsewhere. All this leads to one more unfortunate truth about editing: Just when you have made a major decision, be prepared to see it scrapped by reality.

The senators are taking turns speechifying behind closed doors. They had set time limits for each senator, and early calculations had suggested the possibility of concluding remarks later today, with votes on the impeachment charges some time tonight. Although contingency plans are in place for a historical front page Friday, no one seems willing to bet on a historical show of rhetorical restraint by the senators. It now looks as though the paper's best-laid plans are getting knocked over by wind. When the first few senators broke their time limits, recalculations began to churn. Right now the odds are much better that someone will have to go back to George Smith, scratch tomorrow's plan and start looking at how to book the Saturday paper for an additional four pages in the A section.

Circulation numbers for a typical Friday newspaper are higher than for a typical Saturday paper. If the Senate vote comes Friday rather than Thursday night, there will be far more mystery about whether the paper gets a bounce in its Saturday circulation numbers than in how President Clinton's trial will end.

For nearly eight weeks after Clinton's impeachment in the House, the U.S. Senate trial was a story with an ending in search of a middle and a closure date. Managing Editor Eblen had considered the story's name, or "slug," to be "Acquit," not "Impeach," almost since the House voted for impeachment. But when will the vote come? Editor Luecke predicts an early vote Friday so senators can catch flights home for the weekend break. That's the best guess yet. Eblen asks whether other acquittal-related stories are working. One reporter is trying to get a comment from "a schmuck in jail" who was convicted on charges similar to the ones President Clinton faces. This launches a discussion of why the newsroom switchboard should be alerted to accept collect calls. Inmates cannot use taxpayer dollars to call direct. "That's what all my prisoner friends say," one editor quips. "They have to call here collect."

Any other stories? The business editor foresees a possible story about how the financial markets will *not* react if President Clinton is acquitted. "They won't react unless (Federal Reserve chairman) Alan Greenspan is acquitted," someone jokes. Presentation Editor Dorsey mentions a piece called "10 Ways to Celebrate the Acquittal." Serious heads drop as though an inch was cut off the bottom of their chair legs. This is the kind of story that will get more readership than many serious editors would ever care to know. If the front page carries historical import, this could be a page-two story that attempts to reflect the mood of the American public. Eblen asks to see a copy of the story. Editor Luecke wants to see one, too. No other words need to be spoken.

10:33 a.m.: Critique Time with a Twist

The unusually long morning meeting takes a sharp, introspective turn. It is time to critique Thursday's paper (the sharp part). But more than that, it is time to look at the big picture (the introspective part). Managing Editor Eblen and Editor Luecke's goal is to make the Thursday critique session something different. They explain that is why everyone is in this new setting, complete with baked goods. Some professional journalists are legendary for their ability to find free meals, so offering food to get a staff member's attention is always a good move. Today's focus is the importance of anticipating news events, rather than just reacting to them or to the competition. The conversation will turn naturally to understanding exactly what the competition is and how to respond to it.

A decade earlier, in 1989, the same topics were receiving intense attention. At that time, Knight Ridder, Inc., which owns the *Herald-Leader,* had its so-called weapons laboratory in Boca Raton, Fla., running at full tilt in the form of the "25/43 Project." The goal was to reinvent *The News,* a small daily newspaper, in an experiment to assess how successfully a paper might attract,

(continued) told the *Herald-Leader* on Thursday to expect "for planning purposes" a 2,800-word commentary from the senator on Clinton's acquittal. The commentary, which will be sent by e-mail, translates to 80 column inches—fully two-thirds of a page—rivaling the lead news story on the event. In her position, Gallman must deal with the biggest egos, inside and outside the newsroom. Her new best friend: the world wide web. She ends up running excerpts of McConnell's commentary in the paper and the full text at the paper's website.

How It All Unfolds

What the reader sees as one newspaper page, a press prints as one page of a set of four pages. If you compare front and back pages, you will see that they have been printed at the same time. If there is color on one, you have color to use on the other. Now flip the pages over. See how Page 2 and the inside of the back page were printed at the same time? Are both black and white? See how that would make sense? What we see as four pages, the press sees as one big sheet with two sides. Four printing plates deliver images to the four pages we see. That's why the page count of newspapers moves up in increments of four pages.

satisfy and retain Baby Boom readers (ages 25 to 43 at that time). Meanwhile, senior editors at Gannett Co., Inc., owner of the *Herald-Leader*'s Kentucky rival, the *Louisville Courier-Journal*, were developing News 2000, the blueprint for Gannett's newspapers of the future. By 1992, Michael P. Smith, who had served as managing editor in Boca Raton during the project, and Mark Silverman, then director of News 2000, were teamed together for a presentation on the future of newspapers at the Michigan Press Association winter meeting. Silverman went first, outlining News 2000 with particular attention to understanding the changing nature of the newspaper industry's competition and putting a premium on anticipating change for readers. Among Silverman's points were the following:

- From 1950 to 1990, the population of the United States nearly doubled from roughly 100 million to 200 million; daily newspaper readership stayed virtually the same, rising from 50 million to 60 million copies a day.
- Newspapers can no longer see themselves in competition only with other newspapers. They are in an information business transformed in 1950 by television and now facing competition from niche magazines, newsletters and cable TV programs as well as online, multimedia and new media products.
- Newspapers can no longer be reactive. If reporters see a large housing development under construction, they should begin to project that five years later, when the paper may be running stories about parents calling for a new school in the neighborhood. That story should not be done only at a time of crisis. The newspaper should be proactive in helping the community stay ahead of that curve.

Smith followed with findings from the 25/43 Project. At first he shuffled his papers with a hem and haw. Afterward, he would confide, "Silverman said everything I was going to say." Here two titans in the newspaper industry, Knight Ridder and Gannett, after investing millions in research and brainstorming, had come to many of the same conclusions about how newspapers needed to change. Years later, the echo can be heard in the *Herald-Leader*'s critique session. Perhaps that should come as no surprise. One of Smith's colleagues on the Boca Raton project was Rick Press, who is now features editor at the *Herald-Leader*. When Smith was once asked what newspaper learned the most from the Boca Raton project, he replied the *Atlanta Journal and Constitution*. That is where Eblen had worked as a senior editor before he took the *Herald-Leader*'s managing editor post. The number of newspaper newsroom staff members around the country totals about 75,000. If that does not sound like a small world, consider this: In between his work as News 2000 director and executive editor of the *Detroit News*, Silverman was executive editor of the *Louisville Courier-Journal* for little more than a year. An old saw in the newspaper profession goes something like this: If you work five years in the newspaper business, you can walk into any newspaper newsroom in America and find someone you know or someone who knows somebody you know.

One common bond for journalists is likely to be their experiences with newspaper critique sessions, which have a long, harsh history. From high schoolers to the pros, the term "slash" has been known to replace the word "cri-

According to the Audit Bureau of Circulation, the agency ensuring as much truth as possible in a circulation game where high numbers can translate to big advertising dollars, the *Herald-Leader*'s circulation is 116,205 Monday through Thursday, 139,222 on Friday, 130,295 on Saturday and 158,113 on Sunday. The "Clinton Acquitted" paper was not a big seller at 130,298—only three more copies sold than the *Herald-Leader*'s most recent Saturday average.

Look up the Yiddish word "schmuck" in the dictionary. Would you use the word in a sex scandal story? Why would you not use it to describe any old jerk? For more information, see Chapter 4 on usage.

tique," as in, "You are invited to attend our 'slash' session." This sentence is spoken not only with a straight face but also with a sense of pride, apparently from the speaker's having survived—and learned from—so many of them. At the *Herald-Leader*, the critiques by Tim Kelly, who rose from executive editor to editor to publisher, are remembered for, let's say, their clarity. Today, Managing Editor Eblen begins with praise, citing three or four examples of how the paper had successfully kept readers a step ahead on stories ranging from an all-important tobacco settlement for Kentucky farmers to an all-fun preview of the Academy Awards.

Then he exhorts the troops to be more vigilant. He mentions how the paper got beat on other stories by the competition. He also explains how sloppy writing and proofreading led to information in a chart being different from that in a story; a map missing one of Kentucky's 120 counties; and a caption suggesting that a child pictured was the offspring of a crack addict. The last mistake is why newspapers carry libel insurance.

Eblen continues his critique, suggesting that the paper had been overusing the "collective we." He invokes Mark Twain, who he says once observed that only two kinds of people should use "we": editorial writers and people with tapeworms. Eblen objects to the use of, "We did a little handicapping," in an Oscar preview story. Rather than "we," he suggests using "the *Herald-Leader*." Features Editor Press disagrees and defends the use of "we" in this case. At this tense moment, a colleague suggests that both Eblen and Press are right. "Everyone knows," he says, "that most entertainment writers have tapeworms."

It has been a long meeting. Editor Luecke steps in with a voice of reason: "Breeziness, writing with a voice or an attitude is fine," she says, "but we should use these devices sparingly."

Eblen opens the discussion to larger issues. Features Editor Press takes the lead.

"We shouldn't be so concerned about how stories get played in the *Courier-Journal*," he says. "We're the only ones who care about that. They're not our competition. Television is our competition. What, only 3 percent of our readers also read the *Courier-Journal*? One hundred percent watch TV. We should celebrate when we beat TV."

He ended with one line too many for some of his colleagues. They scoffed at the idea of television news being a serious competitor, except maybe in crime news or in enterprise stories.

"TV beats us enough," Luecke says.

Eblen compliments Press for making a good point.

"TV should be our main competition," Eblen says.

Press is on a roll: "If we are in tune with what television is doing, we will be able to show our value to our readers by doing a better job on the same stories. People will trust us more. That's a way to draw people back to reading newspapers."

Eblen shifts the discussion of television from competitor to collaborator. He updates the staff on the paper's experiment with providing WKYT-TV, the local CBS affiliate, with summaries of top stories in the next day's paper so they could be promoted by the broadcast anchors in a brief segment of the 11 o'clock news. The broadcast station wins by adding a few items to the newscast; the paper hopes to benefit from increased readership arising from the promos.

Breaking the Glass Ceiling

Pam Luecke is the first woman to be editor in the *Lexington Herald-Leader*'s history, which dates back to 1860 for the Herald (morning paper), 1888 for the Leader (afternoon) and 1983 for the *Herald-Leader* (morning). She hired the first African-American journalist to be editorial page editor, Vanessa Gallman, from Knight Ridder's Washington, D.C., bureau. Elsewhere in America, women and minorities remain underrepresented in newsroom leadership positions.

Readers Love—not Buy—It

After a decade of Gannett's experimenting with News 2000, Knight Ridder's playing out the 25/43 Project innovations and other newspapers and newspaper groups' following suit or making their own changes, one thing appears clear: A newspaper can increase its readers' satisfaction, but that does not necessarily mean that more readers will buy more newspapers. The time is right for the next grand experiment. Maybe you will lead it.

The collaborative venture is so new, suspicion is still in the air. One staff member wonders whether the *Herald-Leader* is providing a tip sheet to the station that might result in a television reporter doing a story that makes the paper's story look old.

"That better not happen," Eblen says, "or we'll stop doing it." He explains that the agreement was that the anchors would only read the promos, which arrive at the station late enough that it would be difficult to match the story anyway. If the station wanted to do a follow-up story the next day, Eblen says, that would be OK. Television the enemy becomes television the partner in a strategic alliance. In Chapter 12, we'll discuss other partnerships, including the world wide web.

Is this something new? Dial back a decade. N. Christian Anderson, then editor of the *Orange County Register*, is sitting in his office watching a new local 24-hour cable news program, not CNN but OCN, developed in his newspaper building by his own company.

"Aren't you afraid of losing readers?" he is asked.

"No," he says, "we're just whetting their appetites." Television the competitor becomes television the teaser.

In the late 1980s and early 1990s, the rhetoric was heavy in the air: Look at what happened to the railroad industry when it clung to its shiny engines rather than realizing it was in the transportation business. Newspaper editors were described as clinging to their shiny printing presses rather than viewing themselves as holding the franchise for local news in an information industry. By the mid-1990s, the rhetoric had given way to action at newspapers large and small.

In 1995 the Inland Press Association, the largest independent newspaper association in the country, began the Inland Innovation Awards in cooperation with the School of Journalism and Telecommunications at the University of Kentucky. For the first time, Inland member newspapers competed in categories called "New Technologies" and "Strategic Alliances."

The *Edwardsville Intelligencer* in Edwardsville, Ill., submitted an entry involving only a videotape and a CD-ROM disc. It and another small paper, the *Hunterdon County Democrat* in Flemington, N.J., won for producing public affairs shows for their local cable television provider. Newspaper the competitor had become a television programmer.

The *News-Sentinel* in Ft. Wayne, Ind., won for "talking trading cards," using audiotext to add dimension to baseball cards printed in the newspaper. Fans could call the newspaper and hear a recording about their favorite player.

The *Chicago Tribune* won for launching the "Good Eating" section in the newspaper and supplementing it with a cable television program and online services. Out of the '80s anxiety surrounding newspaper readership trends, the '90s had become the decade in which newspapers looked at television and technological advances, including the world wide web, and began to say, "If you can't beat 'em, join 'em."

10:37 a.m.: Morning News Meeting Ends

After the unusually long 33-minute meeting, Editor Luecke sees Publisher Kelly in the hallway.

The Dangers of Criticism

Publication critiques are high-risk exercises. Fragile egos or strong opinions often get in the way of learning. One technique is to only accent the positive publicly and to deal with the negative privately and individually. In his seminal 1936 book, *How to Win Friends and Influence People*, Dale Carnegie wrote: "Criticism is futile because it puts the person on the defensive and usually makes him strive to justify himself. Criticism is dangerous, because it wounds a person's precious pride, hurts his sense of importance, and arouses resentment."

Carnegie's point is not that you should ignore mistakes or not help someone to improve. The problem is, as he puts it, "ninety-nine times out of a

(*continued*)
hundred, people don't criticize themselves for anything, no matter how wrong it may be." That means criticism is far more likely to lead to counterproductive resentment than it is to correct the problem. To have people learn more rapidly and retain what they learn more effectively, Carnegie suggests that positive rewards be used to reinforce desirable practices.

Another critique technique, outlined in the Chapter 8 discussion of the Maestro Concept, is to have journalists working in teams create a list of goals for evaluation—in this case, readers' questions—before they begin their work. They then review that same list after their work is done to see how many goals were achieved. The Maestro Concept takes Carnegie's advice on positive reinforcement and encourages the use of "Bravo! Boards" to celebrate success in implementing the concept.

"What's the latest?" Kelly asks.

"I don't think they'll vote today," Luecke says of the U.S. senators. "I'm betting on tomorrow."

Kelly, miffed that the senators had voted to close the impeachment trial to media coverage, says: "Of course, that will give the senators one more round of talk shows. I can't believe it—all these senators saying on television what they couldn't say publicly because the trial is closed."

For a newsroom that includes an online operation that broadcasts the local CBS affiliate's 6 o'clock news live to desktop computers, this will not be the last discussion of how television changes the definition of news, when it breaks and how.

In the end, the *Herald-Leader*'s edition of Friday, Feb. 12, 1999, opens with the "Bluegrass classic" front page, displaying "a sense of place" and previews the Senate vote (fig. 1.3).

PART II: ACQUITTAL DAY

Discussion of American history has a way of reducing a president's lifetime to an item or two. For President Clinton, one item will surely be his impeachment, which happened eight weeks earlier. If he is lucky, a second will happen today, Friday, when he is acquitted in the U.S. Senate.

Before he was exhumed journalistically during the Clinton impeachment debate and many were reminded of his acquittal in the U.S. Senate in 1868, President Andrew Johnson had been reduced to just his impeachment in many news stories. A 1999 poll conducted by The Freedom Forum foundation suggests that history will repeat itself. Of the top 100 stories of the 20th century, according to the poll of prominent journalists and scholars, Clinton's impeachment will rank No. 52. His acquittal will not make the list. Discussion of journalism history has a way of reducing a newspaper to a front page or two. How much have you ever seen of America's first newspaper, *Publick Occurrences*? Just the front page? For many, the *Chicago Tribune* has been reduced to a "Dewey Defeats Truman" headline. Does a picture of a beaming, just-re-elected Harry Truman come to mind? He is holding up one edition that *Tribune* editors wish they could have back. The *Herald-Leader* newsroom today, like its counterparts around the country, is running on dual engines: one powered by the energy to produce a historical front page and the other fueled by the anxiety reflected in Pam Luecke's wry comment: "I just hope we don't screw it up."

Friday, Feb. 12, 1999

10:03 a.m.: The Early News Meeting

Managing Editor Tom Eblen convenes the 10 a.m. news meeting (fig. 1.4), just like Thursday. Only this time, the newsroom's leadership has gathered in the usual conference room, and gone are the doubts about what will happen and when in the U.S. Senate impeachment trial. Eblen asks for a roll call of top stories not Clinton related for the Saturday paper. The focus first is on the front pages of the inside sections. The names of the sections are written on a marker board, and the slugs of stories are added as the meeting progresses. Asterisks by story names mean photos are available. A special meeting to discuss the Clinton sto-

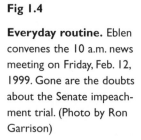

Fig 1.4

Everyday routine. Eblen convenes the 10 a.m. news meeting on Friday, Feb. 12, 1999. Gone are the doubts about the Senate impeachment trial. (Photo by Ron Garrison)

Fig 1.5

Sunday planning.
Assistant Managing Editor
Tonnya Kennedy takes over
for Eblen at the Friday
meeting to lead the same
group in planning the
Sunday paper. (Photo by
Ron Garrison)

ries will follow this one after a critique of today's paper. The section fronts of that paper and yesterday's flank the marker board to provide context for the critique.

Assistant Managing Editor Tonnya Kennedy takes over for Eblen to lead the same group through her primary responsibility, the Sunday paper (fig. 1.5). Planning has been in the works for days for some stories, weeks for others. The big lesson here: If you want an outstanding publication, you cannot concentrate on just one issue at a time. The quality of planning defines the quality of the publication, from high school newspaper staff working on issues twice a year to magazine staff working on Christmas issues in June. For Kennedy, now is the time to double-check how the Sunday paper will follow up the Clinton acquittal story (a page-one analysis will appear). Sunday papers get special treatment because they usually have the highest readership of the week and represent one of the few bright spots in newspaper circulation trends. Another difference from weekdays is that Sunday stories tend to run longer. Editors need to guard against confusing the length of a story with its depth of insight. As one editor who deliberated on Gannett's News 2000 program put it: "The problem with newspapers is not the long story that's long. It's the short story that's long."

12:16 p.m.: The Acquittal Vote

Wire editors at the *Herald-Leader*, as well as their counterparts around the nation and the globe, see a steady stream of updates from Associated Press reporters and editors as the senators vote (fig. 1.6).

Newspapers like the *Herald-Leader* have access to several wire services, ones generated by newspaper groups or other agencies, such as Reuters or Agence France-Presse. But none has shaped American journalism like the Associated Press (AP), which has delivered news to its clients over the last 150 years. Today, AP's news comes silently in the hum of computers. As late as 20 years ago, AP wire machines would have been ringing in the news (ding, ding, ding) as the Teletype machines hammered out words (chunk, chunk, chunk). The more bells and the fewer words, the more important the story. A "flash" might read simply, "Pope shot." After all, how much more do you need to know to start tearing up page one? A notch down in volume and up in words would be a "bulletin." A story marked "urgent" might or might not be urgent depending on whether you were interested in it. Today, "AP News Alerts" arrive silently. What newsrooms have lost in romance they have gained in efficiency. One AP wire practice that transcends the decades, however, is the time stamp for stories. Can you tell the times the news items in figure 1.6 moved on the wire? For a clue, think military time: 1100 is 11 a.m., 1200 is noon and 1300 is 1 p.m.

Another tradition involves moving breaking news stories in pages, or "takes." In the precomputer era, this was done at the typewriter, and every newsroom had a legend about an overanxious city editor who ripped a page out of a slowpoke reporter's typewriter and announced "30," or that the story was finished. Wire editors will see "writethrus," extended or rewritten versions of an AP story, that follow the first take (fig. 1.7). The second version will be marked "first lead writethru," the third version "second lead writethru," and so on until the end of the revisions or the end of a 12-hour cycle. Using Eastern time from the AP's New York headquarters, the PM cycle begins after midnight and works for afternoon, or "p.m.," newspapers. The AM cycle begins after noon and works for morning, or "a.m.," newspapers.

The Clinton acquittal story will hit as the cycles turn from p.m. to a.m.—bad news for the managing editor of a morning paper who wants a fresh

Fig. 1.6

Hot AP wire. The Associated Press sends alerts to update editors as U.S. senators vote at Clinton's impeachment trial.

```
@body copy:
<*J><B>BC-APNewsAlert<B>
<*J>Clinton assured of acquittal on perjury article; "no" votes
surpass one-third of Senate.
<*J>AP-CS-02-12-99 1216EST
<*J>


@body copy:
<*J><B>BC-APNewsAlert<B>
<*J>Clinton assured of acquittal on obstruction of justice article;
"no" votes surpass one-third of Senate.
<*J>AP-CS-02-12-99 1232EST
<*J>


@body copy:
<*J><B>BC-APNewsAlert<B>
<*J>Senate declines to vote on censure today.
<*J>AP-CS-02-12-99 1308EST
<*J>


@body copy:
<*J><B>BC-APNewsAlert<B>
<*J>President Clinton says he's "profoundly sorry"
<*J>AP-CS-02-12-99 1440EST
<*J>
```

```
@body copy:
<*J><B>PM-Clinton-Impeachment, 10th Ld, a0612,120<B>
<*J><B>URGENT<B>
<*J><B>Senate acquits Clinton of perjury<B>
<*C><B>By LARRY MARGASAK<B>
<*C><B>Associated Press Writer<B>
<*J>WASHINGTON (AP) — The Senate today acquitted William
Jefferson Clinton of perjury, nearing the end of a 13-month drama
that catapulted an affair with a White House intern into only the
second presidential impeachment trial in history. The 42nd
president was poised to finish his term in office.
<*J>Senators voted 55-45 to reject the perjury article, with 10
Republicans joining all 45 Senate Democrats in acquittal. "Not
guilty as charged," Chief Justice William Rehnquist declared.
<*J>A smaller margin was expected to reject a second article of
impeachment charging Clinton with obstruction of justice.
<*J>Both charges would have required 67 votes for conviction, a
threshold that senators have known for weeks would not be met.
<*J><B>MORE<B>
<*J>AP-CS-02-12-99 1225EST
<*J>
```

front page. "Tell me something new" is a steep challenge from a newspaper reader who has heard the story at noon on radio or television, then has seen it again on the 6 o'clock and 11 o'clock TV newscasts. Of course, that does not include what the readers might see or hear online or on late-night news or talk shows. At the *Herald-Leader*, Managing Editor Tom Eblen will be looking for ways throughout the day "to advance" the story so it does not look so old Saturday morning.

The Quiet Traditional Newsroom

Reporters and editors will take a break to get their news about President Clinton's acquittal live from television (fig. 1.8). After the vote, a voice calls out, "Hey, did you hear the president was acquitted?" A lone laugh echoes through the barely occupied newsroom. That silence you hear arises from the death of many afternoon newspapers in America, and gone with them are some of the best hours copy editors ever worked: 7 a.m. to 3 p.m. with most of the work done before lunch. If the afternoon papers were not in the hands of the lunchtime crowd, the circulation director would have been furious. This story is breaking for an afternoon paper's deadline, a statement that would have been spoken with urgency 50 years ago. Today the speaker might politely hold back a yawn. Only a relatively few afternoon papers still exist, mostly because of tradition or joint operating agreements with morning papers. Rarely is there still fiery competition among two newspapers in a town, let alone with one reveling that a big story like this one is breaking at this time.

The Busy Online Newsroom

For a glimpse at the hectic afternoon newspaper newsroom of the past, turn to the modern American afternoon paper, the online edition. New World

Fig. 1.7

Writethrus. When the vote is complete, the story moves on the AP wire in "takes," a few paragraphs at a time, and in "writethrus," or updated stories.

The Niche Mentality

To a successful market-driven magazine editor, a freewheeling discussion of who is the competition would be remarkable. The senior executives would have demographic and psychographic information on typical readers and a strong feeling about what niche their magazine fits relative to its competitors. That information would drive advertising, editorial and circulation strategies, the three legs of the magazine stool.

Over the last 50 years, newspapers have become more like magazines in writing, design and market strategy. They have changed in keeping with several forces: the splintering of radio stations into niches; the growth of network and cable television channels; a boom in the specialized magazine market; the rise of high-priced, narrowly focused newsletters; and now the availability of news and information on the world wide web. Newspaper executives have become more marketing focused. Editors speak the same marketing mantra: "We're not in the newspaper business; we're in the news and information business."

(continued on page 21)

Editor Malcolm Stallons had alerted the *Herald-Leader*'s online users that they could patch their computers over to pick up live C-SPAN TV coverage leading up to the acquittal vote. When news of the Senate vote broke on the Associated Press wire, Stallons hurried to edit that story for the online newsroom. He then updated the coverage repeatedly, including a photo of President Clinton giving his response at the White House. That is the kind of old-world flurry you would have seen in 1950s newsrooms when, as one old-timer recalled, someone could attend a fight at Madison Square Garden in New York City and then pick up a paper to read about the results on the subway ride home that night.

Online users will see coverage of Clinton's acquittal Friday, 17 hours before the newspaper typically will arrive on doorsteps by 6 a.m. Saturday (fig. 1.9). Online publications have the edge over traditional newspapers not only in their speed and flexible publication schedule but also in the lack of limitations on story lengths and availability of space to run color photos or graphics. Like traditional broadcast news outlets, they bring the power of audio and video to help tell stories. But online publications are not bound to regularly scheduled editions or newscasts. Online editors publish repeatedly in stages by building the backbone of a story and then adding text, audio and visuals, and links to related websites.

For instance, Stallons plucks a photo of President Clinton off the wires and adds it to the online front page along with an updated story from the Associated Press (fig. 1.10). This kind of change is reminiscent of the "rolling replates" that newsrooms used to do in between multiple editions of the paper. These traditions made more practical and financial sense in an era of competition among newspapers. When the cost of these pull-your-hair-out practices were weighed against the success of beating radio and television on breaking news, they were gradually dropped. Today, many papers like the *Herald-Leader* are down to two editions a few hours apart, an early one to reach outlying areas and a late one to be delivered closer to home.

Fig. 1.8

Quiet traditional newsroom. Reporters at the *Herald-Leader* catch up on coverage of the trial by watching television Friday afternoon. (Photo by Ron Garrison)

The View from the Top

Herald-Leader Publisher Tim Kelly watches television coverage of the U.S. Senate vote (fig. 1.11). He is living his boyhood dream of running a newspaper in the state where he grew up. His advice to young people is that to move up the ladder sometimes you have to move the ladder. For Kelly those moves were as a senior newspaper editor in Los Angeles, Denver and Dallas. A copy editor and wire editor in his day, he rescued one of the old AP wire machines from the trash heap and keeps it in his office as a conversation piece.

Kelly has seen reporting and editing move from paper, pencil, typewriters and Linotype machines to computers, online publications and direct-to-plate production. He oversees not only the newsroom, where his heart still resides, and the editorial pages, where he has a voice, but also advertising, marketing, circulation, production and the business office. He is in charge of many things but really just one thing: the bottom line. For him, like his counterparts around the country and the world, the future of newspapers is no theoretical debate. Kelly and those like him are determining the future with every managerial move. They are usually direct.

"People keep asking me my mission," said one publisher, tired of consultants. "My mission is to sell every damn paper I can."

Is going online the answer to reversing readership trends and dealing with high production costs? At most places like the *Herald-Leader*, the question about online success is not about how much money you are making but how little you are losing. Is the newspaper industry's attempt at online publishing a financial house of cards that will come crashing down? Or is online journalism the same kind of money-loser that FM radio was in its early days? For the really big decisions, you need publishers.

2 p.m.: The Copy Desk

Copy Desk Chief Amy Butters arrives for work at 2 p.m. (fig. 1.12) ahead of her night copy editors, who will arrive in staggered shifts to cover the

Fig. 1.11

Publisher's view. *Herald-Leader* Publisher Tim Kelly watches television coverage of the U.S. Senate vote in his office. (Photo by Ron Garrison)

Figure 1.12

A long day. Copy Desk Chief Amy Butters gets down to work early, before her night copy editors arrive in staggered shifts. (Photo by Ron Garrison)

(continued from page 17)

The heart of what makes newspaper people who they are, however, has little to do with a marketing orientation. Die-hards believe passionately that newspapers represent a higher calling. They believe newspapers are big enough to invest heavily in telling stories about righting the wrongs that oppress the disadvantaged, oblivious to whether that kind of reporting will increase circulation or whether a wealthy core-reader market is being served. Marketing strategies mesh in radio, television, magazines, newsletters and the web; they still clash in newspapers, though the resistance is waning.

paper's first edition and its late edition. She is ready to implement her plan for assigning stories to copy editors who will handle the Clinton coverage and the other stories in the news section of the Saturday paper. For days now, she has solicited headline ideas for the Clinton acquittal story, has posted the suggestions for review by the newsroom staff and has talked with her staff about this big day. Like many of her counterparts around the country, she is short of staff. On this day, the *Herald-Leader* is down five copy editors, one in sports and four in news. It's bad news for the team carrying today's copy load, but good news for any aspiring copy editor with talent. The copy desk is a land of opportunity.

4:03 p.m.: The Everything-But-Clinton Meeting

Longtime copy editor John Ireland runs the first afternoon news meeting (fig. 1.13), which focuses on everything but the Clinton acquittal stories. He will be in charge of getting these stories wrapped up and into the paper early. At the daily 4 p.m. news meeting, there are listeners and there are note-takers. The listeners attended the 10 a.m. news meeting, heard the rundown before and are in the last few hours of their workday. The note-takers are attending the first news meeting of their night shift and are the ones who will see the paper through to completion.

The traditional newsroom operates like an assembly line. A newsroom night shift picks up the chassis created by the dayside staff and completes the newsprint vehicle. Unfortunately, this is not always the best method to produce high quality. The Detroit automotive industry learned this the hard way in the 1980s before it began to adopt the project-based, teamwork-intensive approach to continuous improvement that had helped its Japanese rivals to succeed in the American marketplace. The Total Quality Management revolution is only beginning to take place in tradition-bound newspaper newsrooms.

If the *Herald-Leader* had moved off the assembly line and toward project-based teamwork, how might the newsroom have operated? Well, imagine if a team had been assigned earlier this week to produce 10 pages of Clinton acquittal stories. Having met to lay out their plan yesterday, they could have started today at 10 a.m. By 6 p.m. they would be winding down the project and be ready to head home to their families at a reasonable hour. Locked in tradition, the *Herald-Leader* night shift will just be getting into gear about this time. These editors will arrive home past midnight.

Being a part of a newspaper management revolution involves asking questions like, "Do so many people really need to work nights?" Night shifts put a strain on families and detach journalists from mainstream American life. How that detachment over time can affect news judgment is worth debating. What could have been the 10 a.m. meeting for this team is by tradition the 4 p.m. news meeting.

4:10 p.m.: The Clinton Huddle

After the 4 p.m. news meeting, Managing Editor Eblen huddles with Presentation Director Steve Dorsey and Night News Editor Larry Froelich (fig. 1.14). Eblen considers a twist to the acquittal story headline, something like "Acquitted but not absolved" or "Acquitted but not exonerated." Sometimes it helps to see how such a headline would scream to decide whether it sounds right, so he asks Dorsey to create draft proofs. After the huddle breaks, Froelich is asked whether the 10 planned pages of coverage are coordinated

Fig. 1.13

The night shift. Copy Editor John Ireland runs the first afternoon news meeting, which focuses on everything but the Clinton acquittal stories. (Photo by Ron Garrison)

Fig. 1.14

The triad. Managing Editor Eblen huddles with Presentation Director Steve Dorsey (left) and Night News Editor Larry Froelich. They debate what the lead headline will say. (Photo by Ron Garrison)

Innovative Coverage

The *Herald-Leader* remains largely a traditional newsroom with section editors or assistants aligned with the paper's metro, business, sports and feature sections for local news. The *Orange County Register* was one of the leaders in the early 1990s in aligning editors with topics of readers' interests, rather than with sections of the newspaper. The most talked-about example was the *Register*'s "mall reporter," who ostensibly was free to write stories for any section of the newspaper about a topic near-and-dear to Southern Californian readers: the shopping mall. For more information on experiments in newsroom organization, see Chapters 8 and 12.

with the editorial page. "I don't know," he says, explaining that the separation between the newsroom and the editorial page is "like church and state." In an office adjacent to Editor Luecke's, Editorial Page Editor Vanessa Gallman at first thinks that a same-day editorial might send the wrong message and that time for reflection was necessary to put the event into proper perspective. The Saturday paper, however, will have a short lead editorial on Clinton's acquittal and the Sunday paper will follow with a lengthy editorial as well as a perspective piece from former *Chicago Tribune* editor Jim Squires.

When he was editor, Squires heard tales of the night the *Tribune* proclaimed that Dewey defeated Truman and plenty more about life at the *Tribune* under Publisher Col. Robert McCormick. A detractor once described the colonel as one of the greatest minds of the 14th century. Squires tells the story of the time he noticed that a state was missing from a *Tribune* map of the United States. It turns out that the colonel, upset with a prominent resident of that state, had ordered decades ago that the state's name or likeness never appear in the *Tribune*. Further, the legend goes, the colonel ripped the star representing the state from the American flag in Tribune Tower. At that time and at that paper there was no separation of "church and state."

Back to the Drawing Board

One glance at the "Acquitted but . . ." proofs (fig. 1.15), and the managing editor looks for another tack to tell the story in a way fitting for history but also fresh for readers. He is searching for a forward-looking spin, but the "Acquitted but…" headlines seem more appropriate for an editorial or a column rather than the front page of the news section.

Some newspaper editors, particularly those at tabloids, will write the main headline first, then design the front page around it. How else could these memorable headlines scream from New York City newsstands: "Headless Body in Topless Bar," or "Ford to City: Drop Dead," or, more recently in the Clinton-Lewinsky intern sex scandal, "The Full Monica." They probably were not written to fit "specs," the traditional process of newspaper headline writing in which the page design comes first and the headline sizing follows.

The Budget

Night News Editor Froelich, whose work on big-time stories at the *Detroit Free-Press* has prepared him for this night, circulates a budget of Clinton-related stories segmented by pages and organized by themes (fig. 1.16). This will help to coordinate copy editors' work. "Copy flow," which involves reporter and wire-editor deadlines, and "page flow," which involves copy-editor and production-editor deadlines, are the newsroom's bloodstream. Reporters, wire editors and copy editors may work story by story, but Froelich and Copy Desk Chief Butters must be focused on closing pages for production. Deadlines for pages and their stories are staggered from the press-start time backward. Early pages start the procession of printing plates being added to the press. Late pages accommodate up-to-the-minute changes. Understanding how much time is available to perform a particular newsroom task defines who has management potential and who does not.

Fig. 1.15

Back to the drawing board. This is one of several proofs displaying variations of "Acquitted but …" headlines. None of them feel right to the *Herald-Leader*'s managing editor. (Copyright the *Lexington Herald-Leader*/used by permission)

Fig. 1.16

Impeachment trial budget for Saturday 2/13

Clinton on Trial: Acquitted

(* = story has been moved to Desk)
(rails: body copy, rag right, bfclc all names; use subheds for separate elements)

■ **On the front page (paul)**

13IMPEACH: The Senate votes mostly along party lines to acquit President Clinton on the two articles of impeachment. (45 ins. - the wires - pete)
13IMPEACH-ANALYSIS: What have they wrought? (25 ins. - nytimes - john)
13KYIMPEACH: How did Kentucky's senators, Mitch McConnell and Jim Bunning, vote on the impeachment, and why? by Gibson (mike)
13IMPEACH-NEXT: And you thought it was over? What's next? (the wires) + refers, liftout quote/mug refers and perhaps a By-the-numbers on the ordeal. (amy d.)

■ **Page A2 (dean)**
***13IMPEACH-CELEBRATE:** Ten ways to celebrate the end of the trial w/ illustrations from art dept. (fort worth star-telegram)

■ **Page A3: A day of decision (pete/dean)**
13IMPEACH-RAIL1: How they voted (ap)
13IMPEACH-SCENE: The scene, inside and outside the Senate chamber (18 ins. - nytimes)
13IMPEACH-DEFECT: A look at the 10 Republicans who broke ranks on at least one of the impeachment votes. (18 ins. - nytimes)
13IMPEACH-LEGAL: Why the House managers fell so short in making their case, even when the public seemed to believe Clinton lied and covered it up. (20 ins. - nytimes)

■ **Page A4: The players (kristal/paul)**
13IMPEACH-RAIL2: The senators speak and react. (wires)
***13IMPEACH-STARR:** He just won't go away. (20 ins. - buro)
13IMPEACH-CLINTON: President Clinton plans a statement in the Rose Garden this afternoon in response to his acquittal on impeachment charges. Jodi Enda covers and reports on the mood of the White House. (18 ins. - buro)
13IMPEACH-MANAGERS: Rep. Hyde, in an interview, and other House managers comment on the day's developments. (15 ins. - nytimes)
13IMPEACH-CHRONO: A graphic timeline (continues on next page)

■ **Page A5: Looking ahead (pete/paul)**
13IMPEACH-RAIL3: What did Americans think? (the wires)
***13IMPEACH-ELECTIONS:** Monica Lewinsky is no Anita Hill. And while Americans might be angry at Republicans for dragging out the impeachment of President Clinton, they are unlikely to carry their fury into voting booths in November 2000, political experts say. (19.5 ins. - buro)
***13IMPEACH-FUTURE:** Having won acquittal, Clinton will now run for history. He will spend the remaining 23 months of his presidency and perhaps the rest of his life trying to erase the stain of impeachment. (20 ins. - buro)
***IMPEACH-IMPACT:** One surprise from 13 months of Monica madness is that it may have made America more ready for a woman to be president. (25 ins. - buro)
13IMPEACH-DEM: Democratic senators won a victory, but can scarcely celebrate it. (12 ins. - latimes)
13IMPEACH-CHRONO: A graphic timeline (continuation from second inside page?)

■ **Page A6: In Kentucky (dean)**
13LEXCHAT: A diverse group of local residents agrees to come in and chat about the verdict. We observe and write about it. by Mead. PHOTOS. w/ bioboxes
   w/**13LEXCHATBOX.** Bio box on our participants.
13TRUMAN : Column on why no one cares about the impeachment process and writing about the few

(continued on next page)

Theme pages. The budget of impeachment trial stories will help coordinate copy editors' work. (Copyright the *Lexington Herald-Leader*/used by permission)

5 p.m.: The Late News Meeting

Froelich leads a 12-minute follow-up meeting focused on the Clinton acquittal pages. Newsrooms for morning daily papers typically pause in the late morning, early afternoon and late afternoon for formal planning meetings. Conversation at the late-afternoon meeting usually turns quickly to the best photos for page one. For tomorrow's historic front page, there is nothing good turning up on the wires, mostly just podium shots of President Clinton. A laptop computer loaded with photo possibilities is configured to project images on a television screen (fig. 1.17). One paper adopted a similar method to clarify photo content after editors looking at just the negatives misjudged a car-wreck photo. Only when the photo was blown up on the front page did they notice a severed arm in the picture.

More to Decide

After the late news meeting, a small group huddles for 21 minutes to nail down exactly what stories of particular lengths are going where, especially on page one (fig. 1.18). Hesitation about which stories to play on page one causes a chain reaction of uncertainty. A story bumped off page one will displace another good story on a different page, which will force another story to be moved, and so on. News does not stand still waiting to be packaged: A bomb threat has cleared the Senate floor; Monica Lewinsky's "friend" Linda Tripp says Monica still loves the president; R.W. Apple Jr. of the *New York Times* has filed his analysis. Reaction quotes keep rolling in. Pressing again for a forward-looking front page, Managing Editor Eblen wants to see a segment entitled, "What's next."

The main headline is still up for grabs. "It's over" and "Back to work" are offered, but the first is considered trite and the second pushes the story so far ahead that the historical moment is lost. One option is to run "Acquitted" as large as the paper published "Impeached," but Presentation Director Dorsey feels no obligation toward typographical parity.

Eblen sees a quote buried in a wire story that he wants blown up with a key phrase added to the attribution: "We've got to end the pain, heal the nation and get back to work," says U.S. Sen. John Warner, R-Va., one of 10

Fig. I.16 (continued)

who have been mesmerized by the proceedings, respectively. by Edwards and Truman.

13MADISON: PHOTOS. GRAPHIC. Madison Middle School's 600 students will have a mock vote on Friday for conviction or acquittal of the president. The school's student council decided to get involved in politics. by Richardson.

w/**13MADISONBOX**: Brite on why some schools are going out of their way NOT to get involved in politics. by Blackford.

13IMPEACH-KYHOUSE: We check with the four House members from Kentucky who voted for impeachment. How do they react to the acquittal? by Gibson

■ **Page A7: Winners and Losers (kristal/dean)**
***13IMPEACH-RAIL4**: A timeline on how Clinton fared in the polls during his ordeal. (14 ins. - ap)

***13IMPEACH-COSTS**: The impeachment trial of President Clinton has drawn to a close and it's time for an accounting. This painful episode in American history appears likely to cost everyone involved — taxpayers included — well more than $60 million. And that's not including the millions likely to be added in coming months and years as Independent Counsel Kenneth Starr continues to pursue his prosecutorial targets. (20 ins. - buro)

13IMPEACH-WINLOSE: After almost 13 months of nonstop scandal, there are winners and losers dotting the landscape. From the Starr-crossed lovers to the members of Congress to lawyers and friends. (15 ins. - buro)

***13IMPEACH-AFFECTED**: When the all-clear siren sounds after a huge tornado, you come out and look around to see who lost his shirt and who, with a little luck, survived. Sales quadrupled for novelist Nicholson Baker's "Vox," after the Starr report disclosed that Lewinsky made a gift of the book — a tale of phone sex — to the president. Baker would rather it wasn't so. In Arkansas, a banker tried and cleared finds himself a local folk hero. A look at some people pulled in to the swirl. (15 ins. - buro)

***13IMPEACH-CHANGES**: The long-running Monica Lewinsky scandal produced big and measurable changes in many aspects of American daily life, among them the acceptability of sex talk in public discourse, public sentiment about skeletons in political closets, even Americans' taste in lingerie. (20ins. - buro)

■ **Page A8: From the Front Page (paul)**
JUMPS from **13IMPEACH**, **13KYIMPEACH** and **13IMPEACH-ANALYSIS**

■ **Page A9: The media**
***13IMPEACH-MEDIA**: Journalists are openly grappling with whether "have you ever" questions — involving adultery, drug use or other past embarrassments — are relevant, or at least more acceptable, in the climate fostered by the nonstop coverage of the Lewinsky story. 1,075 words, by Howard Kurtz (Post). Moved.

■ **Page A15: Commentary page**
13IMPEACH-TEXT: Text of Clinton's remarks following verdicts, plus excerpts or full texts of McConnell's and Bunning's statements.

■ **Extra stories for filler**
***13IMPEACH-CONSTITUTION**: If there were any heroes in the impeachment spectacle, they are long dead For Madison, Hamilton and George Mason, the framers of the Constitution, gave Americans the principle that dictated the outcome in Clinton's trial and left the nation shaken but stable. (20 ins. - buro)

***13IMPEACH-CONSPIRACY**: Communist invasions. Mind-controlling "Furbies." CIA plots, feminist coups and the end of the world. And you thought you knew all about the impeachment trial. (15 ins. - trib)

Fig. 1.17

Visual aids. A laptop computer loaded with photo possibilities projects images on a television screen during the late afternoon news meeting. (Photo by Ron Garrison)

Fig. 1.18

Triad reconvenes. After the late news meeting, a small group huddles for 21 minutes to nail down exactly what stories will go where. (Photo by Ron Garrison)

Republicans who broke ranks on at least one vote for Clinton. Figure 1.19 shows a proof of their final headline selection.

Eblen double-checks which promos will be used atop page one to highlight stories in the sports, business and religion sections inside the paper. The story about the list of top 10 ways to celebrate the end of the impeachment trial has made the paper on page two (fig. 1.20); it gets a small promo of its own.

Late Afternoon: Departments at Work

Online

The *Herald-Leader*'s online readership research suggests that computer users have a 9 a.m. to 5 p.m. attention span. After 5 p.m., presumably when web surfers have gone home and are on their own tabs, readership falls like a rock (fig. 1.21). The online journalists' workday harkens back to the afternoon daily staff's hours: an early morning start and then home before dinner.

Photos

Photo Editor Lisa Edmondson works the AP Leafdesk (fig. 1.22), an AP computer terminal that provides a steady stream of images to the newspaper. Among those images are examples of how afternoon papers, such as the *San Francisco Examiner* and the *Seattle Times*, are handling the Clinton story on their front pages. She flags those examples for her colleagues who will decide the shape of the *Herald-Leader*'s front page.

One example from the AP Leafdesk shows a printer in the backshop of the *San Francisco Examiner* making up the front page (fig. 1.23). The large cutout image of Clinton walking drives photojournalists crazy because it messes with the original photo, but it provides a strong visual metaphor: "walks," as in "is acquitted." The photo shows a bold, confident president strutting forward. Is

Fig. 1.19

Page-one proof. The front-page proof shows the final headline, chosen to reflect the historical importance of the story. (Photo by Ron Garrison)

Cyan Magenta Yellow **Black BType**

5 25 50 75 100

A2 Lexington Herald-Leader
Saturday, February 13, 1999

The fat lady sang

Impeachment is history! Here's how to celebrate

As the dust settles, here's a list we've all been waiting for ...

10. Rip out your cable.

9. Sew four gold stripes on the arms of your favorite jacket.

8. Move to France, where presidential adultery doesn't cost taxpayers a dime.

7. Get a bunch of friends together and reserve the Mayflower hotel's $5,000-a-night presidential suite, where your group can re-enact the 23rd deposition of Monica Lewinsky — just for the heck of it!

6. Write a thank-you note to Richard Douglas Llamas, the D.C.-er who fulfilled many a citizen's fantasy last week by standing up during the Senate proceedings and shouting, "God almighty, take the vote and get it over with!"

CHRIS WARE/STAFF

5. Throw a "Celebrate the Acquittal" party. Attempt to whack the Linda Tripp pinata. Exchange gifts; then make people give them back. A "profoundly unsorry" time will be had by all.

4. Pin a scrap of blue cloth to your lapel, in silent commemoration.

3. Get out that glue gun and consult Martha Stewart about the best way to preserve your copy of the Starr Report for the literary enjoyment of future generations.

2. Attempt to locate your own moral compass.

1. Register to vote.

— LIZ STEVENS, FORT WORTH STAR-TELEGRAM

Fig. 1.20

Page-two proof. The second page reflects the mood of many Americans with the "Top 10 Reasons to Celebrate Acquittal" story. (Copyright the *Lexington Herald-Leader*/used by permission)

Fig. 1.21

Online winds down. The *Herald-Leader*'s online newsroom is about ready to close for the day. At 5 p.m. online readership falls like a rock. (Photo by Ron Garrison)

29

it a lie? After all, Clinton showed no hint of bravado at his news conference after his acquittal. In fact, as he walked from the podium, his shoulders were hunched. What's the proper image of a man who survived being beaten to a pulp politically?

Another example (fig. 1.24) from the AP Leafdesk shows the front page of the Friday edition of the *Philadelphia Daily News*, whose newsroom sits one floor below that of the venerable *Philadelphia Inquirer*. Like the *Herald-Leader*, both are Knight Ridder newspapers. This front page stands like a dagger pointed at the heart of critics who suggest that group, or "chain," ownership leads to a homogenization of newspapers. The reaction in the *Herald-Leader* newsroom to their cousin's handiwork ranges from a laugh and shake of the head to a studied response from news artist Chris Ware. He explains how much time and skill is involved in achieving just the right puffiness in Clinton's left eye.

If you think cutouts drive photojournalists crazy, break out the strait-jackets for a discussion of photo manipulation through computer programs such as Adobe PhotoShop. Photo manipulation is as old as photo use in newspapers, which dates to the late 19th century. In the 1980s, newspapers increasingly turned to pagination, the electronic composition of pages. In the early 1990s, the AP dropped its photo proofing machines to introduce the Leafdesk computer system. With these changes, photo reproduction processes changed dramatically. What had been the engraving department of production, which in the early '80s was still using saws to cut blocks of lead for photos at the *Chicago Tribune*, gradually moved to desktop computers. Pagination shifted tasks and responsibilities out of production to newsroom copy editors, and electronic photo handling shifted the engraving department's work to photo editors. In both cases, the burden came with the benefit of control. The same was true in high schools. No longer did newspaper editors have to send photos and text to the printer and then be disappointed with what came back. They could control how those stories and photos looked through their desktop computers.

Unfortunately, the same tools of photo enhancement to improve repro-

Fig. 1.22

Window to the world.
Photo Editor Lisa Edmondson at the AP Leafdesk processes a steady stream of images from *Herald-Leader* wire services. (Photo by Ron Garrison)

duction can be used for photo manipulation that blurs the truth. With the ease of do-it-yourself desktop manipulation, photo illustrations, like the *Philadelphia Daily News* cover, have become more common. In a number of notorious cases, publications crossed the line. For example, a soda can evaporated in a photo of a Pulitzer Prize-winning photojournalist, and *National Geographic* magazine moved one of the pyramids in a cover photo. These cases and others led newspapers and magazines to revisit their ethical guidelines for photo usage. Policies range from "never change anything" to "if you are going to manipulate a photo, it must clearly look phony." The *Daily News* cover of Clinton falls into that latter category.

Photo Editor Edmondson and her boss, Photo Director Ron Garrison, anguish over using a podium shot of President Clinton as the lead photo for the front page (fig. 1.25). Not only is there no strong lead art, there is also no strong secondary photo. Garrison expresses his concern to Eblen about having only mugshots on the front page. Edmondson gets an e-mail from a friend working at another paper wondering what the *Herald-Leader*'s lead photo will be.

At the Leafdesk, photo editors select, crop, size and tone photos for publication (fig. 1.26). Several versions of Clinton's portrait, with shades of difference in his eyes and lip position, are available this day.

Fig. 1.25

Lead art. Photo Editor Lisa Edmondson and her boss, Photo Director Ron Garrison, anguish over using a podium shot of President Clinton as the lead photo for the front page. (Photo by Buck Ryan)

Fig. 1.26

Familiar face. At the Leafdesk, photo editors select, crop, size and tone photos for publication. (Photo by Ron Garrison)

Fig. 1.27

Course is set. A color page one proof at 7:43 p.m. gives senior editors a glimpse into how their work will look to readers. (Copyright *Lexington Herald-Leader*/used by permission; AP/Wide World Photos)

Fig. 1.28

QPS. The Quark Publishing System allows many users to work on the same page at the same time. (Photo by Ron Garrison)

A color page-one proof at 7:43 p.m. gives senior editors a glimpse into how their various decisions would look to readers tomorrow morning (fig. 1.27).

Copy Desk

The *Herald-Leader* copy desk uses the Quark Publishing System, which allows multiple users to work on the same page at the same time (fig. 1.28). The system keeps track of what stories are ready, what stories have been sent to the composing room and what stories should be handled next. The old days of headline orders have been replaced by Quark pages created by the design desk with dummy type where headlines should go. Copy editors write their headlines over the dummy type to see if they fit.

Design Desk

Designer Paul Wallen is used to having a lot of people looking over his shoulder while he assembles the front page (fig. 1.29).

Graphics

Artist Tim Blum draws photos from the *Herald-Leader* library, segments of graphics from various wire services and facts from wire stories to create a timeline graphic that will run across two full pages (fig. 1.30).

9:30 p.m.: The "Oh, My God" Rule

Editor Luecke and Managing Editor Eblen review final proofs for the first edition, which typically has a newsroom deadline of 10:30 p.m. for news and 11:10 p.m. for late sports scores (fig. 1.31). At this point, they are looking to correct only major errors, known in newsrooms as "Oh, my Gods."

After deadline, the newsroom empties out. Many newspapers have a tradition of catering meals on holidays and special occasions, such as election nights (fig. 1.32).

At the *Herald-Leader*, copy editors take turns working in the composing room, where they make sure page proofs are made and circulated in the newsroom (fig. 1.33). A backshop editor is the last set of eyes to see final pages. On this night, a copy editor circled a passage on a proof of the paper's lead editorial: "We watched in open-mouthed amazement as the sexual indiscretions of

Fig. 1.29

In the hot seat. Designer Paul Wallen assembles the historic front page. (Photo by Ron Garrison)

Fig. 1.30

12-column graphic.
Artist Tim Blum puts
events over four years into
perspective. (Photo by Ron
Garrison)

Fig. 1.31

Final checks. Editor Pam
Luecke and Managing
Editor Tom Eblen review
final proofs for the first
edition and see no "Oh, my
God" mistakes. (Photo by
Ron Garrison)

Fig. 1.32

Newsroom cools off.
After the paper closes, all
that's left in the news conference room are empty
pizza boxes. (Photo by
Ron Garrison)

elected leaders became part of the daily news." The word "open-mouthed" was wisely deleted. Composing rooms, once vast areas filled with the deafening sound of Linotype machines, are small and quiet today—if not nonexistent—because of pagination.

Although the editorial and advertising departments are separated at newspapers, readers see both editorial and advertising at the same time. The headline label "Sex, Lies and News Coverage" stands opposite a photo of two women in satin sleepwear (fig. 1.34). Is putting this headline next to this advertisement an "Oh, my God"? Too late now; the presses are ready to roll.

11:30 p.m.: The Pressroom

Not only has pagination shrunk composing rooms, but also computer-to-plate technology has all but eliminated the prepress production department. Tonight 80 percent of the printing plates at the *Herald-Leader* will be created with the push of a button (fig. 1.35). A few weeks later, that number will rise to 100 percent for the first time. In the past, a newspaper page was "pasted up" from type set on paper strips. A page-size negative was shot of the paste-up, then the negative was used to "burn" the plate. With computer-to-plate technology, the plates are burned by a laser image setter, eliminating two steps—and at least two jobs.

The presses began to roll six minutes late (11:26 p.m.) for the Bluegrass edition and on time (1:10 a.m.) for the Metro Final edition (fig. 1.36). Managing Editor Eblen called that a "very good performance, considering the number of extra pages."

The smell of ink, the roar of the presses, the feeling of power can all be very intoxicating to newspaper journalists. They continue an American tradition begun in 1690 with Benjamin Harris's Publick Occurrences. Newspapers have been called "history in a hurry" and "the daily miracle." The Saturday, Feb. 13, 1999, issue of the *Lexington Herald-Leader* is both (fig. 1.37).

Fig. 1.33

Backshop heats up. A copy editor reviews the pages in the composing room. She is the last line of defense against errors. (Photo by Ron Garrison)

Fig. 1.35

Computer to plate. Modern technology that "burns" printing plates directly from the computer has improved quality and saved money. (Photo by Ron Garrison)

A MAESTRO CRITIQUE OF PAGE ONE

The *Herald-Leader* staff produced an impressive front page packed with information for readers. The newsroom process put an emphasis on planning, which included several meetings. The process and the front-page results are intricately linked. In Chapter 8 we will explain the Maestro Concept, which offers a different approach to story and page planning. If the *Herald-Leader* had employed the Maestro Concept, here are a few ways the process and the results might have been different.

As early as the previous week or as late as the 4:10 p.m. huddle on Friday, a "maestro," in this case the managing editor, would have asked a newsroom team to brainstorm on what questions would immediately come to a reader's mind about the Clinton acquittal story. The list of questions might have looked something like this:

1. What was the vote?

2. What was President Clinton's reaction?

3. What happens next?

Fig. 1.36

Stretching deadlines.
Even though the press starts rolling a few minutes late, Managing Editor Tom Eblen calls it a "very good performance, considering the number of extra pages." (Photo by Ron Garrison)

Fig. 1.37

Hot off the press. The Saturday, Feb. 13, 1999, issue of the *Lexington Herald-Leader* is the first take on history. (Photo by Ron Garrison)

4. What was Kentucky's role?

5. How much did all this cost?

Once the team has decided on the top three to five questions, those questions drive the design of the front page and they become the basis of a critique of the page after publication. The questions create a "reader-friendliness index," and the goal is to answer as many of those questions as quickly and as easily as possible for readers.

Journalists traditionally focus on answering readers' questions. In figure 1.38, see how the numbers for the questions we listed correspond with where those questions were answered on the front page. The Maestro Concept refines the tradition to make those agreed-upon questions an organizing tool for page design.

In figure 1.39, all the stories and photos on this "maestroed" page appeared in the *Herald-Leader*'s acquittal coverage. They were rearranged or highlighted to respond directly and neatly to the readers' questions we identified. In a critique after publication, the maestro would reconvene the team, assess the page's reader-friendliness index (i.e., five questions raised, five answered) and discuss how the page might have been more effective and what the team might do differently next time to improve the process.

Fig. 1.38

Same questions answered. The numbers on this page correspond with answers to the questions we listed. Those questions can become an organizing tool for design. (Copyright the *Lexington Herald-Leader*/used by permission; AP/Wide World Photos)

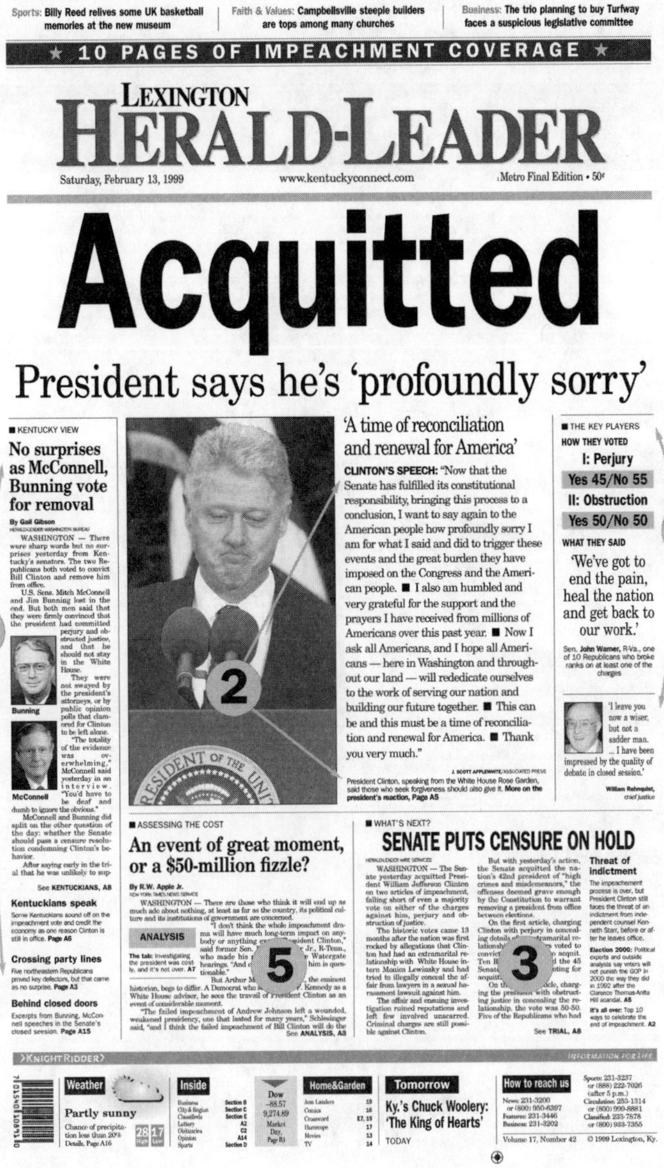
Sports: Billy Reed relives some UK basketball memories at the new museum | Faith & Values: Campbellsville steeple builders are tops among many churches | Business: The trio planning to buy Turfway faces a suspicious legislative committee

★ 10 PAGES OF IMPEACHMENT COVERAGE ★

LEXINGTON HERALD-LEADER

Saturday, February 13, 1999 | www.kentuckyconnect.com | Metro Final Edition • 50¢

Acquitted

President says he's 'profoundly sorry'

■ KENTUCKY VIEW

No surprises as McConnell, Bunning vote for removal

'A time of reconciliation and renewal for America'

CLINTON'S SPEECH: "Now that the Senate has fulfilled its constitutional responsibility, bringing this process to a conclusion, I want to say again to the American people how profoundly sorry I am for what I said and did to trigger these events and the great burden they have imposed on the Congress and the American people. ■ I also am humbled and very grateful for the support and the prayers I have received from millions of Americans over this past year. ■ Now I ask all Americans, and I hope all Americans — here in Washington and throughout our land — will rededicate ourselves to the work of serving our nation and building our future together. ■ This can be and this must be a time of reconciliation and renewal for America. ■ Thank you very much."

■ THE KEY PLAYERS

HOW THEY VOTED

I: Perjury

Yes 45/No 55

II: Obstruction

Yes 50/No 50

WHAT THEY SAID

'We've got to end the pain, heal the nation and get back to our work.'

Sen. John Warner, R-Va., one of 10 Republicans who broke ranks on at least one of the charges

'I leave you now a wiser, but not a sadder man. ... I have been impressed by the quality of debate in closed session.'

William Rehnquist, chief justice

■ ASSESSING THE COST

An event of great moment, or a $50-million fizzle?

■ WHAT'S NEXT?

SENATE PUTS CENSURE ON HOLD

Threat of indictment

Kentuckians speak

Crossing party lines

Behind closed doors

Weather | Inside | Home&Garden | Tomorrow | How to reach us

Ky.'s Chuck Woolery: 'The King of Hearts'

Fig. 1.39

Think like a reader. The stories and photos on this "maestroed" page were rearranged or highlighted to respond directly and neatly to the readers' questions we identified. (Copyright the *Lexington Herald-Leader*/used by permission; AP/Wide World Photos)

2

The Nature of News

——

A good newspaper, I suppose, is a nation talking to itself.
—Arthur Miller

He who asks is a fool for five minutes, but he who does not ask
remains a fool forever.
—Chinese proverb

In all that an editor does, he or she must make decisions about what to change and what to leave alone. In many of these decisions, the editor can find hard and fast guidelines in the dictionary, the stylebook or some other reference book.

Many decisions depend not on solid rules but on good judgment, usually tied to an understanding of news. The editor must know what the story is about and what the writer is trying to accomplish. Is it hard news or a feature? Many features are written in a casual tone where even the rules of grammar might be bent. Is the story noncontroversial or does it include potentially libelous material? Does it require a clever headline or a straightforward one?

COMPARING TWO NEWSPAPERS

News judgment is not guided by a set of concrete, universally held principles. News judgment varies from person to person, from city to city and from publication to publication. Look at figures 2.1 and 2.2, the front pages from the *Chicago Tribune* and *Chicago Sun-Times* on the day after serial killer John Wayne Gacy was executed.

In some ways, the two pages are similar. Both place the Gacy story on page one. Both include Nelson Mandela's election as South Africa's president. But the pages are so different that it's hard to believe they were produced within a block of each other.

Both views of the news are valid, based on several factors:

- *Page size.* Don't discount the physical differences between a broadsheet paper like the *Tribune* and a tabloid like the *Sun-Times*. A broadsheet is about twice the size of a tabloid, 13 inches wide by 21 inches deep, not counting margins. The editors at the broadsheet have the luxury of hedging their bets with more stories on page one. That's what the *Tribune* did here, packaging the Mandela story as a centerpiece and running the Gacy story in the right-hand column. The *Sun-Times* had to be decisive in choosing a top story; it chose Gacy.
- *Personality.* The pattern for "tabloid journalism" was set in the early 1900s by London's *Daily Mirror,* described by Emery and Emery

Figs. 2.1 and 2.2

Same city, different papers. Chicago is a rare city: It still has two competing newspapers. These pages from the *Chicago Tribune* and *Chicago Sun-Times* show how different the two papers can be. Notice especially the play given to the story about serial killer John Wayne Gacy's execution. (Reprinted with special permission from the Chicago Sun-Times, Inc. © 1999; © Chicago Tribune Company. All rights reserved/used with permission)

(1962) as "small, sensational, and amusing." The first tabloid in this country, New York's *Illustrated Daily News,* was launched in 1919. The traditional fare for the tabloid newspaper has been a sensational mix of crime, sex and entertainment; the *Sun-Times* has followed this pattern to varying degrees through several changes in ownership over the last

20 years. It was owned briefly in the 1980s by Rupert Murdoch, who took it to the far edge of tabloid journalism. Today, the *Sun-Times* displays "sophisticated sensationalism," the definition applied to modern tabloid journalism by Dr. Mario Garcia of the Poynter Institute for Media Studies. The *Sun-Times*'s news values are high, but it retains a grittier approach to news than the *Tribune*, evident in its presentation of the Gacy story.

- *Circulation patterns and audience.* The *Sun-Times* takes a large portion of its readership within the city of Chicago while the *Tribune* markets itself heavily in the suburbs. The Gacy story could be interpreted as being a much stronger story within the city, where readers are viewed as more interested in local issues and less attuned to international affairs.

- *News philosophy.* How does a publication position itself within the context of city, state and nation? The *Tribune,* with its longer history and circulation far beyond the city limits of Chicago, places a much higher value on national and international news than does the *Sun-Times.* The *Sun-Times* includes national and international news, to be sure, but it's just less likely to show up on the front page.

NEWS JUDGMENTS, SMALL AND LARGE

As we saw with the example of the Lexington *Herald-Leader* in Chapter 1, news judgment comes into play with almost every decision an editor makes. Some decisions are on the micro level, where a single word choice is involved, and some occur on the macro level, where broad decisions are made about which stories should run where.

News Judgment on the Micro Level

The following is a true story: Years ago in a game against the Detroit Lions, a huge Chicago Bears tackle named Dan Hampton laid a hard block on the Detroit kicker Eddie Murray. The Lions protested that the play was unnecessarily rough considering that Murray, perhaps the smallest player on the field, was hanging back after kicking off. The Bears were quick to point out that Hampton had acted within the rules in carrying out his blocking assignment.

In a follow-up story, a *Chicago Tribune* reporter wrote that the controversy arose when Hampton "blocked" Murray. When the story got to the desk, an editor changed "blocked" to "clobbered," believing the stronger word described better what had happened to the diminutive kicker. At the Bears practice the next day, the reporter was confronted and criticized for his use of "clobbered" for what was, after all, a legal play.

In changing the reporter's word, the editor displayed poor news judgment. The reporter had carefully chosen a neutral word, "blocked," based on the news value of *fairness* to both sides. The editor chose his word based on the competing news value of *conflict,* accentuating the violent nature of the block.

Editors make dozens of decisions every day like the example above. It's news judgment at the micro level. For the editor, every story represents a series of small news decisions, any of which might be complex. An editor might ask:

- *Is this the right word?* This decision rests on knowing usage, on understanding what the story is about and on realizing the editorial spin the reporter wants. Sometimes reporters fall in love with a word without being quite sure what it means; editors are justified in correcting usage. But sometimes an editor can forget that writers today often are pushed by superiors to be more creative and entertaining. An editor who is too mechanical can deaden a writer's prose.
- *Is the sentence put together properly?* This decision requires the editor to understand what element of the sentence is most important and deserves emphasis: who, what, when, where, why or how. The editor needs a firm grounding in grammar and a feel for clarity, simplicity and brevity.
- *Does the paragraph do its job efficiently?* The editor must identify the topic of the paragraph and see to it that each sentence supports that topic. The editor needs an eye for composition. Editing at the paragraph level takes special care because fixing a paragraph often means making a substantial change in the writing. The editor must make sure he or she understands what the reporter is trying to do.
- *Does the story flow properly?* The editor should err on the side of caution when it comes to moving paragraphs around. It takes an understanding of the subject matter and of what's most important. Always consult with a supervisor before making these major changes in a story.

The Good Editor

Everyone in the news business knows at least one of those editors who believe they must leave their fingerprints on every piece of copy they touch. The good editor does just the opposite. He or she makes the story better without changing the writer's style or editorial spin. The good editor, like the physician, follows the maxim, "Above all, do no harm."

The good editor keeps in mind three ideals:

1. Make the simplest fix possible. Some editors see one word that is a mistake and use it as an excuse to rewrite a sentence. This is the way of the hack.

2. For close calls, let the writer's words stand. The editor may not like the sound of what is written, but the writer prevails in matters of taste.

3. When in doubt, seek help by asking questions. Others on the desk are the editor's best resource.

Reasons to Change Copy

The good editor has a valid reason for every change in a story that he or she makes. These reasons may include:

- *Accuracy.* This is the number one reason for changing copy. It includes "killer mistakes," usually errors of fact, as well as spelling, grammar and punctuation. Writers appreciate changes that make the story accurate.

- *Clarity.* If the editor doesn't understand it, will the reader? Problems of clarity often require the editor to ask the reporter what he or she means. Be careful not to "fix" something that is unclear by making it clearly wrong. Check first!
- *Simplicity.* Multisyllabic words are more difficult to read and understand; that may be why the military and government are so fond of them. The rule is, Use the shorter word when no meaning is lost. Sort out the double talk.
- *Brevity.* Long, complex sentences are difficult to read and understand. Studies have shown that the optimum *average* sentence length for readability is 20 words, in a pleasing mix of long and short sentences.
- *Consistency.* News stories must be consistent. Figures must add up. If the lead says five men were arrested, five must be named. Consistency also applies to style. All news organizations have rules about using figures, about capitalization and about abbreviations, among other things. *The Associated Press Stylebook and Libel Manual* is the most commonly used style guide, but many larger news organizations have their own stylebooks.
- *Coherence.* For a story to hang together, it must have smooth transitions. Achieving coherence can be as simple as finding the right conjunction. It may require making sure quotes are attributed logically or less frequently. In extreme cases, it may require shifting the order of paragraphs.

Rewriting versus Editing

As soon as an editor decides to abandon the strategy of making the simple fix and decides to rewrite a part of a story, he or she runs the risk of introducing errors or changing the essential meaning of the original. Remember that reporters are subject to many limitations and pressures; respect what they do and they will respect their editors. Before rewriting, discuss your proposed change with a supervisor, who will often call the writer.

News Judgment on the Macro Level

Good editors soon are invited into the macro level of news judgment. At this level, editors select stories and decide where they go. The traditional process of news selection is a complex mix. Its ingredients include broad news values such as timeliness, proximity or oddity; the personalities and power relationships of those making the decisions; and a large measure of what Robert Giles (1991) calls "critical judgment." Giles, the former publisher of the *Detroit Free Press*, writes that critical judgment involves "intuition, experience, a strong sense of events, and a concern for fairness and balance."

Another term for critical judgment is "gut instinct." In the best sense, it comes from long experience in the news business. At worst, it reflects the biases and interests of the individual.

News Values

Traditional news values include concepts that are useful if editors employ them thoughtfully and without personal bias. Those values are timeliness, audience, prominence, celebrity, oddity, proximity, magnitude, impact and conflict.

Timeliness

The news value of timeliness could be divided into two related elements. The first could be called the scoop mentality: If a newspaper or TV station has a story first, the editors tend to overestimate its importance. The scoop mentality becomes damaging when being first overrides other news values. The result is that the trivial story may be played up because the news organization had it first. Scoop thinking also can be damaging when a news outlet rushes a story to publication, sometimes shortcutting normal reporting practices.

The internet has brought about a return in scoop thinking because of its ability to put the news out instantly. Sometimes news organizations have been burned. In late January 1998, as the story about President Clinton's affair with White House intern Monica Lewinsky broke, editors around the country had to decide whether to put early stories on their websites or wait for further verification. Nontraditional—some would say nonprofessional—journalists on the world wide web such as Matt Drudge complicated the process. Drudge and others were not reluctant to rush the story on to the web. At *Newsweek*, editors agonized over whether to go to press with one of the first stories about taped conversations between Linda Tripp and Lewinsky. On the tapes, Lewinsky discussed her affair with the president. *Newsweek* reporter Michael Isikoff had been developing the story for weeks. As *Newsweek* reported in its Feb. 2, 1998, edition, its editors knew that Drudge was aware of the tapes and of *Newsweek*'s upcoming story, and that Drudge was eager to scoop the magazine. Still, with the reporting process not complete, *Newsweek* held the story a week. Drudge didn't, reporting that at *Newsweek* the story had been "spiked."

Not all publications were as cautious. Here are some examples from an article by Sherry Ricchiardi in the March 1999 issue of the *American Journalism Review:*

- The *Dallas Morning News* reported a story in its early editions of Jan. 27, 1999—and at its website—that a Secret Service agent would testify he had seen Clinton and Lewinsky in a "compromising" situation. The story received prominent play on ABC's "Nightline" and other television broadcasts, all attributed to the *Morning News*. But the story was wrong and had to be retracted in the next edition. "It was a unique situation Monday night when a primary source suddenly reversed field," executive editor Ralph Langer wrote in the retraction. But in rushing to be first, the paper had violated its own rule of requiring two independent sources when reporting information anonymously.
- In a sort of reverse jeopardy, *Detroit News* reporter Rick Blanchard wrote a story describing Monica Lewinsky's home page, available to

anyone searching the America Online directory. The day the story appeared, Jan. 22, AOL pulled the site and announced that it was a hoax "designed to deceive people."

- On Feb. 4 the *Wall Street Journal* posted a story on its website that said a White House steward had told a federal grand jury he had seen Clinton and Lewinsky alone in a study near the Oval Office. The *Journal* had not gotten comments from the White House and the steward's lawyer. On Feb. 9, the paper retracted the story, saying the steward had testified he hadn't seen them together.

These incidents signal a change in how editors do their jobs. In all these cases, pressure from internet competition weighed into news decisions. Bill Kovach, curator of the Nieman Foundation, told Ricchiardi that for years the evidence has been there that the new communication technology would require journalists to reconsider how they do their business. But the signs have been virtually ignored, he says.

"It has been a torturous lesson for a lot of journalists, if you have seen the postmortem shows, Dan Rather sitting there ashamed of what he does for a living," Kovach told Ricchiardi. "You have to ask, 'If journalists are ashamed, what do we do about it?'"

The second component of timeliness has to do with seasonal stories. Ever notice how that story about global warming always crops up in the middle of an intense heat wave? In this sense, timeliness requires editors and reporters to think ahead and anticipate events. A second challenge for editors and reporters is to make cyclical stories fresh each time they come up.

Audience

Editors and reporters must keep in touch with the community where they work. They also need a general idea about what readers will or won't accept. Good taste is an important criterion where it involves pictures of gruesome scenes, stories about lewd behavior or writing that includes profanity.

Several ground-breaking studies have led to the conclusion that reporters and editors do not have a clear idea of what their readers think, or even who their readers are. Flegel and Chaffee (1971) found that reporters were directed in their news judgments by their own opinions more than those they perceived of their editors or readers. Breed (1955) concluded that newspeople "redefine" their values to the level of the newsroom group because it represents the source of rewards. Breed (1956) also theorized that because newspeople are heavy consumers of other media, their views of what's news become standardized. Studies such as these were largely ignored in newsrooms until newspapers faced economic problems in the late 1980s.

In many of today's newsrooms, editors and reporters are more aware of their audiences, due in part to initiatives such as the two we mentioned in Chapter 1—Gannett's News 2000 and Knight Ridder's 25/43 Project—and the civic journalism/public journalism movement, which we talk about later in this chapter. In Chapter 8, we'll discuss another of these initiatives, the Maestro Concept, which urges reporters and editors to "think like a reader."

Prominence

When important people are involved, insignificant details can take on great importance. When President Dwight D. Eisenhower suffered a heart attack in the 1950s, his doctor routinely briefed the media on the president's bowel movements—information that the media made sure got reported.

Celebrity

One important change in news values over the last 20 years has been the increase in news about celebrities. Whole magazines devote their pages to those who are famous. While it's a chicken-and-egg issue as to why celebrities are so fascinating to media consumers, the fact is that news and tidbits about them are well-read and watched. The term "celebrity" extends beyond those on screen, stage and recordings; it also includes those in political, fashion and literary circles, to name a few. Note the difference between "prominence" and "celebrity." The pope, secretary of state and mayor of New York are prominent. Brad Pitt and David Letterman are celebrities.

Oddity

The "man bites dog" story continues to be standard fare for news organizations, and all the more so if the story comes with pictures. Today, when video camcorders are everywhere, viewers are fed a steady diet of unusual happenings on the nightly news and on "reality programs." The danger is that unimportant stories might get major exposure merely because the television station has the tape or the newspaper has a photo.

Proximity

A page-one story in Chicago may be a brief in Miami. Many smaller newspapers and broadcast outlets pursue the "local angle" in almost every story they use; for them, news truly begins at home. The editors at these organizations realize that community news sells, and they are striving for innovative ways of identifying and presenting local stories.

Curiously, many of the large national chains of news outlets have been leaders in promoting local news. Gannett in 1991 began its News 2000 project, a program "to improve editorial content" by focusing on "community interests and reader needs in the planning and production of news." Knight Ridder in 1993 produced its *Local News Idea Book.* Its editors stated that local news "is important because it is the ingredient that allows newspapers to distinguish themselves from other media."

Magnitude

Sometimes an event attracts so many spectators that it must be covered. The Woodstock rock concert in 1968 started out as a minor happening that became a major story when 400,000 spectators attended. The danger is that editors and reporters will ignore stories rich in human interest that attract little attention. Conversely, the bandwagon effect can make a story seem more important than it is. As media organizations strive to outdo each other, a story can receive much more coverage than it deserves.

Impact

Stories affecting many people are important; that's why death and taxes are closely covered. But sometimes a story with impact is not easily identified, especially in its early stages. AIDS was treated as a minor medical curiosity when it was first diagnosed in the 1980s among what was seen as a select group. News organizations were slow to respond to it as a serious threat to the population at large.

Conflict

It's a key element in any drama, but sometimes those involved in a story complain that only angry words get reported even if conflict was a minor part of a happening. Some editors have decried how news organizations cover public life as a game, with everyone divided into winners and losers.

The movement of public journalism arose in reaction to the "horse race" coverage given elections, with an emphasis on who's ahead in the polls and who has the best campaign strategy. Public journalism, also called civic journalism, sought to take election coverage back to a debate of issues relevant to the community. Rosen (1994) writes that public journalism seeks to encourage "civic participation or regrounding the coverage of politics in the imperatives of public discussion and debate."

Topics as News Values

News organizations have come to realize that their readers and listeners have interests that differ from the traditional news values outlined above. Knight Ridder in its *Local News Idea Book* edited by Smith and Rhodes (1993) states that when readers are asked about the things they want to see, 10 topics appear on almost every list:

1. Education: What's happening in the schools

2. Parenting: Family issues

3. Environment: Earth issues, quality of life, development

4. People: Stories about people like me

5. Career: How to get ahead, successful people

6. Work: Issues of the workplace

7. Money: How to make, save it

8. Time: How to find it, spend it

9. Health: Fitness, nutrition, leisure

10. Consumerism: Getting value for your dollar

The News Meeting

News judgment on the macro level finds its expression in the news meeting, sometimes called the doping session, budget meeting or news huddle. As we saw in Chapter 1, these meetings are held several times a day. At newspapers, the first daily news meeting may occur in the morning with the last happening in the early evening, five or six hours before the last piece of copy is sent to the composing room. Some sections of the newspaper, such as features or special Sunday sections, will plan editions weeks in advance similar to the way magazines work. At broadcast stations, the final news meeting may happen much closer to broadcast time.

How a newsroom makes its decisions ranges from a senior editor barking out instructions to a vote by everyone in the news meeting. This process can take place in a closed conference room or out in the middle of the newsroom. The principals involved can include a small core of newsroom leaders or can extend to readers of the newspaper. News meetings at many newspapers have changed over the last 20 years in three important ways: first, more diversity in the participants with more women and minorities represented; second, more democracy and less top-down decision making; and third, more planning that has permitted decisions in a 10 a.m. meeting that used to be reserved for 4 p.m. or even 5:30 p.m. meetings.

At a newspaper, the news meetings will be attended by section editors: national, metropolitan, features, sports, business, photo and possibly graphics. At broadcast stations, the assignment editor, news editor, top writer, producer and maybe the news anchor will attend.

News meetings have three goals:

1. Decide on the all-important lead story and on other front-page stories. Often the opinions of editors from other sections are valued.

2. Avoid duplication between sections. An important sports person dies; does the story go on page 1 or on the obituary page?

3. Discuss the competition: What do the wire services have? What do other news outlets have?

When editors meet to decide on news, the results depend on who is calling the shots. When the editor-in-chief or the news editor presides over the news meeting, power is always part of the equation.

By nature, news people are competitive types, and the news meeting may be their one chance a day to impress the boss. Argyris (1974), in his classic study of the *New York Times* newsroom, found that a "win-lose dynamic" affected judgment; *Times* employees he interviewed said the news meeting could become "a forum for 'outshining' others, and for gaining visibility with the leader."

In these meetings, news judgment is affected by two factors:

1. Who can make the best argument. Editors often succeed on charisma. Or sometimes it's just who can talk the loudest. The

smart editor knows that not every story he or she likes can go on page one. Instead, this editor pushes those stories that have real news value; he or she soon gains respect for good news judgment.

2. Who owns the press or transmitter. The owners of news outlets vary from the starched-collar conservative to the Barnum-like showman.

Right and wrong can be elusive because our tools are weak for measuring success: whether our audience is served by our decisions. Many editors prefer it that way, believing their job is to present news that readers need, but in today's environment, editors must balance what they believe readers need to know with what they want to know.

The largest gap in a newspaper newsroom tends to be between word people, where status resides, and visual people, where often it does not. At the best magazines, the art director plays a pivotal role in bringing words and visuals to a page with impact. At many newsletters, the role of editor and designer tends to blur into a production role. Over the last 20 years, newspapers have moved closer to an art director model by elevating design positions into senior management with titles such as "assistant managing editor for graphics and design" or, more recently, "presentation editor."

Designers often live tortured existences in newspaper newsrooms. They struggle under the burden of being considered lightweights because their backgrounds and their interests generally do not run deeply into news reporting and writing, the base on which many section editors and senior editors have built their careers. Designers often feel they endure the ramblings of editors obsessed with stories that average readers could not care less about. And when the designers think they might find allies in photojournalists and photo editors who appreciate the power of visual communication, they are more likely criticized by them for running photos too small.

Visual storytelling has been the domain of photojournalists and graphics artists as long as technology has permitted reproduction of their work. The term "visual journalist," which was coined to elevate the role and to foster appreciation of designers and graphics artists in the newsroom, is beginning to catch on, though it's a long road to equality. Photographers are still striving to be recognized—and deployed—as photojournalists, not just shooters. Ironically, they are out of the loop because they spend so much time out of the newsroom and in the community. When visual people are quiet and reserved, they tend to be overmatched rhetorically in news meetings.

Changing Values

News organizations are moving away from classic standards of news judgment, spurred by increasing competition from new media. Editors and publishers are realizing that traditional approaches to news judgment were formed in part by the biases of past editors and publishers rather than from a concern for readers. The only thing certain is that editors and reporters must expect change and handle it with an open mind.

AN EDITING STRATEGY

An editing strategy becomes necessary because of deadlines: You'll find that you'll always want more time than you have to edit a story and to write a headline. The following strategy is based on the premise that editing errors do not carry the same weight. Some errors will kill your credibility, some errors will embarrass you, and some errors will go unnoticed by the reader. Before you finish editing, you must eliminate all the killer mistakes and embarrassing errors, and clean up as many of the other mistakes as time allows.

Many errors in grammar, punctuation, usage and style are not killer mistakes. Editors usually can't afford to spend much time on them, but the language still is important. The solution is to have language skills down cold. One reason we stress language skills is so you can fix language problems automatically.

The Killer Mistakes

You must pay special attention to the killer mistakes. We've listed seven here:

1. *A flawed lead.* You must sweat every word, every letter of the lead. Make sure it has no typos, no erroneous information and no missing information. You may have to rewrite a lead, but any changes there must be approved by your supervisor. You won't have time to treat every part of the story like this. The lead deserves the special attention because it may be the only part of a story that someone reads.

2. *A flawed headline.* Like the lead, you must sweat every letter of the headline: no typos, no erroneous information, no missing information that's vital to telling the story. The headline deserves special attention because any error will be set in large type and because far more headlines are read than story leads. Headlines and leads are high-visibility areas.

3. *A misspelled name.* Whether it's the name of a person, a place or a thing (organization, disease, animal, whatever), it must be spelled correctly. Fixing a misspelled name does not require reading comprehension, just concentration and respect for the importance of getting names right.

4. *A libelous statement.* Anytime you're dealing with charges, accusations or negative comments, you must be fair to both sides.

5. *A wrong location.* If a story contains an address that appears unreasonable or if it mentions a neighborhood that doesn't sound right, check it out. It helps an editor to know the community and how it's laid out.

6. *A problem quotation.* Make sure that each quotation deserves to be there and that it does not just repeat something paraphrased before.

7. *A mistake you introduce.* This is the worst mistake you can make. Your job is to improve copy. If you do a great job of cleaning up a story, but through your rewriting you introduce a typo, all that hard work goes for naught. Be especially careful that any time you change copy you do not create a new mistake.

The Embarrassing Mistakes

Here are mistakes that will embarrass you:

- *A spelling error of a word other than a name.* As we've noted, misspelled names fall under the killer mistake category. Editors soon find that readers know how to spell and willingly notify the paper of errors.
- *A grammatical mistake.* This is a sure way to look bad.
- *A punctuation mistake.* A misplaced punctuation mark is a good way to trip a reader and irk a supervisor.

The Tedious Mistakes

Some mistakes probably will go unnoticed by readers, but not by a supervisor, someone the editor must impress. Here are three of those errors:

1. *A style mistake.* Unless it's a glaring inconsistency or oddity, readers won't be bothered by style. Making a style mistake, however, is a big deal to a supervisor. He or she is likely to conclude that you don't know your stylebook or what it takes to be a good editor. Moreover, of all the things that a supervisor has to worry about, style should not be one of them. Style problems should be cleaned up by you before they get to the supervisor.

2. *A usage mistake.* Readers aren't always aware of the niceties of standard English usage, but some readers will notice. More important, the supervisor will notice. The same fallout that an editor suffers from a style mistake applies here as well.

3. *A lack of tightening.* Although readers may get an uneasy feeling about all those words passing before their eyes, they still will read loose writing if the content is interesting enough. The supervisor, however, will take pride in omitting needless words, phrases or clauses. If the supervisor has to do too much of this, it will reflect poorly on the editor. Tighten writing, but don't fall into the trap of tinkering with words when time and big mistakes are passing by. Also, stories can be edited too tightly. Any time an editor makes a change, he or she should ask if meaning has been lost.

Getting in the Swing

A good editor knows when to slow down and when to speed up. Correcting some mistakes will take the same time for experienced editors as for beginners. For example, an old-timer probably won't be any quicker at checking something in a phone book than a rookie.

Other mistakes may bog down some editors and not others. For example, some editors do not have to look up how to spell certain words; others do. Likewise, some editors don't have to turn to a grammar book or style book to correct mistakes. These small points add up to the difference between a good, fast editor and a slow editor, who by definition is not that good. Speed is important in editing.

Approaching each story with a systematic method, such as the one we have outlined below, will help you develop into a good editor.

A Step-by-Step Approach

The key to editing success is to approach each story systematically and to make sure you're spending your meager amount of time appropriately.

You cannot edit a piece properly without going over it at least twice. Although several steps are listed here, the editing process at its simplest breaks down like this:

- Make one sweep to read the story to catch as much as you can.
- Write a headline.
- Make a second sweep to clean up everything else, particularly any mistakes you may have introduced on your first edit.

Deadlines being what they are, you may find on the job that you have time for only a first sweep and a headline. In practicing to become a good editor, you should follow the seven-step process below until it becomes automatic.

1. Do the little stuff.

Get the small, mechanical but important parts of the job out of the way first:

- *Check the slug.* The slug is a one-word name usually assigned by the news editor. It becomes the official reference for all things relating to that story. For a story slugged TRIAL, you may have a TRIAL caption, a second story slugged TRIAL SIDEBAR, and for later editions, a substitute story slugged SUB TRIAL. On the computer, put the correct slug in the appropriate directory field. Getting the slug right is important for tracking and locating stories as your shift wears on.
- *Check the column width and type styles.* Some computers require that you type the correct measure, or column width, and type style in the directory field. On other systems, this information may go at the top of the text as a code. Make sure it's right, because a mistake here can mean missing a deadline. Most systems have a default that sets copy in body type at the standard width, usually about 12 picas or 2 inches.
- *Mark up the byline or other special type.* On the computer, a code must be entered for the byline and any title that may follow, such as "staff writer." Not all stories have bylines; wire stories often do not. If there is one, make sure it's right.

- *Clean up paragraphs.* Sometimes on the computer, the paragraphs may not be inserted properly, especially if the copy was received from a different system or from a reporter in the field.
- *Clean up the bottom of the story.* On the computer, go to the bottom of the story and remove any unnecessary type that may result from electronic transmission. On some computer systems, identifying information finds its way here.
- *Write the specifications for your headline.* You'll have to enter the headline code either in the directory field or at the top of the story. You'll receive headline orders from your supervisor, who gets them off the page layout.

2. Make your first sweep.

Your goal on the first sweep is to clean up the glaring errors and get a good sense of what the story is about. On your first sweep of the story, fix any mistake that (1) doesn't require you to look up the answer and (2) doesn't make you lose track of the story's meaning. Editing skill can be defined by the number of corrections you can make on this first sweep without turning to a reference book.

Look for mistakes in: grammar, punctuation, spelling, style, usage and typos. Tighten the copy by omitting needless words. This step is directly related to your speed. Speed is everything when you're editing. About the only other place you can gain speed is with headline writing. The ability to write good headlines quickly can free up time for other editing chores.

Flag key points that you know you'll want to check later. Most computer systems let you put in nonprinting notes. Use these to mark names so you can check at a glance whether each mention of a name is spelled the same way. On the first sweep, you shouldn't stop to check anything, but you should flag everything that bothers you, or you may forget it later. The notes will not be printed by the typesetting machine if you forget to take them out later.

Pay special attention to the parts of the story that make you stumble. If you have to reread something to understand it, that's a problem. Be sure to flag it, and later when you go back to fix it, do not make the mistake of rereading the segment repeatedly and then talking yourself out of making a change. Trust your first impression and ask for help from your supervisor if you need it.

3. Sweat the lead.

After making the first sweep, you now begin to concentrate on the mistakes that can kill you. And there's no better place to begin than with the lead. Sweat every word, every letter. Decide whether the lead needs to be rewritten to include more information or to make it consistent with information lower in the story. Before you rewrite a lead, however, check with your supervisor. Many publications do not allow changes in the lead without clearing them with the writer.

4. Write the headline.

A few stories, such as the obits you'll do at first, will not require a headline; some get just a boldface name line, some other label or nothing at all. In those rare cases, you can skip this step and move on to the next.

When writing a headline, start by examining the lead. A weak lead will make for a weak headline. That's why you shouldn't skip step 3. At the same time, you shouldn't wait until the end to write the headline. You never know how long it will take you. Start it now. If you can complete the headline quickly, do it. If you get stuck, don't waste time. Go back to your editing for a while and try the headline again later. Sometimes taking a step back from the headline helps. The advantage of trying to write a headline at this point is that you get a second chance if the headline doesn't come to you immediately. If you wait to write the headline at the end, you have no second chance.

Before you continue to the next step, check the words in your headline against the ideas in the lead. If your headline takes a different angle, either your headline is bad or your lead is bad. Use this headline-writing step as a way to double-check your editing of the lead. If you were right to include an angle in the headline that's not in the lead, then consider rewriting the lead.

Never turn in a headline with a misspelled word. That makes the headline worthless. Check every letter before you are finished with your headline. Chapter 9 can help you to write good, interesting headlines.

5. Eliminate other killer mistakes.

At this point, go back to the problem areas you flagged on the first sweep and concentrate on the biggest problems first.

Since time is of the essence, be suspicious of a name only if it is spelled more than one way or if the name is unusual. You never want to be caught with a misspelled name, but you won't have time to check everything. Other major concerns are locations, quotations and libel.

- Locations

  Are the addresses right? Does the neighborhood name jibe with the address listed? When time is short, check addresses only if they look suspicious or if the story hinges on directing people to a particular location, be it for a funeral or a lecture at the public library.

- Quotations

  Do they advance the story? If they just repeat a previous paraphrase, then edit out the quote or the paraphrase.

- Libel

  If it is a crime story, look for potentially libelous statements. Make sure you are being fair and charges are clearly attributed. See chapter 6 for guidelines.

6. Clean up what you've missed.

The first place to look is for mistakes you introduced through sloppy editing. Be careful. Introducing a mistake is a mortal sin.

You may have been distracted on your first sweep and missed a point of grammar, punctuation, spelling, usage or style. Or you may have to look up something. You may find writing that should be tightened. But don't fall into the trap of tinkering with words and wasting time that could be better spent clearing up a big mistake or rewriting your headline.

7. Double-check the headline.

After more thought about the entire story, you may come up with a better idea for a headline. The best way to improve writing is to rewrite, and that particularly applies to headlines. Headlines are important enough to spend any extra time on them.

FINAL NOTE ON DEADLINES

The process outlined above is complex; it takes practice. Success depends in part on knowing your news organization and your community. You'll find that deadlines become easier to meet as you gain experience. You should know, too, that not all stories are created equal. Many complex stories will reach your desk early in your shift when you can give them the time they deserve. In some sections of a newspaper, such as features, little editing is done on deadline. Magazines also are edited well in advance of publication. You have more time in magazine editing, but be warned: The standards for accuracy are much higher. Magazines routinely check every fact in an article.

RULES FOR GOOD WRITING

An old newsroom joke says that editors separate the wheat from the chaff—then print the chaff. The joke rings true for many in the news business who have had their copy weakened by *hack editors,* those who make changes without really knowing why. To avoid being this kind of editor, you should have clear ideas about what makes good writing. Here are a few guidelines that will help you critique the copy you edit.

I. Use sentence structure to emphasize what is important.

Good writers know what they want to emphasize and how to express it. Think of a sentence as having three parts: a beginning, a middle and an end. The beginning and the end are the most emphatic; the least emphatic part is the middle. Whether a phrase should go before a clause or after depends on what you want to emphasize. The greatest emphasis falls on what you say last. Take this sentence:

In the heat of the night, he left the house.

As written, his act of leaving is emphasized. If *the heat of the night* is what you want to emphasize, then write:

He left the house in the heat of the night.

Keep emphasis in mind when editing news stories. Take this lead:

> *Firefighters battled for hours to contain an inferno that engulfed and destroyed the Empire State Building Thursday night.*

Although the verbs are strong, the emphasis is wrong. The lead has two main points: the destruction of the Empire State Building and the cause, fire. They should be in the two emphatic parts of the sentence. Here, as in most straight news stories, the time element is of secondary importance. It should be buried in the middle of the sentence. Compare that lead with this:

> *The Empire State Building was destroyed Thursday night by fire. Firefighters battled the blaze for hours to no avail.*

In a straight news story, the first few words of a lead should identify the topic of the story. In the first lead, you have to pass over 14 words before you get to the two main points buried in the middle of the sentence. Note that in the first lead, the time element (Thursday night) was emphasized at the end.

In the second lead, the first four words sum up the topic of the story. The minor time element is rightly buried in the sentence, and the cause of the destruction is emphasized by its placement at the end.

Note also the difference in sentence length between the first lead and the second. Writers mix long, medium and short sentences for variety and rhythm. They use short sentences for emphasis. The stark second lead has added impact.

One more thought on emphasis and the end of a sentence: Attribution is almost always best at the end of a sentence in newspaper writing. (In broadcast writing, the attribution comes first.) When attribution is tacked on to the end of a sentence, the emphasis is on what preceded it. Consider this:

> *Police said John Franklin, 23, of 2113 N. Sedgwick St., was charged with rape and murder.*

Although *police said* is an important part of the sentence, readers would be more interested in the name of the suspect and the charges he faces. The sentence should read:

> *John Franklin, 23, of 2113 N. Sedgwick St., was charged with rape and murder, police said.*

Here, more emphasis is on *John Franklin* and on *rape and murder* than on *police said*.

2. Use passive voice only when necessary.

Passive voice, despite what you may have heard, is not all bad. Sometimes it is preferable to active voice. You must be able to identify passive voice and to determine if it is the best way to make a point.

Passive voice means the subject of a sentence is the receiver of the action expressed by the verb. For example:

The car was driven by him.

The subject, *car*, is receiving the action *was driven.*

Passive voice has three characteristics: (a) a form of the verb to be (in this case, was), (b) a past participle (driven), (c) the preposition *by*, either present or understood.

You should avoid passive voice for two reasons: It's wordy, and the verb is weakened. Compare the passive voice example above with this active voice version:

He drove the car.

The sentence in the active voice is shorter and more dynamic.

You should use passive voice for two reasons:

1. Sometimes the receiver of the action is more important than the doer of the action. Many news-story leads are written in the passive voice to accent the receiver of the action. Remember the passive voice lead above that began *The Empire State Building was destroyed.* Compare that with the active voice lead that began *Firefighters battled for hours.*

2. Sometimes the doer of the action is not known or not important, for example:

   The murder suspect was arrested.

   In this case, the authorities making the arrest don't need to be mentioned.

   The mysterious fire was set in the office.

   In this case, the doer is unknown (and the preposition *by* is understood, not expressed).

By using passive voice only when necessary, the writer varies sentence length and structure, which enhances writing.

Understanding passive voice helps you avoid "false passives." An example:

The student was given the answers by the teacher.

In the true passive, the subject is the receiver of the action. *The student was given* is a false passive because the student was not given, the answers were. It should read:

The answers were given to the student by the teacher.

Or better yet:

> *The teacher gave the student the answers.*

False passives often show up in headlines like this: *Mayor given award.* Make it *Mayor gets award.*

3. Don't turn verbs into nouns or adjectives.

The verb is the most important part of speech. Bad writers take good dynamic verbs and turn them into nouns, often by adding the suffixes *-tion* or *-ing.* They use verbs such as *to make, to conduct* or *to hold,* or even *to be,* the weakest of all verbs. In each of the following examples, the first sentence uses a strong verb; the second uses a verb as a noun:

- *The panel will examine the problem.*
  The panel will make an examination of the problem.
- *He is studying the project.*
  He is conducting a study of the project.
- *The group meets this week.*
  The group is holding a meeting this week.

A related problem is turning verbs into adjectives, particularly with *-ful* endings. In each of the following, the first sentence has a strong verb, the second a verb as adjective:

- *He hopes he will win the race.*
  He is hopeful he will win the race.
- *We are watching the situation.*
  We are watchful of the situation.
- *Money helps our cause.*
  Money is helpful to our cause.

Resist the temptation; save and use vivid verbs.

4. Use parallel construction.

Similar thoughts should be expressed in the same way. Look at this sentence:

> *He wants to attend college, to graduate and get a job.*

This is lazy and wrong. Make the last item parallel by saying:

> *He wants to attend college, to graduate and to get a job.*

In this example, infinitives are used correctly throughout:

> *We plan to go home, to get dressed, to go outside and to go swimming.*

In this sentence, present participles are used correctly:

> *He specializes in running good pass patterns, catching the ball and scoring touchdowns.*

Notice in this sentence how each title follows the name:

> *The speakers were Rudolph Giuliani, mayor of New York; Madeleine Albright, secretary of state; and Mark Yudof, president of the University of Minnesota.*

Don't mix the order by saying: *New York Mayor Rudolph Giuliani; Madeleine Albright, secretary of state; and Mark Yudof, president of the University of Minnesota.*

Newspapers often set off a list of items with a colon after an introductory clause. Each item is listed in a separate paragraph, usually with a "bullet." For example:

> *The friend gave the couple these options:*
> * *A divorce.*
> * *A separation.*
> * *An annulment.*
> * *A session with a marriage counselor.*

The bulleted list is a useful device if the items are kept parallel as shown; an article begins each item. Otherwise, it can get confusing. Don't do it this way:

> *The president promised:*
> * *Lower taxes.*
> * *An improved leadership condition.*
> * *Higher income.*

Make the second item *Better leadership.*

Use parallel construction for neither/nor and either/or statements. What follows neither/either must be in the same form as what follows the nor/or. Write it this way:

> *We want neither to go nor to stay.*

The two infinitives are parallel. Don't write it like this:

> *We want neither to go nor stay.*

Here's an example using gerunds:

> *He liked either running or fishing.*

Don't write it:

> *He liked either running or to fish.*

The same holds for the not only/but (also) construction, often misused. What follows the *not only* must be in the same form as what follows the *but (also)*.
Here's an example using two adverbs:

> *We like being not only there but also here.*

Don't write it like this:

> *We not only like being there but also here.*

This parallel construction uses two verbs with their helping verbs:

> *We not only can go but will go.*

Don't write:

> *Not only can we go, we will go.*

Starting a sentence with *not only* can easily get you in trouble.

5. Keep subjects near verbs and modifiers near words they modify.

In this example, the subject *Mayor Richard M. Daley* is separated from the verb *stated* by 13 words:

> *Mayor Richard M. Daley in his first address to the City Council in almost a month succinctly stated that he runs the city.*

Here's an improved version:

> *In his first address to the City Council in almost a month, Mayor Richard M. Daley stated that he runs the city.*

When modifiers, adjectives and adverbs get separated from the words they modify, the result can be humorous—and embarrassing. Here's an example:

> *Skating all out, the puck rocketed into the net on Hull's slap shot.*

Sort it out this way:

> *Skating all out, Hull rocketed the puck into the net with a slap shot.*

6. Choose a short word over a long word when no meaning is lost.

The two words *start* and *initiate* mean the same thing. Use *start*. Say *try* rather than *endeavor*. Say *trouble* rather than *inconvenience*. Appendix D provides a list of words and phrases that can be simplified.

When injuries are mentioned, put the medical terms into everyday language. Instead of *lacerations, contusions* and *abrasions*, make it:

> *The man suffered cuts, bruises and scrapes.*

Beware of those who write with a thesaurus in hand; they seek out elegant variations, often out of an unwarranted fear of repeating themselves. Use the same word over and over if the alternative is an elegant variation. *Chicago* written 20 times is still better than one *Windy City* in a news story.

7. Try to keep one idea to one sentence.

Beware of the dasher, the writer who uses the dash to stuff as many ideas as possible in a sentence:

> *The City Council enacted an ordinance Wednesday that would virtually ban the sale or use of drug paraphernalia—an ordinance supported by Mayor Richard M. Daley's allies but fought by independents—by a vote of 45–5.*

Instead, write:

> *The City Council enacted an ordinance Wednesday that would virtually ban the sale or use of drug paraphernalia. The ordinance was supported by Mayor Richard M. Daley and his allies but was fought by independents. The vote was 45–5.*

8. Use contractions properly.

Avoid using contractions in straight news stories, except in quotations. Reserve them for light feature stories. In this example from a news story, the contractions are inappropriate:

> *The jurors didn't convict the man of murder because they couldn't reach a consensus.*

Make it:

> *The jurors did not convict the man of murder because they could not reach a consensus.*

> Use formal writing for a formal event. Also, shun odd contractions, such as *he'd* for *he would* and *it'll* for *it will*.

9. Avoid *-ize* verbs.

Using *-ize* obscures meaning or unnecessarily adds syllables. Don't say *The family was Chicagoized.* Say *The family was acclimated to Chicago.* Don't say *utilize,* say *use.*

10. Don't split infinitives unless absolutely necessary.

An infinitive is split when one or more adverbs come between the *to* and the verb. For example, *to really emphasize.* In general, avoid splitting infinitives but know that occasionally a split cannot be avoided to make a succinct, clear statement. For example:

The president sought to sharply reduce taxes hindering business investment.

Split infinitives also may be acceptable when you want to really emphasize a point. Here are some do's and don'ts:

Don't write: *You have the chance to swiftly and conveniently deactivate the system.*
Make it: *You have the chance to deactivate the system swiftly and conveniently.*

Don't write: *He asked me to not help her.*
Make it: *He asked me not to help her.*

11. Tighten by making clauses into phrases, phrases into words.

A clause contains a subject and a predicate. Clauses beginning with relative pronouns such as *who, that* and *which* often can be reduced to phrases. For example: *Alvin Jones, who is president of the fan club, arrived.*

Make it: *Alvin Jones, president of the fan club, arrived.*

Or: *Fan club President Alvin Jones arrived.*

Another example: *The president is achieving his main goal, which is reducing spending.*

Make it: *The president is achieving his main goal: reduced spending.*

Yet another example: *The councilman attacked the plan that is being considered by the panel, which was set up by the mayor.*

Make it: *The councilman attacked the plan being considered by the panel set up by the mayor.*

WORKOUT: SENTENCES

A natural progression in learning how to edit is to understand first how the language works, then how to edit sentences, then how to edit stories. Here, we'll concentrate on sentences.

In editing, you need to know where to direct your energy. Working with sentences limits the variables and helps focus your attention on what needs to be changed and what should be left alone. Take time to think about how you would edit each sentence. Then we'll explain how we would do it and talk about how others have edited these sentences.

Sentence 1

■ It was his intention to do research on the subject so that he could conduct an intelligent interview with his guest.

Let's take this concept by concept: *It* is used either as a pronoun or as an expletive. An expletive is a word or phrase not needed for sense but used to fill out a sentence grammatically. Take this sentence: *The book is funny; it is my favorite.* The word *it* is a pronoun taking the place of the noun *book.* Now, consider only this sentence: *It is my favorite.* Try to drop the *it* and say the same thing by rephrasing the other words in the sentence. You can't. That's a sign that you're dealing with a pronoun, not an expletive.

Now look again at sentence 1. What is *it* replacing? The answer is nothing, so *it* can't be a pronoun. It's an expletive. Try to drop *it* and say the same thing by rephrasing the sentence. Rather than saying, *It was his intention,* you can say, *He intended.* Being able to drop *it* is a sign that you're dealing with an expletive.

You don't always have to delete expletives. Sometimes you'll use them in features and columns because they lend a light tone to writing. They also show up in quotations because that's the way people speak. Sentence 1, however, can be tightened and improved by deleting the expletive.

When you're editing, tune into noun endings, such as *-tion, -sion, -ance, -ence, -ment* and *-ing.* Then ask yourself, are there strong verbs crying to get out? If so, free them and improve your writing.

In sentence 1, which nouns have trapped verbs? We talked about one already, *intention,* and we freed the verb *intend.* We see two others: *research* and *interview.* Don't write *to do research;* make it *to research.* Don't write *He could conduct an intelligent interview with his guests;* make it *He could interview his guests intelligently.*

So here's how we would have reworked the sentence:

He intended to research the subject so that he could interview his guests intelligently.

A common question that arises is, do you need the word *that?* Most often *that* belongs or doesn't belong as a matter of style. Make sure you read the entry on *that* in the *Associated Press Stylebook.*

Here's some of the thinking behind our style: Sometimes the possibility of confusion determines if you use *that.* Take this sentence:

The company declared a dividend would not be issued.

Without *that* after *declared,* it sounds first as if the company declared a dividend, a specific business term. The missing *that* distracts the reader—exactly what we don't want to do.

Sometimes using *that* depends on how a sentence sounds. Take this sentence:

The mayor said that the program would begin in June.

In this case, *that* is unnecessary and should be dropped to tighten the writing. A *that* immediately after *said* can almost always be dropped. But compare this sentence:

The mayor said Saturday that the program would begin in June.

In this case, *that* becomes necessary because reading the sentence is too difficult without it *(The mayor said Saturday the program).*

Sometimes using *that* depends on tone. Including *that* after *so* in sentence I seems fitting because the sentence was written in a formal tone. The same idea expressed in an informal tone would go something like this: *He was going to study so he could look good as an interviewer.* With an informal tone, drop *that.*

Where you place *intelligently* also is related to tone. What's the difference between saying, *He could intelligently interview his guests,* and saying, *He could interview his guests intelligently?* Well, when you place an adverb between the helping verb *(could)* and the main verb *(interview),* the tone of your sentence is more informal. Many newspaper stories are cast in an informal tone. Feature stories are an obvious example, but stories with an informal tone can be found in news, sports and business sections. Some articles, such as obits and crime stories, are written in a formal tone because the topics are so serious.

The point is to realize how small parts of writing add up to create a formal or an informal tone. The placement of adverbs is one factor; the use of expletives is another. Contractions weigh into this. Using them adds a light tone to writing; not using them helps set a formal tone.

Word choice is another important factor. Whether you say "take a bus" or "catch a bus" depends on the appropriate tone for your story. When you're writing or editing, decide what tone is most appropriate for a story and follow through.

Here's another way to edit sentence I:

He intends to research the subject before interviewing his guests.

There are a few mistakes here. First, the tense changes from past *(was in the original)* to present *(intends).* This is sloppy editing. Sometimes it's better to use present tense, but not here. The original said he intended to do something. You don't know whether he did it or whether he still intends to do it.

Second, the editor edited too tightly. Anytime you cut a sentence ask, *Have I lost important meaning?* The interviewer is concerned about looking intelligent. That idea is lost. Another editor dropped *with his guests* when editing the sentence. Was the subject going to interview sources for a story or guests on a show? Again, the problem is editing too tightly. How about this version?

He intended to research the subject in order to intelligently interview his guests.

The editor changed *so that he could* to *in order to*. The editor used three words instead of four, but is it really a good change? Notice that either version uses the same number of syllables (four) to say the same thing. Readability studies show that as you decrease syllables you make writing more understandable. Here, one version is not better than the other; remember that ties go to the writer. Also, *in order to* is a phrase that is stilted and is overused. We don't consider this type of change worth the effort. Of course, the biggest mistake is splitting the infinitive *to interview*.

Along the same lines, another editor changed *subject* to *topic*. Since the meaning is the same, we consider this hacking, not editing. Such changes waste valuable editing time that could be better spent other ways. When words mean essentially the same thing, the writer's way stands. The writer was there first with *subject*, so leave it as is.

Fixing things that aren't broken is a common editing mistake. The motive for doing this often is that the editors feel uncomfortable with what was written because it's not the way they would have done it. That's not a good enough reason to change copy. When you're editing, you're judging not how the writer stacks up against you but how well the writing will communicate with readers.

Sentence 2

■ He could not get an extention of his work schedule.

This is an extension of what we just talked about. (Did you notice the spelling error?) Knowing where to focus is important. Some editors would just change the spelling and move on. Others, remembering what we said about turning verbs into nouns, would rewrite the sentence: *He could not extend his work schedule*. The problem is that the sentence still doesn't make much sense. A common mistake in editing is tinkering with words rather than concentrating on what they mean.

This is a sentence one of the authors had to edit on the job. He wasn't sure what the writer meant, so he asked him. The meaning was, *He could not get time off*. Hard to believe, we know. The point is that you can't edit what you don't understand. Good editors don't try to be mind readers. They ask the writer. Sometimes that's impossible because of deadlines. It's often better to delete an ambiguous statement than to try to reword it. Much to the writer's dismay, editors tend to change things that are unclear to make them clearly wrong.

Here are some other bad ideas on how to edit this sentence:

- Changing *could not* to *was not able to*. We want to say the same thing in fewer words.
- Changing *could not* to *couldn't*. You can't make this change without knowing the tone of the story.
- Changing the sentence to *He could not get a work-schedule extension*. Now the phrasing is not only ambiguous but also awkward.

Sentence 3

■ I would like to give you assistance in making alterations in your vacation plans before you come to a
conclusion on them.

What nouns are trapping strong verbs? We see three: *assistance (assist* or *help), alterations (alter* or *change)* and *conclusion (conclude, complete* or *finish).*

    Would like is the kinder, gentler way of saying *want.* Remember writing
friendly letters in grade school? Well, *would like* is more appropriate for that kind of
writing, and *want* is more appropriate for news writing. Again, it's a question of word
choice and tone. Here's our first crack at editing the sentence:

    I want to help you decide on your vacation plans.

Anytime you make a change that radical, stop and ask, Have I lost important meaning?
Sometimes editors get heavy-handed and edit too tightly when they run into bloated
phrasing. The editor ends up wielding an ax rather than a scalpel.

    Look again at the original. Our major change involves the last half, *in mak-
ing alterations in your vacation plans before you come to a conclusion on them.* On second thought, it sounds more like the request was to help with tentative vacation
plans. This is better:

    I want to help you fine-tune your vacation plans.

    The original writing was sloppy, but that doesn't justify sloppy editing. When
you edit weak writing, you are more likely to make a mistake. You are not exactly
sure what was meant, and after muddling through bad sentence after bad sentence,
you tend to change copy out of frustration. Chances are great that at some point you
will go overboard. A classic confrontation in the newsroom is the hack writer squar-
ing off with the good editor who vastly improved an article but changed one unclear
statement to make it clearly wrong. The hack writer complains; the editor is repri-
manded. Nothing is said about how everything else in the story was improved. After
all, that's what the editor gets paid to do.

    Here's another thought on how to rework the sentence:

    I want to help you change your vacation plans before they are final.

This editor is good at condensing and simplifying individual thoughts, but think about
what the whole statement says. It sounds as though the person is more interested
in manipulating than helping. That wasn't our impression of the original statement.
You would have to ask the writer to be sure.

    Another editor changed the beginning of this sentence to *Let me help you.*
Remember the sloppy editor who changed the verb tense? Well, this sloppy editor

changed the verb mood. The original is in the indicative mood, a straight statement of fact. This is in the imperative mood, a command. Not a good change.

Would you say, *I want to help you finalize your vacation plans?* No, because *finalize* is not better than *fine-tune* in this case. *Finalize* is used to mean *complete, finish, end* and *put in final form.* The more possible meanings a word has, the less effective it is.

Good editors make clauses into phrases and phrases into words without losing meaning.

Sentence 4

■ The candidate, who has announced that she will make a run for the presidency, will give a talk on politics at the university.

We hope you see two incidents of verb bashing here. First *make a run* can be simply *run.* Second, *give a talk* can be just *talk.*

Look at this clause: *who has announced that she will make a run for the presidency.* Can you make the entire clause one word? *Presidential* would work. Again, any time you make such a radical move, consider whether you've lost important meaning.

When you're looking to make a clause into a phrase or into just a word, tune in to the pronouns *who, which* and *that* when they are matched with the verbs *to be* or *to have.* The verb *to be* may show up as *am, is, are, was* or *were.* The verb *to have* may show up as *has, have* or *had.* So far we have this:

The presidential candidate will talk on politics at the university.

Now what does *on politics at the university* mean? Does it mean the university's inner-office politics, or does it mean that the candidate will speak at the university on politics in general? Your job as an editor is to make sure that a writer speaks with one voice. If something can be read the wrong way, it will be. In this sentence, words would have to be added or rearranged to make the writer's point clear.

Let's talk about how you should not have edited this sentence:

- By changing *talk* to *speak* or *lecture.* What's the difference between *talk* and *speak?* Both mean the same thing and both are one syllable. Which do you go with? What the writer wrote. *Lecture* is bad on two counts: It has two syllables and it has a bad connotation: Who wants to get lectured on anything by a politician? Again, readability studies suggest that we should change multisyllabic words to one-syllable words, if we do anything. Also, not all talks are lectures, so changing *talk* to *lecture* changes the meaning as well.
- By changing *has announced* to *announced.* *Has announced* is in the present perfect tense; *announced* by itself is in the past tense. The meaning is different. *Has announced* suggests that the declaration came a while ago. *Announced* implies that it just happened.
- By changing *talk on politics* to *talk politics.* It's a question of tone. To say, *I want to discuss the matter* is to speak in a formal tone. To say,

Let's talk turkey is to speak in an informal tone. Formal tone seems more appropriate for sentence 4.
- By changing *talk on politics* to *talk about politics*. Again, you're fixing something that's not broken, and you're saying in two syllables what you can say in one.
- By capitalizing the "U" in *university*. AP style says no.

Sentence 5

■ The patients were given examinations by the doctor on a one-to-one basis.

One problem with this sentence involves not just passive voice but a false passive. With passive voice, the subject receives the action expressed by the verb. With false passive, the wrong word receives the action of the verb. Consider this statement as a full sentence: *The patients were given.* What does this mean? Given up to the gods? What the writer meant to say was that the *examinations* were given to the patients.

You may have resurrected the verb *(The patients were examined)* or used active voice *(The doctor examined)* without noticing this discrepancy. False passive shows up in headlines such as this one: *Mayor given award.* Again, the mayor wasn't given; the award was given to the mayor. A better headline would be *Mayor gets (or wins) award.*

Another problem with sentence 5 is the word *basis.* Like the word *manner, basis* is almost always a tip-off to tightening. Here's how we would have reworked this sentence:

The doctor examined the patients individually.

This also could do the trick: *The doctor examined each patient.* Some editors, however, err by dropping the "one by one" angle. The writer is trying to emphasize that the examinations weren't done two by two or en masse. Here's a change that would make some writers' skin crawl:

The patients received personal medical examinations.

The *-tion* problem is just rearranged and the meaning is obscured. Medical examinations can be done by nurses or nurses aides or technicians, not necessarily doctors. The editor moves the writing from the specific to the general. That's going the wrong way.

Sentence 6

■ The politician skirted the issue in a clever manner, as he does on a regular basis.

We can change *in a clever manner* to *cleverly,* and *on a regular basis* to *regularly* or *often.* Here's how we would have reworked the sentence:

The politician skirted the issue cleverly, as he does often.

When we edit, we try to keep the same sentence structure used by the writer. It isn't always possible to do, but if you can, your improvements will be clearer to the writer and you'll be less likely to bungle something. There's no need to leave your mark on everything you edit. Our goal is to have writers thank us for helping them but still feel as though the work is theirs.

Let's talk about other ways to edit this sentence. Consider this:

The politician cleverly skirted the issue as he always does.

Putting the adverb *cleverly* there changes the original structure and separates the subject from the verb. Usually it's best to keep the subject and verb together. Placing *cleverly* between the subject and the verb doesn't really change the tone, but it does slightly shift the emphasis. Here it doesn't make much difference, but consider how the meaning of this sentence changes as the word *only* moves around:

Only I slapped him in the face.
I only slapped him in the face.
I slapped only him in the face.
I slapped him only in the face.

Think twice before you move modifiers around.

The ending *as he always does* is a problem. *Often* and *always* don't mean the same thing. This is sloppy editing. Other editors came up with *typically* and *as usual* to express *on a regular basis.*

How a sentence sounds is a factor in editing. This sentence not only misfires but sounds bad:

Typically, the politician skirted the issue cleverly.

Who said editing is easy? Try this example:

The politician, as usual, skirted the issue cleverly.

This version changes the structure and splits the subject and verb, but it could work.

Another person changed *skirted,* a perfectly good word, to *avoided.* Lazy editors change words that make them feel uncomfortable rather than turn to a dictionary to see if the word is used properly.

Sentence 7

■ Charles Jones, who is president of the club, handled the controversy in an adept manner.

Let's see how much you've learned. *Who is* should have jumped out at you. That clause can become a phrase just by dropping *who is* or by condensing and moving the title before the name, as in *Club President Charles Jones.* Note that *president* is lowercase after the name but capitalized before the name, according to AP style. Also, *in an adept manner* can become *adeptly.* So here's how we would rework this sentence:

Club President Charles Jones handled the controversy adeptly.

We didn't put *adeptly* between *Jones* and *handled* to maintain the original structure. One editor changed *in an adept manner* to *well*. It's better to stick with a variation of the writer's word than to insert your own.

Sentence 8

■ He took strong exception to the judgment and made no mention of the crime.

By now we hope you're focusing on *exception* and *mention*. The use of *exception* is a more complicated problem because it's part of the expression *to take exception*, meaning to object or to feel offended. Before you can change the wording, you need to know what was meant. In this case, the phrase probably is closer in meaning to *object* or *disagree*. If the writer meant *He was offended by the judgment*, then you see the problem of rewriting such an expression.

Let's say the context of the story points us to *object*. Saying *He objected to the judgment*, however, is not enough. You need to preserve the idea of *strongly*. At the very least, it must be:

He strongly objected to the judgment.

When writers use adverbs to modify verbs, they usually are better off looking for stronger verbs. In this case, what verb combines the ideas of strong objection? *Condemn* might work. But by changing the phrasing to *He condemned the judgment*, you're taking two steps away from what the writer wrote. *Took strong exception* became *strongly objected*, and that became *condemned*. The further you move from the original, the riskier it gets. That's why it's important to consult the writer about changes. Is *condemned* overstating the reaction? It could be. On the job, with the writer unavailable, we would be more likely to go with *strongly objected*. *Made no mention of the crime* is easier. That can become *did not mention the crime*. So here's the safest way to play it:

He strongly objected to the judgment and did not mention the crime.

Put *strongly* after the subject rather than after the verb because *objected to the judgment* needs to be kept together. A big mistake is changing *did not mention* to *failed to mention* or *ignored*. *Failed* implies that he should have; who are you to say what the man should have done? *Failed* is a loaded word that should be used with care. *Ignored* is another example of taking two steps away from the original and heading down the wrong path. It implies that he deliberately disregarded something when, in fact, he may have just forgotten.

One editor did this:

Taking strong exception to the judgment, he didn't mention the crime.

This shows a relationship between the actions that wasn't expressed in the original sentence and may not exist. Also, the contraction adds a lighter tone than what was expressed in the original.

Sentence 9

■ **The car which he wants is too expensive.**

Stop anytime you see *which* introduce a clause like this. Grammatically, the word is called a relative pronoun, and the alternative is *that.* Your first inclination should be to change *which* to *that* because the two are commonly confused. But the meaning and emphasis of a sentence changes depending on which word you use. If you use *which*, you should also use commas. Think of your choices as *that* or *comma/which*. Here are two ways this sentence could read:

The car, which he wants, is too expensive.

Here the emphasis is on the clause *The car is too expensive.* The idea of *which he wants* becomes secondary; it's more of an afterthought. Grammatically, the *which* clause is considered nonessential to the meaning of the sentence. Compare that sentence with this:

The car that he wants is too expensive.

Here, *that he wants* defines the car we're talking about. Which car is too expensive? The car he wants. Grammatically, the *that* clause is considered essential to the meaning of the sentence.

Now which sentence is correct? Probably the second one, but it depends on what the writer meant. If you edited this sentence by just deleting *which,* making it *The car he wants is too expensive,* you decided on the second meaning. The word you really deleted is *that.* Here's another example to illustrate the difference between nonessential (which) clauses and essential (that) clauses:

Students who don't know grammar shouldn't argue with teachers.

This is a warning to only those students who don't know grammar. The clause *who don't know grammar* restricts the meaning of *students.* Now consider this:

Students, who don't know grammar, shouldn't argue with teachers.

This means all students don't know grammar and all students shouldn't argue with their teachers. The clause is nonrestrictive.

Before we leave sentence 9, consider this change:

He wants a prohibitively expensive car.

This is the work of a frustrated editor longing to be a writer. Good editors rewrite only monstrosities, not simple sentences. Compare this version with *The car he wants is too expensive.* The point here is made in nine syllables. The alternative takes 12 syllables. Just another reason it's a mistake.

Sentence 10

■ He is hopeful that his group can revise its profit picture upward.

Strong verbs get lost not only in nouns but also in adjectives. The suffix *-ful* is a common culprit. Not *He is hopeful,* but *He hopes.* A news writing convention is to say *He says he hopes.* Writers are advised not to get into people's heads and to report just what those people say. This keeps writers from getting duped by people saying they hope something happens, but they really don't. The same applies to *think, believe* and *feel.* You don't always have to qualify such statements with *says* or *said,* however. The rule applies to sensitive or questionable information. Sentence 10's context suggests that *he hopes* is fine.

Always beware of jargon that obscures meaning. Don't say *revise its profit picture upward,* when you can say *increase profits.* Don't say *down-sized cars;* say *smaller cars.* Here's how we would have reworked this sentence:

He hopes his group can increase profits.

Including *that,* an optional move, would lend a formal tone. One editor changed the present-tense *can* to the past-tense *could.* That would work only with, *He hoped his group could increase profits.*

These sentences show that editing is a complex task. Even a seemingly routine change can hinge on understanding the news, the tone of the story or the writer's intentions. One editor at the *Chicago Tribune* always advised new employees, "Don't be the Lone Ranger; ask questions." Asking questions of reporters and of your fellow editors will give you the understanding you need and deliver you from error. When in doubt, ask.

CHAPTER

3

Get Me a Quote

By necessity, by proclivity—and by delight, we all quote.
—Ralph Waldo Emerson

I never said most of the things I said.
—Yogi Berra

Editors need to take special care when handling quotations. For the reader, quotation marks signal a speaker's exact words, whether they are or not. For many news people, quotes are untouchable, and editing them may be considered a grave mistake. When you first take your place on a copy desk, ask your supervisor about the news organization's policy on quotes before you do anything.

What is a quote? It is any part of the copy that is enclosed in quotation marks and attributed to a source. This is not a fine distinction. No quotation marks? No quote. For a number of reasons, an editor may choose to remove the quotation marks. Then the copy becomes a paraphrase and can be edited like any piece of copy.

Because of newsroom policy that discourages editing quotes, many editors feel uncomfortable doing anything when they see quotation marks. But many stories can be improved when editors read quotations with the same critical eye they use on other copy.

We would be naive to think that what reporters present as quotes are always the exact words of the speaker. Instead, reporters give us their best representation of what a speaker said. The exact words of the speaker are filtered by the reporter's hearing, note-taking, attention to detail, news judgment, typing skills and language skills. Even so, the editor must defer to the writer when handling quotes.

The AP stylebook advises not to change quotes even for grammatical changes. We've found that many publications allow one-word grammar fixes. But take note: Anything beyond that requires special punctuation or paraphrasing. We may be preaching heresy when we say that quotes are not untouchable. But we still advocate caution. What the editor does with a quote requires good judgment and a thorough understanding of the story.

QUOTES: THE FEW, THE STRONG

Quotes should be strong. They should advance the story. Quotes should not repeat what's in the paragraphs preceding them. Quotes should be consistent with the content of the story. As editors, you need to understand how quotes get into a story before making changes.

The Origins of Weak Quotes

Weak quotes come from several places.

- *Publicists.* Smart publicists use long quotes in their press releases because they know writers and editors are hesitant to dig in and cut quotes. Such quotes usually hold little news value and often are self-serving to the publicist's client. In targeting broadcasters, publicists know the value of actualities, taped quotes that the newscaster can insert into the broadcast. And television producers see more and more "video press releases," with ready-made "interviews."

  Although quotes in press releases often are attributed to people in high positions, the quotes likely were written by the publicist and approved by the person "quoted." The quotes become their words. The same goes for taped actualities; the questions asked contain no surprises and result in planned responses. For these reasons, many quotes from press releases, typed or taped, are empty of real news value.
- *Lazy writers.* A story filled with quotes requires less thinking on the part of the author. Some reporters practice "tape-recorder journalism." By letting the tape recorder run and by using the quotes at length, the writer lets the story write itself, becoming a stenographer rather than a reporter. This often results in meaningless and repetitive quotes, or paragraph after paragraph of unbroken quotes.
- *Desperation.* A writer sometimes will use a quote because he or she got it right. It may not say much, but it's right. The writer may be under pressure to produce quotes in the story; the days of news editors barking, "Get me a quote!" are not dead.

The Indispensable Quote

Quotes are almost mandatory in news stories of any length. Here's why:

- *Quotes lend authority.* The quotation marks say to the reader, Here are the exact words. Along with this sense of authority comes the appearance of accuracy, even though the reporter may not get all the words right.
- *Quotes give visual relief.* Just as a long, unbroken series of quotes can be boring, so too can the long story unrelieved by quotes.

In printed matter, quotes relieve grayness in copy. A quote should begin with a new paragraph. In one news-writing formula, the first two paragraphs set up a quote in the third paragraph.

In broadcasting, too, quotes provide welcomed relief from news being read by reporters. The popularity of the sound bite comes in part from this ability of quotes to add variety.

- *Quotes draw in readers.* Quotes make the story feel more human; they put the reader in touch with the speaker. Quotes are an excellent way to characterize a subject, much better than a description.

When to Quote

Not all quotes are created equal. A quote usually is worth keeping if it comes from an important person, it is unique, or it was said uniquely.

- *Someone important says something important.* The emphasis is on who and what. When the U.S. Senate was sworn in by Chief Justice William Rehnquist at the beginning of President Clinton's impeachment trial, the *Minneapolis Star-Tribune* ran the entire oath in bold type above the headline "Senate Becomes Jury."
- *Someone says something unique.* Often the quote will be a straightforward, newsworthy statement. The emphasis is on what is said.

  News conferences often produce routine material not worth quoting. Such is not the case when the news conference is used to announce a rare occurrence with real news value. When basketball star Michael Jordan retired in January 1998, his news conference was totally predictable. Nevertheless, Jordan's words were quoted at length, in newspapers and magazines, and on radio and television. Even National Public Radio used actualities of Jordan's news conference on its news show "All Things Considered." The unique quality of the event made the routine statement newsworthy.
- *Someone says something uniquely.* When a source has a way with words, good quotes result. Often such a quote brings out the human dimension of an otherwise complicated or dull story.

  Stories about economics often fit this description. In a December 1998 story about low prices for farm commodities, the *Minneapolis Star-Tribune* ran this quote from Karen Richter, who farms with her husband, Dave, near Montgomery, Minn.:

  "I think we'll get through this. I hope we'll get through this. You know, part of the land Dave's dad owns was given to a Civil War widow. I wonder what she would have thought of what's happening now."

  The rest of the story gave statistics on pork prices, numbers made more meaningful by Karen Richter's words.

STRATEGY FOR EDITING QUOTES

Before you evaluate a quote, keep in mind the importance of punctuation: The quote is what goes between the quotation marks. Words contained within quotation marks have special status, so be careful.

Adding Quotation Marks

In editing quotes, the editor has one hard and fast rule that must never be violated: Don't add quotation marks to something just because it sounds like a quote. Here's an example:

Baghdad will fire on warplanes violating Iraqi airspace, Vice President Taha Yassin Ramadan said.

The novice might make it:

"Baghdad will fire on warplanes violating Iraqi airspace," Vice President Taha Yassin Ramadan said.

Even if the sentence is essentially what Ramadan said, placing it in quotation marks allows the charge to be made that Ramadan wasn't quoted accurately. Sources sometimes make such charges to discredit stories critical of them.

Tactics for Saving Quotes

Saving a quote means that the editor preserves at least part of what's said in quotation marks. Sometimes this means removing material and using the partial quote. Sometimes this means adding explanatory words in brackets. Ways to save quotes include using snippets, ellipses, brackets and one-word grammar fixes.

Snippets

A snippet is a partial quote, sometimes as short as one word. A full quote can contain more words than it's worth but still have critical language that must be quoted.

In the example cited above, the U.S. Senate took this oath on Jan. 7, 1999, from Chief Justice William Rehnquist:

"Do you solemnly swear that in all things appertaining to the trial of the impeachment of William Jefferson Clinton, president of the United States, now pending, you will do impartial justice according to the Constitution and laws: So help you God?"

An Associated Press story for afternoon papers of Jan. 7 boiled that down to this:

Senators today were taking an oath to "do impartial justice," and Chief Justice William Rehnquist was assuming his role as presiding officer for Clinton's trial on charges of perjury and obstruction of justice.

But don't overuse snippets; they can make the reader eye-weary. See below.

Original:
Sen. Trent Lott of Mississippi said the best way for senators to remain "cool and calm" would be to "hear each other" and to "talk to each

other," adding that the Senate was in "uncharted waters." At the White House, Joe Lockhart, Clinton's press secretary, said the president's lawyers would make a "compelling case" for acquittal.

Edited:
Sen. Trent Lott of Mississippi said the best way for senators to remain "cool and calm" would be to hear and talk to each other, adding that the Senate was in "uncharted waters." At the White House, Joe Lockhart, Clinton's press secretary, said the president's lawyers would make a "compelling case" for acquittal.

Be careful not to introduce an ungrammatical or awkward shift in pronouns when you use a snippet.

Original:
In a brief statement issued by the association, Bourassa said he was quitting for health reasons. His doctor "has recommended that I immediately discontinue all stressful activity. Therefore, I hereby resign as president of the Smith Mountain Lake Association effective May 24, 1985."

Edited:
In a brief statement issued by the association, Bourassa said he was quitting for health reasons. He said his doctor had recommended that he "immediately discontinue all stressful activity."

"Therefore, I hereby resign as president of the Smith Mountain Lake Association effective May 24, 1985," Bourassa said.

Ellipses

An ellipsis signals that words have been removed from the quote. A good quote with a stretch of useless or repetitive information in the middle of it can be shortened with ellipses.

Be aware, however, that ellipses can serve two purposes: to mark where material is missing or to indicate a pause. Here is a confusing use of ellipses:

On the day he stabbed bus driver Luther Crowder, Edmonds said that "Queen Isabella stomped me with her foot to my mind . . . there was no way to base my mentality . . . no way to survive . . ."

In the example above, ellipses serve only to draw attention to what's missing. Ellipses are unnecessary at the beginning of the second sentence in the quote below, too:

"The safest thing will be to bow out now and let everyone know," said Bill Houck, vice president in charge of public relations for Festival Park. ". . .A lot of people probably put a lot of time into it and we know they'd like to be in that water, but it's just too dangerous."

Brackets

Sometimes one or two words of explanation in brackets or parentheses can save a quote from being meaningless or hard to understand.

Original:
"He is making a mockery of the United States justice system," the senator said.

Edited:
"He [Clinton] is making a mockery of the United States justice system," the senator said.

One-Word Grammar Fixes

When the emphasis is on what is said, not who is saying it, clean up the grammar. It's not fair to hold people to mistakes in grammar; people don't talk as neatly as they write. Mistakes get in the way of what is being said and distract the reader.

Original:
"That little girl is very brave," Hanson said. "She was laying there with half her arm off, but she laid there and behaved herself and did exactly what we told her to do."

Edited:
"That little girl is very brave," Hanson said. "She was lying there with half her arm off, but she lay there and behaved herself and did exactly what we told her to do."

In the example above, a story about rescuing a child from an accident scene, the speaker's grammar mistakes only serve to distract the reader from what's important in the story: the little girl's bravery and the drama of the rescue. But note that only the words *laying* and *laid* were changed. To change more—and leave the quotation marks in place—would be a big mistake.

Sometimes grammar has a bearing on the story. For example, a story was written about a man who wanted to educate his son at home and was being prosecuted under state truancy laws. Here is one of the few quotes from the story:

"My son won't go to these schools," Hermanstyne said. "They cannot teach him nothing in the sciences."

Should the editor change it to "anything about the sciences"?

A question the story explored was if the man was capable of educating his son at home. His grammar would seem relevant to answering that question. Even so, the editor who handled the story recognized that the quotes were sparse. Did he speak perfect English for most of the interview, only to have one of his rare slip-ups selected for the story? To do so would have characterized the speaker unfairly.

The editor checked with the reporter before fixing the grammar. The reporter said the man used atrocious grammar for two hours. The quote was not unfair, and because grammar had a bearing on the story, it was left as written.

When the emphasis is on who is speaking, leave grammar alone. In feature stories about people, quotes often are used to characterize the subject, bad grammar and all. But be careful of phonetic spellings used to convey dialect. Consider this quote:

> *"I'm gonna draw my pay and then I'm takin' me a little vacation," Bonner said.*

The phonetic spellings make the quote hard to read. Are they really necessary or fair? Many of us drop our g's or say "gonna" or "wanna" instead of "going to" and "want to." One of our former presidents used to talk about the *zekative branch of gummint*, but writers always translated it into *executive* and *government*. Writers seem to use dialect only when the speaker is from a rural area.

Another problem is that writers aren't consistent with phonetic spellings. Consider this:

> *"I'm gonna draw my pay and then I'm takin' me a little vacation," Bonner said. "Upon my return, my wife and I will look into buying the quaint English Tudor on the hill."*

How do you fix the inconsistency? Translate the phonetic spellings into common spellings.

When a Quote Can't Be Saved

In sizing up a quotation, an editor may decide that the information is valuable but that more than one-word grammar fixes are needed to make the quote readable. In this case, the editor can paraphrase the quote. At other times, the editor may decide to delete the quote.

Paraphrasing

Remember that paraphrasing is not a way to save a quote. The first step is to remove the quotation marks. In doing so, the editor is saying, these are no longer the exact words of the speaker. It is no longer a quote.

After you remove the quotation marks, you can edit the words like any other piece of copy.

> Original:
> *"On subsequent investigation of the terrain, CENCOM determined that a vertical insertion of troops would best facilitate success of the planned interdiction," Ridgeman said.*

> Edited:
> *After mapping out the terrain, the central command decided using paratroopers would be the best way to make the attack a success, Ridgeman said.*

Paraphrasing also is a useful tool when a writer lets quotes run for several paragraphs. After the quote runs for two or three paragraphs, the editor can look for a change of direction or a change of subject, then paraphrase a sentence or two. This adds variety and also can supply a valuable transition to the story.

Deleting the Quote

If you can't paraphrase the quote, or if it's not worth saving, then delete it. Anything irrelevant, wrong, libelous, unnecessary or inconsistent should be cut.

In this example, the quote is libelous and irrelevant:

> *"We nailed the rapist,"* an unidentified bystander said. *"Now, we just hope some do-gooder judge doesn't let him go."*

This quote is libelous because the person arrested in the case has been convicted in print as a rapist—and by an anonymous person. It's irrelevant because it expresses an extreme opinion of the court system. The best thing to do would be to delete the quote.

One More Time—Carefully

Because people don't speak as neatly as they write, virtually every quotation you see in a newspaper could be said better in a paraphrase. Keep in mind the importance of having quotes, and remember that the editor's first approach is to try to save them.

Two of the most common mistakes are:

- Making more than one-word grammar fixes and not removing the quotation marks
- Killing a quote worth saving

Finally, context is sometimes more important than what a person said. Consider this excerpt from a Newsweek story about radio personality Don Imus:

> *Does Imus go too far? "I'm the f—-ing I-man!" he explodes. "What do you mean too far! What, are you crazy?"*

The quote above is just as it was written except some of the context has been removed. It makes Imus seem like an egomaniac. But here's the quote as the reporter, Evan Thomas, actually wrote it:

> *Does Imus go too far? "I'm the f—-ing I-man!" he explodes, or pretends to. "What do you mean too far! What, are you crazy?"*

Now the quote takes on a playful nature and tells us much more about the personality of the speaker. Context makes the quotes mean different things.

Broadcasters, with their time pressures, must be vigilant against what Walter Cronkite calls the "malquote." This is a quote taken out of context or without explanation of what question the speaker was answering.

A Few Words on Profanity

In 1950, the actor Jack Webb created a sensation when he said the word *damn* during a TV episode of "Dragnet." Today, profanity is inescapable: on street corners, on television and in the news.

Reporters more and more will find sources who use profanity in answering even routine questions. In the quote from Don Imus, it's instructive that he dropped the F-word without hesitation on a reporter from a national news magazine.

When a reporter runs into a source who swears, the reporter may believe the profanity must be included if quotes are to be accurate. Then the editor has to make the decision on whether to cut out the swearing or leave it in. How does he or she decide?

Using Profanity

Don't go out of your way to offend. When profanity is necessary, don't rub the reader's nose in it. It's one thing to use profanity in a story; it's quite another to put that profanity in a headline, a teaser or a pull quote (a quote set in larger type).

When selecting a pull quote, make sure something inoffensive doesn't become offensive when it is removed from the context of the story. Remember that many readers scan these pieces of larger type and never get to the story. Here's an example:

In the November 28, 1987, edition of the *Chicago Tribune*, a travel writer told about a trouble-filled trip he took to England. In the story, he quoted a British cabby as saying, "Keep your *pecker* up, sir," carefully explaining that pecker to the British means *chin*, as in "Keep your chin up, sir." The pull quote, in 14-point bold type set smack in the middle of the page, used the quote without the context, running the risk of unnecessarily offending readers.

WORKOUT: HANDLING QUOTES

Here are some sentences and paragraphs that include quotes. Edit each example, then see how we would do it.

Remember that in editing quotes, the words within the quotation marks must remain the same. You can punctuate or shorten quotes, insert words in brackets or make one-word grammatical fixes. Or you can paraphrase: remove the quotation marks and edit what would then be just another piece of copy.

This first sentence is from a news story about the budget, and the speaker's evaluation is just one of many presented.

■ 1. "Between you and I, the budget is too fat and getting fatter," said Bruce Fosdick, the mayor's special assistant for finances.

First, size up the quote. Is it worth saying? Even without the context of a story, this looks like a good quote because it says something in a unique way. We would keep this quote.

That decision being made, let's turn first to the attribution. For the most part, you'll use the subject-verb construction in your attributions: *Fosdick said.* But when a long appositive follows the name, one that would separate the subject and verb, then go to the construction we have in sentence 1.

The next problem is grammar. *Between you and I* should be *between you and me.* Do you fix it? That depends on emphasis. If this were a profile of Bruce Fosdick, and if the reporter had good reason to characterize him as a man who doesn't use good grammar, then the emphasis would be on who is speaking. You wouldn't fix it. But the context, a news story about the

Publication Policy

In making such a decision, the editor must respect the news organization's policy on profanity. Most newspapers see themselves as family publications and forbid most profanity.

When a newsmaker utters a profanity that is important to the story, the editor must find a way to convey that to readers without offending them. In the Don Imus quote, *Newsweek* attempted to soften the force of Imus's profanity by making it *f—ing* while leaving the word in to retain Imus's irreverent nature. Some publications would just delete the offending word, believing that using hyphens doesn't really hide the word from readers.

Many publications have no reluctance to let profanity stand if it is important to the context of the story. *The New Yorker*, surely one of the most dignified magazines on the newsstand, routinely allows all varieties of profanity to appear in its pages.

Writer Freedom

Columnists, especially highly paid stars, are allowed to take their writing where other reporters can't. Often they are encouraged to be controversial and to take risks. Editors may warn their supervisors about what a columnist has written, but the editor can't make even small changes without the columnist's consent.

Sometimes the columnist will use profanity, usually in a quote. Mike

budget, puts the emphasis on what is being said. In that case, make the one-word grammar fix.

Sentence 1 should read like this:

"Between you and me, the budget is too fat and getting fatter," said Bruce Fosdick, the mayor's special assistant for finances.

Remember, we're talking about one-word grammar fixes. Now look at this sentence from a story on a hearing to determine if contraceptives should be distributed at an inner-city high school:

■ **2. "Where was you peoples when we needed you?" the pregnant teen-ager told the education committee.**

Do you clean up the grammar in this quote? First, consider the context. The quote is good because it characterizes the consequences of teen-age pregnancy; the teen-ager's loss of education is clear from her language. If the emphasis is on who is speaking, then leave the grammatical errors.

Caution: You should know that what used to be simple matters of editing are complicated today by concerns about sensitivity toward disadvantaged groups. In the end, many editors will feel uncomfortable with this quote because it may reinforce a stereotype of a racial or social minority. Be aware of how your fellow editors feel about this, especially your superiors, and be up to date on the policies of your news organization.

How about this quote?

■ **3. When asked who authorized the break-in, the president said, "It wasn't me."**

Several factors would lead us to leave this quote as is:

• The tone is conversational; fixing the grammar ("It wasn't I") would substantially alter the tone.

• We would leave the contraction as is. You should avoid contractions in news writing to preserve a formal tone, but allow the language in quotes to be conversational.

• The president, being an important person saying something important, will be quoted widely on this, probably on television. It wouldn't pay to use something other than his exact words.

(continued)
Royko, of the *Chicago Tribune,* who died in 1997, had a more profane style than most; his columns were routinely questioned by editors. In the vast majority of cases, Royko won because, well, he was Royko.

The danger is that other writers will see the columnist using profanity and sneak some into their writing. Feature writers often try this, and because features tend to be looser and freer with language, editors sometimes let the swearing stand. This pattern of creeping obscenity usually ends when the managing editor or editor-in-chief notices it and cracks down.

Broadcasters have the added burden of the Federal Communications Commission. For much of broadcasting's history, the FCC allowed no profanity on

■ 4. "I was just pullin' your leg," Jester said. "I wasn't going to steal it."

Fixing this quote involves a variation on the grammar fix: making phonetic spellings consistent. If Jester says *pullin'*, why doesn't he say *goin'*? Phonetic spellings should be used only in profiles or features where it is necessary to characterize the speaker, and then they should be consistent. Otherwise, convert them to the standard spellings. Make No. 4 read:

"I was just pulling your leg," Jester said. "I wasn't going to steal it."

The AP stylebook also says to avoid "abnormal spellings" such as *gonna* and *wanna,* especially in news stories.

■ 5. "The mayor suffered lacerations on his upper torso, abrasions of his face and contusions to his legs," the officer said.

This sentence is grammatically correct, but is it clear? *Jargon* is specialized or technical language used in various professions. In quotes, jargon presents a problem for editors. Often reporters are unwilling to sort through technical language, believing it is more accurate than everyday language. But jargon is difficult to understand and sometimes downright deceptive. Reporters and editors do readers a disservice by not translating for them.

Do we just change words, such as *lacerations* to *cuts*? Not without removing the quotation marks and paraphrasing. Paraphrasing does not save the quote! When you eliminate quotation marks, you eliminate the quote. Paraphrasing here can be done in two ways.

The first approach would be to change the jargon to simpler words: *The mayor suffered cuts on his chest, scrapes on his face and bruises on his legs, the officer said.*

Note how these medical terms are translated: *abrasions* equals *scrapes, upper torso* equals *chest* or *back* (you may need to check out which), *contusions* equals *bruises, fracture* equals *break, lacerations* equals *cuts* and *hemorrhage* equals *bleeding.*

The second approach to sentence 5 would be the minimalist scheme: *The mayor suffered minor injuries, the officer said.* The more important the person, the more detail you'll include.

■ 6. "No other facts were released, and the investigation is continuing," police said.

An editor can make a good case for eliminating this unnecessary sentence: It tells us nothing of importance. Remember

(continued)
the airwaves and had elaborate procedures a station must perform if one of the "seven deadly words" were spoken into a live microphone. The seven deadly words were all of four letters and referred to either a bodily function or a part of the anatomy.

Today, in the age of deregulation and cable television, broadcasters feel much freer to use profanity, to the point where one of the seven deadly words, *piss,* pops up regularly on talk shows and entertainment shows. News shows can't be far behind.

that you also would strike a quote that was libelous, irrelevant, wrong or inconsistent.

■ **7. The man in the street looked "dead," the witnesses told police.**

A lot of one-word snippets make their way into copy. The AP Stylebook says to reserve snippets for sensitive or controversial words that must be identified as coming from the speaker. A writer also may wish to use a snippet to emphasize a speaker's words: *The mayor said he was "directly opposed" to hiring more workers.*

Or a snippet may be used when the writer doesn't want the reader to think the words came from her: *The victim darted into the street without "even looking," the bus driver said.* In No. 7, the quotation marks are unnecessary; the word *dead* fits none of these criteria.

■ **8. Falk said that because he is off welfare, he is "happy I don't have to dance to the state's tune."**

When a partial quote is constructed carelessly, the words can come out as something confusing or impossible for the speaker to say. Here, the shift in pronouns from third person (he) to first person (I) produces the confusion. Make it:

Falk said that because he is off welfare, he is happy he doesn't have "to dance to the state's tune."

See how you would handle this paragraph:

■ **9. "We walked on eggshells as we approached the suspect," Sgt. Frank Lewis said concerning the arrest of Smith on the murder charge. "We took all the usual precautions you would take. We arrested him following ordinary procedure. We took him away. He'll be locked up for a long time; Wrigleyville can rest easy for another day," Smith said.**

Several approaches are possible with these sentences. All involve cutting down an overly long quote to save what is interesting. An editor could use an ellipsis like this:

"We walked on eggshells as we approached the suspect," Sgt. Frank Lewis said concerning the arrest of Smith on the murder charge. "We took all the usual precautions. . . . He'll be locked up for a long time; Wrigleyville can rest easy for another day."

Matter from the middle of the quote has been removed, so we've used an ellipses. Note that the ellipsis completes a thought, so we need four dots. If the word before the ellipsis constitutes a grammatically complete sentence, put a period at the end before the ellipsis. Leave a space before and after the ellipsis. Here is another approach:

"We walked on eggshells as we approached the suspect," Sgt. Frank Lewis said concerning the arrest of Smith on the murder charge. "We took him away. He'll be locked up for a long time; Wrigleyville can rest easy for another day."

Here, the ellipsis isn't necessary. Ellipses are not used at the beginning or end of quotes because it is assumed something always precedes or follows.

Note also that we've eliminated the second attribution, which says *Smith,* not *Lewis.* Mixing up names is a common mistake. Note that usually only one attribution is needed even if a quote spills across more than one paragraph.

How would you change these paragraphs?

■ 10. "Can we justify all those lost lives for about 4 percent of the oil we use here in the United States?" Sheldon asked. "Can we manage without that oil better than we can manage without those precious lives?"

"These are hard questions, Mrs. Schroeder, but they need to be asked," Sheldon concluded. "And they need answers before we get into a shooting war."

You should do two things: remove the close-quote after *precious lives?* and remove the second attribution. When a quote continues across two paragraphs, don't end the first paragraph with quotation marks, but do begin the second with quotation marks. Make it:

"Can we justify all those lost lives for about 4 percent of the oil we use here in the United States?" Sheldon asked. "Can we manage without that oil better than we can manage without those precious lives?

"These are hard questions, Mrs. Schroeder, but they need to be asked. And they need answers before we get into a shooting war."

Notice how this reads fine without the second attribution. The first attribution is best at the first logical break, usually at the end of the first clause. Partial quotes need different treatment. Edit this:

■ 11. Charles R. Woltz complained that the Bosnians have treated his son Troy as "a dishonored interloper. If my only son must end the Woltz line and give his life for our country, I believe he and the rest of the troops should be accorded a little of the warm fuzzies they deserve. Please intercede."

The jump from partial quote to full quote is uncomfortable. Start a new paragraph with the full quote:

Charles R. Woltz complained that the Bosnians have treated his son Troy as "a dishonored interloper."

"If my only son must end the Woltz line and give his life for our country," Woltz said, "I believe he and the rest of the troops should be accorded a little of the warm fuzzies they deserve. Please intercede."

Notice that the attribution for the full quote comes at a logical break, but that the sentence continues. That's why the comma is used after *said* and not a period.

Here's our next sentence:

■ 12. "This plan will really do a lot to reduce the deficit," the senator smirked.

How do you smirk something? Don't make a verb do more than it can. Variations on this theme are *he smiled, he laughed* and *he grinned*. More acceptable is *he joked*, but even that should be saved for when the speaker is really telling a joke. Here's how we would fix sentence 12:

"This plan will really do a lot to reduce the deficit," the senator said sarcastically.

Or:

"This plan will really do a lot to reduce the deficit," the senator said with a smirk.

A big mistake would be to make it simply *the senator said*. Without the context of his smirk, the quote would be misconstrued as a straight statement of fact and not sarcasm. Tone is important when twisting the language. Try this one:

■ 13. "I believe we should work to benefit all mankind, not just the rich," she noted.

Another case where the attribution is off the mark. Make it *she said*. Reserve *noted* or *pointed out* for a statement of fact, as in this sentence: *"Of course, the canal zone isn't located in Honduras," he noted.*

In news writing, *said* is preferred over other verbs because it is neutral. *Claimed,* for instance, implies doubt about the speaker's truthfulness. *Contended* and *asserted* are fine when the speaker talks with conviction. Avoid overworked forms such as *remembered* and *stressed*. Reserve *stated* for quotes from written reports or documents, or for formal statements that are spoken. Use *added* only when the statement immediately follows another.

Many writers are in love with the attribution *according to*. We wonder how it's different from *said* when a speaker is being quoted—other than it's wordier. *According to* can be useful when the quote comes from a book or a report. It certainly carries too much of a hard-news edge for feature stories.

Can you see what's wrong with this sentence?

■ 14. "The problem with this city is the mayor," officials of the fair-housing group said.

This sentence probably was the result of a reporter taking something directly from a press release. The reporter didn't hear the officials say this together, unless they also were a barbershop quartet. The easiest fix for sentence 14 is to remove the quotation marks.

■ 15. "Sen. Percy is a pain in the neck as far as the Pentagon is concerned," the admiral said.

This is a style point. The AP stylebook says to spell out titles in quotes with the exceptions *Dr., Mr.* and *Mrs.* Those always are abbreviated. Make it: *"Senator Percy is a pain in the neck as far as the Pentagon is concerned," the admiral said.*

■ 16. "Muslim scholars have issued a fatwa against any American who pays taxes to his government," bin Laden told Newsweek.

Here is a case where a word of explanation inserted with brackets can improve the quote. Make it:

"Muslim scholars have issued a fatwa [a religious order] against any American who pays taxes to his government," bin Laden told Newsweek.

The next three examples contain problems with quote lead-ins. Quotes should not appear in a story out of thin air. They need to be set up with a lead-in, a sentence that sets the scene and often introduces the speaker. The trick to writing a good lead-in is to connect the quote to the copy without being unnecessarily repetitive. For the first example, consider the two paragraphs to be from the middle of a story in which the speaker already has been introduced. How would you evaluate the lead-in?

■ 17. Brett was born with a hereditary disease in which a missing enzyme in the brain causes severe brain damage and loss of muscle control.

"For reasons that we don't fully understand, missing this enzyme interferes with normal early brain growth and development," De Vivo said. "This disease has put him in a chronic stage of sleep."

This lead-in works well. It describes the disease and its cause without stealing the essence of the quote. The two paragraphs have just enough repetition to connect them.

Now look at these paragraphs:

■ 18. The flood on Piney Creek caused $500,000 in damage and forced more than 160 people from their homes.

The Army Corps of Engineers has studied the creek since 1957, when floods "almost wiped the town out," Mayor Doris Landreth said. Now, she said, what the area doesn't need is another study.

"We don't need another study," the mayor said. "We need the damn creek fixed. Take what money would be spent on the studies and get in there and do some corrective work."

This is an example of unnecessary repetition in the lead-in and the quote. You could edit it two ways: Remove the repetitive part of the lead-in or remove it from the quote. The simplest approach would be to eliminate *We don't need another study* from the quote. The quote is strong enough without it, and leaving the phrase in the lead-in gives the reader a sharp entry into the quote.

Here's how the paragraphs would read:

The flood on Piney Creek caused $500,000 in damage and forced more than 160 people from their homes.

The Army Corps of Engineers has studied the creek since 1957, when floods "almost wiped the town out," Mayor Doris Landreth said. Now, she said, what the area doesn't need is another study.

"We need the damn creek fixed," the mayor said. "Take what money would be spent on the studies and get in there and do some corrective work."

You may wonder about the use of *damn*. Profanity should be considered carefully and handled according to newsroom policy. Some news organizations are more liberal about the use of profanity than others, but most would not object to the use of the word *damn*. (See our discussion of profanity earlier in this chapter.)

Here is one more example:

■ **19. A psychiatrist not connected with the state study of teenage suicides said he was not surprised by the results.**

> *"Nothing surprising here," Dr. Jan Fawcett, chairman of the department of psychiatry at Rush-Presbyterian-St. Luke's Medical Center, said. "You can't keep kids from committing suicide by just educating them about the problem and telling them where to get help. It's not an intellectual exercise. There's more to it than that."*

A couple of things could be handled better in this quote. First, use the lead-in to introduce the speaker. That way, you avoid breaking up the quote with a long appositive, and you keep *said* from dangling at the end of the sentence. Second, avoid the direct repetition in the lead-in and the quote. Here's how you could handle the paragraphs:

> *Dr. Jan Fawcett, chairman of psychiatry at Rush-Presbyterian-St. Luke's Medical Center, was not connected with the state study of teenage suicides but was not surprised by the results.*

> *"You can't keep kids from committing suicide by just educating them about the problem and telling them where to get help," Fawcett said. "It's not an intellectual exercise. There's more to it than that."*

Finally, let's look at a longer example, an item from an action-line column. In an action-line column, readers call in with problems and a reporter helps them solve them. Read the question, then edit just the answer. When you've finished, check how we did it.

> *Q—I hope you can help us. There is a family in the 6400 block of South Evans Avenue that has three or four cars parked in front of our doors. The people are taking parts from one car to the others. The man works night and day and has a flat bed truck that he hauls them on. There are also three or four big dogs barking all night. We can never park out front because of all this. Can you help?*

> *—The church and neighbors, South Evans Avenue*

> *A—"Please be advised," Police District Commander Julius Watson said, "that an investigation was initiated by this district's tactical unit and it was ascertained, after a four day surveillance, that vehicles were in the process of being repaired and a flat bed truck was also parked there, which had been used for transportation of said vehicles. The owner of the vehicles was contacted and stated that the vehicles were his and he would clear them away as soon as possible. A special attention was effected and vehicles will be cited if*

*found to be in violation. A continued surveillance of the area will be
monitored by the 3rd District abandoned vehicle officer."*

The first step would be to remove the quotation marks and paraphrase
the whole thing. Most of it needs to be translated from legalistic language; almost none of it is unique in what he says or how he says it. (The idea of a vehicle officer being abandoned was interesting, however.) Here's one approach:

*A—Cmdr. Julius Watson of the 3rd District said an investigation
found, after four days of surveillance, that vehicles were being re-
paired at the Evans Avenue address. A flat bed truck also was
parked there. The owner told police that the vehicles were his and
that he would clear them away as soon as possible. If they are not
removed, they will be ticketed, Watson said. Police will continue to
watch the area.*

Quotes require all the skills an editor can bring to bear, especially news
judgment, punctuation, grammar and style. Don't get in the habit of passing
over quotes with the idea that they can't be fixed. Careful editing can make quotations even more valuable to the story.

CHAPTER

4

It's the Language, Stupid

—

Grammar and logic free language from being at the mercy of the tone of voice. Grammar protects us against misunderstanding the sound of an uttered name; logic protects us against what we say having double meaning.
—Eugen Rosenstock-Huessy

The language skills—grammar, punctuation, spelling, usage and style—are the journalist's tools. What often surprises those new to the news business is how unsure many writers and editors are in using those tools. Their use of the language is governed by a list of do's and don'ts built up through years of experience. If you asked them why they did things a certain way, they would be hard pressed to answer. A common response is, "My former editor at the *Klaxon-Star* told me to do it that way, and he's a journalism legend." Too often, what that legendary editor told them was wrong.

In our section on editing strategy, we classified language mistakes as embarrassing errors. But misspellings, ungrammatical language and misused words undermine reader confidence in a publication, just as shoddy workmanship drives away a carpenter's customers. A study commissioned by the American Society of Newspaper Editors and released in December 1998 stated that a newspaper's credibility often is undermined by language mistakes. More than one-third of respondents said they see spelling or grammatical mistakes in their newspapers more than once a week, and 21 percent said they see them nearly every day.

In the sections that follow, we'll cover the five language skills every journalist must master: spelling, grammar, punctuation, usage and style. After each section, you'll find a workout that asks you to solve problems then compare your work with how we would do it.

SPELLING

Nobody in the news business likes misspelled words. A misspelled word in a story makes the writer or editor look bad. A misspelled word in a headline blares incompetence.

If writers and editors had to rely only on memory, spelling would be worse than it is. In today's newsrooms, however, journalists have more tools than ever to fight the spelling battle. Besides the traditional tools of stylebook and dictionary, journalists now can run their stories through computer spell-checkers, and many editing systems come with online dictionaries. For names and places, the Internet gives editors a way to go right to the source to check spelling.

Spelling can be broken down into two types of problems: The first concerns names of people and places and requires special resources. The second involves more common words and involves dictionary skills. In solving either of these problems, the first rule is *when in doubt, look it up.* That means understanding reference books.

Checking References

If you were to visit the desk of a daily newspaper as editors come in for their shifts, you would see them unpacking briefcases or visiting their lockers to get their reference books. Most editors have a "kit" of references they bring to their workstations. All editors need a stylebook and a dictionary. Editors on the news desks might add an almanac, a map of the city and perhaps state and local government guides. Sports editors might replace government guides with sports encyclopedias and press guides for the local teams. On the business desk, editors might add guides for looking up the names of firms.

When an editor's personal stock of reference books doesn't hold the answer, he or she will check other references on the desk. The list below includes some sources an editor might consult:

- *The telephone book.* The phone book contains names, addresses and phone numbers, as well as a wealth of information about the community. Phone books often contain white pages of residential listings, "gray pages" of business listings and "blue pages" for government listings.

  Some phone books are less useful than others because of how names are organized. To save space, some phone books list a surname, usually in capital letters, followed by the first names and addresses of those who share that surname. The problem arises with names that have unusual sequences of capital and lowercase letters, MacDonald for instance. In the phone book, it might read MACDONALD, leaving the editor in the dark as to proper capitalization. In those cases, further checking may be required.

  Sometimes the consumer and business yellow pages are helpful because they offer classified listings: all the auto repair shops are in one place, all the tire dealers in another.

- *City directories, or "crisscrosses."* A crisscross has two sections: one lists addresses in order of street and house number, then gives the names of who lives there; the second lists phone numbers in order by prefix, then tells who has that number.

- *Phone books for other cities, for nearby colleges and universities, and for large local organizations.* A newspaper in a large city will have dozens of phone books for its suburbs, but even a news organization in a small city will have phone books for towns in its circulation area.

- *Almanacs.* For names of people and places, and for historical facts, editors can turn to an almanac like *The World Almanac and Book of Facts.* It contains listings of prominent people with place and date of birth. It also has listings of all cities of more than 5,000 in population and all two-year and four-year colleges, among many other facts. Many editors don't place total trust in the almanac; it's put together under deadline and has been known to contain errors. If facts are critical to a story, a second source should be used for verification.

- *Encyclopedias.* People and places from around the world can be checked in an encyclopedia. A handy one-volume edition, such as the *Columbia-Viking Desk Encyclopedia,* can be kept right at the desk.

- *Who's Who.* The names and short biographies of prominent people from many fields are in these volumes. It's especially useful for editing obituaries.

- *State and National Directories.* For the names and titles of politicians and other government facts, turn to the state register, often called the "blue book" or "red book." Some states also publish a handbook of state government. For the national government, the *Congressional Directory* is useful.

    These same facts can be found on the Internet. All federal agencies have websites as do all state governments and many counties and cities. Editors today can access these sites from their editing terminals.

- *Place Name Tools.* A gazetteer, such as the *Columbia Lippincott Gazetteer of the World,* lists geographical locations in dictionary form. The U.S. Postal Service publishes complete listings of zip codes. Maps and atlas often are the quickest way of checking place names, especially hard-to-find ones like state and city parks.

- *Other News Outlets.* Often an editor will turn to other news outlets for information. Most desks keep numbers handy for their news services. The *Editor & Publisher* yearbook provides a comprehensive list of newspapers; *Broadcasting* magazine puts out a similar volume for radio and television.

- *Reference Room.* When resources on the desk have been exhausted, the editor can turn to the reference room. At large news organizations, the reference room may resemble a small library with a reference librarian on hand to answer queries. At smaller news outlets, the reference room will contain just the essentials: encyclopedias, almanacs, maps and the all-important clip files of past stories organized by topic. Very often, reference room materials, including story archives, are available through the news organizations internal network, or intranet, website.

The Spelling Hierarchy

To enforce consistency in spelling, news organizations have a hierarchy of sources. At the top, the stylebook overrules all other sources. It may be *The Associated Press Stylebook and Libel Manual,* or it could be the news organization's own stylebook. The AP stylebook, for the most part, agrees with *Webster's New World College Dictionary, Fourth Edition.* When that dictionary is silent on a particular point, the AP stylebook says to turn next to *Webster's Third New International Dictionary.*

For words not listed in the AP stylebook, editors turn to the dictionary and find the preferred spelling. All editors and writers should be working from the same edition of the dictionary, including online varieties.

Sometimes writers will try to justify spelling a word a certain way by saying, "Well, it's in the dictionary." That's not good enough; note that we said "preferred spelling." What is the preferred spelling?

1. It's the first spelling in the dictionary entry. This goes for suffixes, too, such as *-ation* or *-able. For example,* the dictionary lists *cancel,* and after the definition gives the variants as *canceled* or *cancelled.* The first ending given, *-celed,* is the preferred spelling.

2. If a word has two separate listings, then use the one with the definition. For instance, *usable* is listed in the dictionary with a definition. *Useable* is listed second but with no definition.

3. Do not use spellings that are introduced by *also, var.* (variant), *alt.* (alternate spelling) or *Brit.* (British spelling).

4. What if a word is listed two ways with different definitions? For instance, *voluntarism* had been the preferred spelling, with *volunteerism* listed as *also.* But the new edition of the dictionary lists the words separately with slightly different definitions. House style, which is set by the publication, then settles the issue, choosing one spelling or allowing both. We know of one large newspaper where the editors have decided to use *volunteerism* for all usages.

Electronic Aids

Today's editing terminals, often just personal computers with special configurations, are capable of much more than just word processing. A writer or editor often has access to a variety of electronic resources:

Spell-checking Programs

The spell-checker can speed the editing process, if the editor understands how it works. The spell-checker must use the news organization's dictionary of choice. One advantage is that the spell-checker dictionary can be customized to reflect local style. Spell checkers don't catch misused words—*their* instead of *there,* for instance. They can be unreliable with names. But used right, the spell-checker gives the editor an undeniable advantage on deadline.

Online Clipping Services

Most large newspapers and many smaller ones have electronic "morgues," online clipping files with some going back more than 10 years. Some of these files require special terminals, usually found in the reference room, but more and more news organizations allow an editor or writer to access the electronic morgue from the editing terminal. In addition, some news organizations may be a part of a collective electronic clipping service such as Lexis-Nexis. These services allow the writer or editor to search clipping files from newspapers and magazines using key words. Just one warning is in order: Using past articles to check facts works only if those articles were correct in the first place. Sometimes checking a spelling against a clipping only perpetuates a mistake.

The Internet

Many newspapers make the Internet available to editors through their editing terminals. For checking obscure spellings on deadline, the Internet may be of limited value because of the time involved in making Internet searches and because many websites are poorly edited. On the other hand, finding a specific organization or company on the Internet usually takes little time, and a company website would be considered an authoritative source for spelling the names of company officers. For example, the wire service *Agence France-Presse* was mentioned in Chapter 1. An Internet search engine quickly turned up a listing that confirmed the hyphen. The Internet is a vast source of information, but editors must learn to use it efficiently.

WORKOUT: SPELLING TEST

Here is a spelling test of commonly misspelled words. These words and additional words on the list in Appendix A have been gleaned from our personal experience as editors; they are words that give journalists trouble. Some words sound similar but have different meanings; see *complement* and *compliment*, for example. Consult the dictionary to understand the difference.

Circle the word that is spelled correctly in each pair. Choose the preferred spelling. After you've gone through all 69 items, read the answers and the explanations that follow.

1.	adviser	advisor
2.	protester	protestor
3.	impostor	imposter
4.	judgment	judgement
5.	harass	harrass
6.	embarrass	embarass
7.	accommodate	accomodate
8.	dietitian	dietician

9. longtime   long-time

10. re-create   recreate (to create anew)

11. counterproposal   counter-proposal

12. Realtor   realtor

13. rock 'n' roll   rock and roll

14. OK   okay

15. backward   backwards

16. toward   towards

17. afterward   afterwards

18. a lot   alot

19. surprise   suprise

20. restaurateur   restauranteur

21. disastrous   disasterous

22. paid   payed

23. receive   recieve

24. weird   wierd

25. desperate   desparate

26. separate   seperate

27. maneuver   manuever

28. liaison   liason

29. cemetery   cemetary

30. occurred   occured

31. occasionally   occassionally

32. referring   refering

33. canceled   cancelled

34. preferred   prefered

35. preferable   preferrable

36. possessive   possesive

37. responsibility   responsiblity

38. familiar   familar

39. fluorescent   florescent

40. grammar   grammer

41. misspell   mispell

42. memento	momento
43. minuscule	miniscule
44. definitely	definately
45. cannot	can not
46. consensus	concensus
47. assassinate	assasinate
48. Philippines	Phillipines
49. Muhammad	Mohammed (prophet of Islam)
50. Muslim	Moslem
51. black	Black (race)
52. African-American	African American
53. Ph.D.	PHD
54. nickel	nickle
55. usable	useable
56. sizable	sizeable
57. argument	arguement
58. bureaucracies	buracrasies
59. regardless	irregardless
60. succeed	suceed
61. proceed	procede
62. secede	seceed
63. precede	preceed
64. supersede	supercede
65. exonerate	exhonorate
66. acquitted	aquitted
67. Colombia	Columbia (South American nation)
68. ordnance	ordinance (artillery shells)
69. volunteerism	voluntarism

Spelling Answers

All of the correct answers are in the first column. Here are the correct spellings with the primary sources for each:

1–3. For *adviser* and *protester*, the AP stylebook specifies "not advisor" and "not protestor." The dictionary lists *-er* before *-or* for both. Compare those with *impostor.* The stylebook and dictionary agree on *impostor.*

4–8. The stylebook makes a preemptive strike on these four commonly misspelled words. It lists *judgment* and warns specifically, "not judgement." *Harass, embarrass* and *accommodate* are all troublesome words listed in the stylebook and dictionary no other way. For *dietitian,* the stylebook warns "not dietician," a spelling given in the dictionary as "also (now rare)."

9–11. The wrong use of a hyphen counts as a misspelling. These are three examples. *Longtime* is listed solid (no hyphen) in the stylebook and dictionary; it is never hyphenated. For *re-create,* you have to interpolate what the stylebook has to say. Under *re-* it says that for many words, "the sense is the governing factor" as to whether or not it gets a hyphen. AP gives as examples "recover (regain) and re-cover (cover again)"; "resign (quit) and re-sign (sign again)." Note how *resign* and *re-sign* differ in pronunciation. Judging from this entry, it makes sense to hyphenate *re-create* (create anew) as compared with *recreate* (enjoy leisure time). The stylebook lists *counterproposal* under an entry for the prefix *counter-.* It's never hyphenated.

12. *Realtor* is a trademark of the National Association of Realtors and must be capitalized. The stylebook says *real estate agent* is preferred; use *Realtor* if you have a reason to indicate that the individual is a member of the National Association of Realtors. Companies and organizations guard their trademarks jealously and will write stern letters if an editor fails to capitalize words such as *Xerox, Kleenex, Jell-O* and *Styrofoam.*

13–14. Expressions such as *rock 'n' roll* and *OK* have emerged from slang into common usage. The AP stylebook prefers *rock 'n' roll,* while the dictionary, obviously believing the music has grown up, has it as *rock and roll.* It's *OK, OK'd, OK'ing* and *OKs* in the stylebook.

15–17. For some reason, some of us want to tack an "s" at the end of these words. All are in the stylebook. For *backward,* the dictionary lists *backwards* as a variant; *toward* is the dictionary spelling with the definition; and for *afterward,* the dictionary lists *afterwards* as "also."

18. It's *a lot,* two words. Sometimes you have to come by the correct spelling through elimination. In this case, *alot* isn't listed in the AP stylebook or the dictionary, so we assume the word doesn't exist.

19. Pronunciation is no help with some words, for instance, *surprise.*

20–21. The root words, *restaurant* and *disaster,* don't match up with these forms, *restaurateur* and *disastrous.* They are spelled no other way.

22. For *paid,* the dictionary lists *payed* as "obs," meaning obsolete.

23–24. Remember the old spelling rule, "I before E except after C or when sounded like A as in neighbor and weigh"? It holds true for *receive,* but not for *weird.* That's what makes the English language so much fun: weird spellings like this. The stylebook lists *weirdo* but not *weird.*

25–26. Don't confuse words like *desperate* (in trouble) and *disparate* (distinct), or for that matter, don't confuse *separate* with *desperate.* All are in the dictionary.

27–29. Three more words that give journalists fits: *maneuver, liaison* and *cemetery.* The last two are in the stylebook; the dictionary gives no other listing for any of them.

30. The AP stylebook and the dictionary give no other spelling for *occurred.*

31. *Occasionally* is spelled no other way in the dictionary.

32–35. Here's a handy rule for whether to double the last letter when adding a suffix. If the emphasis in pronunciation is on the last syllable (re-FER), then double it: *referring.* If the emphasis is on the first syllable (CAN-cel), then don't double: *canceled.* But don't be confused by single-syllable words that double down depending on sense: *busing* (going by bus) and *bussing* (kissing). *Preferred* agrees with this rule, but is *preferable* an exception to the rule? No. Note how the pronunciation changes: PREF-er-a-ble.

36. Don't have a dictionary? You can find *possessive* in the stylebook—as an entry on how to punctuate possessives.

37. Dropping an "I" out of *responsibility* is a common typo. Sometimes you need to slow down and look at every letter.

38. Don't confuse *familiar* with *similar. Familiar* is in the stylebook.

39. The stylebook and dictionary agree on *fluorescent* for the spelling for the type of lights in most public buildings.

40–41. Being a good editor is knowing when to slow down and knowing when to look closely at spelling because it would be embarrassing if it got in your publication wrong. *Grammar* and *misspell* are two good examples. Both are in the stylebook.

42. If you want to be laughed at by others in a newsroom, spell it *momento* instead of *memento,* although the dictionary does list *momento* as an "erroneous spelling of memento."

43. Remember that *minuscule* comes from *minute;* it's in the stylebook.

44. AP lists *definitely,* and the interesting thing is the definition the stylebook gives us: "Overused as a vague intensifier. Avoid it."

45. The stylebook and dictionary give no other spelling for *cannot*.

46. Stylebook or dictionary, *consensus* is the only way it's spelled.

47. The stylebook lists *assassin* but not *assassinate*, which is in the dictionary.

48. Many commonly used place names are in the stylebook and dictionary, *Philippines* among them. Be aware that the people of the Philippines are *Filipinos*, with a capital "F" according to the stylebook.

49–52. The stylebook gives Muhammad as the preferred spelling. The dictionary lists *Mohammed Ali,* not the boxer but rather the viceroy of Egypt in the 19th century, also known as *Mehemet Ali.* This goes to show that dictionaries are great sources of information, geographical, historical and biographical.

   Muslim is preferred by the stylebook. *Moslem* was listed as preferred in past editions of the AP stylebook, with the note that some followers of Islam in this country go by *Muslim.* The latest stylebook says that the term *Black Muslim* is considered derogatory, but still uses black, lowercase, as the "preferred usage for those of the Negro race."

   These words are examples of how news organizations try to refer to racial and ethnic groups in the way that they prefer. A few years ago, the *Chicago Tribune* changed to *Muslim.* In a note to the *Tribune* staff, Managing Editor Dick Ciccone noted that the *Washington Post* and the Associated Press use *Moslem,* but that the *Los Angeles Times* and the *New York Times* went with *Muslim.* Ciccone quoted *New York Times* Managing Editor Al Siegel as saying that his paper changed to *Muslim* in October 1988 because most authoritative articles and books on the Islamic faith went with *Muslim.* Ciccone said the *Tribune* "identifies several groups and individuals by their preferences (African-American, Hispanic-American) and would do the same with Muslim."

   The words *black* and *African-American* are two more examples. In the 1960s when Tom Bradley was elected mayor of Los Angeles, the *Chicago Tribune* called him in a headline the city's "first Negro mayor." Now *black* is falling into disuse, replaced by *African-American* (note the hyphen). Newspapers have accepted the use of *African-American* because black people seem to prefer it and because it is accurate, probably more accurate than *black.* Newspapers will fall back on *black* in headlines, though, because that term isn't considered derogatory.

53. The stylebook lists it as *Ph.D.* but prefers that writers say the person holds a doctorate and name the specialty. See also *academic degrees.*

54. *Nickel* is the preferred spelling in the dictionary; it lists *nickle* as "alt. sp. of" nickel.

55–57. To "E" or not to "E"? In all three of these words, *usable, sizable* and *argument,* the "E" drops out when the suffix is added.

58. Again, you have to slow down and look at every letter of *bureaucracies.*

59. Use *regardless* or be a laughing stock. The dictionary lists *irregardless* as "non-standard or humorous."

60–64. These words—*succeed, proceed, secede, precede, supersede*—are commonly confused. Note that *succeed* and *proceed* are the double "E" words. That helps narrow it down, but you just have to learn them.

65–66. Neither *exonerate* nor *exorbitant* has an "H" in it; putting one in is a common error. So, too, is dropping the "C" from *acquitted.*

67. Misspelling the name of a country, like *Colombia,* in a headline or story harms you beyond embarrassment; it hurts your credibility. People think you don't know anything about the country.

68. *Ordnance* means artillery shells; *ordinance* means a municipal law. You have to know the definition to spell it right. Know the difference.

69. For reasons mentioned above, use *volunteerism* for all usages.

THE GRAMMAR SURVIVAL KIT

Welcome to the grammar survival kit. We hope it saves you time and embarrassment, and delivers you from error. But before you dig in, you must have the right attitude. Know this:

Grammar is learned. The idea, "I am old, therefore I know grammar," is false. A person may write with good grammar based on years of hearing it spoken, but the writer who knows the craft knows more: He or she understands the rules. Understanding is the highest form of learning. That's why we stress knowing the rules and how they work.

Knowing grammar will make you popular in the newsroom. Let them overhear you say, "My God, doesn't this writer know that you use a comma before the conjunction when joining two independent clauses!?" and they will flock around you.

We said in our section on news judgment that even grammar is affected by the type of story we write. Most news stories require a formal tone, meaning painfully correct grammar. Light news stories, feature stories and many columns take an informal tone, meaning the rules of grammar are relaxed and sometimes broken. Writers and editors of those stories need an even greater understanding of the rules.

The first step toward understanding grammar is knowing the parts of speech and the job each one does.

Parsing and Parts of Speech

To parse a sentence means to determine the part of speech of each word in a sentence and label each word accordingly. It may seem tedious, but parsing holds the key to understanding the language—and to writing and editing with confidence.

This first part of the grammar survival kit will reacquaint you with terms used to describe the language. First, you need to know the eight parts of speech: noun, pronoun, verb, adjective, adverb, preposition, conjunction and interjection.

Noun

A noun is the name of a person, place, thing, idea or quality. A guide to help you when parsing: Nouns answer the question who? or what?

Pronoun

A pronoun takes the place of a noun. The noun it replaces is called the antecedent. Look at this sentence: *Eric has no money because he gave it away.* The noun *Eric* is the antecedent for the pronoun *he.*

Verb

A verb expresses action or state of being. Here's an action verb: *He painted the house.* Here's a state of being verb: *He is a painter.*

Adjective

An adjective can be a word, phrase or clause used to modify a noun or pronoun. It answers the questions which one? how much? or how many? Here's an adjective as a word: *pretty.* Here's one as a phrase: *in the garage,* as in *The car in the garage is mine.* Here's an adjective as a clause: *who talked,* as in *The boy who talked is my brother.*

Clause versus Phrase

Before we go further, make sure you know the difference between a clause and a phrase. A clause has a subject and a verb; a phrase doesn't.

Adverb

An adverb is a word, phrase or clause used to modify a verb, adjective or another adverb. It answers the questions how? when? or where? Here's an adverb that is a word: *slowly.* Here is a phrase used as an adverb: *into the store,* as in *The man walked into the store.* Here is a clause used as an adverb: *when she entered,* as in *The crowd stood when she entered.*

Preposition

A preposition is used in a phrase and takes a noun or pronoun as its object. The preposition shows a relationship. Example: *like*, as in *He runs like me*. The object of the preposition is *me*, and the phrase shows the relationship between how he runs and how I run. Here are some of the more frequently used prepositions: *aboard, about, above, across, after, against, along, amid, among, around, at, before, behind, below, beneath, beside, between, beyond, by, down, during, except, for, from, from among, from between, from under, in, into, of, off, on, out, outside, over, round, round about, since, through, throughout, to, unto, under, underneath, up, upon, with* and *within*.

Conjunction

A conjunction connects words, phrases or clauses. Conjunctions are of three types:

1. Coordinating conjunctions connect two words, two phrases or two clauses of equal rank; one does not depend on the other for meaning. Coordinating conjunctions include *and, but, for, or, nor, so, yet*. Conjunctive adverbs also are used to connect clauses of equal rank. Examples: *however, then, therefore, thus*.

   Here's an example of a coordinating conjunction connecting words: *You and I are twins*. Here's an example connecting phrases: *He went to the doctor but not to the dentist*. Here's an example connecting clauses: *I'll bring milk and you bring flour*.

2. Subordinating conjunctions connect dependent clauses to independent clauses. Subordinating conjunctions include *as, as if, because, before, if, since, that, till, unless, when, where, whether*. Relative pronouns, such as *who, whom, whose, which, what* and *that*, also are used as subordinating conjunctions. Here's an example: *We'll all go down to meet her when she comes*. The clause *she comes* is dependent on the other clause.

3. Correlative conjunctions are used in pairs, such as *both/and, either/or, neither/nor, not only/but also, as (so)/as*. Example: *Neither rain nor snow can stop the mailman*.

Interjection

An interjection expresses strong feeling, such as *oh! hurrah! wow!*

The Right Part of Speech

A word can be a different part of speech depending on its use in a sentence. Look at this example:

The football team moved down the field after getting a first down as the fans in their down coats cheered, "Get down!"

The word *down* is used first as a preposition, then as a noun, then as an adjective and finally as an adverb.

Words or phrases can work as adverbs. In the sentence above, the prepositional phrase *down the field* acts as an adverb, telling where the team went. When parsing, you also could mark the expression *"Get down!"* as an interjection.

When in doubt about what part of speech a word is, consult the dictionary. The dictionary may list several parts of speech for the same word, so be guided by how the word is used in the sentence.

Being able to parse is important. Editors must know usage. Bad writers stretch the use of words to the breaking point. For example, look at this sentence:

The man was shotgunned to death.

Although a dictionary may list the noun *shotgun* also as a verb, good editors draw the line for formal tone or precision. The word *shotgun* is best held to its preferred use as a noun, the one listed first in the dictionary. One way to rewrite the sentence:

A shotgun blast killed the man.

See that perfectly good nouns are not turned into awkward verbs.

Another example of bad writing:

The Cubs downed the Giants.

Of all the synonyms for defeat, the writer chose to stretch the versatile word *down* to the breaking point by making it a verb. Some usage experts believe the word *but* should be restricted to its use as a conjunction: *I went home, but no one was there.* Avoid using *but* as a preposition, as in *All but John went.* Make it *All except John went.*

Parsing Tricks

Good writers know the parts of speech for a word and hold the word to its primary use. Sometimes a misused word is hard to spot. Here are a few tricks you'll run across while parsing:

Expletives

Remember that a pronoun must have an antecedent, a word that comes before it to give it meaning. Look at this sentence:

John picked up the book and read it.

The pronoun is *it* and the antecedent is *book.*
But what about this sentence:

It is cold in Chicago.

In this case, *it* can't be a pronoun because it has no antecedent. In this sentence, *it* is an expletive. You often can improve and shorten a sentence by rewriting the expletive out: *Chicago is cold.*

The word *there* may be used as various parts of speech, but sometimes it is used as an expletive. In this example, *there* is used as an adverb: *Go there.*

In the next example, *there* is used as an expletive: *There is a dog in the closet.*

Rewrite it as *A dog is in the closet.*

Be alert to expletives. In feature stories, they can add a lighter tone when used sparingly. In most cases, edit them out if you can.

One more word about pronouns and antecedents: Use pronouns, especially *it,* sparingly; they may lead to confusion. Here's an example:

The dog dragged in the cloth, and it was muddy.

Question: Is the dog or the cloth muddy?

Infinitives

An infinitive is the "to" version of a verb; it is part of the verb. The infinitive of the verb *walk* is *to walk.* When parsing, don't mark an infinitive as a preposition.

Proper Nouns

Consider a proper noun such as *John Jones* as one noun.

Articles

The articles *a, an* and *the* are a special class of adjectives.

Contractions

Note that contractions often contain two parts of speech. The contraction *it's* contains a pronoun, *it,* and a verb, *is.*

WORKOUT: PARSING I

Now, put all this knowledge into action. Parse the following sentences by writing the correct abbreviation above each word: N for noun, PRO for pronoun, V for verb, ADJ for adjective, ADV for adverb, PREP for preposition, CON for conjunction and INT for interjection.

Put proper names in parentheses *(John Jones)* and mark them as nouns. Put infinitives into parentheses *(to hike)* and mark them INF. Articles can be marked ART. Mark expletives EXP.

1. Bill kicked the ball down the street, and she followed.

2. Swimming is really fun to do when you are young.

3. Oh, to go to movies is my favorite pastime.

4. Alice is the woman who gave Bill the book.

Answers:

1. Bill (N) kicked (V) the (ART) ball (N) down (PREP) the (ART) street (N) and (CON) she (PRO) followed (V).

2. Swimming (N) is (V) really (ADV) fun (ADJ) to do (INF) when (CON) you (PRO) are (V) young (ADJ).

3. Oh, (INT) to go (INF) to (PREP) movies (N) is (V) my (PRO) favorite (ADJ) pastime (N).

4. Alice (N) is (V) the (ART) woman (N) who (PRO) gave (V) Bill (N) the (ART) book (N).

Sentence Function

Sentence functions should not be confused with parts of speech. Knowing the functions of words in a sentence will help you understand when to use *who* or *whom*, *good* or *well*, *lie* or *lay* and other sometimes troublesome words. Knowing sentence functions will save you embarrassment.

A little background: A sentence is an independent clause. A dependent clause depends on an independent clause for meaning. Take this sentence:

> *While consumers remain blissfully ignorant, programmers are sending clients dire warnings about the Y2K bug, which is very much a national threat.*

This is really three clauses combined in one sentence.

First comes a dependent clause *While consumers remain blissfully ignorant*. Then comes an independent clause: *programmers are sending clients dire warnings about the Y2K bug*. Finally, we have another dependent clause: *which is very much a national threat*.

Here are the functions of words in this sentence:

Subjects: *consumers, programmers* and *which*

Predicates: *remain, are sending* and *is*

Direct object: *warnings*

Indirect object: *clients*

Object of a preposition (about): *Y2K bug*

Predicate adjective: *ignorant*

Predicate nominative: *threat*

Definitions

Subject

A subject does what the predicate expresses; it's the "who" or "what" that goes with the predicate. Generally, the subject comes before the predicate.

Predicate

Predicate is another term for the verb, transitive or intransitive. "Predicate" is a useful term because it can include more than one verb. Example:

The guitar can be played with a pick or with fingers. Can be played is the predicate.

A transitive verb is an action verb such as *run*. An intransitive verb is a linking verb such as *is*. Transitive verbs take direct objects. Intransitive verbs take a predicate adjective modifying the subject or a predicate nominative clarifying the subject.

Direct Object

The direct object receives the action expressed by the verb. For example, *mail carrier* is the direct object in this sentence: *The dog bit the mail carrier.*

Indirect Object

The indirect object receives the direct object. In this example, the direct object is *letter* and the indirect object is *George*:

The mail carrier gave George the letter.

Object of Preposition

A noun or pronoun that follows a preposition in a prepositional phrase is the object of the preposition. *From* is the preposition and *work* is the object of the preposition in this sentence:

The woman came home from work.

Predicate Adjective

It is an adjective modifying a subject and connected by a linking verb. Here's an example:

His room was messy.

The subject is *room* and the predicate adjective is *messy*.

Predicate Nominative

The predicate nominative is a noun or pronoun referring to the subject and connected by a linking verb. In this example, *Maria Callas* is the subject and *soprano* is the predicate nominative:

Maria Callas was a soprano.

WORKOUT: PARSING II

Now, parse these sentences again, marking the sentence function. You'll notice that most modifiers can be ignored. Use these abbreviations when parsing for sentence function: S for subject, P for predicate, PA for predicate adjective, PN for predicate nominative, OP for object of preposition, DO for direct object and IO for indirect object.

1. Bill kicked the ball down the street, and she followed.

2. Swimming is really fun to do when you are young.

3. Oh, to go to movies is my favorite pastime.

4. Alice is the woman who gave Bill the book.

Here are the answers:

1. Bill (S) kicked (P) the ball (DO) down the street (OP), and she (S) followed (P).

2. Swimming (S) is (P) really fun (PA) to do when you (S) are (P) young (PA).

3. Oh, to go (S) to movies (OP) is (P) my favorite pastime (PN).

4. Alice (S) is (P) the woman (PN) who (S) gave (P) Bill (IO) the book (DO).

Pronoun Basics

Pronouns take on different forms, or *cases*, for different uses. To *decline* a pronoun is to give its form in its three cases: nominative, objective and possessive. Pronouns used as subjects are in the nominative case. Those used as objects are in the objective case. Those used to show possession are in the possessive case. Here's an example of a pronoun declined into its three cases:

Nominative: who

Objective: whom

Possessive: whose

Some pronouns have two possessive forms, such as *my* and *mine* for *I*. Consult the dictionary for the forms of pronouns in the three cases.

WORKOUT: PRONOUNS

Decline these pronouns. The nominative case is given; provide the objective case and the possessive case:

Nominative	Objective	Possessive
I		
you		
he		
she		
it		
we		
they		
who		

Answers:

Nominative	Objective	Possessive
I	me	my, mine
you	you	your, yours
he	him	his
she	her	her, hers
it	it	its
we	us	our, ours
they	them	their, theirs
who	whom	whose

Who and Whom

Many writers and editors struggle when they have to decide between *who* and *whom*. *Who* is the nominative case and is used as a subject or a predicate nominative. *Whom* is the objective case and is used as a direct object, indirect object or object of a preposition. The same rules apply to *whoever* and *whomever*.

The problem arises when a writer or editor has trouble determining the sentence function of the pronoun. Remember these three points:

1. Every predicate has a subject, either stated or understood.

2. The first step in deciding between *who* and *whom* is to identify each predicate in a sentence, then find its subject.

3. If the pronoun is the subject, use *who*. Once the subject is determined, the remaining nouns and pronouns are easier to parse.

Here are examples of when to use *who* and *whoever*:

Give the package to the man who comes to the door.

The verbs are *give* and *comes*. What is the subject of *give*? It's *you* and it's understood. What is the subject of *comes*? Right, it's *who*.

Note: We use *who* instead of *that* because the antecedent is *man*. The rule is to use *who* and *whom* with people and with animals with names. Use *that* with anonymous animals and inanimate objects. Now look at this sentence:

Give it to the man who he said will come to the door.

Identify the predicates: *give, said, will come*. The subjects are *you* (understood) *give, he said* and *who will come*.

In this sentence, the clause *he said* interrupts the clause *who will come to the door* but does not affect the pronoun. *He said* is parenthetical.

Give it to whoever comes to the door.

Although *whomever* seems natural, *whoever* is the subject of the verb *comes*. The entire clause, *whoever comes to the door*, is the object of the preposition *to*.

Here are some examples of when to use *whom* and *whomever*.

Give the package to whom I named.

Start with the predicates: The subject of *give* is *you* understood. The subject of *named* is *I*. All the verbs have subjects, and all the verbs are action verbs. Chances are good that what's left is a direct object, indirect object or object of the preposition; *whom* is the direct object of *named*.

The clause, *whom I named,* is inverted. Turn the clause around (*I named whom*) then substitute another pronoun for *whom* to see if you want the nominative or objective case: *I named him; I named whom.*

Give whom the book?

Here *whom* is the indirect object. Again, the subject of *give* is *you* understood: *You give whom the book.* Because you would say *You give her the book,* not *she,* the objective case is correct.

The letter was delivered to whom it was addressed.

Here *whom* is the object of the preposition *to*. Again, all the verbs have subjects (*letter was delivered, it was addressed*).

Predicate Nominative

The predicate nominative is used with the verb *to be* and all its forms: *be, am, is, are, was, were* and *been*. Think of the verb as an equal sign: What's on one side of it is the same as what's on the other side, especially when it comes to pronoun case.

For example, when you answer a phone and someone asks for you, you should say, *This is he* or *This is she*. You know the subject is in the nominative case. Because *is* can be considered an equal sign, what's on the other side of it should also be in the nominative case. *He* or *she* is the predicate nominative. Going by the rules, you should say *It is I*. Through widespread use, however, *It's me* has become acceptable.

Don't let adverbs such as *not* and *certainly* or other words throw you off. These sentences are correct:

> *That certainly wasn't he.*
> *He was thought to be I.*
> *The woman in the car was thought to be I.*

Subject of the Infinitive

Look at this sentence:

> *He thought her to be me.*

This involves another rule: The subject of an infinitive is always in the objective case. Here the subject of the infinitive *to be* is *her*. Because *to be* is an equal sign, *me*, the objective form of *I*, is correct. Another example:

> *He thought the young woman in the back row to be me.*

The subject of the infinitive is *the young woman*.
Here is a quick *who* or *whom* quiz: Is this correct?

> *Award the prize to whomever you believe to be deserving.*

Answer: *Whomever* is correct. It is in the objective case because it is the subject of the infinitive *to be*, and *you believe* is parenthetical.
How about this:

> *Everyone wondered who the mystery man would be.*

Answer: *Who* is correct because it is the subject of an inverted clause with a predicate nominative. When turned around, the clause is *who would be the mystery man*, and both *who* and *mystery man* are in the nominative case.
Another example:

> *If I had known who he was, I would have acted differently.*

Undo the inverted clause and you have *he was who*, with *who* being the predicate nominative.

Possessive before Gerunds

A gerund is the *-ing* form of a verb used as a noun. The same *-ing* form also serves as the present participle, which can be used as an adjective. For example:

> *Swimming is fun.*

Swimming is a gerund in this sentence, and it's the subject. Another example:

> *A swimming fish gathers no moss.*

Fish is the subject of the predicate *gathers; swimming* is a present participle used as an adjective to modify *fish*.

A possessive is used before a gerund:

Ellen's playing the tuba was obnoxious.

And the possessive case of a pronoun is used before a gerund:

His swimming is fun for us to watch.

Some confusion may arise in sentences such as this:

Did you enjoy his playing the guitar?

Whether we use *his* or *him* depends on the emphasis of the statement. In the sentence above, the act of playing the guitar is emphasized, and the possessive form of the pronoun *he* is used with the gerund *playing*.

But say that 2-year-old Chuckie picks up the guitar and hammers out "Jumpin' Jack Flash." Later, you would ask:

Did you enjoy him playing the guitar?

That's because the emphasis is on Chuckie, not the music. In this case, *playing* is not a gerund; it's a present participle used as an adjective modifying *him*. The subject is *you*, the predicate is *did enjoy*, and *him* is the direct object.

Pronouns and Antecedents

Remember that pronouns are the same as their antecedents in number, singular or plural. Which of these is correct?

He is one of those students who is always late for class.
He is one of those students who are always late for class.

At first you may be inclined to write *who is* rather than *who are*. But *students* is the antecedent for *who*; the plural *are* is needed so that the antecedent and pronoun agree in number.

Sometimes double pronouns are used for emphasis or clarification. Which of these is correct?

Let's you and I look for the dog.
Let's you and me look for the dog.

Parsing comes in handy to understand why the answer is *you and me. Let's* is the contraction for *let us. You and me* explains what is meant by *us*. Because *you and me* is the same as *us*, all the pronouns must be in the same case, the objective case.

At first glance, you may think *you and me* is the subject of the sentence and therefore think *me* should be *I*. But the sentence is a command. The subject is *you* understood, *look* is the predicate, *for* is a preposition and *dog* is the object of the preposition. Other examples:

> *It was we editors who made the difference.*
> *We* and *editors* are predicate nominatives.
> *The teacher gave us students the answers.*
> *Us* and *students* are indirect objects.

Pronouns after Conjunctions, Prepositions

Which of these is correct?

> *She is as tall as I.*
> *She is as tall as me.*

Knowing which pronoun to use depends on knowing that *as* is a conjunction; the correct pronoun is *I.* Remember, conjunctions join clauses. In this case, the first clause is *she is,* and the conjunctive phrase *as tall as* joins it to the second clause *I (am).* Although *am* is not spoken, it is understood; the speaker chose not to finish the sentence. Now, which of these is correct?

> *He swims like me.*
> *He swims like I.*

Again the answer depends on knowing that *like* is a preposition; the correct pronoun is *me* because it is the object of the preposition and must be in the objective case.

One more time; which is correct?

> *She likes him better than I.*
> *She likes him better than me.*

It's a trick question because both sentences may be correct; it depends on what you mean. You could mean:

> *She likes him better than I (do).*

Then the correct pronoun is *I* because it is the subject of the suppressed verb, *do.* But you could mean:

> *She likes him better than (she likes) me.*

Then the correct pronoun is *me* and the clause *she likes* is suppressed. In each case, *than* is used as a conjunction.

One more note about *as/as* constructions: When a negative word like *not* or *never* is used with the construction, the first *as* becomes *so.* Here are examples:

> *She is as tall as Bill.*
> *She is not so tall as John.*
> *She never will be so tall as Fred.*

Reflexives

These are the *-self* forms of pronouns. They are often used for emphasis and are often unnecessary:

I myself rescued the woman.

But the biggest problem with reflexives is that they are used incorrectly by writers unsure of grammar. Instead of saying *between you and me*, some will say *between you and myself*. That is just as wrong as saying *between you and I*. So, just between us (and not *just between ourselves*), catch those who hide behind reflexives.

That and Which

Clauses and phrases can be classified as essential or nonessential. Here are three guidelines for using *that* and *which* (see also our discussion in Chapter 2):

1. Use *that* when what follows is an essential part of a sentence.

2. Use *which* when what follows is nonessential; it would be said in a low tone of voice.

3. Use commas with *which* but not with *that*.

Say you have two bikes for sale. One is in the garage, and the other is on the lawn. A bike's location, then, is essential to identifying it. A buyer who doesn't like the one on the lawn would say:

The bike that is in the garage is the one I want.

If you had only one bike, however, and it was in the garage, the buyer would say:

The bike, which is in the garage, is what I want.

Be alert to *whiches* in copy; they often should be *thats*.

One exception to the rule is when two *thats* are used closely together in a sentence. In such a case, make the second *that* a *which*:

He contended that the case which involves his friend is phony.

No commas are used before and after the *which* clause because it is essential to the sentence. See the AP stylebook entry under Essential Clauses.

Subject-Pronoun Agreement

Be aware of the singular pronouns: *each, every, either, neither, one, everyone, anyone, someone, nobody, anybody, somebody* and *everybody*. When these pronouns are subjects, any related pronouns in the sentence must agree in number. For example:

> *Neither is happy in his job.*

A common mistake is to use the plural, *their job.* Writers sometimes use *their* because they want to avoid using the masculine pronoun *his* after a singular subject. In a group that includes men and women, the formal rules of grammar would have us say:

> *Everyone must do his own work.*

That's sexist when *everyone* includes women. In such a case, make the subject plural and use a plural, sexually neutral pronoun:

> *All must do their own work.*

Another option, though not as neat:

> *Everyone must do his or her own work.*

Because it relies on accepted usage, this is better than yielding to other "solutions": new words such as *hir* to replace *his,* or creative punctuation such as *s/he* or *she/he.*

Subject-Verb Agreement

Subjects and verbs must agree in number: If the subject is singular, the verb must be singular. The same for plural. Problems arise in isolating the subject and determining its number. Knowing how to parse helps. Here are some rules:

- In *neither/nor* and *either/or* constructions, the verb agrees with the closest subject. For example:
  Neither the boys nor the girl is going.
  Either the girl or the boys are going.
- Singular pronouns as subjects take singular verbs. Make it:
  Neither is going, not *Neither are going.*
- Don't be confused by parenthetical subjects in phrases using *as well as, together with* or *along with.* They usually are set off by commas. The main subject of the sentence is what counts. For example:
  Bill, as well as Jim and Sally, is going.
- Some phrases that appear to be plural actually are singular because they are inseparable in meaning. For example:
  Biscuits and gravy is on the menu.
  Salt and pepper is what I want.
- Some plural words, such as *media* and *phenomena,* are often mistaken for singular ones. The singular of *media* is *medium.* The singular of *phenomena* is *phenomenon.* These examples are correct:

New media compete directly with television.
Cosmic phenomena are often mistaken for UFOs.
For guidance, follow the AP stylebook. See the entries on *media* and *collective nouns.*

• *None* is either singular or plural depending on its meaning. When deciding which, try to make *none* read as singular; if you can't, then it's plural. *None* is singular when:

  1. It means not one: *None of the apples is ripe.*

  2. It means no one: *None of my uncles is bald.*

  3. It is followed by a prepositional phrase with a singular object of the preposition: *None of the gasoline was spilled.*

• *None* is plural when:

  1. It means no two: *None of the wrestlers face each other today.*

  2. When it stands for something that has no common singular: *None of the U.S. forces have been deployed.*

  3. When it is the subject of a sentence with a plural predicate nominative: *Of those who became doctors, none were women.*

See the AP stylebook entry *none.*

Adjectives and Adverbs

Adjectives have three degrees: positive, comparative and superlative. The positive expresses a quality without comparison:

He is fast.

The comparative explains the relationship between two persons or things:

He is faster than she.

The superlative describes someone or something top-rate:

He is the fastest.

Watch out for superlative adjectives because they are sloppily overused. Few people or things deserve to be called the best, as in *She is the best doctor in the world.* That would be tough to prove.

Some adjectives have no comparative or superlative form and instead rely on qualifiers: *abundant, more abundant, most abundant.*

Some adjectives come only in the superlative: *unique, perfect, square, straight, endless, perpendicular, pregnant* and *dead* are common ones. Don't do this: *That is very unique.* Something is unique (one of a kind) or it isn't.

Remember predicate adjectives? They are "linked" to subjects by linking verbs. The most common linking verb is *to be.* Others such as *feel, smell, look, taste* and *sound* are related to the senses. Other verbs used sometimes as linking verbs are *seem, become, appear, prove, remain, turn, grow, stay* and *continue.*

Don't confuse adjectives and adverbs. For example:

He looks bad.

This means he is pale and drawn. The predicate adjective *bad* modifies the pronoun *he.* Compare that sentence with this:

He looks badly.

This means his eyes are poor; the adverb *badly* modifies the verb *looks.* In the first sentence, *looks* is an intransitive, or linking, verb; in the second, *looks* is a transitive, or action, verb.

Good is an adjective. *Well* is usually an adverb: *It works well.* When the meaning of *well* is *not sick, well* is an adjective:

I'm glad he is well again; he looks very healthy now.

In this sentence, *well* is a predicate adjective.

The position of an adverb in a sentence changes the meaning of the sentence. Consider these examples using the word *only:*

Only he seems interested in boating.

Nobody else seems interested.

He only seems interested in boating.

He's not really interested.

He seems interested in only boating.

Boating apparently is his one interest.

Verbs

You know what *tense* means just before you go to the dentist, but what does *tense* mean in its grammatical sense? It means time. In English we have six tenses to distinguish various points in time. Some Native American languages have just one tense; some Native Americans might say, *I go today, I go tomorrow, I go yesterday.*

The English language has not only six tenses but also three moods to worry about, not to mention progressive forms. Ours is a complicated language; ask any foreigner trying to learn it.

Verbs are the most important part of speech. Good writers are separated from bad ones by their use of verbs. To use verbs properly, you need a thorough knowledge of their properties, and you need to know the terminology.

Principal Parts

The principal parts of the verb *to run* are:

1. Present tense: *run*

2. Past tense: *ran*

3. Past participle: *run*

4. Present participle: *running*

How do you find the principal parts of a verb? Consult a good dictionary. Look up the infinitive form, which is also the present-tense form. That will be followed by the past-tense form and the past participle. Sometimes more than one past-tense form or past participle will be listed; we're interested in the one listed first. The present participle of a verb is the *-ing* form of the present tense.

The dictionary may not list the principal parts of "regular" verbs such as *to walk* because they follow this standard rule for past and past participle forms: Add "-ed" to the present tense form. Therefore, the principal parts of the verb *to walk* are:

1. Present tense: *walk*

2. Past tense: *walked*

3. Past participle: *walked*

4. Present participle: *walking*

When in doubt, test for the different forms by substituting the verb in the sentences below:

1. Present tense: *I run today.*

2. Past tense: *I ran yesterday.*

3. Past participle: *I had run.*

4. Present participle: *I am running.*

Beware of "irregular" verbs, such as *broadcast.* Its principal parts are:

1. Present tense: *broadcast.*

2. Past tense: *broadcast.*

3. Past participle: *broadcast*

4. Present participle: *broadcasting.*

Let the dictionary be your guide.

Tenses

Tense means time; the form of the verb used in a sentence governs when that sentence takes place in the mind of the reader.

- **Present.** The present tense expresses action going on or action that occurs always, repeatedly or habitually. Examples:

  The boys are ready to go.

  They go to school by bus.

  She eats cereal for breakfast.

  The present tense may express the future:

  The train leaves in five minutes.

- **Historical present.** The historical present refers to an event completed in the past but described as occurring in the present:

  The bandit goes to the bank. The police arrive. He flees the scene.

  The historical present is used in headlines:

  Ingrid Bergman dies.

- **Past.** A verb's past tense expresses action completed at a definite time in the past. Examples:

  He lay down yesterday.

  He wrote the letter last Tuesday.

- **Future.** The future tense expresses action that will occur:

  He will write a letter tomorrow.

- **Past perfect, present perfect, future perfect.** The "perfect" tenses include a form of the helping verb *to have* plus a past participle. The tense is determined by the tense of the helping verb.

  Present perfect consists of *have* or *has* plus a past participle. It expresses action completed or action continuing in the present:

  He has written a letter to his uncle. (completed action)

  I have lived here for many years. (action continuing)

  Past perfect consists of *had* plus a past participle. It expresses action completed before a stated or known time:

  The man testified that he had written the letter.

  Future perfect consists of *will have* plus a past participle. It expresses action that will be completed before a stated or known time in the future:

  He will have written the letter before we arrive tomorrow.

Voice

Verbs are in either the active voice or passive voice. A verb is active when the subject of the sentence is the doer of the action expressed by the verb. (See also our discussion in Chapter 2.) For example:

John hit the ball.

The subject, *John,* is doing the action, the hitting.

A verb is passive when the subject of the sentence is the receiver of the action:

The ball was hit by John.

The subject, *ball,* is receiving the action, being hit.

Passive voice has three elements:

1. A form of the verb *to be*. In the sentence *The ball was hit by John,* the *to be* verb is past tense, *was.*

2. A past participle, in this case *hit.*

3. The preposition *by,* either present or understood. Here is a case of an implied by: *The ball was hit.*

Be aware of the false passive:

Jane was given the ball.

Jane, the subject of the sentence, does not receive the action; *ball* does. Make it:

Jane got the ball or *The ball was given to Jane.*

See our discussion of false passives in chapter 2.

Mood

Mood is the property of a verb that indicates how the writer or speaker feels about the statement being made. Mood adds nuance and richness to the language. Verbs come in three moods: indicative, imperative and subjunctive.

- Indicative mood makes a statement of fact or asks a question:
  John hit the ball.
  Did John hit the ball?
- Imperative mood gives a command or makes a request that is not a question:
  Hit the ball.
  Will you please return the book.
  Note that neither example uses a question mark.
- Subjunctive mood offers the greatest challenge to editors because it is being eroded by misuse. It expresses:

Doubt: *I wonder if it be true.* In the subjunctive mood, *be true* is correct rather than the indicative *is true.*

A wish: *I wish I were a rock singer.* It's *were* rather than *was.*

A prayer: *Peace be with you.* It's *be* rather than *is.*

A demand: *I insist that he go.* It's *he go* rather than *he goes.*

A necessity: *The board had no choice but that she be dismissed.* It's *she be* not *she is.*

A resolution or motion: *I resolve that he investigate the matter.* It's not *he investigates.* Another example: *I move that the meeting be adjourned.*

A condition contrary to fact: *If I were you, I would go.* It's *were,* not *was.*

Don't confuse this last use of the subjunctive with conditional statements, in which the indicative mood is used. Conditional statements also use the word *if*, but the meaning is entirely different.

Let's say a friend was at a party, and you did not see him. You might say:

If he was there, I didn't see him.

You are making a simple statement not contrary to fact, so the indicative *was* is used. Now let's say your friend couldn't make the party, and as a result you had a lousy time. Then you might say:

If he were there, I would have had a great time.

In this case, the subjunctive *were* is used because your friend was not there; you are stating a condition contrary to fact. One word makes the difference.

Here are two examples of conditional statements in the indicative mood:

If I was there, I don't remember.
If you are telling the truth, I will apologize.

Knowing the difference between the subjunctive and the indicative in the last example could save you a punch in the nose. Compare it with this:

If you were telling the truth, I would apologize.

You are calling someone a liar.

The subjunctive mood also is used in clauses introduced by *as if* and *as though.* This is correct, in the subjunctive mood:

She yelled as if she were hurt.

It's not *was hurt.*

Subjunctive mood also is used in idioms: *if need be, God bless you, God forbid, so be it.*

Conjugation

Understanding how verbs are conjugated will help you better understand the subjunctive mood, subject-verb agreement and sometimes troublesome verbs such as *lie* and *lay.* Verbs are conjugated by tense, voice and mood in first person, second person and third person, and in plural and singular.

Here is the conjugation of the verb *to be* in the present tense, active voice, indicative mood:

First person singular: *I am*

Second person singular: *you are*

Third person singular: *she is*

First person plural: *we are*

Second person plural: *you are*

Third person plural: *they are*

Compare that with the verb *to be* conjugated in the present tense, active voice, but subjunctive mood:

First person singular: *I be*

Second person plural: *you be*

Third person singular: *she be*

First person plural: *we be*

Second person singular: *you be*

Third person plural: *they be*

You can see why we use *he be* in the sentence *I demand that he be executed*. Instead of using the third-person singular, present tense in the indicative, *he is*, you must use the third-person singular, present-tense form in the subjunctive, *he be*.

Here is the verb *to be* conjugated in the past tense, active voice, indicative mood:

First person singular: *I was*

Second person singular: *you were*

Third person singular: *he was*

First person plural: *we were*

Second person plural: *you were*

Third person plural: *they were*

Compare this with *to be* conjugated in the past tense, active voice but subjunctive mood:

First person singular: *I were*

Second person singular: *you were*

Third person singular: *she were*

First person plural: *we were*

Second person plural: *you were*

Third person plural: *they were*

You can see why we use *I were* in the subjunctive statement *If I were you, I would go.* The past tense indicative form is *I was.*

If you learn how the subjunctive and indicative forms of the verb *to be* differ in the first and third person, and the present and past tense, you will have a handle on the subjunctive mood.

For other verbs in the subjunctive, the infinitive form is used for the third-person singular in the present and past tense. For example, *go* from the infinitive *to go* is used rather than *goes* in the subjunctive mood:

> *I demand that he go.*

It's the same in the past tense:

> *I demanded that he go.*

When verbs are conjugated in the passive voice, consisting of a form of the verb *to be* plus a past participle, the tense is governed by the helping verb *to be*. This is the conjugation of the verb *to drive* in the present tense, passive voice, indicative mood:

First person singular: *I am driven*

First person plural: *we are driven*

Second person singular: *you are driven*

Second person plural: *you are driven*

Third person singular: *he is driven*

Third person plural: *they are driven*

Progressive Form

The progressive form of a verb expresses action still continuing. It consists of the verb *to be* and a present participle. The verb *to be* may be conjugated in any of the tenses, voices or moods. Some examples of the progressive form:

> *I am seeing the ball game.*

The verb is present tense, active voice, indicative mood.

> *I am being seen on television.*

This is present tense, passive voice, indicative mood.

> *I have been seeing her.*

This is present perfect tense, active voice, indicative mood.
The last sentence consists of the present tense of the helping verb *to have* plus the past participle of *to be* plus the present participle of *to see*. Note: Strictly speaking, the progressive is not a tense.

Verbals

Verbals are forms of verbs often used as other parts of speech. The verbals are the infinitive, the gerund and the participle.

- The infinitive is the "to" form of a verb. The present infinitive would be *to go*. The perfect infinitive would be *to have gone.*
- The gerund is a verbal noun. It can be used as a subject:
  Walking is fun.
  And it can be used as an object:
  Doug enjoys reading.
- The participle is a verbal adjective. It can be the present participle, the past participle or the perfect participle.
  This sentence uses a present participle as adjective:
  Sitting here, we saw the parade.
  Sitting modifies *we.*
  A common error is the dangling participle. The noun or pronoun modified by the participle must immediately follow the phrase containing the participle. Here is a dangling participle:
  Sitting here, the parade passed by us.
  The sentence is wrong because the parade was not sitting.
  This sentence uses a past participle as adjective:
  The terms suggested by the committee were fair.
  Suggested modifies *terms.*
  Here is a perfect participle as adjective:
  Having finished the work, I left.
  Having finished modifies *I.*

Helping Verbs

Helping verbs are also known as auxiliary verbs. *Do* is an example. *Do* often is used for emphasis; most often it is unnecessary. For example:

He did bring his book.

You can make the sentence into:

He brought his book.

Lie and Lay

These verbs continue to plague writers and editors.
To lie means to recline: *You lie down if you're sick.* Its principal parts are:

Present: *lie, lies*

Past: *lay*

Present participle: *lying*

Past participle: *lain*

To lay means to place: *First we must lay the groundwork.* Its principal parts are:

Present: *lay, lays*

Past: *laid*

Present participle: *laying*

Past participle: *laid*

Lie is intransitive, meaning it does not take a direct object: *The wounded man lay down on the ground.*

Lay is transitive and takes a direct object: *He laid the book on the table.* The direct object is *book*.

Confusion arises most often with *lay:* It's the present tense *to lay*, and it's the past tense of *lie*. Get used to sentences such as this:

I lay down all day yesterday.

One way to keep the verbs straight is to remember that lay means either *place* (present tense) or *reclined* (past tense), and that laid can mean only *placed* (past tense). Substitute those words in your mind when deciding on *lay* or *laid*.

The AP stylebook includes an entry on *lay and lie*.

WORKOUT: GRAMMAR

The key to solving grammar problems is being able to recognize the parts of speech and the functions of words in a sentence. To that end, make sure you understand the exercises in parsing sentences in the grammar survival kit.

Part A

Circle the correct answers in the following sentences:

■ 1. (Who/whom) is responsible?

Who is the subject of the intransitive verb *is*. Remember that *who* is the nominative case; it is used for subjects and predicate nominatives. *Whom* is the objective case; it is used as a direct object, indirect object, object of a preposition or subject of an infinitive.

■ 2. This is (who/whom).

Again it's *who* because it's the predicate nominative. Forms of the verb *to be* show a state of being; what is on one side is equal to what is on the other. Note that you can reverse the sentence: *Who is this?*

■ 3. This is the man (who/whom) was indicted.

Did you pick *who*? First find the verbs. The first verb is *is*; its subject is *this*; the predicate nominative is *man*. The second verb is *was indicted*; the subject is *who*, and as a subject, it must be in the nominative case. *Was indicted* is the past tense, passive voice. Note that *who was indicted* is a dependent clause that modifies *man*. The whole clause acts like an adjective.

■ **4. This is the man (who/whom) the grand jury indicted.**

This time it's *whom*. The first verb is *is;* the subject is *this;* the predicate nominative is *man.* The next verb is *indicted;* the subject is *grand jury. Indicted* is a transitive verb; it takes a direct object, in this case *whom* in the objective case. Again, you can reverse the clause: *The grand jury indicted whom.* This is another dependent clause working as an adjective.

■ **5. Police wanted (whoever/whomever) would surrender first.**

It's *whoever.* The first verb is *wanted;* its subject is *police.* Next verb is *would surrender;* the subject is *whoever. Wanted* is a transitive verb and takes an object, but in this case, the whole dependent clause plays the role of direct object.

■ **6. Police wanted (whoever/whomever) they could get.**

Make it *whomever.* The first verb is *wanted;* its subject is *police.* The next verb is *could get;* its subject is *they* and the direct object is *whomever.* To make this clear, reverse the sentence and substitute the pronoun *him* for *whomever: they could get him.* (*He* clearly won't work.) Note how this sentence is similar to sentence 4.

■ **7. Police wanted to know (who/whom) the guilty man was.**

Did you figure out that *who* was the predicate nominative? The first verb is *wanted;* its subject is *police.* The next verb is *was;* the subject is *guilty man;* the predicate nominative is *who.* What is *to know?* It's an infinitive modifying *wanted.*

■ **8. Police wanted to know (who/whom) the newspaper said was the guilty man.**

Don't be fooled on this one. It's *who.* This sentence is similar to sentence 7, except that the clause *the newspaper said* is inserted into the second clause as a modifier. The first verb is *wanted;* its subject is *police.* The next verb is *said;* its subject is *newspaper.* The next verb is *was;* the subject is *who.* The predicate nominative is *guilty man.*

■ **9. Police believed (he/him) to be (I/me).**

Use the objective case pronouns *him* and *me.* This sentence is something entirely different. The first verb is *believed;* the subject is *police*. Next, go to the infinitive *to be*; the subject of the infinitive is *him*; remember, the subject of the infinitive is in the objective case and the verb *to be* shows a state of being. What goes on one side of the verb must be equal to what goes on the other, so the second pronoun is *me*. You can reverse them: *me to be him*.

■ 10. He wondered (who/whom) is guilty.

It's *who*. The first verb is *wondered;* the subject is *he*. The next verb is *is;* the subject is *who*. The predicate adjective is *guilty*. Take away the first clause, *he wondered,* and you have exactly the same thing as sentence 1.

■ 11. He wondered (who/whom) police say is guilty.

Sentence 11 is *who*. This sentence is a twist on sentence 10. We insert the short clause *police say* into the second clause, *who is guilty,* but that doesn't change the subject-verb relationships. The first verb is *wondered;* its subject is *he*. The second verb is *say;* its subject is *police*. Third verb is *is;* its subject is *who;* the predicate adjective is *guilty*.

■ 12. He wondered (who/whom) police believe is guilty.

Sentence 12 is *who,* again. The reasoning is the same as for sentence 11, except the second verb is *believe* instead of *say*. Everything else is exactly the same.

■ 13. He wondered (who/whom) police believe to be the guilty man.

Make it *whom*. This one requires a bit more unraveling. First, remember that the subject of the infinitive is in the objective case. Now look at the verbs: The first verb is *wondered;* the subject is *he*. The second verb is *believe;* the subject is *police*. The next verb is the infinitive *to be;* the subject is *whom*. *Guilty man* follows the same rules as a predicate nominative, only it would be in the objective case, too, if it were a pronoun. Remember that the verb *to be* is like an equal sign.

■ 14. He wondered (who/whom) police believe the guilty man is.

It's *who,* but this one is a bit tricky. You can figure it out if you start with the verbs. The first verb is *wondered;* the subject is *he*. The second verb is *believe;* the subject is *police*. The third verb is *is;* the subject is *guilty man; who* is the predicate nominative. You can reverse the clause: *The guilty man is who*.

■ 15. (Who/whom) is the guilty man?

Who is the subject of the verb *is; guilty man* is the predicate nominative.

■ 16. He is a president (who/that) never forgets.

This is something different. It's *who*. The rule is to use *who* when it refers to a person or an animal that has a name. Use *that* with inanimate objects and nameless animals. This is correct: *Secretariat is a horse who won the Triple Crown.* This is also correct: *I will catch the squirrel that ate a hole in my roof.*

■ 17. He is one of those dogs that always (comes, come) when called.

Sentence 17 is *come,* the plural form. Remember that the pronouns *who* and *that* are chameleons; they take on the qualities of their antecedents. The clause, *that always come when called,* describes a group of which this dog is just one member, so the antecedent is *dogs* and is plural. Compare that with this sentence: *He is the only one of the dogs that comes when he is called.* Now the clause describes just one dog, so the antecedent is *one* and is singular.

■ 18. Can you imagine (his/him) running for president?

Go with *his.* Usually the context of the sentence or of the surrounding paragraph will tell us which is right: *him* or *his.* When the context doesn't provide a clue, go with the possessive. In sentence 18, we lack that context, so we'll go with the possessive *his.*

■ 19. Can you imagine (his/him) running for president, how tough that must be?

Clearly it's *his.* Here the context tells us we're emphasizing the act of running for president, a tough task. The gerund *running* serves as a noun and is the direct object of the verb *imagine.* The pronoun *his* modifies *running.*

■ 20. Can you imagine (his/him) running for president, that idiot?

In this sentence, use *him.* The context tells us that the emphasis is on the person running; he's an idiot. Now we go with *him* as the direct object of the verb *imagine* with the participle *running* as the modifier.

■ 21. Keep this between you and (I/me).

Me is correct. Using I is a common mistake; some people believe *between you and I* sounds better, but the pronouns *you* and *me* are objects of the preposition *between*. They both belong in the objective case.

■ 22. If I (was/were) you, I'd quit.

Go with subjunctive mood, *were*. Subjunctive mood is used because the statement is contrary to fact; I can't be you unless I'm skilled in performing Vulcan mind-melding.

■ 23. (We/us) the people have inalienable rights.

Find the verb, *have*. Find the subject, *we (the people)*.

■ 24. Give (we/us) the people our rights.

This time, make it *us*. To sort out some sentences, we must supply understood parts. Here, the verb is *give;* the subject is *(you)* understood. *Us* is the indirect object; *rights* is the direct object. Use the objective form, *us*.

■ 25. I am (as/so) tall as my father, but I will never be (as/so) tall as Wilt.

In the first instance, use *as;* in the second, use *so*. With comparisons of this type, use *as/as* when the comparison is positive; use *so/as* when the comparison contains a negative. In the second clause, *never* is the negative.

Part B

Edit the following sentences to correct grammar mistakes. Do not rewrite the sentences; just make one-word changes. If a sentence is correct as written, just mark an "OK" next to the number of the sentence. Then see how we would do it.

■ 1. The company put their best products on the market first.

Replace *their* with *its*. This is a case of pronoun-antecedent agreement; *company* is singular, so *its* must be used.

■ 2. I feel badly for him, but he feels good.

Replace *badly* with *bad*. The key: Remember that the verb *feel* can be transitive or intransitive. The trick is figuring out which. In both clauses, the verb *feel* is intransitive; it shows a state of being. In the first clause, *I* is the subject and *bad* is the predicate

135

adjective; it modifies *I*. If you used the adverb *badly*, it would modify the verb *feel*, and it would mean you couldn't feel things; maybe you just had a skin graft on your fingertips. In the second clause, the subject is *he* and *good* is the predicate adjective.

■ **3. The car which I bought is over there.**

The key to this sentence is deciding if the clause *which I bought* is essential or nonessential. You could justify it either way and handle it three ways:

• If you decide the clause is essential, you would change the pronoun to *that: The car that I bought is over there.*

• If you decide the clause is essential, you could just strike the word *which: The car I bought is over there.*

• If you decide the clause is nonessential and keep the pronoun *which*, you must enclose the clause in commas: *The car, which I bought, is over there.*

■ **4. The cat, which is related to the lion, is a popular pet.**

The clause *which is related to the lion* is clearly nonessential. The sentence is OK as written with the clause enclosed in commas.

■ **5. The merger of the 10 American companies, the six Japanese firms and the two Australian businesses have left Wall Street reeling.**

Change *have* to *has*. This is a problem in subject-verb agreement. The trick is connecting the subject *merger* and the verb *has* (singular). The long prepositional phrase that intervenes has no effect on subject-verb agreement here.

■ **6. The dog just laid there as I lay the book on the table.**

Change *just laid* to *just lay*, and change *I lay* to *I laid*. The verbs *lie* and *lay* are confusing but not impossible to learn. Some editors conquer the problem by writing the conjugation in the front of their stylebooks so they can look this up quickly.

Remember that *to lie* is the intransitive verb meaning to recline. The conjugation is, *I lie down, I lay down yesterday, I have lain among the lilies. To lay* is the transitive verb; it takes a direct object and means *to place: I lay the book on the table, I laid the book on the table yesterday, I have laid the book on the table.*

■ **7. He likes football better then me.**

Change *then* to *than. Then* is an adverb telling when or an adjective as in *then-President Reagan.* In this sentence, we want the conjunction *than.*

Is *me* correct? It would be if you meant he would rather watch football than spend time with you—in which case it may be time to find a new friend.

■ 8. A number of us has decided to attend the gala.

Change *has* to *have*. The problem again is subject-verb agreement. Here, *number* means more than one of us, so it takes a plural verb. *Number* can be singular, as in *The lotto number for today is 1441.*

■ 9. A MGM film, done brilliantly, can become an historic event.

Change the first article *a* to *an*. When the word following the article begins with a soft vowel sound, go with *an*. *MGM* is pronounced *em-gee-em;* the soft sound requires *an*.

In the second part of the sentence, change *an* to *a*. *Historic* starts with a hard *h* sound, so use *a*. This is the form stated in the AP stylebook. Compare that with *an honorable man*. Use *an* because *honorable* starts with the soft *h* sound.

■ 10. A Wilmette couple was injured Monday when their car skidded off the road and hit a tree.

Change *was* to *were* for two reasons: The two people were injured as individuals, and the pronoun *their* is plural. If you were to insist on keeping the verb singular, then you would have to change the pronoun from *their* to *its*. That makes the sentence sound awkward.

■ 11. None of the passengers were injured in the train wreck.

Change *were* to *was*. *None* usually is singular but not always. Here it is singular because it means *not one* was injured.

■ 12. Five people were on the plane, but none was hurt.

This sentence is correct as written. *None* means *not one* was hurt.

■ 13. None of the gasoline was lost.

It's correct as written. *None* stands for *gasoline,* a word that is singular.

■ 14. None of her income taxes was paid.

Change *was* to *were*. In this sentence, *none* stands for *no amount of taxes* and is plural.

■ 15. None of the negotiators agrees.

Change *agrees* (singular) to *agree* (plural). Because you need two to negotiate, *none* must mean *no two* and is plural.

■ 16. The United States will deploy its forces, but none are expected to see combat.

■ 17. We looked for the police, but none were around.

None stands for *forces* and *police*, words that have no singular in the sense they are used. Can the United States deploy its force? Do we look for a police? Both sentences are correct as written.

■ 18. None of the construction workers are men.

This is correct as written. We use a plural verb because *men*, the predicate nominative, is plural. Remember that words on either side of the verb *to be*, the subject and predicate nominative or predicate adjective, are equal. Because *men* is plural, consider *none* as plural.

Part C

Rewrite the incorrect sentences to make them grammatical. If a sentence is correct as written, just mark an "OK" next to the number of the sentence. If you need more information before you can correct a sentence, explain the ambiguity. Then see how we did it.

■ 1. The sea gulls entertained the sun worshippers on the beach. Often swooping near the tanned bodies, the lifeguards delighted in their antics.

An example of the so-called dangling participle, in this case *swooping*. It describes the birds, but the nearest noun that it might modify is *lifeguards*. Did the lifeguards swoop? The simplest fix is to rewrite it:

Often swooping near the tanned bodies, the birds delighted the lifeguards with their antics.

■ 2. Jimmy Carter was the first resident of Plains, Ga., to be elected president in 1976.

Another misplaced modifier, the prepositional phrase *in 1976*. It sounds like a second or a third also was elected in 1976. The least that should be done is to move *in 1976* to the beginning of the sentence. Some may want to make it: *In 1976 Jimmy Carter became the first resident of Plains, Ga., to be elected president.* That's not a problem, but further changes aren't necessary.

■ **3. The tax reform measure is easy to understand, easy to implement and requires no special approval.**

In the name of parallel construction, don't mix verbs of differing forms in a series. Here you have two infinitives, *to understand* and *to implement,* mixed with a present tense, *requires.* Change it to:

The tax reform measure is easy to understand and to implement, and it requires no special approval.

Note that good editing sometimes requires you to add words.

■ **4. Albright asked everyone to do their best.**

Here's a case where the classic rules of grammar clash with modern sensitivities. The rule says that if we speak of one unidentified member of a group of mixed gender, we use the masculine. On the other hand, we want to be sensitive to sexism. This problem is easily solved by going to the plural:

Albright asked them all to do their best.

If you went strictly by the grammar rules, the sentence would read: *Albright asked everyone to do his best.* AP tells us not to assume maleness, so we must rework the sentence.

Here are some things you would not do:

• Mix plural and singular, as the original sentence does. In formal writing, bad grammar is unacceptable.

• Use oddball pronouns such as *hir, s/he* and the much discredited *te.* Less of a problem is *he or she.* Some people, in bending over backwards to be fair, recommend that you alternate between *he or she* and *she or he.* This is a wordy construction no matter who goes first; it's often much simpler to use a plural form.

■ **5. The players praised their coaches and reflected on their successes this season.**

The ambiguous pronoun *their* can't be fixed without asking: Does the second *their* refer to players or coaches? It could refer to both. Check sentences like this before making a fix.

■ **6. Trump told Griffin he could improve his profits.**

Again, check before fixing. The pronouns *he* and *his* suggest several permutations: Trump could improve Griffin's profits, Trump could improve Trump's profits, Griffin could improve Trump's profits, Griffin could improve Griffin's profits. You get the point.

■ 7. The Falcons played without discipline, which bothered coach Dan Reeves.

Which is the offending pronoun. The antecedent for a pronoun usually is the noun that most immediately precedes it, in this case *discipline*. But does discipline bother a guy like Dan Reeves, a typical football coach? Not hardly. You could make a simple fix that is less prone to misunderstanding: *The Falcons played without discipline, and that bothered coach Dan Reeves.* Or you could rewrite this to say: *The Falcons' lack of discipline bothered coach Dan Reeves.* You might note that the context of the story often will help the editor sort out these things.

■ 8. Either the lawyers or the president have reason for concern.

We need the singular verb *has.* The rules say that in *either/or* and *neither/nor* constructions, the verb agrees with the closest element of the subject. In this case, *president* is closest and is singular. If it had said *Either the president or the lawyers,* then the verb would be *have.*

■ 9. The Bills will either play the Broncos or the Steelers.

Make it: *The Bills will play either the Broncos or the Steelers.* Be careful of *either/or, neither/nor* and *not only/but also* constructions, known as co-relative conjunctions. Don't separate these conjunctions from the words they are joining.

■ 10. The Sabres will not only defeat the Oilers but also the Kings.

Make it: *The Sabres will defeat not only the Oilers but also the Kings.* This is the same as sentence 9. Writers who start out a sentence with *not only* often find themselves in a pickle because so many words will intervene between the *not only* and the *but also* part of the conjunction.

■ 11. The block has 10 houses, and all but one have white shutters. The house which has green shutters is Ann's. Monica's house which has white shutters is old.

Make it: *The block has 10 houses, and all except one have white shutters. The house that has green shutters is Ann's. Monica's house, which has white shutters, is old.*

We're looking at two problems here.

a. The first has to do with holding words to their primary meaning. Avoid using *but* as a preposition, as it is here. Its primary use is as a conjunction. The preposition *except* works better here.

b. The second problem has to do with essential and nonessential clauses. In the second sentence, we need to change *which* to *that* because the clause is essential; we need to know that Ann's house is the one with green shutters. But because all the other houses have white shutters, that fact is nonessential in identifying Monica's house in the third sentence. Keep *which* and set off the clause with commas.

■ 12. Although the lawyer's opinion was rejected, he vowed to find another legal wedge to free his client.

The pronoun *he* has no antecedent because *lawyer's* is not really a noun; it's a possessive used as a modifier. Make it: *Although his opinion was rejected, the lawyer vowed to find another legal wedge to free his client.*

■ 13. She received a higher grade than anyone in her class.

In news writing, we strive to be precise. In this sentence, *anyone* includes the person with the highest grade; what we mean to say is *anyone else*.

PUNCTUATION

In music, composers use rests to provide pauses that give a song its phrasing, its emphasis and a good deal of its rhythm. Long rests signal the end of one phrase and the beginning of the next, while short rests add texture and meaning to the music without separating related phrases.

So it is with punctuation marks. In working through the punctuation exercises that follow, you may find it helpful to relate the most-used punctuation marks with musical rests: a period equals a whole rest, a semicolon equals a half rest, a colon or a dash equals a quarter rest, and a comma equals an eighth rest (fig. 4.1).

In addition, a pair of dashes or parentheses add a certain dynamic to the writing, like crescendo-decrescendo marks. What a writer places between dashes is emphasized, to be read in a louder voice. Writing enclosed in parentheses is read with a lowered voice.

The rules of punctuation can seem complicated, but they all fall under one broad rule: Punctuation should add clarity. Good writers use punctuation to show relationships clearly. They join related ideas with commas and semicolons, add emphasis by setting off ideas with colons and dashes, and separate unrelated ideas with periods and parentheses. When in doubt about a punctuation mark, ask if it helps make the writing clearer.

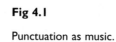

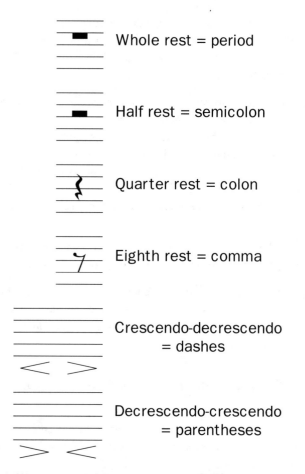

Fig 4.1

Punctuation as music.

The Comma

Commas are used for clarity; they stop your eyes from running into trouble. Take this sentence:

Ever since the boy has been better.

Put a comma after *since,* and you have a sentence. Without it, you have a run-on mind-boggler.

Commas and Conjunctions

Commas are used with conjunctions to join related clauses. Here are rules for the conjunction *and*:

- If no subject follows *and,* then no comma should come before it.
  I finished studying and then went to a movie.
- If the subjects of clauses joined by *and* are the same, and the clauses are closely related, then don't use a comma before *and.*
  I finished reading the material and then I wrote the paper.
- If the subjects of clauses joined by *and* are the same but the clauses are not closely related, use a comma before *and.*
  I finished reading the material, and then I called my sister.

- If the subjects of clauses joined by *and* are different, use a comma before *and*.
  I wrote the paper, and my roommate edited it.

Here are rules for the conjunction *but*:

- Use a comma before *but* if a second subject, same as the first or different, is stated after *but*.
  Dole ran for president, but I did not vote for her.
  Dole ran for president, but she did not win.
- If no subject follows *but*, then no comma should come before it.
  Dole ran for president but did not win.

Rules for the conjunctions *or* and *for* when they join two clauses:

- Use a comma before *or* when the second subject is different.
  Denise is the best on the team, or Northwestern wouldn't have given her a scholarship.
- When the subjects before and after *or* are the same, no comma should come before it.
  Denise is the best on the team or she thinks she is.
- Always use a comma before the conjunction *for* to show that it is not being used as a preposition.
  The pirate told them where to look, for he knew where the treasure lay.

Commas and Rhythm

Using simple sentences in a series adds rhythm to writing, and light punctuation can set the tone. Use commas when semicolons would interrupt the rhythm. Just as you would use a comma to separate a simple series of words such as *red, white and blue,* use a comma to separate simple sentences in a series:

> *He came, he saw, he conquered.*
> *It was sunny today, it was sunny yesterday, it will be sunny tomorrow.*
> *Reagan intervened in Grenada, Bush sent troops to the Persian Gulf, but Clinton preferred air strikes.*

Introductory Phrases

Use commas after introductory clauses or phrases. If the phrase is short, three words or less, the comma may be omitted.

> *In the bright summer of 1982, he left for the circus.*
> *In 1982 he left for the circus.*
> *When he finally made his grand entrance, we ate.*

Sometimes clarity dictates a pause:

> *When he came, we ate.*
> *Climbing the fence, he ripped his pants.*
> *The job being done, we went home.*

Use commas after *yes* and *no* and interjections not requiring an exclamation point: *ah, oh, well, why.*

> *Yes, you may go to the show.*
> *Oh, well, we'll survive.*

Essential and Nonessential

Set off nonessential clauses and phrases, and parenthetical words, with commas. Remember, in this case, commas come in pairs, one before and one after the clause or phrase. Omit the commas with essential clauses or phrases:

> *Robert Redford, who starred in "The Horse Whisperer," is an American actor.*

The nonessential clause beginning with *who* is set off with commas.

> *Students who come to class get good grades.*

The essential clause *who come to class* needs no commas. Another way to think of it is as a restrictive clause. It restricts the meaning to only those students who come to class.

> *The soldier, seeing the grenade, ducked.*

Seeing is part of a nonessential phrase.

> *The man throwing the popcorn is my father.*
> *Throwing* is part of an essential phrase.
> *My only brother, Harry, helped.*

Harry is nonessential.

> *My sister Elaine met me and my other sisters.*

Elaine is essential.

> *He came from Tempe, Ariz., to see us.*
> *She was born on Dec. 28, 1956, in New York.*

The state in the first sentence and the year in the second are considered nonessential. These sentences agree with AP style. Note the style for just month and year, where a comma is not used.

> *Our daughter was born in April 1985.*

Quotations

Use commas to set off simple quotations:

> *The runner said, "Ah, well, I'll win next time."*
> *"Ah, well, I'll win next time," the runner said.*
> *"Ah, well," the runner said, "I'll win next time."*

In quotations of more than one sentence, attributions should be placed at the first logical break, usually at the end of the first clause. Sometimes in divided quotations, punctuation stronger than a comma is necessary:

"We must go now," she said. "I have to get up very early tomorrow."

No comma is needed when a quotation within a sentence is closely related to the rest of the sentence:

His reaction was always "Ah, well, maybe next time."
He said the "time is now" for action.

Coordinate Adjectives

Adjectives having the same weight are joined by commas. These are called coordinate adjectives:

The tall, slender, graceful girl approached.
The tall, slender and graceful girl approached.

To test if adjectives are coordinate, see if *and* could be substituted for the comma. If it can, the adjectives are coordinate:

The sleek, anxious man laughed.

It works if you replace the comma with *and: sleek and anxious.*

The sleek Yale man laughed.

No comma because *Yale* has more weight.
Another test: If the adjectives can be reversed, they are coordinate.

The tall, handsome man arrived.
The handsome, tall man arrived.
The tall log cabin burned down.

Note that *the log tall cabin* doesn't work.

The Semicolon

The semicolon is one of the most underused and misused punctuation marks. Get used to it and use it freely.

Use semicolons to link ideas to show direct relation or contrast. They replace conjunctions when two sentences are joined:

They asked many questions; he answered them all.
John liked the show; Bill was bored.

Using a comma would be wrong, as in: *John liked the show, Bill was bored.* This is called a comma splice.

Semicolons lend clarity by blocking off elements separated by commas in complex constructions.

The survivors included his wife, June; two sons, Walter and Theodore; and a brother.

Note the semicolon before *and.* Here are two more examples:

The speakers at the meeting were Hiram Hills, president of the company; Mitch Pickett, chairman of the board; and Iris Inman, corporation counsel.

John will be late, I am told; but because of the importance of the dinner, we must start on time.

Note the use of the semicolon and the conjunction *but* here. It is an exception to an earlier rule. The two clauses are complex with commas used in each. Stronger punctuation than another comma is needed for clarity.

Use semicolons to separate sentences joined by conjunctive adverbs, such as *therefore, however, hence, nevertheless, accordingly, thus, then.*

The team did not block well; therefore, it could not expect to win.

We laughed until our stomachs hurt; however, the best was yet to come.

Use a semicolon before *as, namely* or *thus* when introducing examples:

Three singers signed for the concert; namely, Elton John, Bob Seger and Elvis Costello.

When only one example follows, a comma suffices:

One fruit was eaten, namely, apples.

The Colon

It is a useful yet underused mark. Use colons to introduce or emphasize words or ideas.

He suggested three colors: blue, green and red.
He had only one idea in mind: drinking.
She left us with this promise: All will be well tomorrow.

Note that when a complete sentence follows a colon, the first word is capitalized, according to the AP stylebook.

Use a colon rather than a comma to set off long quotations, especially if they run more than one paragraph. For example:

John Glenn, who resigned from NASA in 1964 after years of frustration, said: "It was only years later that I read in a book that [John F.] Kennedy had passed the word that he didn't want me to go back up.

"I don't know if he was afraid of the political fallout if I got killed, but by the time I found out, he had been dead for some time, so I never got to discuss it with him."

Note that there is no end quotation mark after *back up.*

The Hyphen

Hyphens are used primarily for clarity and sometimes for conciseness. If confusion would result otherwise, use a hyphen to join compound modifiers: *He went to the modern art museum.* This means he went to a museum with modern conveniences.

He went to the modern-art museum. This means he went to a museum displaying modern art.

She had four great grandchildren. Her grandchildren are great kids.

She had four great-grandchildren. Her daughter's daughter has four children.

He has a full-time job. Note how this sentence is different: *He works full time.*

The 3-year-old girl hit her brother. Note how this sentence is different: *He is 2 years old.*

Keep some compound modifiers hyphenated when they are used after the verb *to be* to avoid confusion:

The senator was soft-spoken. A hyphen prevents the hurried reader from coming up with this: *The senator was soft.*

Here are other examples:

The comic was quick-witted.
The team was second-rate.

Hyphens are not used to join adjectives to adverbs, especially *-ly* adverbs:

It is a specially manufactured product. Don't make it *specially-manufactured.*

It is a uniquely crafted table. Not *uniquely-crafted.*

One exception to this rule, according to the AP stylebook, is the adverb *well* when used with participial adjectives such as *known.* According to the stylebook, this is right: *He is a well-known man, and she also is well-known.* You wouldn't think of hyphenating the adverb *very* with the adjective *good: We saw a very good show.* Sometimes a hyphen is a must.

He covered the roof and re-covered it.

Note how this sentence is different:

He fell off the roof and recovered.
The NATO nations need to re-ally their forces.

Note how this sentence is different:

NATO really needs to realign its forces.

Suspended hyphenation is used for brevity. Just be careful to provide a space where needed.

The rapist received a 20- to 30-year sentence.
The class calls for 1- and 2-year-olds.
One-, two- and three-bedroom apartments are available to low- and middle-income families.

The Dash

Beware of the "dashers." Such writers use the dash when a colon or comma would do nicely, or when they want to pack as many ideas as possible into one sentence.

The mayor proposed a tax hike—it was unprecedented—to bail out the schools.

Make it: *The mayor proposed an unprecedented tax hike.*

She listed the qualities—intelligence, charm and wealth—that she liked in men.

Make it: *She listed the qualities she liked in men: intelligence, charm and wealth.*

Alf Landon—the perennial presidential candidate—arrived.

Make it: *Alf Landon, the perennial presidential candidate, arrived.*

Occasionally a dash may be used to set off an emphatic word or phrase. Such a sentence often ends with an exclamation point:

We will vacation in Monaco—if I get a raise.

She found the perfect mate: tall, charming, rich—and a man!

Parentheses

Parentheses within a sentence usually are a good sign that the sentence should be recast. They often clumsily interrupt the flow of ideas:

John Glenn (he recently went back into space after being the first American to orbit the Earth) is the senior senator from Ohio.

Make it: *John Glenn is the senior senator from Ohio. He recently went back into space after being the first American to orbit the Earth.*

Sometimes parentheses are an acceptable way to tighten writing if the information included in them is short and succinctly answers a question in the reader's mind, an answer that needs no elaboration.

Mario Cuomo ran for mayor in 1977 (he lost), and he decided he had had enough of politics for a while.

WORKOUT: PUNCTUATION

Punctuate the following sentences properly. You may have to insert punctuation marks or delete them. Do not rewrite the sentences; just touch them up. Note: Some of the sentences are correct as written; mark them OK. Then see how we would do it.

■ 1. The flag is red white and blue.

Use commas to separate elements in a series, but do not put a comma before the conjunction in a simple series. Not all grammar books agree that this last comma, the so-called serial comma, should be left out; *The Elements of Style* by Strunk and White, for instance, says to use the serial comma, but the AP stylebook says leave it out. We'll follow the AP stylebook. Punctuate it like this: *The flag is red, white and blue.*

■ 2. Tension builds the gun sounds and the race begins.

In sentence 2, some will argue that clauses require the serial comma, but the stylebook says to do that only with a series of complex clauses or phrases. Sentence 2 contains obviously simple clauses. Make it: *Tension builds, the gun sounds and the race begins.*

■ 3. I'll have toast, coffee, and ham and eggs.

This is correct as written. A comma is needed before the conjunction in a series if an element of the series, in this case *ham and eggs,* also contains a conjunction.

■ 4. The minister is survived by his wife Alice two daughters Sarah and Mary and a son Joseph.

Two things are at work here.

First, the names are set off because they are nonessential. The man has only one wife, so her name is not really necessary to identify her. He has only two daughters, so again the names are nonessential and are set off by commas. He has only one son, so the name is nonessential. Compare that with this sentence:

He took his son James hunting while the rest of the boys stayed home.

No commas around *James* because his name is essential in identifying him.

Second, we use semicolons to separate elements in a series when the individual elements contain commas. Note that we use a semicolon before the last conjunction: *The minister is survived by his wife, Alice; two daughters, Sarah and Mary; and a son, Joseph.*

■ 5. He is survived by his wife Alice and a son Edward.

We set off the names with commas because they are nonessential. We do not use a semicolon because two elements do not make a series: *He is survived by his wife, Alice, and a son, Edward.*

Consider the next two sentences together:

■ 6. Elaine gave her only brother Buck a gift.

■ 7. Buck gave his youngest sister Elaine a gift.

In both sentences, the names are nonessential. In the first case, Buck is the only brother; in the second case, he can have only one youngest sister, so her name also is nonessential. The AP stylebook has a good section on essential and nonessential. Punctuate sentences 6 and 7 like this:

Elaine gave her only brother, Buck, a gift.
Buck gave his youngest sister, Elaine, a gift.

Here is another pair of sentences:

■ 8. The Bijou is showing the suspense thriller, "L.A. Confidential."

■ 9. The filmmaker Leland's movie "Mud" was a flop.

In both sentences, the definition of what is essential comes into play. In sentence 8, the title of the movie is obviously essential; more than one suspense thriller has been made in the history of film. Delete the comma: *The Bijou is showing the suspense thriller "L.A. Confidential."*

In sentence 9, you might ask if "Mud" is Leland's only movie. The key is his title of filmmaker. Somewhere in his past, he must have made another movie of some sort, so the title is essential. No comma is needed: *The filmmaker Leland's movie "Mud" was a flop.*

■ 10. The bigamist's wife Joan was upset with her husband's other wife Sally and Sally's only brother Tom.

Sentence 10 is an example that what is essential and nonessential can change between the beginning and end of a sentence. We say the man is a bigamist, then name a wife. Because a bigamist has two wives, her name is essential and does not take commas. Then we name his other wife. Now, because we cannot mistake who we're talking about, her name is nonessential. Some may argue that we eventually name both wives, so the first name should be nonessential, too. Our guideline is, Don't do something early in a sentence that readers can't understand until they read the whole thing, not if you can help it. Of course, we need a comma before the only brother's name: *The bigamist's wife Joan was upset with her husband's other wife, Sally, and Sally's only brother, Tom.*

■ 11. Congress passed the bill, the president vetoed it.

A common error is the comma splice, where a comma joins independent clauses. Some grammarians refer to this as a run-on sentence. The key is that the clauses are independent.

You could fix this sentence three ways. You could put in the semicolon, and that's what we prefer because it's the simplest edit. You could put in a period and capitalize *the,* making it two sentences. That is grammatically correct but damages the close relationship of the clauses. You also could put in a comma and the conjunction *and.* Again, that tends to separate the clauses more than we'd like. We'd do it like this: *Congress passed the bill; the president vetoed it.*

■ 12. Feed a cold starve a fever.

The editor has to think about the understood elements of this sentence to get it right:

(You) Feed a cold (and) starve a fever.

Feed and *starve* make up a compound verb with one understood subject. We can replace *and* with a comma, not a semicolon: *Feed a cold, starve a fever.*

■ 13. Nothing ventured, nothing gained.

The sentence is correct as written. This time the clauses are connected with a comma, not a semicolon, because they aren't independent.

■ 14. He came he saw he conquered.

Here you have three short independent clauses. You could connect them with semicolons, but remember that different punctuation marks require different pauses, like the rests in music. In sentence 14, a semicolon would be too much of a pause. You can use commas and the sentence is still perfectly readable.

He came, he saw, he conquered.

■ 15. The program, which will not be repeated caused a furor.

Commas often come in pairs, like parentheses. You need the commas because the clause *which will not be repeated* is nonessential: *The program, which will not be repeated, caused a furor.*

Handle these next two sentences as a pair:

■ 16. The Grand Rapids, Mich. man suffered the injury on Jan. 4, 1982, in his home.

■ 17. Write to the dean at 1845 Sheridan Road Evanston Ill. 60208.

Place commas after *Mich.* and *1982* in sentence 16, and after *Road* and *Evanston* in sentence 17. These are required according to AP style. But note the difference between *Jan. 4, 1982,* and *January 1982*. In the first, with a full date, the year is set off by commas. In the second, without a full date, no commas are used and the month is not abbreviated. In sentence 17, note that the ZIP code is not set off with commas:

The Grand Rapids, Mich., man suffered the injury on Jan. 4, 1982, in his home.

Write to the dean at 1845 Sheridan Road, Evanston, Ill. 60208.

■ 18. At the end of World War II he joined the company as a clerk.

The rule is to set off long introductory clauses or set off introductory clauses where misunderstanding is possible. How long is long? More than three words. Sentence 18 requires a comma because the introductory clause contains seven words:

At the end of World War II, he joined the company as a clerk.

Consider the next three sentences together:

■ 19. In 1981 he joined the company as a clerk.

■ 20. When he retired from the company he felt sad.

■ 21. When he retired he felt sad.

All three involve introductory clauses. Sentence 19, with an introductory phrase of two words, does not need a comma. Sentence 20, introduced by six words, requires a comma. Sentence 21 doesn't need a comma.

In 1981 he joined the company as a clerk.
When he retired from the company, he felt sad.
When he retired he felt sad.

Here is another pair of sentences:

■ 22. Ever since she was a good girl.

■ 23. After the lonely lumberjack sawed his last log cabin fever overcame him.

In sentence 22, the introductory phrase is short, but comprehension would be hindered by not putting a comma after *since*.

The same applies to sentence 23: The introductory clause is long, but more than that, leaving out the comma would leave the sentence open to misunderstanding.

Ever since, she was a good girl.
After the lonely lumberjack sawed his last log, cabin fever overcame him.

■ **24. When the water rushed in, Smith said he held his breath.**

The key to this sentence is recognizing that *Smith said* and *held his breath* cannot be simultaneous actions. Anytime you put the attribution in the middle of a sentence, set it off with commas. If you were editing this beyond punctuation, which you are not, you could put the attribution at the end: *When the water rushed in, he held his breath, Smith said.* That's not really better. Make it: *When the water rushed in, Smith said, he held his breath.*

These three sentences deal with similar problems:

■ **25. Walt Johnson, of Evanston, was elected to the board.**

■ **26. Walt Johnson of Joplin, Mo., was elected to the board.**

■ **27. Walt Johnson, 42, of Evanston, was elected to the board.**

Prepositional phrases, like most modifiers, are not set off from the words they modify. You wouldn't write *Walt Johnson, of Evanston,* any more than you would write *the Prince, of Wales.*

In sentence 25, then, delete the commas. Sentence 26 is OK; the state is set off with commas according to AP style. See sentence 16. In sentence 27, we set off Walt Johnson's age, but not the prepositional phrase *of Evanston.* Warning: Don't edit too quickly or mechanically. Take a look, recognize what is being set off, then put in punctuation.

Walt Johnson of Evanston was elected to the board.

Walt Johnson of Joplin, Mo., was elected to the board.

Walt Johnson, 42, of Evanston was elected to the board.

Consider these two sentences together:

■ **28. Yes I did it. Ah, well, I'll face the consequences.**

■ 29. Look over there officer. The man, who robbed me, is No. 3 in the lineup.

Set off words of direct address with commas. In sentence 28, *yes* is set off in the first sentence. *Ah, well,* is set off in the second. In sentence 29, *officer* is the word of direct address. In the second sentence, eliminate the commas around *who robbed me*. That clause is essential in identifying whom we are talking about:

Yes, I did it. Ah, well, I'll face the consequences.
Look over there, officer. The man who robbed me is No. 3 in the lineup.

■ 30. The mayor thought long and hard about the measure, but he couldn't accept it.

This sentence is OK as written. The rule: When the conjunction *but* connects two clauses, put a comma before it. Another way to think about it: If a subject is stated after *but,* use the comma. Notice how this sentence is different: *The mayor thought long and hard about the measure but couldn't accept it.* No subject comes after *but;* what you have is a compound verb: *thought but couldn't accept.*

■ 31. The mayor thought long and hard about the measure and sought advice from his aides who knew the importance of the matter. But, he couldn't accept it.

Compare the first part of this with sentence 30. No comma before *and* because it connects compound verbs *thought* and *sought.* You do need a comma after *aides* to set off the nonessential clause *who knew the importance of the matter.* Strike the comma after *but.* This is a common error. Go back to sentence 30. We doubt anyone felt it necessary to put a comma after *but* in sentence 30. It's the same for sentence 31, except that the sentence, not just a clause, begins with *but.* Make sentence 31 read: *The mayor thought long and hard about the measure and sought advice from his aides, who knew the importance of the matter. But he couldn't accept it.*

■ 32. The mail carrier delivered the package and he asked to use the phone.

Looking at sentence 32 and the ones that follow, you might review the rules for using commas with conjunctions. In sentence 32, the subject is the same for both clauses: *the mail carrier* and *he.* But because the clauses are not closely related, use a comma before *and: The mail carrier delivered the package, and he asked to use the phone.*

The next three sentences concern similar problems:

■ 33. The mail carrier delivered the package, and asked to use the phone.

■ 34. The mail carrier delivered the package, and was asked if he had a pen.

■ 35. The mail carrier delivered the package and he asked the recipient to sign for it.

In sentence 33, delete the comma; no subject is stated after *and,* so no comma is needed: *The mail carrier delivered the package and asked to use the phone.*

In sentence 34, delete the comma; no subject is stated after *and,* so no comma is needed: *The mail carrier delivered the package and was asked if he had a pen.*

Sentence 35 is OK as written. The subject, *mail carrier,* is restated in the second clause, but the clauses are closely related, so no comma is used: *The mail carrier delivered the package and he asked the recipient to sign for it.*

■ 36. The mail carrier delivered the package, but did not have a receipt.

Strike the comma after *package* because no subject is stated after *but.* This is just a compound verb: *The mail carrier delivered the package but did not have a receipt.*

■ 37. The mail carrier delivered the package but he did not have a receipt.

A comma is needed before *but* because the subject is restated. Note how the rule for *but* is different from the rule for *and.* That's because but can be used as a preposition as well as a conjunction: *The mail carrier delivered the package, but he did not have a receipt.*

Consider these two sentences:

■ 38. The cheap ugly coat was offensive.

■ 39. The cheap fur coat was offensive.

Coordinate adjectives are equal in strength and are separated by a comma. The test: Can the adjectives be reversed and still make sense? In sentence 38, it doesn't matter if you say *the cheap, ugly coat* or *the ugly, cheap coat.* You need to insert a comma. Note how sentence 39 is different; you wouldn't say *the fur cheap coat.* The adjectives are not coordinate adjectives:

The cheap, ugly coat was offensive.
The cheap fur coat was offensive.

■ **40. The coach called Jones "A shining example."**

With sentence 40, we begin punctuating sentences with quotations. Sentence 40 illustrates how to handle a partial quote, or a snippet. The first letter of the quote is lowercase: *The coach called Jones "a shining example."*

Note that the period goes inside the quotation marks. Commas and periods always go inside quotation marks, even when the quotation marks go around something like a movie title: *We saw "Gone with the Wind."*

■ **41. The coach said Jones is a stellar performer.**

Sentence 41 is OK as written. Woe to the editor who adds quotation marks to copy without at least checking with the writer. You never can assume something is a quote just because a *he said* is attached to it.

■ **42. The coach said "Phil Jones is a shining example."**

When an attribution introduces a quote of one sentence, use a comma. The AP stylebook says to use a colon when the quote is two or more sentences. Make it: *The coach said, "Phil Jones is a shining example."*

■ **43. "Phil Jones is a shining example" the coach said "I wish him the best."**

Sentence 43 requires straightforward punctuation. Insert a comma inside the quotation marks after *example.* The attribution ends a sentence, so a period is inserted after *said: "Phil Jones is a shining example," the coach said. "I wish him the best."*

■ **44. "Phil Jones is a shining example" the coach said "and I wish him the best."**

Note how sentence 44 is different from sentence 43. The attribution comes in the middle of a sentence. Insert a comma after *example* inside the quotation marks and use a comma after *said,* not a period: *"Phil Jones is a shining example," the coach said, "and I wish him the best."*

■ 45. "Phil Jones is a shining example" the coach said "his teammates don't compare."

In sentence 45, the editor has to recognize that what follows the attribution is obviously a new sentence; put a comma after *example* and a period after *said* and capitalize *his*: *"Phil Jones is a shining example," the coach said. "His teammates don't compare."*

■ 46. "Phil Jones" the coach said "is a shining example."

This is another continuing quote; insert commas after *Jones* and *said*.

Putting the attribution here is OK once in a while for emphasis, but it can be ridiculous, too. Consider this sentence: *"I think," Descartes said on the anniversary of his greatest discovery, "that I shall have some cake."* The attribution should come at the first logical break, usually at the end of the first clause. But we'll go with this: *"Phil Jones," the coach said, "is a shining example."*

■ 47. The coach said "Phil Jones is a shining example. I can't remember a scholar-athlete held in higher regard by his teammates, teachers and fans. "I wish him the best. I know Northwestern will be a better place because of him."

Take your time to sort this out. Use a colon after *said* because the quote contains more than one sentence. What about the open-quotation mark before *I wish*? You could handle it by starting a new paragraph or by deleting the quotation mark. What we want to get across is how to punctuate quotes that continue over more than one paragraph. The first paragraph does not end with quotation marks, but the second paragraph begins with them. Here's how it should look:

The coach said: "Phil Jones is a shining example. I can't remember a scholar-athlete held in higher regard by his teammates, teachers and fans.
"I wish him the best. I know Northwestern will be a better place because of him."

The next two sentences address similar issues:

■ 48. "Is that right" the president asked.

■ 49. Was that a "handshake agreement?"

Question marks used with quotes can be tricky because, unlike commas or periods, question marks sometimes go outside the quotation marks. In sentence 48, the question mark goes inside because the quoted material is the question. In sentence 49, the quoted material is not a question; it just falls within a question. The question mark goes outside the quotation marks:

"Is that right?" the president asked.
Was that a "handshake agreement"?

These two sentences deal with colons:

■ **50. Consider this We drop all charges and go back to business.**

■ **51. I can't believe this Northwestern won a football game.**

Use a colon to introduce lists, concepts, ideas. If what follows the colon is a complete sentence, begin it with a capital letter. In sentence 50, all you need is a colon after *this:*

Consider this: We drop all charges and go back to business.

In sentence 51, the colon after *this* introduces the clause and helps to emphasize it. That emphasis makes it better than a period or semicolon. Some will prefer a dash, but editors should be careful about inserting dashes into copy. Dashes provide strong emphasis that the writer may not have desired. Make it:

I can't believe this: Northwestern won a football game.

■ **52. The city approved a 10 year plan for establishing a hazardous waste dump.**

Hyphens are used to eliminate confusion. This is done by connecting things that belong together. In making those connections clear, we aid the reader in understanding. Sometimes hyphens are required as a matter of style even though the odds of misunderstanding are slight. In sentence 52, a hyphen is required in *10-year plan* as a matter of style.

In *hazardous-waste dump,* the hyphen is needed to eliminate possible confusion. It's a dump for hazardous waste, not a hazardous dump: *The city approved a 10-year plan for establishing a hazardous-waste dump.*

■ **53. The 25-year old man faces a burglary charge.**

The second hyphen in *25-year-old man* is dictated by AP style under the entry ages: *The 25-year-old man faces a burglary charge.*

Look at these two sentences together:

■ 54. First and second rate products were for sale.

■ 55. The city owned and operated building burned down.

These deal with suspended hyphenation. The key is to understand what is being hooked together with hyphens. In sentence 54, we're hyphenating *first-rate* and *second-rate*. A space is needed after *first-* because we're not connecting *first-and*. In sentence 55, we're obviously not connecting *and-operated*, so the space comes after *and*. Make the sentences read:

First- and second-rate products were for sale.
The city-owned and -operated building burned down.

You should be aware that some computer editing systems require that the editor insert a special space, sometimes called a *fixed space*, or else the computer will automatically close up the space after a hyphen.

■ 56. The multi-million dollar project would help the community.

For further guidance about when to use hyphens, consult the AP stylebook entry under specific prefixes, such as *multi-,* and under prefixes in general. The entry under *multi-* says to make it "solid" in most usages: *The multimillion-dollar project would help the community.*

Note that *multimillion-dollar* is hyphenated as a compound modifier.

Consider these two sentences together:

■ 57. Its wrong to spend like that.

■ 58. The kangaroo put the wallet in it's pouch.

Slow down for words such as *its* and *it's*. In sentence 57, we need the apostrophe because we want the contraction of the words *it is: It's wrong to spend like that.*

In sentence 58, we eliminate the apostrophe because we want the possessive pronoun *its: The kangaroo put the wallet in its pouch.*

■ 59. A weeks work for a days pay.

Guidance for phrases such as *a day's pay* is in the stylebook under *possessives/quasi possessives*. The phrases *a week's work* and *a day's pay* take apostrophes: *A week's work for a day's pay.*

These two sentences deal with similar problems:

■ **60.** A teachers' strike was averted.

■ **61.** She was looking for a writers' guide.

In both sentences, eliminate the apostrophes because *teachers* and *writers* are not possessives but rather descriptive words. A way to test this is by turning it into a prepositional phrase. If you would say *a strike by teachers,* then you do not have a possessive. Or if you would say *a guide for writers,* it's not a possessive, either. But if you had a phrase such as *the books of teachers,* you could make it into a possessive, *the teachers' books.* Make the sentences read:

A teachers strike was averted.
She was looking for a writers guide.

■ **62.** What the problem is is not clear.

Use a comma to separate repeated words that would be confusing: *What the problem is, is not clear.*

THE USAGE SURVIVAL KIT

You learned about grammar, punctuation and spelling in elementary school, but terms like style and usage may be new to you. They refer to other rules we need to follow when writing and editing. Style simply means a set way of doing things to ensure consistency throughout a news organization. For most journalists, style is governed by *The AP Stylebook and Libel Manual,* with additional rules falling under *local style.*

Usage is a clipped term meaning *standard English usage,* which is the way words are used to express ideas.

In France, a government agency oversees usage of the language. The French recognize the link between usage and culture, so they guard their language jealously against intruding foreign words.

Great Britain had H.W. Fowler, who wrote a *Dictionary of Modern English Usage.*

In our country, usage experts are self-appointed. You may have read books or articles by the likes of Edwin Newman, William Safire and Theodore Bernstein listing the do's and don'ts of word choice.

We struggle with usage rules because the language changes through misuse and because different rules apply depending on whether you're using formal tone or informal tone. When people talk, they use an informal tone. But when we write news stories, we want formal usage.

Why care about formal usage? It's more precise. When you mix up words like *anxious* and *eager,* you leave yourself open to misinterpretation even though most people may know what you mean. And precision is a key ingredient in journalism.

Right Usage

The first and simplest rule of usage is this: Make sure you know what a word means before you use it. Just because it sounds neat doesn't mean it's right.

One sportswriter at the *Chicago Tribune* often referred to wacky pitcher Steve "Rainbow" Trout of the Cubs as "the quixotic left-hander." What does *quixotic* mean? The dictionary says it means "of or like Don Quixote; 2. extravagantly chivalrous or foolishly idealistic; visionary; impractical or impracticable." It was quite a stretch to apply that to Steve Trout, who did things such as treat a blister on his pitching hand with pickle juice. What the writer might have meant was *quirky*.

Correct or Politically Correct?

Some questions of usage come under the heading of what offends people. For instance, years ago we referred to people with mental disabilities as *retarded*. But this word came to be a derogatory term, so the preferred usage became *mentally handicapped*.

But disabled people began to protest the use of *handicapped*, which means "having a disadvantage that makes achievement unusually difficult," especially "a physical disability." It was seen as too harsh a word. The point is a fine one. Those who are disabled don't like to think of themselves as limited in what they can do, and they certainly don't want others, especially employers, to think that way, either. *Disabled* became preferred and news organizations went along with the general consensus because any of those terms were accurate in communicating meaning. *Mentally disabled* followed.

But the dictionary defines disabled as "deprived of physical, moral, or intellectual strength." That has its own negative connotations. One preference some groups have expressed is *a person with a disability*. The reasoning here is that the emphasis then is on the person, not that the person is disabled. Some news organizations find that construction overly wordy.

Some people now prefer *challenged*, as in *physically challenged* or *mentally challenged*. The problem here is that *challenged* takes in a lot more territory than *disabled*. In the name of communicating precisely, news organizations have resisted using *challenged* as a synonym for *disabled*. It really is a euphemism that has spawned many jokes, such as older people saying with a laugh that they're *chronologically challenged*.

But let's take it a step further. We've read articles in which *special children* were mentioned, and we were left to figure out that the writers meant *mentally disabled children*. Saying *special children* may display well-intentioned sensitivity, but it doesn't communicate effectively.

Those who insist on these changes of usage are not just squeamish; they know that words carry strong connotations that can be translated into attitudes and even laws. Still, news organizations have a duty to communicate effectively and should resist the more far-out attempts.

Name Brands, Trademarks and Legal Names

Some usage involves trademarks or legal titles. These are easy to deal with if you are aware of them. Words like *Styrofoam*, *Jell-O* and *Xerox* are trade names and belong to specific products from specific companies. The AP stylebook includes those three and many others. It says specifically to not use words like *Xerox* as a verb, as in *I xeroxed the proclamation.* Make it: *I photocopied the proclamation.*

Cutting the Fat

Finally, a big part of editing as it concerns usage is doing away with wordiness or redundancy. To do that, you have to know what words mean. For example, if something is *complete,* it's all there. It can't be *very complete.*

Beware of buzzwords, the trendy words or phrases that characterize an era or event. In the 1960s a common phrase was *diametrically opposed* to the war. However, the second dictionary definition for *diametric* is "completely opposed or opposite." So the two words were redundant.

Primary Meaning

Sorting out usage problems requires knowing how to use the stylebook and the dictionary. Let's look at some examples:

The man was shotgunned to death.

The question is, Should you use shotgun as a verb? The stylebook offers no guidance, so turn to *Webster's New World College Dictionary,* Fourth Edition. You see *shotgun* listed first as a noun. In this dictionary, definitions are listed in historical order. The first definition of a word relies more on etymology, the word's origin. The most common, present-day uses are listed toward the end of an entry. The second use listed for shotgun is as a verb meaning "to shoot, force or threaten with a shotgun." So is this sentence correct?

Well, not really. The dictionary is saying that people use *shotgun* as a verb, but it's not necessarily saying that they should. (See also our discussion of this in Chapter 2.) This is where usage experts come in. Depending on the expert, you'll hear that yes, it's OK, or no, it's not. But twisting nouns into verbs isn't a good idea. *Shotgunned* sounds strained and awkward. Let's hold words to their primary usage. We would rewrite the sentence to say: *A shotgun blast killed the man.*

We could make it simply *The man was shot to death.* Now we've lost meaning; was he shot with a shotgun, a pistol or a BB gun? In editing this sentence, you must preserve the ideas of *shotgun* and *death.*

Here's another example:

For more information, contact the city Health Department.

Knowing where to concentrate is an important editing skill. Some editors will rewrite this sentence and miss the point, which is whether *contact* should be used as a verb. This is a good example of how usage changes through misuse. *Contact* is like *shotgun* in that both started out as nouns and then became verbs. The difference is that *contact* is further down the road of misuse and, therefore, more acceptable.

We'll use the *New York Times* stylebook to explain. At one time the rule for *contact* was "Do not use as a verb." Here's the latest entry: "Although it has gained acceptance [as a verb], it remains graceless and has also achieved triteness. On those grounds, avoid it where possible."

What has happened is that so many people have knowingly or unknowingly violated the earlier usage rule that the verb *contact* has moved from out of bounds to center field. Can't you just see the stylebook writer's teeth grind when he writes *graceless* and *triteness*? That's the problem with knowing usage rules. Because most people don't, you live a tortured life of reading and hearing words used improperly, then seeing those mistakes become acceptable practices over time. The precise writer and editor pays attention to not only what's acceptable but also what's preferred.

How then would we edit the sentence? We would leave it as is. In an earlier life, following the old *New York Times* rule, we would have made it: *For more information, get in contact with the city Health Department.* What was right then is too wordy now.

Our problem with *contact* is not so much its use as a verb as its vague meaning. Does it mean call or write? Is there a fax number? Lazy writers use *contact* rather than a specific word. If the writer provided phone numbers and addresses, it would make the reader's life easier. Sometimes it's unnecessary or impossible to be specific. Then *contact* is fine. But if an address is listed, say *write*. If a phone number is listed, say *call*. Would you use *phone* as a verb? No, because it would be a noun twisted to serve as a verb.

This next sentence is another example of a misused word:

The Cubs bested the Dodgers.

Twisting a noun into a verb makes usage experts wince; twisting an adjective into a verb makes them scream. Look up *best* in the dictionary and you'll see it listed first as an adjective and fourth as a verb meaning "to defeat." Some writers think twisting words like this makes writing fresh. It doesn't; it just makes writing twisted.

Some sportswriters grow bored with words like *defeat;* they reach for phrasing like *The Indians scalped the A's* and *The Bisons stampeded the Mud Hens.* All of which doesn't make much sense and certainly isn't fresh. The energy is misdirected. Good writing is marked by depth of meaning. These puns dance along the surface and call attention to themselves.

In our example, we would do better just to say: *The Cubs defeated the Dodgers.*

Now look at this sentence:

I have studied your $1 million offer and decided to accept same.

What is the primary use of the word *same*? Our dictionary lists it first as an adjective and gives several examples. It is used here as a pronoun. That's the usage problem. The more appropriate pronoun is *it*. We also would add *have* before *decided* to keep the verbs parallel, or in the same form. Both should be in the present perfect tense. So the sentence would read: *I have studied your $1 million offer and have decided to accept it.*

One more:

She has authored many books.

Again, usage is keeping words to their primary meaning. *Author* is first a noun. Here it is twisted into a verb. The sentence should read: *She has written many books.*

Unambiguous Words

Look at this sentence:

We ate during halftime.

Should it be *during halftime* or *at halftime*? *During* could mean two things: *at* or *throughout*. Imagine your cholesterol level if you ate throughout halftime, about 20 minutes straight. Usage rules demand precision in the language. We want words to speak with one clear voice. We would make it: *We ate at halftime.*

Tired Words

Some words become disabled through overuse. Here's an example:

The mayor will unveil her three-point plan.

Unveil is questionable on two counts. First, it's overused. When a word is used often, it soon becomes trite and even draws attention to itself. Words should not distract readers. Second, *unveil* implies that the plan is now hidden and will soon be revealed. Our guess is that the writer means something more like *announce, introduce* or *present*. Each would work, but for the record, we would write, *The mayor will present her three-point plan.*

If the plan really had been kept secret, we would prefer *reveal*. Good usage is restricting words to their most appropriate uses. For *unveil* that means when objects are literally uncovered.

Some overused words are part of the wiseguy lingo journalists use, especially in headlines. A case in point:

Police promised that they would investigate the case and probe any possible suspects.

Probe has an unfortunate medical connotation. We would just delete it. Words like *probe* are used as last resorts by headline writers who can't say *investigate* because it's too long. They reach into their bags of "headlinese" and come up with *probe*. The real problem starts when writers see these words and begin using them as a matter of first choice. Before long someone is writing: *The company's head mulled a bid to probe his foe.* What they mean is: *The company's president considered a proposal to investigate his rival.* Anytime you see these headlinese words in copy, don't hesitate to change them. Realize that good headline writers hate to use them.

Here's a sentence with an overused word that borders on being a cliché:

The major New York book publisher made major inroads in examining the major issues of the day.

There's another point here beyond overuse. Sometimes words fail you not because they are bad but because of the words that precede or follow them. Taken separately, each use of the word *major* is fine. Taken together, this sentence won't work.

To fix it, you must drop two *majors*. If you leave the first one, you can delete the second (after all, making inroads means doing important things) and change the last one to *significant: The major New York book publisher made inroads in examining the significant issues of the day.*

The Right Word for the Right Place

Some words become inappropriate because of their context:

The trio of robbers scoffed at the idea.

If there were four robbers, would you call them a quartet? So let's say: *The three robbers scoffed at the idea.* Again, good usage means keeping words to their primary use. Reserve *trio* for stories about musicians.

Sometimes we make a word do too much work in a sentence:

He served as a priest, a vice president and a third baseman on the softball team.

The problem here also relates to parallel construction. The verb *served* has three objects, but it makes sense for only the first two. You can say he served as a priest and served as a vice president, but no one serves as a third baseman. You need to find a verb that works with all three, and *was* is simplest:

He was a priest, a vice president and a third baseman on the softball team.

The Color of a Word

Look at this sentence:

He claimed she hit him and later claimed first prize in the liars contest.

Just as we see colors in relation to other colors, we decide some usage questions based on the words around us.

This is one of the few sentences in captivity in which the verb *claim* is used properly two times. *Claim* isn't usually a problem when it means to lay claim to something, such as first prize. The usage problem arises when it is used instead of *said, asserted, contended* or *charged*. If you look up *claim* in the dictionary, you'll see the definition "to assert in the face of possible contradiction." The problem with *claim* is that it carries doubt with it. Take this sentence: *She claimed she was innocent.* It sounds as if you're saying, *She claimed she was innocent, but she's really not.*

In news writing those connotations make statements unfair. The word *said* has the advantage of being neutral. No problem with this: *She said she was innocent.* If you wanted to reflect emphasis in the speaker's voice, you would write, *She asserted that she was innocent,* or *She contended that she was innocent.*

WORKOUT: USAGE

Edit the following sentences to correct miscues, to omit needless words or to improve word choice. Don't rewrite the sentences; just touch them up. If a sentence is correct as written, just mark it OK. Then see how we would handle it.

■ 1. He compared this year's results to last year's.

In this sentence, we're comparing differences, so use the preposition *with.* See the AP stylebook on this, then edit it to read: *He compared this year's results with last year's.*

■ 2. He compared love to a rose.

The sentence is OK as written. This time, we're comparing similarities, metaphorically, so we'll use *to.* See the stylebook again.

■ 3. Killed were five women, three men and eight children.

A stilted usage that is unnecessary. Make it: *Five women, three men and eight children were killed.*

■ 4. He could not convince the mayor to take a stand on the issue, said O'Brien.

Remember, it's *persuade to* and *convince that. Persuade* shows action; *convince* shows a state of mind. Also, observe the subject-verb order with attributions. Make it: *He could not persuade the mayor to take a stand on the issue, O'Brien said.*

■ 5. The show was as good or better than last year's.

You need to complete the as/as comparison. Make it: *The show was as good as or better than last year's.*

■ 6. The mayor-elect vowed to effect change.

Sentence 6 is OK as written; see the stylebook under *affect, effect. Effect* as a noun means result; *effect* as a verb means to bring about. *Affect,* a verb, means to influence.

■ 7. Alcohol effected his decision.

In sentence 7, make it *affected,* meaning influenced: *Alcohol affected his decision.*

■ 8. The effect of alcohol can be debilitating.

Sentence 8 is OK as written.

■ 9. The pro-life demonstrators totally destroyed the clinic.

News organizations try to go along with what people want to call themselves—until it obscures understanding. The issue in question here is abortion, and it's more accurate to say *anti-abortion demonstrators*. What about *pro-choice demonstrators*? Many in so-called pro-choice groups make the point that they support only the right to have an abortion, not the act of abortion itself. In news accounts, you'd be more accurate to say *abortion rights demonstrators* and save *pro-choice* for those tight headlines.

One more thing: *Totally destroyed* is a sloppy redundancy that is worth eliminating. Just make it *destroyed*. See the stylebook under *demolish, destroy*. We'll make sentence 9 read: *The anti-abortion demonstrators destroyed the clinic.*

■ 10. A couple more coins and the total would be over $1 million.

Two fixes are needed: First, *Couple* is a noun, not an adverb, so you need *of* before *more*. Second, *over* should be saved to show a physical relationship of something on top. See the AP stylebook. Make it: *A couple of coins more and the total would be more than $1 million.*

■ 11. The Easter Sunday service was very unique.

Eliminate redundancy! Isn't Easter always on Sunday? And *unique* means one of a kind; an intensifier like *very* is unnecessary: *The Easter service was unique.*

■ 12. Some 10,000 marchers stormed the building, and a guard was strangled to death.

Some is misused here; we mean *about*. *Strangle* means "to choke to death," so eliminate the redundancy: *About 10,000 marchers stormed the building, and a guard was strangled.*

■ 13. The defendants' lawyer refuted the plaintiff's argument, then the plaintiff's lawyer refuted the defendants' claims.

Know what a word means. *Refute* means "to prove wrong," something that seldom happens in a court of law. Some words that might be used instead are *rebutted, challenged* and *disputed.* Make it: *The defendants' lawyer rebutted the plaintiff's argument, then the plaintiff's lawyer challenged the defendants' claims.*

■ 14. The boxer was chomping at the bit.

This is a common mistake. The correct term is *champing: The boxer was champing at the bit.*

■ 15. The mayor died suddenly in his sleep.

The dictionary has an entry for *sudden death.* It means a death that is unexpected *and* instantaneous. In this case, *unexpected* is what we mean; we don't know if he died instantaneously. Make it: *The mayor died unexpectedly in his sleep.*

■ 16. The resident implied that the mayor was a schmuck.

Again, when you use a word, make sure you know what it means—especially non-English words or phrases. *Schmuck* is a Yiddish term for penis. The dictionary lists *jerk* as a synonym: *The resident implied that the mayor was a jerk.*

■ 17. Speaking to the police, the informant inferred that the mayor was involved in the scheme.

In sentence 16, you may have been tempted to change *implied* to *inferred.* Remember that the speaker or writer implies, or indicates indirectly; the listener or reader infers, or derives a hidden or indirect meaning. Sentence 16 was correct, but sentence 17 is not. See the AP stylebook entry, and make the sentence read: *Speaking to the police, the informant implied that the mayor was involved in the scheme.*

■ 18. He tried to throw the discus further than anyone else.

Use *farther* when something can be measured with a ruler. For everything else, time, degree or quantity, use *further.* See the stylebook: *He tried to throw the discus farther than anyone else.*

■ 19. The boy was anxious to get an ice cream cone.

Anxious takes its meaning from *anxiety:* apprehensive uneasiness or brooding fear. Unless this boy has an allergy to dairy products, *anxious* is misused here. Make it: *The boy was eager to get an ice cream cone.*

■ 20. Rain was not anticipated for Tuesday, the forecaster said.

Anticipate means to give advanced thought; it implies the act of planning for something, as in, *I anticipated rain by bringing my umbrella.* See the AP stylebook. What we mean here is this: *Rain was not expected for Tuesday, the forecaster said.*

■ 21. The mayor and his cohorts comprised the Chicago contingent at the convention.

Use the primary meaning of words. *Cohort* means a group or a band. Better to say *The mayor and his followers.*

Comprise means to contain. The Chicago contingent would *comprise* the mayor and his followers; but the mayor and his followers would *compose* the Chicago contingent: *The mayor and his followers composed the Chicago contingent at the convention.*

■ 22. The funeral service was running late, the pastor admitted.

Funeral service is redundant. *Admitted,* like *claimed,* has a negative connotation. It implies that the speaker is giving up information unwillingly. Make it: *The funeral was running late, the pastor acknowledged.*

■ 23. If we had less variables, there would be less confusion.

If you can count individual items, use *fewer.* For quantities or continuous measurements, use *less.* See the AP stylebook and make it: *If we had fewer variables, there would be less confusion.*

■ 24. The truck collided with the parked car.

Because the parked car isn't moving, the truck is obviously to blame for the accident. *Hit* is better than *collided* because it's so much shorter. See the stylebook: *The truck hit the parked car.*

■ 25. The event was postponed due to snow.

Use *because of* to introduce a phrase modifying a verb: *The event was postponed because of snow.* Use *due to* when the phrase modifies a noun: *The postponement was due to snow.* Could you make it *The event was snowed out?* No. *Postponement* means "to hold back to a later time." Don't confuse that with *cancel,* meaning "to call off" without expecting the event to be made up later. *Snowed out* does not make a distinction between these two. Be specific.

■ **26. Schools will be closed in Chicago and Evanston on Monday and Tuesday, respectively.**

Respectively seldom saves space and is harder for the reader to sort out. Make it: *Schools will be closed Monday in Chicago and Tuesday in Evanston.*

■ **27. My past experience insured success.**

All experience is in the past; eliminate redundancy. Reserve *insure* for the act of issuing an insurance policy. See the stylebook and make it: *My experience ensured success.*

■ **28. A handful of people attended the exhibit by the famous sculptor Leland.**

Imagine a handful of people. Sort of silly, isn't it? Avoid clichés like that. Also, *famous* is a suspect word. Truly famous people need no such introduction. Make it: *A few people attended the exhibit by the sculptor Leland.*

■ **29. The attorney refused to comment on the case.**

Refused goes in the same category as *claimed* and *admitted*: words that carry negative meaning. *Refuse* seems to say that the person should have talked but didn't. Make it: *The attorney declined to comment on the case.*

MATTERS OF STYLE

"Style" is simply a way of doing things. Style is the way news organizations ensure consistency in their presentation. For the writer and editor, style mainly concerns how language is used, including everything from how to abbreviate California to whether Harry S. Truman's middle initial takes a period. (It does, according to the Associated Press. Although the initial doesn't stand for anything, Truman said in the 1960s, "It makes no difference." Since then, AP has gone with the standard practice of using the period.)

The Rise of the Associated Press

The Associated Press Stylebook and Libel Manual has become the industry standard mostly by default. Years ago, the AP and United Press International competed as equals in providing services to news organizations. In the 1980s, UPI went into sharp decline. The Associated Press says in its stylebook that it now provides "state, national and international news, photos, graphics and broadcast services to newspapers, radio and television stations around the world."

By its own count, it serves 1,550 U.S. newspapers and 6,000 U.S. radio and television stations and networks. It provides information to more than 15,000 news outlets worldwide.

Part of the AP's success is due to its status as a cooperative of its members. It remains sensitive to the needs of its customers because they are its owners. The flip side is that much of what the AP distributes comes from its members.

If you think about the wide reach of the Associated Press, you will realize that consistency in its use of language isn't just a journalistic nicety; it's an economic necessity. If its members all used their own style, the AP would spend countless employee hours correcting style errors. For news outlets, adapting to AP style eases the workload on editors who handle primarily AP wire copy.

Not that other wire services don't exist. Reuters is a service that specializes in international news. The *New York Times*, the *Los Angeles Times* and the *Wall Street Journal* offer wire services, as do news conglomerates such as Gannett, Knight Ridder, Newhouse and Tribune Media. Each of these wire services may have its own style following its parent organization. Wire editors soon become adept at picking up the differences between, say, the *New York Times* and the Associated Press.

Local Style

Large newspapers usually have their own stylebooks. These may agree to a large extent with AP style, but they also will include "local" style: exceptions and additions to AP style. These are standard ways of referring to local government, organizations or locations.

News organizations that use the AP stylebook also will develop local style sheets. These may be printed collections of style points or simply computer files where the copy desk chiefs post style points.

Common Ground

The people who write stylebooks today seek to conform to the most commonly used rules of grammar, punctuation and usage. This has not always been so. In the 1930s, Col. Robert McCormick, the eccentric owner of the *Chicago Tribune*, attempted to recast the English language into simplified spellings. The *Tribune*'s style was his main engine of change. For many years, the *Tribune* stylebook dictated spellings such as *frater* for *freighter* and *thru* for *through*.

Not until the 1980s were the last of these truncated spellings eliminated from the *Tribune*'s stylebook. *Cigaret*, replaced by the preferred *cigarette*, was one of these last words to go.

In his foreword to the latest edition, AP President Louis D. Boccardi states that the goal of the AP stylebook has always been to "make clear and simple rules, permit few exceptions to the rules, and rely heavily on the chosen dictionary as the arbiter of conflicts."

Boccardi adds that journalists aren't unanimous in their approach to style. "Some don't think it is really important," he writes. "Some agree that basically there should be uniformity for reading ease if nothing else. Still others are prepared to duel over a wayward lowercase." We have run into all three.

The first type, those who think style is not important, waste our time by expecting us to fix their style errors. This type of sloppiness is unprofessional, and it damages the confidence editors have in a writer.

The third type, those who think stylebooks must answer to some higher order for every period and abbreviation, have wasted our time in unproductive argument. In the end, somebody has to decide a common way to do things, and not everyone will agree.

We fall into the second category. If style is based as much as possible on accepted practices, then the professional thing to do is learn proper style and use it.

The Most Used Entries

Appendix B provides a guide for studying AP style. It's based on our own experiences and on studies that have determined the most-used entries to the stylebook.

Almost every news story contains names, titles, addresses and dates. After a few nights on a desk, editors come to apply style in these areas by force of habit. Here, in alphabetical order, are the AP stylebook entries that you'll use the most and that are most worthy of study:

Abbreviations and acronyms

Addresses

Capitalization

Courtesy titles

Datelines

Dimensions

Directions and regions

Essential clauses, nonessential clauses

Essential phrases, nonessential phrases

Numerals

Organizations and institutions

People, persons

Plurals

Possessives

Quotation marks

State names

That

Time element

Times

Titles

United States

Verbs

WORKOUT: AP STYLE

Correct the following sentences to make them conform to AP style. Use your stylebook! If a sentence is correct as written, just mark an "OK" next to the number of the sentence. Then see how we would do it.

■ 1. Madeleine Albright, Secretary of State, appeared at the press conference.

See the AP stylebook entry *titles*. It says not to capitalize but to spell out titles that are set off from a name by commas. Also see the entry for *press conference*; it says *news conference* is preferred. Make it: *Madeleine Albright, secretary of state, appeared at the news conference.*

■ 2. The Senator urged his workers to listen to the Pope.

Again, the entry *titles* says not to capitalize but to spell out titles when they are not used with a name. Make it: *The senator urged his workers to listen to the pope.*

■ 3. The girl handed mayor Richard Daley a rose.

The entry *titles* says to capitalize formal titles used directly before a name. Make it: *The girl handed Mayor Richard Daley a rose.*

■ 4. Five to ten people were arrested for assault in the attack on the company Chairman, Steve Wilson.

See *numerals* under *sentence start*. It says to spell out numbers when they begin a sentence. Under *other uses*, it says to spell out whole numbers below 10 and use figures for 10 and above.

Under *arrest*, it says not to use the construction *arrested for*. Also don't capitalize the title *chairman*. Make it: *Five to 10 people were arrested on charges of assault in connection with the attack on the company chairman, Steve Wilson.*

■ 5. The panel voted five to two in favor of the 1st Amendment.

Under *numerals* and *some punctuation and usage examples*, the stylebook gives the proper form for votes, 5–2. Under *figures or words?* it gives the correct form as *First Amendment*. Make it: *The panel voted 5–2 in favor of the First Amendment.*

■ 6. The address will begin at 8 p.m. Saturday night at Soldier Field.

See the AP entry *times*. Eliminate redundancy! Make it: *The address will begin at 8 p.m. Saturday at Soldier Field.* Note that this sentence follows the formula *time-date-place*. This formula provides the most succinct way of ordering these essential elements.

■ **7. The president said that he would veto the bill.**

See the AP entry *that (conjunction)*. It says not to use *that* after *said* unless the time element intervenes. Make it: *The president said he would veto the bill.*

■ **8. The president said Friday he would veto the bill.**

Use the same entry, *that (conjunction)*. Here the time element is present. Make it: *The president said Friday that he would veto the bill.*

■ **9. The lawyer contended her client was innocent.**

Again, the entry *that (conjunction)* applies. Make it: *The lawyer contended that her client was innocent.*

■ **10. The company declared a dividend on its blue-chip stock would not be granted this year.**

The AP entry *that (conjunction)* applies again, but note that clarity alone would lead us to add *that* after *declared*. Make it: *The company declared that a dividend on its blue-chip stock would not be granted this year.*

■ **11. The mayor said he believed the alleged bribe was paid in August and that the recipient was the alderman.**

See the AP entry *allege*. It says first that the word "must be used with great care." *Alleged* is OK as used here. Under the entry *that (conjunction)*, it says to include *that* when it aids in clarity. Make it: *The mayor said he believed that the alleged bribe was paid in August and that the recipient was the alderman.*

■ **12. The program is scheduled for 5:00 p.m. August 15th at 5200 North Clark Street.**

The relevant AP entries are *time, dates, months* and *addresses*. Make it: *The program is scheduled for 5 p.m. Aug. 15 at 5300 N. Clark St.*

■ **13. The candidate discussed United States foreign policy at a rally along North Clark Street.**

The relevant AP entries are *United States* and *addresses*. Make it: *The candidate discussed U.S. foreign policy at a rally along North Clark Street.*

■ 14. The population of the U.S. is more than 230,000,000.

The relevant AP entries are *United States* and *numerals*. Make it: *The population of the United States is more than 230 million.*

■ 15. She worked part-time in a small town before getting a full time job in Mesa, Arizona.

The relevant AP entries are *part time, part-time; full time, full-time;* and *state names.* Make it: *She worked part time in a small town before getting a full-time job in Mesa, Ariz.*

■ 16. The sick boy was well received.

See the AP entry *well.* Make it: *The sick boy was well-received.*

■ 17. The paper in Austin, Tex., was looking for help.

See the AP entry *state names.* Note that the Associated Press does not use the two-letter Postal Service abbreviations. A memory aid: All state names with five or fewer letters, plus Alaska and Hawaii, are spelled out. Note that the comma after Texas is correct. Make it: *The paper in Austin, Texas, was looking for help.*

■ 18. The three-year-old colt was running 35 m.p.h. when he set the record in Sept., 1973.

The relevant AP entries are *ages, animals, miles per hour* and *dates.* To understand why we say *he set the record,* you have to know that *colts* are young male horses while *fillies* are young female horses. You can find these definitions in the sports area of the stylebook under *horse racing.* Make it: *The 3-year-old colt was running 35 mph when he set the record in September 1973.*

■ 19. More than four thousand applied for the factory job.

See the AP entry *numerals.* Make it: *More than 4,000 applied for the factory job.*

■ 20. The media is to blame.

See the AP entry *media.* It says the word is plural. Make it: *The media are to blame.*

■ 21. The city ethics committee voted to withdraw their recommendation.

See the AP entries *collective nouns* and *committee*. Note that you would capitalize *ethics committee* only if that were the body's formal name. Assuming that's true, make it: *The city Ethics Committee voted to withdraw its recommendation.*

■ 22. The Committee voted rarely.

See the AP entry *committee*. Make it: *The committee voted rarely.*

■ 23. The U.S. state department was hurt by the social security tax cut.

See the AP entries *governmental bodies* and *Social Security*. Make it: *The U.S. State Department was hurt by the Social Security tax cut.*

CHAPTER

5

Obituaries

___

The palest ink is better than the best memory.
—Chinese proverb

An obituary is a story recounting the life of someone who has died. "Obits" are worth closer study for several reasons.

- Obits are a well-read section of any newspaper or news magazine. A good obituary section will include an interesting mix of the famous and not-so-famous. Their stories provide lessons in the history of their city, state and country.
- Obits often are among the first stories assigned to beginning editors and reporters. And until medical science finds the universal cure, obits will always be there.
- Obits and crime stories require careful handling. You'll read about crime stories in Chapter 6. Obits require special care because they involve a sensitive topic, death, and because they have special meaning for the friends and family of the deceased. A mistake made in an obit can cost a news publication a subscriber.
- Obits provide a special lesson in news judgment. Obits are a good place to start in getting you into editing paragraphs and whole stories.

Keep in mind that an obituary is a news story and is different from a *death notice,* a paid announcement that includes personal information on the deceased. Much of what follows comes from an investigation performed in the early 1990s and published internally by a staff review group at the *Chicago Tribune.* In their investigation, the group talked to editors and reporters at several major newspapers.

QUALIFICATIONS FOR GETTING AN OBIT

The most obvious qualification for getting an obit is that the person be dead. Beyond that, the more famous a person is, the more likely that person's death will be news.

At the *Chicago Tribune,* the lead obit writer searches through the paid death notices, other Chicago-area papers and the wire services looking for out-of-the-ordinary but not necessarily prominent people who merit an obituary with a headline. But many people who aren't that interesting and certainly not famous get obits. Funeral directors often are the source for these obits.

Sometimes newspapers run obits of little-known people who happen to be employees or their relatives or friends. These "courtesy obits" are a function of the newspaper's compassion for its employees.

"National" newspapers such as the *New York Times* run obits only on prominent people. Specialists in various departments such as sports, business, science or drama may advise the news desk on whether a person deserves an obit and how long it should be.

Some papers try to run an obit on every area person who dies. At the *Detroit Free Press,* reporters call every funeral home daily and the obits often fill four columns. For most newspapers, then, people must make some impact during their lives to warrant an obit.

Every obituary has common news elements. Some, such as the person's age, major accomplishments and personal history, are usually not controversial. Others, such as cause of death and list of survivors, can create problems that require careful news judgment.

CAUSE OF DEATH

Cause of death is one of those areas that require special sensitivity. First, note that news organizations have done away with most of the euphemisms that used to fill obit pages. No more "passed away," "gone to meet his maker," "shuffled off this mortal coil," "gone to that big aircraft carrier in the sky."

Cause of death can be a touchy subject because of the stigma attached to some diseases. Once upon a time, that stigma was attached to cancer, so the euphemism "died after a lengthy illness" often appeared.

That euphemism was attached to AIDS for a time, and the topic of AIDS caused newspapers to examine whether the cause of death is something important in a routine obit. Today, that stigma has faded as AIDS advocates have urged victims not to hide their affliction.

What about privacy and family feelings? Family members usually do not want the cause of death mentioned in an obit that likely will be clipped, copied and sent to relatives. One reporter at the *Chicago Tribune* noted: "We're finding parents who first learned their kids were gay when they contracted AIDS. How will those parents feel when we put AIDS into the obit?"

Others believe that if a person is prominent enough to warrant an obit, then the cause of death is news. The problem is finding out that information. Often a news organization doesn't have a reliable source for the cause of death. Family members rarely volunteer the information and sometimes don't tell the truth. And an autopsy is almost never completed by the time an obit appears. One editor advised that a news outlet has no choice but to go with the family's account unless it clearly conflicts with the facts or another reputable source, such as the police. If the cause of death can't be discovered, many news organizations will say that the cause of death was unavailable. This signals the readers that an effort was made to get the information.

One news editor said his paper follows normal reporting methods to determine the cause of death without harassing the bereaved. In reporting the death of a well-known person, reporters may feel freer to press for details within the bounds of compassion. If the information given about the cause of death is suspect, the reporter should give a specific attribution.

SURVIVORS

At most papers, only blood or legal relatives are listed as survivors: spouses, children, parents, siblings. Often, other groups such as grandchildren and great-grandchildren will be mentioned but not named: *He is survived by his daughter, Ethel, three grandchildren and five great-grandchildren.*

If a more distant relative is particularly famous, that relative should be mentioned somewhere in the story. For instance, if former Los Angeles Dodgers catcher Steve Yeager were to die, his obit should include the fact that his uncle is retired Air Force General Chuck Yeager, the first man to break the sound barrier.

The survivors question becomes a sensitive issue with the deceased's family when live-in companions are involved. Many news outlets do not list live-in companions among survivors but mention the companion in the narrative, as in "His longtime companion, John Smith, was at his bedside when he died." Another solution is to quote the companion: *"He was a wonderful man who kept his sense of humor right up to the end,"* said Ralph Runion, his longtime friend.

FAMOUS PEOPLE

Do the famous get different treatment? When former Vice President Nelson Rockefeller died, newspapers showed little reluctance to mention that he died in his girlfriend's bedroom. For people that famous, negative facts (such as a jail sentence) or personal habits (such as actor John Wayne's heavy smoking) that may have contributed to death are more likely to get in the obit.

What does famous mean? If a person is famous, you have to do the obit; you don't have a choice. Sometimes the story moves off the obit page and onto the front page as it approaches being a hard-news story.

THE FORMULA

Obits are important to people and embarrassing to news organizations if they are messed up. That's why, like crime stories, obituaries follow a form. Accuracy is the key ingredient; imagine reading a close relative's obit and having the name misspelled. Look over this obit:

R A ZVTCZCRYR
BC-TURYN-OBIT (UNDATED)
c. 1981 N.Y. TIMES NEWS SERVICE

Alexander Turyn, a classics scholar who was a member of the Center for Advanced Study at the University of Illinois at Urbana-Champaign, died Wednesday at his home after a long illness. He was 80 years old.

Turyn's specialty was the textural transmission of works by the Greek tragedians. His research in codicology, the study of manuscripts, and in paleography, the study of ancient handwriting, earned him several important awards in philology.

Among his numerous publications were "Studies in the Manuscript Tradition of Aeschylus" in 1943, "Studies in the Manuscript Tradition of Sophocles" in 1952 and "The Byzantine Manuscript Tradition of the Tragedies of Euripides" in 1957.

He was the recipient of the Golden Cross of the Order of the Phoenix from the Greek government in 1934. In 1959 he was a Guggenheim Fellow, and in the following year he received the Goodwin Award of Merit, the highest award of the American Philological Association.

Two volumes of commissioned articles by leading scholars in the field were dedicated to him this year in honor of his 80th birthday by the classics department at the University of Illinois.

Turyn, who was born in Warsaw, studied at the University of Warsaw and the University of Berlin. He received his doctorate in 1923 from the University of Warsaw, where he was named professor extraordinary of classical philology in 1935.

He left Poland in 1939 and came to the United States in 1942 to teach at the University of Michigan. In 1942, he began teaching at the New School of Social Research in New York.

He joined the University of Illinois in 1945 and was appointed professor of classics two years later and professor Emeritus in 1969.

He was a member of the Polish Academy of Krakow, the Academy of Athens and the Epistemonike Hetaireia of Athens and a former member of the board of advisers of the Dumbarton Oaks Center for Byzantine Studies. He was also a research collaborator with the Vatican Library.

He is survived by his wife, the former Felicia Leontine Sachs; a son, Andrew Stanislaus Gustavus Turyn of Kingston, R.I.; and a brother, Adam Turyn of London.

NYT-08-31-81 0009EDT

This undated obit was done in advance, as is common with prominent people.

Note key lead elements:

- His most significant accomplishments follow his name.
- Age is always important to include.
- "Long illness" appears as the cause of death; in this case, with someone 80 years old, it may be the best description.

The second, third, fourth and fifth paragraphs state his main accomplishments. Note that "codicology" and "paleography" are explained, but "philology" is not. Should it be? We think so. It's the study of literature.

The sixth through eighth paragraphs give the chronology of his life. Note that the dates must make sense, or you must do a bit of research. For instance, if he died in 1981 at the age of 80, then he was born in 1901. That would make him 22 in 1923, when he received his doctorate from the University of Warsaw. That's a bit young, but well within reason for a brilliant scholar.

Last come the survivors and the time-date-place of services, if news of his death is fresh and services aren't in the lead. In this example, no information on services was available.

Note that the last line gives date and time the obit moved on the wire.

WORKOUT: OBITUARY OF A FAMOUS PERSON

A common task for editors is to edit obituaries of famous people. Unless the person has a local connection, the obit probably will come from a wire service, as in this case. With the famous, an editor can check virtually everything in the obit because information on the person is readily available.

Edit this obituary using the editing strategy outlined in Chapter 2. Then hone the lead and check facts. Pay attention to grammar, punctuation and style. You'll need an almanac, dictionary and stylebook. Edit as if this were running in December 2000.

WASHINGTON (AP)—Funeral services for Neil Armstrong, an ex-Navy pilot who in 1969 became the first man to set foot on the moon, will be held Friday at 11 a.m. in Baltimore, Md.

He succumbed Wednesday at age 69.

Born on July 5, 1930 in Wapakonetka, Ohio, Armstrong was a U.S. Navy pilot in Korea prior to becoming a test pilot for the X-15 rocket plane program. He became an astronaut in 1962.

During the Apollo 11 mission in July, 1969, he and lunar landing module pilot Buzz Aldrin became the first two people to walk on the moon. Armstrong also commanded the Gemini 8 mission in March of 1966.

Mr. Armstrong served as deputy associate administrator for aeronautics at the National Aeronautics and Space Administration (NASA) in 1970-71, and as a professor of aerospace engineering at Cincinnati University in 1971-79.

Mr. Armstrong will be interred in St. Joseph's Cemetary in Washington.

Survivors include his father, Stephen, his wife, Janet, and two sons, Eric and Mark.

Let's take this paragraph by paragraph.

WASHINGTON (AP)—Services for Neil Armstrong, ~~an ex-~~ a former Navy pilot who in 1969 became the first man to set foot on the moon, will be held ~~Friday~~ at 11 a.m. <u>Friday</u> in Baltimore~~, Md~~.

- On your first sweep through this story, you would fix some things automatically, such as inserting a dash for the two hyphens.
- *Funeral services* is redundant, as would be *funeral mass.* You can make them just *services* or *mass.*
- You'll see the prefix *ex-* used a lot in obituaries, especially in headlines. Don't use it in a story when you can use a less-harsh and more appropriate word such as *former* or *retired.* Note also that *former* and *retired* don't mean the same thing. *Former* could mean the person quit or was fired. The biggest problem here with using *ex-* is that it is misplaced. He is an *ex-pilot,* not an *ex-Navy.* In headlines, where space is at a premium, *ex-* may be more acceptable, but do everything you can to avoid a headline like this: *Rites set for ex-Chicago mayor.*
- In all stories you edit, observe the form *time-date-place.*
- *Baltimore* takes no state according to the AP stylebook entry for datelines.

He ~~succumbed~~ <u>died</u> Wednesday at ~~age 69~~ <u>70</u>.

- No euphemisms in obituaries. No *passed away,* no *met his maker,* no *gone to that final space station.*
- Let's not use *age,* a noun or verb, as an adjective to modify *70.* He's 70. See below how you would determine this.

~~Born~~ <u>Mr. Armstrong was born</u> on ~~July~~ <u>Aug.</u> 5, 1930, in ~~Wapakonetka~~ <u>Wapakoneta,</u> Ohio. He was a ~~U.S.~~ Navy pilot in Korea ~~prior to~~ <u>before</u> becoming a test pilot for the X-15 rocket plane program. He became an astronaut in 1962.

- When is age important? In obits, for sure. When an age is stated in reference to other dates, you must do the arithmetic to assure that all the years agree. In this obit, which we're editing as if this were December 2000, the next paragraph has Armstrong's birth date as 1930; that works out to 70 years old, not 69. Which do you fix? You

*have to look it up. You can't guess! The almanac, under noted per-
sonalities, gives his birth date as Aug. 5, 1930, making him 70.*

- *The entry also lists his hometown; note the spelling. The prudent editor might want to check another source just to make sure the almanac isn't in error. You'll find that the Columbia Encyclopedia and
Who's Who agree with Aug. 5, 1930, and Wapakoneta.*
- *Born is an awkward way to start a sentence. Grammatically, born
modifies Armstrong.*
- *Many news outlets use courtesy titles in obits. Make sure that the one
chosen is appropriate, if not Mr., Miss, Ms. or Mrs., then one by which
the person was commonly known. Neil Armstrong had been out of the
military since 1955; Mr. would be most appropriate.*
- *Prior to is a stilted substitute for before.*
- *You can tighten to just Navy without losing meaning.*

During the Apollo 11 mission in July, 1969, he and ~~lunar landing module pilot~~
Edwin "Buzz" Aldrin, the lunar landing module pilot, became the first two
people to walk on the moon. Mr. Armstrong also commanded the Gemini
8 mission in March ~~of~~ 1966.

- *You can check out the dates for space missions in the almanac under
space developments. That's also where you'll find the full name of
"Buzz" Aldrin.*
- *Note how nicknames are handled according to AP style.*
- *Remember, don't string modifiers before a name.*
- *The stylebook also guides us on how to use the month and year alone:
no comma, no of.*

Mr. Armstrong served as deputy associate administrator for aeronautics at
the National Aeronautics and Space Administration ~~(NASA)~~ in 1970- and
1971 ~~,and as~~ He was a professor of aerospace engineering at the University
of Cincinnati ~~University~~ ~~in~~ from 1971- to 1979.

- *The AP stylebook says not to follow the name of an organization with
its acronym or abbreviation.*
- *The stylebook also has an entry for the National Aeronautics and
Space Administration, saying that NASA is acceptable on first refer-
ence. So just NASA would be OK, too.*
- *You'll find the University of Cincinnati in the almanac under Colleges
and Universities.*
- *Keep one idea to a sentence; this paragraph is better as two sentences.*
- *Avoid the awkward use of hyphens with years. A rare exception
would be the 1990–91 school year.*

Mr. Armstrong will be ~~interred~~ buried in St. Joseph's ~~Cemetary~~ Cemetery in
Washington.

- *More often than not, people are buried in cemeteries (note spelling).
Interred is used with mausoleums.*

Survivors include his father, Stephen;; his wife, Janet;; and two sons, Eric and Mark.

- *Include* is OK here because this is a partial list. He has more family members than this.
- Note the punctuation. Semicolons are used when items in a series are separated by commas, and unlike the rule for commas, a semicolon is used before *and*.
- The order of relatives listed usually goes from closest to most distant.

WORKOUT: OBITUARY OF AN AVERAGE PERSON

With people who are not famous, the editor has a more difficult task in checking facts. Often the editor must employ the telephone to check facts with the reporter or a funeral home. Here's an example.

Anthony Douglas Carroll, 1155 W. Grace St., apparently died Thursday in Northwestern Memorial Hospital of a coronary seizure. He was 75.

He served as a copy editor and makeup editor for The Chicago Tribune for 35 years before retiring. He also belonged to the St. Luke's Parent-Teacher Association, the Society of Professional Journalists and Citizens United for Baseball in Sunshine.

Anthony was a long-time resident of Urbana, Ill. before coming to Chicago.

Survivors include his wife, Debbie; and two sons, Milo and Harry.

Services are pending.

Let's tackle this as a whole:

Anthony Douglas Carroll, <u>a copy editor and makeup editor for</u> ~~T~~<u>the Chicago Tribune for 35 years before retiring,</u> ~~1155 W. Grace St., apparently~~ died Thursday in Northwestern Memorial Hospital <u>apparently</u> of a heart attack ~~coronary seizure~~. He was 75.

~~He served as a copy editor and makeup editor for The Chicago Tribune for 35 years before retiring.~~ He ~~also belonged to~~ <u>was a member of the</u> St. Luke's Parent-Teacher Association, the Society of Professional Journalists and Citizens United for Baseball in Sunshine.

~~Anthony~~ <u>Mr. Carroll</u> was a long-time resident of Urbana, Ill.<u>,</u> before coming to Chicago.

Survivors include his wife, Debbie<u>,</u>~~;~~ and two sons, Milo and Harry.

~~Services are pending.~~

- Do not use addresses in obituaries; it makes the home of the deceased an easy target for burglars during the funeral.
- The time-tested formula for obituaries calls for listing the deceased's major accomplishments after his or her name in the lead.
- Be careful of misplaced modifiers; the result can be embarrassing as in this case, where we say Mr. Carroll *apparently died*. What we mean is that Carroll died, *apparently of a heart attack*. You can simplify the medical terminology.
- We moved up his major accomplishments and lowercased *the* in *the Chicago Tribune*. The AP stylebook under *newspaper names* says to capitalize *the* if a newspaper does it that way. But how do you know? Most news outlets just make *the* lowercase.
- *Belonging to* an organization is informal tone; we want formal tone in obits. If this obit needs to be trimmed for length, some of these marginal organizations could be dropped.
- Do not use first names for adults. Often newspapers will refer to children (under the age of 18) by their first names, but common sense should prevail. You wouldn't write, *Timmy was charged Monday with strangling an alleged drug dealer*. We would say *Jones*, not *Timmy*.
- If you were editing this story in Illinois, *Urbana* and other well-known area cities would be on your local list of cities that don't need a state. Note the comma after *Ill.*
- With just two items in our list of survivors, use a comma, not a semicolon.
- The last sentence is useless; it tells us nothing. Don't report what you don't know.

We include a chapter on obituaries here because they provide a lesson in how routine news stories often follow a formula but still require good news judgment and attention to detail. Crime stories require this and more. They are the subject of our next chapter.

CHAPTER

6

Editing Crime Stories

It has long been an axiom of mine that the little things are infinitely the most important.

It is a capital mistake to theorize before one has data.
—Sir Arthur Conan Doyle

Stories about crime are standard fare for news organizations. Those crimes range from petty theft to national scandals. Crime stories at all levels demand careful treatment from writers and editors. Both must be aware of the potential for libel, and they must know how to avoid it.

When we say *libel*, we mean any statement that is *potentially* libelous. The legal definition of libel, including topics such as public figures versus private individuals or actual malice, is important.

We're concerned with truth and accuracy, the ultimate defenses in an actual libel suit, but we want to go beyond that to *fairness*. Objectivity is impossible, so fairness is our standard. When you judge the fairness of a story, ask yourself how you would feel reading it if your name were inserted in place of the suspect's.

When a news organization is sued, it loses, even if it wins in court. It pays in the form of legal fees, reporters' lost time and, most of all, respect in the public eye. The best way to win a libel suit is not to be sued in the first place.

Not all news organizations agree on how some things should be handled, but here are a few ideas about how to avoid libel suits.

ASSUMING INNOCENCE

Don't convict someone in print. The courts have the job of deciding guilt or innocence. We must always assume that someone arrested is innocent until proven guilty. One way to be fair is to separate the suspect from the crime. Treat the suspect and the "perpetrator" as two people; that's the best way to ensure fairness.

Writing about Suspects

What can we say about the suspect?

- *Identity.* Some newspapers will not print a suspect's identity until he or she has been charged with a crime. Other papers believe all arrest information is public record. Know your organization's policy. Always use full names and addresses; in a big city, many people may have the same name. A suspect's identity need not be attributed, assuming it comes from police records.
- *Address.* Use it to identify suspects, but avoid giving a victim's address when it can cause harm. Consider this lead:

    A wheelchair-bound man was beaten and his apartment at 1234 Main St. was burglarized Monday for the third time this month.

    What will happen when this gets in the paper? Right, he'll be robbed a *fourth* time.
- *Circumstances of arrest.* Often this is incriminating, so it needs to be attributed to a *privileged source,* such as a police agency. Here's an example: *Smith was arrested with a diamond bracelet in his pocket, police said.*
- *Personal details, including criminal history.* Be careful here. Personal details such as the *suspect lived alone* seem to apply to some crimes but usually are irrelevant. Some publications refuse to use a suspect's criminal history; others go with it only when they believe it is pertinent. It's always better to err on the side of fairness.
- *Unconfirmed allegations never should make the news!*

Writing about the Perpetrator

What can we say about the perpetrator? Remember that in assuming a suspect is innocent, we create another unknown person who actually committed the crime. The court decides if the suspect and that person, the perpetrator, are one and the same. Because we make no attempt to identify the perpetrator as a real person, we have more freedom in what we can say.

Description

News organizations routinely print descriptions of perpetrators, what they look like, what kinds of vehicles they drive, their clothes. The more complete the description, the more useful it is.

Race

This is a sensitive issue. Mention race when it is an integral part of the story, such as a race riot, minority election or missing person. Use race in a description of a perpetrator only when the description is thorough and complete. Otherwise, the information serves only to point the finger at a large group of people. If all you have is that the perpetrator was a black teenager, how many young people do you put on the spot by running the information in a story?

THE CIRCUMSTANCES OF THE CRIME

The imaginary construct of the perpetrator is most useful in describing the crime; it keeps the suspect out of things. Consider this: *An assailant attacked a business man on the elevated platform and the suspect was arrested two blocks away, police said.* The sentence is thorough and yet fair to the suspect. Remember, our goal is to separate the suspect from the crime as much as reasonably possible.

All circumstances of the crime must be attributed to privileged sources.

ATTRIBUTE HOT INFORMATION

Attributing information to a privileged source protects the news organization from libel suits. An attribution, such as *a police spokesman said,* tells the audience this is not our interpretation of the facts but one from authorities. Privileged sources include the police, prosecutors, court records and testimony, regulatory agency proceedings and Congress in session.

How do you know if an unattributed statement came from police? You have to ask your supervisor, a source editor or the reporter.

All "hot" information must be attributed to authorities. That's anything incriminating or that tends to implicate a person in a crime, including accusations, evidence, charges or claims. Anything that makes it look like the suspect did it *must* be attributed.

This applies to quotations. *A witness who refused to be identified* is not a solid attribution. *A witness told police* is usable.

Alleged is overworked; sprinkling the word *alleged* liberally in a news story won't protect you from libel suits. The story must state clearly who is doing the alleging, and often that person must be a privileged source. The more complete the attribution, the better. If you have a police representative releasing information, use his or her full name.

Consider this sentence:

The alleged embezzlement took place Friday after bank hours.

This example is OK, if all you know is that money is missing.

It's also correct to call someone an *alleged* accomplice or an alleged *killer* but, again, make sure you state who is doing the alleging. Often *alleged* is misused, as in *alleged meeting* or *alleged robbery*. Such events either take place or they don't.

WORDS THAT ASSIGN BLAME

Avoid words that assign blame. Strike *arrested for* and *indicted for* from your vocabulary. It's the same as saying the suspect was arrested for committing the crime. Instead, write that the suspect was arrested *in connection with* or *arrested on a charge of,* if charges have been filed.

Passive voice is useful to avoid convicting someone in print. Compare these examples:

> *A West Side man was arrested after he shot a woman to death in a bar Saturday.*

This convicts the subject.

> *A West Side man was arrested after a woman was shot to death in a bar Saturday.*

This separates the suspect from the crime.

Note that many often-used words tend to assign blame if we consider their formal meaning. If we say *a car hit an oncoming truck,* the car's driver seems to be at fault. If we say *a car and a truck collided,* blame isn't assigned to either one. But note that the simplest form should be used when blame is obvious, as in *a car hit a utility pole.* The pole certainly wasn't going anywhere.

STYLEBOOK LIBEL MANUAL

The *Associated Press Stylebook* includes a libel manual as well as many style entries guiding the editor for crime stories. A good one is the entry for *innocent* that advises us to avoid using *not guilty* because the word *not* might inadvertently be omitted, convicting the suspect in print.

WORKOUT: CRIME STORIES

Some problems of usage and style crop up again and again in crime stories. Some of these fall under the categories of tedious or embarrassing errors, but some affect the fairness of a story. Sentence 1 is a good example:

■ **1. Smith was arrested for assault and battery.**

The AP stylebook says not to use the phrase *arrested for* because it suggests that the person is guilty. Make it: *Smith was arrested on an assault charge.* Notice that we've dropped *and battery,* a legal distinction lost on most readers. We can say just *assault.* Read the AP entry *assault.*

How would you handle sentence 2?

■ **2. Smith was arrested for beating a woman in a Loop parking lot.**

You could make it *Smith was arrested in connection with the beating of a woman in a Loop parking lot.* That's OK but a bit cumbersome. This is a case where passive voice can be used to avoid assigning blame: *Smith was arrested after a woman was beaten in a Loop parking lot.* If Smith was not only arrested but also charged, you could make it: *Smith was charged with beating a woman in a Loop parking lot.*

Remember that some terms such as *assault* represent formal charges and can't be used unless that charge has been filed. You wouldn't say *Smith was arrested after a woman was assaulted in a Loop parking lot* unless an assault charge had been filed.

■ **3. A Chicago man was arrested Thursday after a woman was murdered in her home. Ed Johnson, 43, 1545 West Addison, was being held in the Belmont lockup. No charges have been filed.**

Let's take this lead a piece at a time:

- If you can get the man's full name, including middle initial, use it. In a big city like Chicago, many people may share the same name; such information helps to identify which Ed Johnson we mean. Be as formal and exact as you can. Use his address for the same reason.

- You would check 1545 W. Addison and note that Addison is a street. In a metropolitan area like Chicago, you might have to check that any other locations, such as neighborhoods or suburbs, are correctly identified and that addresses jibe with those locations.

- You would change *murdered* to *killed* or *slain*. *Murder* is a formal charge for the malicious premeditated taking of a life. In this sentence, no charges had been filed. See the AP entry under *homicide*.

- When a person's age is followed by a numbered address, insert the preposition *of* before the address. This separates the numbers for easier reading. Also, you would correct the style of the address.

The final product would read like this:

A Chicago man was arrested Thursday after a woman was slain in her home. Edward Johnson, 43, of 1545 W. Addison St. was being held in the Belmont lockup. No charges had been filed.

You might wonder what we mean by *lockup*. It's a holding cell at a neighborhood police station where a suspect can be placed for a few hours until charges are filed. We say *was being held* because that's the best we know at deadline. He may be released by the time the paper hits the streets.

■ 4. Overcrowding at the state jail forced early releases.

A *jail* is a city or county facility. A suspect might be taken from a lockup or holding cell to the city jail. Use the term *prison* for state and federal facilities: *Overcrowding at the state prison forced early releases.*

■ 5. The suspected rapist was to be arraigned before a Cook County Criminal Court judge.

- This sentence is unfair if not potentially libelous. As it stands, calling a person a *suspected rapist* misses the mark, and if the qualifier *suspected* were lost along the way, we would end up calling the person a rapist. That would be libelous. The person is a *suspect in a rape case* or *a rape suspect*.

- Note the difference between suspect and defendant. Those arrested and charged with crimes are suspects until they enter the courtroom. Then they become defendants.

- What about the phrase *Cook County Criminal Court judge*? The AP stylebook says not to use *court* as part of a judge's title unless confusion would result. Here, you need *court* to avoid calling the person a *criminal judge*. The same would be true of *juvenile judge;* make it *juvenile court judge*. But this would be correct under AP style: *Cook County Circuit Judge William Jones.* In sentence 5 the best thing to do would be to drop *judge* and make it: *The rape suspect was to be arraigned in Cook County Criminal Court.*

■ 6. The convicted rapist was sentenced to 10 years.

Compare this sentence to sentence 5. Here, the person has been convicted and can be called a rapist without being libeled. If the qualifier *convicted* gets lost, the sentence might not be quite as fair, but it wouldn't be libelous. Still, some will try to write around this to be completely fair because innocent people sometimes are convicted and win on appeal. You could make it: *The defendant was sentenced to 10 years for the rape conviction.* (Notice it's not 10 years for rape.) You also could make it: *The man convicted of rape was sentenced to 10 years.*

■ 7. Edward Johnson was convicted for stabbing the woman to death.

No real problem using *for,* though *of* sounds more natural. Make it: *Edward Johnson was convicted of stabbing the woman to death.*

■ 8. The boy received a broken arm. He was rushed to Henrotin Hospital.

- We prefer that you say *suffered* instead of *received*. How this is handled varies from newsroom to newsroom and from editor to editor. But we've found that most editors prefer *suffered* to *received* or *sustained*. Look at these sentences: *The boy broke his arm. The boy had his arm broken.* Both are open to misinterpretation. The first sounds like he snapped it himself while the second sounds like he had a mobster do it in a cover-up.

- Avoid clichés such as *rushed to the hospital*. Ambulances never meander, do they? This sentence should read: *The boy suffered a broken arm. He was taken to Henrotin Hospital.*

■ 9. He was treated and released from the hospital.

This is a case of asking the word *from* to do too much. Take each part separately: Would you say *He was treated from the hospital?* No. Make the sentence read: *He was treated at the hospital and released.*

■ 10. The firemen were in good condition at Northwestern Hospital.

- Avoid sexism by making it *firefighters*. Also, use *police officers* instead of *policemen*.

- Make it *listed in good condition*. When a hospital lists someone's condition as good, its staff has evaluated that person's chances for recovery; it doesn't mean that the person is feeling good.

- Always double-check the correct names of hospitals. Although you couldn't be expected to catch it here, reporters often use a shortened form of the hospital's formal name. Make the sentence read: *The firefighters were listed in good condition at Northwestern Memorial Hospital.*

■ 11. The knife-welding man injured three passer-bys, Violent Crimes Unit Detective Julie Jones of the Belmont Precinct said.

- The first thing to do is make *knife-welding* into *knife-wielding* and *passer-bys* into *passers-by*.

- When someone is shot or stabbed, use *wounds* or *wounded* rather than *injuries* or *injured*.

- The term *Violent Crimes Unit* describes the detective's assignment within the department, similar to *homicide squad* or *drug enforcement unit.* Such a designation is more important to the source than the reader. Usually it can be deleted. You would figure that homicide detectives investigate killings.

Make the sentence read: *The knife-wielding man wounded three passers-by, Belmont Precinct Detective Julie Jones said.*

■ 12. **The Cook County coroner pronounced the woman dead upon arrival at the hospital. She had been shot with a 22 caliber rifle.**

- *Coroner* is a somewhat outdated title for what had been an elected position. Most places in the country have a *medical examiner.* Check that you have the correct title. You could leave the medical examiner out of it unless some importance was attached to who declared the person dead.

- It's *dead on arrival.*

- Make it *.22-caliber;* see the AP stylebook under *caliber.* You may see that period before the number come up in a quote like this: *He was packing a .22.*

The sentence should read: *The woman was pronounced dead on arrival at the hospital. She had been shot with a .22-caliber rifle.*

■ 13. **The northbound car hit the southbound truck on the expressway.**

Remember not to use words that assign blame. Make it: *The northbound car and southbound truck collided on the expressway.*

■ 14. **The car hit the guardrail and flipped over early Sunday morning.**

- In this case, *hit* (or *struck*) is preferred. The guardrail will not testify in court.

- What about the phrase *early Sunday morning?* For some people, that may mean 11 a.m. As a guide in news writing, consider the early morning hours to be from a minute after midnight to 4 a.m. If the accident occurred at 2 a.m., then the sentence is OK as written.

■ 15. **He pleaded not guilty to manslaughter.**

Make it: *He pleaded innocent to manslaughter.* The AP stylebook says to use *innocent* rather that *not guilty.*

■ 16. **The suspect was charged with robbery in the apartment break-in.**

- Some might be inclined to make it *burglary* instead of *robbery* because of the break-in angle, but that would be wrong if the *charge* is robbery. The AP stylebook states that robbery involves the use of violence or threat in stealing something. Robbery also can mean a plundering or rifling of a person's possessions, so people can be robbed even if they aren't home. It's also proper to say the home was robbed, just as you would say a bank was robbed. Review the AP entry under *burglary*. It also addresses robbery and theft.

- In the second part of the sentence, make it *in connection with the apartment break-in*. You can shorten this to *in* for headlines, but not in the story. We don't want readers to think we mean during the break-in. The sentence should read: *The suspect was charged with robbery in connection with the apartment break-in.*

■ 17. **The couple was robbed of their jewels when they were vacationing.**

- *Couple* is used with a singular verb *was* but plural pronouns *their* and *they*. Make the verb plural because the meaning of couple here is two people. See the AP entry *couple*.

- Is *robbed* OK? Yes, under the definition given after sentence 16.

- When we speak collectively of ornaments such as rings, brooches and necklaces, make it *jewelry*, not *jewels*. Use *jewels* or *gems* when referring just to stones. Make it read: *The couple were robbed of their jewelry when they were vacationing.*

■ 18. **The boy was drowned in the boating mishap.**

- The AP stylebook notes that people don't die in something as minor as a mishap. Make it *accident.*

- Using passive voice, *was drowned,* implies that a killer was involved, that somebody drowned the boy. Unless this was suspected, make it: *The boy drowned in the boating accident.*

■ 19. **The actor was charged with drunk driving.**

Use *drunken* as an adjective modifying a noun: *The actor was charged with drunken driving.* See the AP stylebook entry. You may use *drunk driving* in a headline if *drunken* doesn't fit.

■ 20. **John Wayne Gacy, the convicted mass murderer, flaunted the law by pulling off a daring escape.**

- Often, those convicted of heinous crimes become known by their full names, again in the interest of identifying them specifically. *John Wilkes Booth* and *Lee Harvey Oswald* are two other examples.

- What about calling Gacy a *mass murderer?* That would indicate a massacre, the killing of many people at once. Gacy killed his victims one at a time over several years. A more accurate term would be *serial murderer.*

- *Flaunt* means to make an ostentatious or defiant display. What we mean here is *flout*, to show contempt for.

- Let's not glorify criminals by calling them daring or ingenious. Many crimes are committed for publicity. Let's not fuel the fire. The sentence should read: *John Wayne Gacy, the convicted serial murderer, flouted the law by escaping.*

■ 21. The eight-man, two-woman jury failed to convict the Teamsters Union leader.

- Criminal juries have 12 members, so numbers need to be checked. You might find out that this jury had four women members.

- Why do we need to break the jury down by sex? You wouldn't unless some aspect of the case made gender meaningful. Let's say a trial was about a woman who killed her husband and pleaded self-defense on the grounds that he was abusing her. Gender might be relevant, but even then you wouldn't use the awkward construction of this sentence. You would make it *the jury of eight men and four women.* In this sentence, gender doesn't seem to be relevant.

- What about the phrase *failed to convict?* It implies that the jury shirked its duty. Maybe the man was innocent; then the jury did its duty. This thinking also applies to sentences like *The legislature failed to pass the bill.* This implies that the bill should have been passed. That's conjecture that belongs in a news analysis, not a news story.

- Make *union* lowercase. The word *union* does not appear in the organization's formal title, *International Brotherhood of Teamsters, Chauffeurs, Warehousemen and Helpers of America.*

The sentence should read: *The jury acquitted the Teamsters union leader.*

■ 22. The police chief refused to answer questions.

This would be correct only if the chief was being unreasonable or hardheaded in not answering questions after repeated attempts. He may not have been able to give more information and simply was acknowledging the fact. In that case, make it: *The police chief declined to answer questions.*

■ 23. The man's ex-wife admitted that she was a suspect in his murder.

- *Admitted* implies that the person has something to hide. Would you say *The Irish boy admitted he was Catholic?* No. It's no crime to be Catholic and it's no crime to be a suspect.

- Usually we'll prefer *former* to *ex-*, but *ex-wife* and *ex-husband* are common terms.

Make it: *The man's ex-wife acknowledged that she was a suspect in his murder.*

■ 24. The policeman shot and killed the rabid dog.

Make this sentence read: *The policeman shot the rabid dog to death.*

The phrase *shot and killed* is useful when the cause of a person's death is in question. With a rabid dog, no doubt exists that the shot caused death, nor does it really matter. With people, use *shot to death* if little doubt exists that the bullet caused death, or if you know for sure after an autopsy. If a person dies after being shot in the chest during a robbery, it's OK to say *shot to death*. But the cause of death isn't always clear. If police find a body in a burned-out home and the person had been shot, they won't know whether the person was shot to death or died as a result of smoke inhalation.

■ 25. The man died of a bullet wound to the chest. An autopsy to determine the exact cause of death was scheduled.

- Here's a case where we want to hedge on the cause of death because the results of the autopsy are still out. When you say *of*, you define the cause of death.

- An autopsy is a procedure that determines the exact cause of death. Edit out the redundancy.

Make it: *The man died after he was shot in the chest. An autopsy was scheduled.*

■ 26. The suspect turned himself into police.

A common mistake and a joke unless, of course, the suspect is a magician. Make it: *The suspect turned himself in to police,* or *The suspect surrendered to police.*

■ 27. Witnesses gave police a description of the robber.

- This goes back to the Rules for Good Writing (chapter 2): Don't turn strong verbs into nouns. Make it: *Witnesses described the robber to police.*

- Make sure you don't use this construction: *Witnesses described the suspect to police.* Unless a witness is able to identify the suspect by name, not usually the case, separate the suspect from the crime. Remember that we assume the suspect is innocent and refer to the person who committed the crime as an unidentified perpetrator: *the robber, the killer* or *the assailant.*

■ **28. Police are looking for two Hispanic youths, 15 to 17 years old.**

We need to be sensitive about mentioning race; it can lead to stereotyping. By using race here, we indict all 15- to 17-year-old Hispanics. Race isn't meaningful unless the description is full and specific. Here's an example when mentioning race is OK:

Police have been hampered in their investigation because few victims have seen their assailant. Police said he has been described as being black, in his early- to mid-20s, 5 feet 8 inches tall and weighing 140 to 150 pounds. He wears a dark-green or black coat, possibly an Army jacket, and dark pants.

■ **29. The 5-year-old boy was convicted of mugging the 82-year-old woman.**

- The ages are stated this way for emphasis and contrast. But avoid using age as a modifier, as in the *43-year-old professor.*

- Some might question the phrase *convicted of mugging.* The actual charge would be something like assault or robbery, but remember that those are legal charges for acts that may be described in everyday terms. In some cases, this construction is useful for writing concise but fair leads. Here's an example:

A West Side man was charged Thursday with breaking into a North Side mansion, tying up its occupants and stealing a collection of valuable paintings.

Then later in the story, you can list the formal charges of burglary, unlawful restraint and larceny.

■ **30. In the old West, rustlers were hung for their crimes.**

We say *Stockings were hung by the chimney with care.* When *hang* means to suspend, the verb is conjugated as *hang* (present tense), *hung* (past tense) and *hung* (past perfect tense). But when we mean execution by rope, the verb is conjugated like this: *hang, hanged, hanged.* Make the sentence read: *In the old West, rustlers were hanged for their crimes.*

■ **31. The alleged mobsters attended the alleged meeting of Mafia bosses.**

- Sprinkling *alleged* through a story does not protect us from charges of libel. It makes a difference who is doing the alleging. Still, the word is useful in hedging to be fair. *Alleged* as it is used first in this sentence is OK. Other words that may be used include *reputed* or *purported*.

- Alleged is misused in the second case; the writer means reported. Make the sentence: *The alleged mobsters attended the reported meeting of Mafia bosses.*

Note: *Mafia* is not synonymous with *mob* or *organized crime*. The Mafia is just one type of crime organization.

■ **32. The suspect was held on $10,000 bail.**

A suspect can be *released on bond* or *held in lieu of bail*. *Bail* is set by a judge and can be satisfied by payment of property or, more commonly, cash payment of a deposit called *bond*. Bond usually is 10 percent of bail. If a suspect does not appear for trial, he or she will be liable for the entire amount of bail. In this sentence, make it: *The suspect was held in lieu of $10,000 bail.*

■ **33. The investigation centered around the eyewitness's lawsuit.**

- If something is in the center, everything else is around it. So we mean to say *centered on*.

- Stay away from clichés like *eyewitness*. The sentence should read: *The investigation centered on the witness's lawsuit.*

■ **34. A passing motorist hailed the passing patrolman, who nabbed the burglar.**

- The word *passing* is unnecessary in both cases.

- Avoid informal usages like *nabbed;* cops and robbers language gives the sentence a feeling of bias against the suspect.

- Make it *burglary suspect*. The person arrested hasn't been convicted of anything. The sentence should read: *A motorist hailed the patrolman, who arrested the burglary suspect.*

Like it or not, crime will always be with us, and it always will be news. In today's environment of newspapers competing with television stations competing with websites, writers and editors face pressure to get the news first—and some would say the more sensational the better. Despite this pressure, those stories in which a person is accused of a crime still demand care and good judgment.

7

Stats, Graphics and Maps

There are lies, there are damn lies and there are statistics.
—Benjamin Disraeli

Editors run into statistics constantly. Statistics show up in stories based on polls, in graphics summarizing financial data and in baseball stories on the sports pages. Stories containing statistics require careful editing for content and for accuracy because, as Disraeli knew well, numbers are only as good as the person interpreting and reporting them.

SURVEYS AND POLLS

Here are two cautionary tales about surveys:

• In 1936, Alf Landon, the Republican governor of Kansas, ran for president against Franklin D. Roosevelt, the incumbent Democrat. *The Literary Digest*, as it had done successfully since 1916, conducted a poll of voters. The magazine sent 10 million ballots to two groups: a list of "prospective subscribers" who were mostly upper- and middle-income people, and a list of people selected from telephone books and motor vehicle registrations. This second group was chosen to "correct for bias" from the first list. About 25 percent of the ballots (2.4 million) were returned, with Landon predicted to win by a huge margin of 57 percent to 40 percent.

   History shows that FDR won with about 60 percent of the vote and that the *Literary Digest* soon went out of business.

- The 1948 presidential election pitted New York's Republican governor, Thomas E. Dewey, against Harry S. Truman, who had assumed the office of president when Roosevelt died in 1945. The Gallup organization conducted a poll on the election, as it had done for every presidential race since 1936. Gallup used a representative sample of about 3,000 voters based on geographic location, community size, socioeconomic level, gender and age. Gallup went to press six weeks before the election with the prediction that Dewey would win. The message was echoed on election night by the banner headline "DEWEY DEFEATS TRUMAN" in the early editions of the *Chicago Tribune*. The photo of the victorious Truman holding the newspaper aloft has become an enduring icon of journalism history.

Both cases still receive attention today in college courses such as the research methods class taught by J. Stephen Downie at the University of Illinois. Downie's analyses of these cases, published on the website, provide valuable lessons about survey methods.

In 1936, the *Literary Digest* used what would be a huge sample by today's standards. But the magazine made two mistakes Downie writes:

1. In the group of "prospective subscribers," Republicans were heavily overrepresented. And in 1936, voters in Roosevelt's Democratic coalition of workers, farmers and minorities did not own telephones, did not drive cars and did not subscribe to literary magazines.

2. The respondents were self-selected; ballots were returned only by those who cared enough to do so.

Gallup's sampling methods in 1948 were much more reliable, but Downie writes that Gallup made two crucial mistakes:

1. The organization stopped polling too soon. In the last six weeks of an election, voters can change their minds.

2. Gallup assumed that "undecided" respondents could be split between the two candidates because they were, after all, undecided. But voters who report themselves as "undecided" often have strong leanings one way or the other.

Organizations that conduct surveys today remain undaunted if more cautious, and the poll story is a staple of the election season. News organizations also use survey research methods to gather information and opinions on the issues of the day, a practice described in the 1970s by Philip Meyer in his book *Precision Journalism*.

The charge has been made that the polls sometimes drive events. The impeachment and Senate trial of President Clinton over the winter of 1998–99 is an example. A *Newsweek* poll of Jan. 28–29, 1999, published a week before the president was acquitted on Feb. 12, was typical of many surveys concerning the president's problems. *Newsweek* reported that only 28 percent of those interviewed said Clinton should be removed from office; 54 percent said the Republican Party had been hurt by the way it handled the impeachment process.

The president's high "approval ratings" during the impeachment process was cited in the press as a strong influence on the Senate leadership to seek an "exit strategy." Did *Newsweek*'s poll and similar ones influence the decisions Congress made? People in the media believed so. The *Newsweek* story described the Senate proceedings as a "show trial" and said that nothing in the process had "much to do with Clinton's guilt or innocence. But it has everything to do with the real stakes: how the voters—and history—will treat Clinton's accusers and defenders."

The story wasn't Clinton's guilt or innocence, but rather how Republicans were going to deal with poll results, the very ones conducted and reported by *Newsweek* and other publications. These polls took on the qualities of self-fulfilling prophecies.

EDITING STORIES ABOUT SURVEYS

Editors need to slow down when they read stories about survey results. Some things to consider are sources, samples, margins of error and healthy skepticism.

The Source

Large newspapers and magazines often conduct surveys in partnership with an academic institution. Sometimes print media outlets and broadcast outlets form alliances. This is necessary because a well-conducted poll is expensive.

Editors should make sure that the participants in the survey and its sponsors are reported. Sometimes this is done as part of the graphics package. *Newsweek,* for instance, reports its sponsorship and its partnership with a Princeton University research group.

Be careful of polls conducted for industry groups, political parties or individual candidates. If the story is about research into road wear, and the research is paid for by Citizens for Better Roads, that fact should be reported. If Citizens for Better Roads is a coalition of paving companies, that should be reported, too. Know whom you're dealing with.

The Sample

Survey research relies on sampling to make its methods affordable. Researchers interview a few people, then apply the results to the population at large. In the *Newsweek* poll mentioned above, the researchers interviewed 751 adults by telephone. While it may seem risky to let 751 people speak for the adult population of the United States, 751 actually is a large sample, statistically speaking.

Think of it this way: If 10 people were interviewed and three said Bill Clinton should be removed from office, that's 30 percent. But let's say two people didn't answer truthfully. Maybe they didn't understand the question, or maybe they wanted to please the interviewer. If only two people out of 10 had stated a false opinion, then the correct percentage could have been 50 percent—or 10 percent. In any survey, you'll have a few people who don't respond truthfully. The larger the sample, the smaller the effect these people have on the outcome. In a sample of 751, where 28 percent said Clinton should be removed, two untruthful responses change the outcome by about a quarter of a percentage point.

Researchers will increase the reliability of a survey by using a *systematic* or *stratified* sample. They will divide respondents by sex, marital status, age, income, education and party affiliation, then choose randomly from within those groups in proportion to the population as a whole. The results also can be reported by group where comparisons are meaningful. In the poll mentioned above, *Newsweek* separated the responses of Democrats and Republicans.

Margin of Error

Even using a very large sample, a survey always can produce the wrong conclusions. Researchers know how to calculate the likelihood of being wrong as a statistical probability. For opinion surveys, the *margin of error* is stated as plus or minus percentage points. A typical figure for a political poll is plus or minus 4 percentage points. When the results are conclusive, the margin of error is not significant. But let's say a poll finds that one candidate is leading another 52 percent to 48 percent, with a margin of error of plus or minus four. The result has to be interpreted as a virtual tie.

A scientific study will report a *confidence level*, the probability that the results are due to chance rather than a real effect. The confidence level is stated as a decimal, such as .95, meaning the result could be expected to happen by chance only five out of 100 times. In the social sciences, studies with a confidence level of equal to or greater than .95 are considered *statistically significant*, and the results are considered meaningful.

Healthy Skepticism

Victor Cohn, in his book *News and Numbers,* says reporters and editors must be willing to ask questions about statistical stories. The two questions he suggests again and again are, *How do you know?* and *Have you done a study?* The first question concerns the methods by which reporters come to their conclusions. The second asks if that method follows the rules of a formal study, including scientific sampling, pretesting of questions and proper statistical analysis.

Another question always worth asking is, *Compared to what?* Have other studies been done? Are the results consistent? Have the results changed over time?

If an editor maintains a healthy skepticism, questions will always come to mind as he or she reads the statistical story. An editor should never be afraid to ask such questions of reporters and other editors.

CHECKING THE NUMBERS

Here are a few notes to help you edit statistical stories (be sure to use your calculator):

- To figure a percentage, divide the small number by the larger and multiply by 100. For instance, to find what percent 15 is of 60, divide 15 by 60 to get .25, then multiply by 100 to get 25 percent.
- Often you'll see the phrasing *one out of 80* or words to that effect. To figure this out, divide the larger number by the smaller number. For 15 out of 60, divide 60 by 15 to get 4; 15 out of 60 can be stated as one out of four.
- Beware of phrasing such as *five times more than* and *five times as much.* For example, if a building is worth $10,000 and you paid five times *more than* it's worth, then you would pay $60,000 (the $10,000 plus five times $10,000). If a building is worth $10,000 and you paid five times *as much as* it's worth, you would pay $50,000.
- In stating an increase or decrease, use phrasing such as *the sales tax increased to 6 percent from 1 percent.* The phrasing *from 1 percent to 6 percent* might be misinterpreted as anywhere between 1 percent and 6 percent.
- Beware of the phrasings *more than* and *less than.* Check them out. For instance, let's say a story claims, *More than 17 percent said they preferred chocolate chips.* You work out the arithmetic and get .1699999. That figure would round off to .17, but it's not *more than* .17, or times 100, 17 percent. You can state it simply as 17 percent.
- To figure the percentage of change between two numbers, find the difference between the two numbers and divide by the original. For instance, if the increase is to 6 from 4, the difference between the numbers is 2. Because you started with 4, it is the original figure. So, 2 divided by 4 equals .5; multiply by 100 and you have an increase of 50 percent.

  The percentage of increase often can be more than 100 percent. If the hotel tax goes to $9 from $3, then the difference between the numbers is 6; the original number is 3, so divide 6 by 3 to get 2.00; multiply by 100 to get an increase of 200 percent.

  For a decrease, it works the same. If the number of doctors in a county goes to 10 from 20, the difference is 10. Divide that by 20, the original number, to get .50 or a 50 percent decrease.
- Any breakdown of percentages should add up to 100. If not, you have to check the original figures to find the mistake. Don't guess! One number could be wrong, or a category could be missing.
- If you calculate a group of percentages, beware of rounding errors. First you'll decide on how many decimal places you'll want to report. For news stories, one decimal place is usually enough. Second, follow the rule of rounding upward from 5 or more.

  Let's say you figure percentages and get these three numbers: .45455, .36364 and .18182. You round them off and multiply by 100 to get these percentages: 45.5, 36.4 and 18.2. You add them up and get 100.1 percent.

  To fix this problem, you could adjust one or two of the numbers. If the difference from 100 percent is large, more than 1 percent, then you might consider carrying the percentages out to another decimal place. Some publications simply report that the percentages add up to more than 100 "due to rounding errors."

• Beware of the difference between a "10-percent increase" and "an increase of 10 percentage points." If government spending for space programs increases to 20 percent of the budget from 10 percent, that's an increase of *10 percentage points*, or a *100-percent increase.*

INFORMATION GRAPHICS

An information graphic is any visual representation of information. This broad definition includes charts, tables, maps and what are called process or "how to" graphics.

A well-done information graphic allows readers to make visual comparisons and to interpret differences in numbers in meaningful ways. The best graphics present more than one variable, such as oil production over time by country.

In its simplest form, the information graphic contains four parts: the headline, the "chatter" explaining the graphic, the body of the graphic, and the source and credit lines (fig. 7.1).

Fig. 7.1

In its simplest form, the information graphic contains four parts: the headline, the "chatter" explaining the graphic, the body of the graphic, and the source and credit lines.

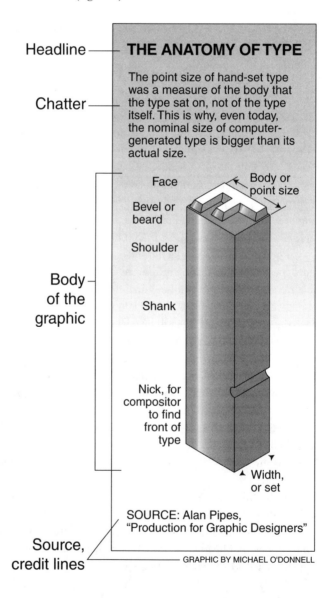

Headline — **THE ANATOMY OF TYPE**

Chatter — The point size of hand-set type was a measure of the body that the type sat on, not of the type itself. This is why, even today, the nominal size of computer-generated type is bigger than its actual size.

Face

Body or point size

Bevel or beard

Shoulder

Body of the graphic

Shank

Nick, for compositor to find front of type

Width, or set

SOURCE: Alan Pipes, "Production for Graphic Designers"

Source, credit lines

— GRAPHIC BY MICHAEL O'DONNELL

Fig. 7.2

A table is the simplest information graphic, one that editors or reporters may be called upon to produce.

MORE MEMORY FOR LESS MONEY
Prices for random-access memory (RAM) continue
to fall with overproduction and reduced demand.

Size (MB)	Type	Speed (Bits)	Speed (ns)	Price
1	SIMM	32	70	$33.99
2	SIMM	32	70	$49.00
8	DIMM	64	70	$189.00
16	DIMM	64	70	$329.49
32	DIMM	64	70	$649.00
64	DIMM	128	70	$1,359.49

GRAPHIC BY MICHAEL O'DONNELL

Editors should read graphics like any piece of copy, checking for inconsistencies, misspellings and factual errors.

Tables

A table (fig. 7.2) is the simplest information graphic, one that editors or reporters may be called upon to produce. It lists figures by categories in columns and rows, allowing the reader to make comparisons. Tables can be done using the newspaper or magazine's text-editing system, without resorting to special graphics software.

Here are a few tips in building tables:

- Use tables when the range of numbers would make another type of chart impractical. For instance, a series of numbers that begins with five and ends with 5 million could not be represented in a meaningful way with a bar chart or line chart.
- Use tables if a plotted chart turns out to be a tangled mess. Often this is related to information overload, and space may be saved by setting numbers in type as a table.
- Use a table when the exact numbers are important. In figure 7.2, the reader must know the exact specifications to find the right memory module and know the exact cost.
- Use tables when the numbers do not represent the same thing, the "apples and oranges" situation. In figure 7.2, the specifications are measured in megabytes (MB), bits, nanoseconds and dollars.
- Make sure the numbers are aligned correctly. Note in figure 7.2 that the MB and bits columns align right, meaning the ones, tens and hundreds are aligned in columns. For prices, note that the numbers align on the decimal point. Also note that the last number in the price column ($1,359.49) includes the comma.

PIE CHARTS

The first and most important rule for using a pie chart is that it must represent 100 percent of the data. In figure 7.3, federal taxes are expressed in percentages, but dollars could be used, as long as the segments still add up to the entire amount of taxes collected.

Fig. 7.3

The first and most important rule for using a pie chart is that it must represent 100 percent of the data.

THE FEDERAL GOVERNMENT DOLLAR

Individual income taxes will raise an estimated $900 billion in 2000. Social insurance payroll taxes—the fastest growing category of federal revenues—include Social Security taxes, Medicare taxes, unemployment insurance taxes and federal employee retirement payments. Corporate income taxes will raise an estimated $189 billion.

WHERE IT COMES FROM

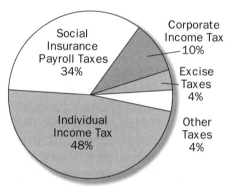

WHERE IT GOES

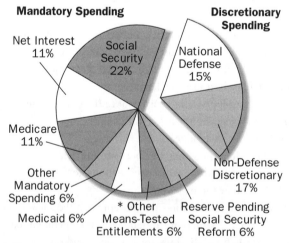

* Means-tested entitlements are those for which eligibility is based on income. The Medicaid program is also a means-tested entitlement.

SOURCE: Office of Management and Budget

GRAPHIC BY MICHAEL O'DONNELL

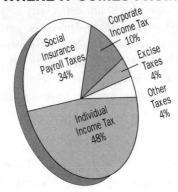

WHERE IT COMES FROM

Corporate
Income Tax
10%

Social
Insurance
Payroll Taxes
34%

Excise
Taxes
4%

Other
Taxes
4%

Individual
Income Tax
48%

Fig. 7.4

Graphic artists use fore-shortening to give charts a three-dimensional quality. Here, perspective has been applied to part of the tax chart. Do the segments maintain the proper proportions?

Look for these problems with pie charts:

- Segments too numerous or extremely small. One common guideline is that a pie chart should be limited to a maximum of seven segments. But notice that one pie in figure 7.3 has nine segments. It still is readable because none of the segments are too small, less than 6 percent. When the slices become very small, consider combining categories.

- Segments don't match the data. When editing pie charts, try to gauge the proportion of each slice with its percentage. It's not as hard as you might think. In figure 7.3, the slice for individual income tax is 48 percent, or about half. Mentally divide the pie in half to quickly judge its accuracy. Other slices can be compared according to similarity. The slices for 15 percent and 17 percent should be about the same size; the slices for 6 percent should all be the same size and should be noticeably smaller than the slices for 11 percent.

- Segments distorted by perspective. Graphic artists use foreshortening to give charts a three-dimensional quality. In figure 7.4, perspective has been applied to part of the tax chart. While a chart using perspective can be eye-catching, do the segments maintain the proper proportions? The visual honesty of a chart should not be sacrificed for attractiveness.

Bar Charts

Use bar charts to show comparisons between individual numbers within a series. Bar charts can be used when some numbers are missing or when the time periods are irregular. Figure 7.5 shows high temperature readings for several days compared with the average high temperature for each date. Note that it doesn't matter what time of day the high temperature was recorded because the bar chart shows only one measurement for one day.

When many measurements are available, the bar chart may become impractical, and a line chart can be used.

Line Charts

Line charts also are known as fever charts or trend charts. Use them when the numbers cover a long time. The emphasis is on movement rather than the individual numbers. Sometimes a line chart can show projected data, as is the case with figure 7.6. Line charts are especially good for showing seasonal changes or comparing two trends over the same time periods, as figure 7.6 does.

Avoid making too many comparisons on one line chart, the "spaghetti bowl" syndrome. As with bar charts, line charts are not practical when the data jump from a small amount to a huge amount. Finally, line charts aren't very valuable if they show just random variation or no variation.

Pictographs

A pictograph is a special type of bar chart that uses pictures to dress up statistical information. The pictograph symbol should be simple and easy to identify. It also should have relevance to the data. Figure 7.7, a pictograph for oil production, matches barrel symbols with the data expressed in millions of barrels a day. Because comparisons may be more difficult to make visually than with a plain bar chart, numbers often are included, as is the case with figure 7.7.

Process Graphics

Process or "how to" graphics use pictures and diagrams to show how something works or how something is done. Often these involve "cutaway" drawings to reveal the inner parts of an object. Figure 7.8 shows a complex process graphic that combines digital photos with figures rendered in a computer drawing program.

An editor who is proofing a process graphic must pay attention to detail. Here's an example: Many newspapers, the *Chicago Tribune* included, have used graphic "depth charts" for previewing important sporting events. These charts often were miniature playing fields with miniature players representing the two teams. Graphic artists produce these charts by drawing one figure, say, a baseball player in fielding position, then copying and pasting it to fill in all the positions. But what if some of the players are left-handed? What if some of them are African-Americans? When the chart goes out to 750,000 readers, you can be sure more than one will notice these mistakes—and write to let you know about it.

Fig. 7.5

Use bar charts to show comparisons between individual numbers within a series. Bar charts can be used when some numbers are missing or when the time periods are irregular.

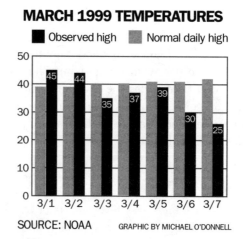

MARCH 1999 TEMPERATURES

■ Observed high   ▨ Normal daily high

SOURCE: NOAA   GRAPHIC BY MICHAEL O'DONNELL

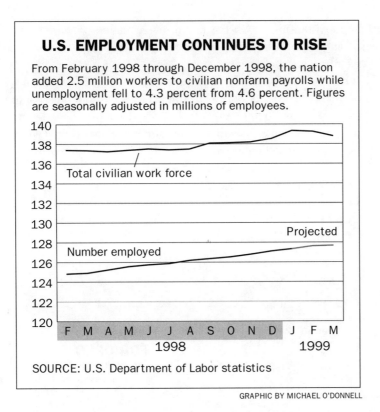

U.S. EMPLOYMENT CONTINUES TO RISE

From February 1998 through December 1998, the nation added 2.5 million workers to civilian nonfarm payrolls while unemployment fell to 4.3 percent from 4.6 percent. Figures are seasonally adjusted in millions of employees.

Total civilian work force

Projected

Number employed

F M A M J J A S O N D J F M
1998   1999

SOURCE: U.S. Department of Labor statistics

GRAPHIC BY MICHAEL O'DONNELL

Fig. 7.6

Sometimes a line chart can show projected data.

Maps

Newspapers and magazines have used maps for more than a hundred years. In his book, *Maps with the News,* Mark Monmonier says that *The Times of London* began using a daily weather map in 1875 with the *New York Herald* following a year later.

The introduction of computer graphics into the newsroom has eased the way for increased use of maps for two reasons. First, maps, once drawn, can be stored electronically and easily altered to serve new stories. Second, maps can be downloaded from graphic services and altered to fit a publication's style for typography, color and texture.

The Persian Gulf War in 1989 produced an explosion of maps, along with other information graphics, because access to the battle zone was tightly controlled by the Pentagon and because many readers were unfamiliar with the Middle East. In an informal analysis of 50 or so newspapers, we found that the same base maps, weapons graphics and charts appeared in almost all of the papers. They were downloading the material from the same graphic services, mainly the Associated Press. But the newspapers varied greatly in how they recombined the images, altered the typography and mixed in color as they sought some individuality.

Maps range from small "locator" maps to full-page extravaganzas that include demographic data or show the progress of a news event. Adding data to a map can result in a satisfying graphic that allows readers to make comparisons at the macro and micro levels. Figure 7.9 shows a map of Minnesota that includes percentages of people who work at home by county. Readers taking the macro view can quickly see that stay-at-home workers tend not to be clustered around metropolitan areas. On the micro level, readers in Minnesota can see how their county stacks up against other counties. Maps like this can add power to stories analyzing social trends.

When editing maps, the first question has to be, does the map reflect geographic reality? Savvy editors know their cities and often can spot inaccurately drawn streets and neighborhoods. Editors also must check labeling of geographic landmarks. Sometimes this means going back to original sources, such as the atlas. Are the street names and other names spelled correctly? Are streets labeled as streets, avenues as avenues and boulevards as boulevards?

Next, the editor must ask if the map clearly shows what it is supposed to show. Locator maps sometimes show a small area in very little detail and no context. Or they show unnecessary detail that can be confusing. If the editor is confused, then the reader certainly will be.

Fig. 7.7

A pictograph for oil production matches barrel symbols with the data expressed in millions of barrels a day. Because comparisons may be more difficult to make visually than with a plain bar chart, numbers often are included.

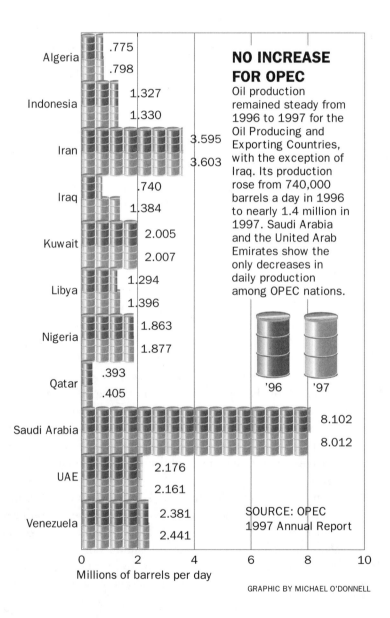

NO INCREASE FOR OPEC
Oil production remained steady from 1996 to 1997 for the Oil Producing and Exporting Countries, with the exception of Iraq. Its production rose from 740,000 barrels a day in 1996 to nearly 1.4 million in 1997. Saudi Arabia and the United Arab Emirates show the only decreases in daily production among OPEC nations.

SOURCE: OPEC 1997 Annual Report

GRAPHIC BY MICHAEL O'DONNELL

A GUIDE TO PIXEL DEPTH

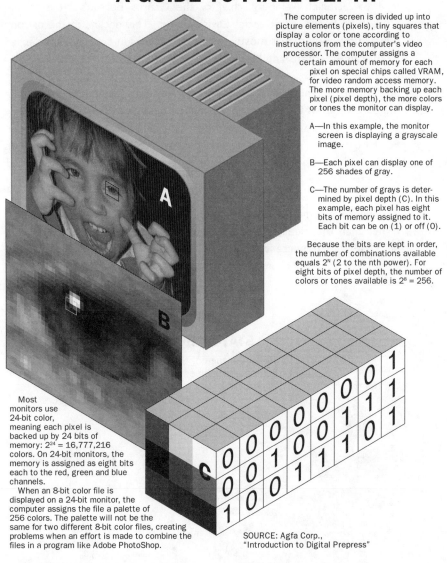

The computer screen is divided up into picture elements (pixels), tiny squares that display a color or tone according to instructions from the computer's video processor. The computer assigns a certain amount of memory for each pixel on special chips called VRAM, for video random access memory. The more memory backing up each pixel (pixel depth), the more colors or tones the monitor can display.

A—In this example, the monitor screen is displaying a grayscale image.

B—Each pixel can display one of 256 shades of gray.

C—The number of grays is determined by pixel depth (C). In this example, each pixel has eight bits of memory assigned to it. Each bit can be on (1) or off (0).

Because the bits are kept in order, the number of combinations available equals 2^N (2 to the nth power). For eight bits of pixel depth, the number of colors or tones available is $2^8 = 256$.

Most monitors use 24-bit color, meaning each pixel is backed up by 24 bits of memory: $2^{24} = 16,777,216$ colors. On 24-bit monitors, the memory is assigned as eight bits each to the red, green and blue channels.

When an 8-bit color file is displayed on a 24-bit monitor, the computer assigns the file a palette of 256 colors. The palette will not be the same for two different 8-bit color files, creating problems when an effort is made to combine the files in a program like Adobe PhotoShop.

SOURCE: Agfa Corp.,
"Introduction to Digital Prepress"

Fig. 7.8

A complex process graphic, combining digital photos with figures rendered in a computer drawing program, requires planning and time.

WORKOUT: STATISTICS

Edit this story, paying special attention to the way numbers are presented. You'll need your stylebook and a calculator.

■ POVERTY

WASHINGTON, D.C.—Three years of positive growth in real median income have restored household income and poverty rates to their 1989 prerecessionary levels, according to reports released today by the Commerce Department's Census Bureau.

Nationwide, the proportion of the population living below the poverty level declined from 13.7 percent in 1996 to 13.3 percent in 1997.

"The 1997 rate was not statistically different from the pre-recessionary rate in 1989," Daniel Weinberg, chief of the Census Bureau's Housing and Household Economic Statistics Division, said. "This decline in the nation's overall poverty rate was mostly caused by declines in poverty experienced by African Americans and Hispanics."

To illustrate, the number of poor African Americans dropped by more than 6.2 percent, from 9.7 million to 9.1 million between 1996 and 1997, while their poverty rate fell nearly 2 percent, from 28.4 percent to 26.5 percent. For Hispanics, the number in poverty declined 4.5 percent, from 8.7 million to 8.3 million, and their poverty rate dropped from 29.4 percent to 27.1 percent.

The median income of White households in 1997 ($38,972) was 56 percent higher than the median income of African American households in 1997 ($25,050) and 46 percent higher than Hispanic households ($26,628).

Fig. 7.9

Adding data to a map can result in a satisfying graphic that allows readers to make comparisons at the macro and micro levels.

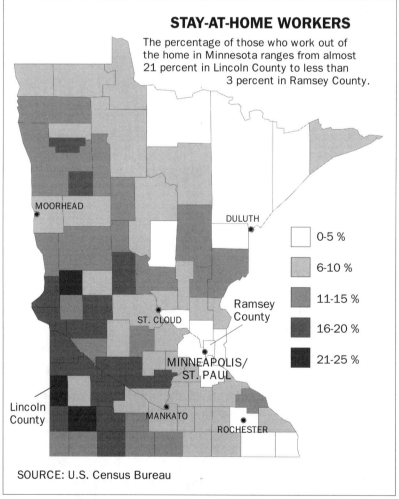

SOURCE: U.S. Census Bureau

GRAPHIC BY MICHAEL O'DONNELL

Some groups had poverty rates in 1997 that were lower than their adjusted 1989 rate: persons 65 and older; residents of the Midwest and the South; African Americans; married-couple families; African American married-couple families; and African American female householder families.

The data are from the March 1998 Current Population Survey. As in all surveys, the data are subject to sampling variability and other sources of error.

Let's take the first two paragraphs:

■ POVERTY

WASHINGTON, ~~D.C.~~ —Three years of ~~positive~~ growth in real median income have restored household income and poverty rates to their 1989 pre-recessionary levels, according to reports released today by the Commerce Department's Census Bureau.

Nationwide, the proportion of the population living below the poverty level declined ~~from 13.7 percent in 1996~~ to 13.3 percent in 1997 <u>from 13.7 percent in 1996</u>.

Washington does not take a *D.C.* after it, according to the *Datelines* entry in the AP stylebook. *Positive* is an unnecessary word; isn't *negative growth* an oxymoron? The opposite of growth would be *decline*.

When talking about a change in numbers, use the formula *to . . . from. . . .* This avoids confusion with a range, such as *he earned from $20,000 to $30,000 a year from free-lance work.* Let's tackle the next two paragraphs:

"The 1997 rate was not statistically different from the pre-recessionary rate in 1989," <u>said</u> Daniel Weinberg, chief of the Census Bureau's Housing and Household Economic Statistics Division~~, said~~. "This decline in the nation's overall poverty rate was mostly caused by declines in poverty experienced by African-Americans and Hispanics."

~~To illustrate, t~~The number of poor African-Americans dropped by ~~more than~~ 6.2 percent,<u> to 9.1 million</u> from 9.7 million ~~to 9.1 million~~ between 1996 and 1997, while their poverty rate fell nearly 2 percent<u>age points, to 26.5 percent</u> from 28.4 percent~~ to 26.5 percent~~. For Hispanics, the number in poverty declined ~~4.5~~ <u>4.6</u> percent,<u> to 8.3 million</u> from 8.7 million~~ to 8.3 million~~, and their poverty rate dropped <u>to 27.1 percent</u> from 29.4 percent~~ to 27.1 percent~~.

See the section on quotes in the AP stylebook and review Chapter 3 about attributing a quote when a long title follows a name. We'll hyphenate *African-American;* see Chapter 4 on spelling.

If you do the arithmetic, you'll find that the exact decline is .0618556 (9.7 minus 9.1 equals .6, divided by 9.7). Times 100, that would round up to 6.2

percent but would not be *more than* 6.2 percent. Note the difference between *2 percent* and *2 percentage points*. Finally, 8.7 minus 8.3 equals .4, divided by 8.7 equals .045977, times 100 rounds off to 4.6 percent.

> The median income of White households in 1997 ($38,972) was 56 percent ~~higher~~ <u>more</u> than the median income of African-American households in 1997 ($25,050) and 46 percent ~~higher~~ <u>more</u> than that of Hispanic households ($26,628).

> Some groups had poverty rates in 1997 that were lower than their adjusted 1989 rate: ~~persons~~ <u>people</u> 65 and older; residents of the Midwest and the South; African-Americans; married-couple families; African-American married-couple families; and African-American female householder families.

> The data are from the March 1998 *Current Population Survey.* As in all surveys, the data are subject to sampling variability and other sources of error.

Use *more than* or *less than,* and save *higher* and *lower* for differences in dimension. Are the figures correct here? Yes, if you remember that the low number is the original number in our comparison. It's the same as figuring an increase: Subtract the smaller number from the bigger number and divide by the smaller.

Clean up the next to last paragraph; see the AP entry under *people, persons.*

The story doesn't give a sampling error or a sample size. These might be facts worth reporting, and they may be available from a Census Bureau website.

The reporter or editor who understands numbers is a valuable addition to the newsroom. A course in statistics is a good addition to any prospective journalist's education. If current trends continue, statistics will become available to newsrooms in a bewildering array, disseminated through websites and updated almost instantly. We've only scratched the surface here. Your challenge is to embrace statistics and keep your news organization accurate and honest.

8

The Maestro Concept

Teamwork is sorely needed throughout the company. Teamwork requires one to compensate with his strength someone else's weakness, for everyone to sharpen each other's wits with questions.
—W. Edwards Deming

The best way to integrate words and visuals on a page is to have verbal and visual journalists working hand in hand toward a common goal. This does not happen naturally. There must be a method to ensure collaboration, and that method is the Maestro Concept. Teamwork, managing time and managing change are essential to its success, and when the concept clicks, the results are an impressive number of awards for writing, editing, photojournalism and design. The Maestro Concept has captured the attention of high school and college journalists working on newspapers and yearbooks; professional editors of trade magazines and newsletters; and staffs of weekly and major daily newspapers here and abroad.

Take a moment to jot down a few questions that occur to you about the concept. We'll compare notes below.

Here's the format for this chapter: First, we'll explain the concept's "idea-group" meetings. Second, we'll talk about the importance of coaching writers. Third, we'll address the challenges of hurdling newsroom traditions. Fourth, we'll see a maestro session in action. Fifth, we'll get a lesson in critiquing, following up on some of the ideas expressed in Chapter 1.

Concluding the chapter, a "Q&A" segment gives answers to four questions about the Maestro Concept: (1) What is it? (2) What are the results? (3) How does it work? (4) Where did the idea come from? How do these questions compare with the ones you have written? A central challenge in the Maestro Concept is trying to anticipate readers' questions, then answering them quickly on a page. The sharper the skill in anticipating these questions, the more engaging and relevant your publication will be to your readers.

The Maestro Concept process begins with a great story idea, often generated in an idea-group meeting. The concept applies to only the best stories, especially those that require photography, design and information graphics. Routine stories can be handled in routine ways. Opportunities for high impact and readership are lost when great stories get routine presentation. A common misconception is that somehow the Maestro Concept must apply to all stories all the time. Instead, the focus is on choosing one great story idea and creating one team to bring it to life on a page. Once the story idea emerges, the focus turns to preliminary reporting by a writer and in some cases a photographer.

Why do we need a writer and photographer working together during preliminary reporting? One example involves a newspaper that set out to do the definitive profile of the city's mayor. The reporter's lead focused on how the mayor slipped off his suit coat, rolled up his sleeves and played basketball with neighborhood kids. There was no photo of this because the reporter had been working weeks on the profile, reporting and writing, before anyone thought to get a photographer involved. With the Maestro Concept, as soon as the paper had committed to spend this kind of time on such a story, a maestro would have had the reporter matched with a photographer.

At newspapers, depending on how the concept is applied in different sections of the newsroom, maestros may be editors or managing editors, section editors, assignment editors, designers or photo editors. Regardless of their positions, as maestros, they are dedicated to managing time for quality by everyone involved in a story.

The time management begins with coaching writers through the reporting process. A "pre-maestro check" involves testing whether enough reporting has been done to ensure that a story is solid. Before writing starts, the maestro convenes a maestro session to engage others who will be involved in the storytelling, such as copy editors, photographers, designers and graphics artists. At times, library researchers will join maestro sessions. The maestro session focuses on readers' questions to develop a plan for more reporting as needed, for writing leads and sidebars, for editing and writing headlines and for photo assignments. Readers' questions drive the design of the story package. The team members assembled in the maestro session follow through on the plan, which is recorded on a maestro form. They make adjustments, large or small, as the story demands.

When readers see the story package in the paper, they find their most pressing questions answered in high-visibility points, such as photos, headlines, captions and information graphics. If all goes well, readers will be fully engaged, and they will read more of the story and understand it more completely than usual.

After publication, the team members reconvene for a brief critique, or "audit," of the story package. The readers' questions generated in the maestro session create a "reader-friendliness index." The more questions answered quickly with impact on the page, the more appealing the story package is to readers.

From story idea to critique, this is a brief outline of the Maestro Concept process. It has as many variations as there are publications using the concept.

1. IDEA-GROUP MEETINGS

Traditionally, story ideas come from either writers or their assignment editors. Reporters are expected to come up with interesting story ideas, though if you ask assignment editors, you would find that the reporter who is constantly bursting with exciting story ideas is a rare and valuable person. Many times assignment editors are tossing ideas to reporters, who must juggle these work assignments with their own ideas. The advantage of reporters coming up with their own story ideas is that they work on articles interesting to them. If a reporter suggests a story idea, however, he or she is expected to follow through on it. This reality tends to inhibit reporters with great ideas from expressing them right away. Instead those ideas sit on a mental shelf and often get lost over time.

The traditional approach to generating story ideas limits creativity, if only because of the limited number of people involved. The Maestro Concept creates a new setting for generating story ideas through idea-group meetings. These meetings free assignment editors and section editors from the burnout burden of having to be the font of creative ideas all the time. The meetings also create an environment for reporters to think big without limitations. The reporters are no longer confined to suggesting only the stories that they have the time and skills to complete. In idea-group meetings, big ideas often lead to the formation of teams across departments, a rare occurrence in traditional newsrooms.

Idea-group meetings are short (15 to 20 minutes), routine, open to anyone and structured. There are three rules:

1. Anyone can suggest any story idea for any reason.

2. Just because a person thinks of a story idea, he or she doesn't have to do it.

3. No critiquing, evaluating or challenging of story ideas is allowed. The ideas are just listed. Later, top newsroom decision makers will assemble the list, set priorities and make assignments.

Who Attends

The purpose of the idea-group meetings is to draw on as much creativity and knowledge as possible, and to use as many contacts as an organization has to offer. Regular participants in these meetings include the newsroom's top editor, section editors, star reporters and others known for their creativity. These people form the inner circle of the idea-group meetings and often represent many of the traditional sources of story ideas.

The next ring of the circle includes copy editors, photographers, designers, graphics artists, newsroom librarians and editorial assistants. These creative people understand the publication and the community but are traditionally outside the decision-making power loop. They usually lack the access to assignment editors that reporters have and face a credibility barrier in the traditional newsroom if only because it's not their job to generate story ideas. Once they are in the comfort of an idea-group meeting and have the ear of newsroom leaders, the value of their contributions becomes readily apparent.

An anecdote from the first newspaper to fully adopt the Maestro Concept illustrates this point. At the *Pharos-Tribune* in Logansport, Ind., a photographer told this story: When he first arrived in Logansport, he noticed what he thought was a llama farm on his way to work. He mentioned it to his boss, the photo editor, but the idea went nowhere. He later mentioned it to the city editor, who asked him to "write it up." He explained the story idea in a memo and delivered it to the city editor. Later when he checked on its disposition, the city editor said somehow the memo got lost. More than a year later, after the paper adopted the Maestro Concept, the photographer attended the first idea-group meeting. He mentioned the llama farm idea, and a story about it ended up in the paper in a few days.

Photographers tend to spend as much time out in the community as reporters, sometimes more. Copy editors see story ideas in what they read each day. Designers and graphics artists see the world in unique ways. Newsroom librarians may be the most careful readers of the newspaper. News assistants are often plugged into a youth culture that escapes an older reporter or assignment editor. They all are valuable resources for story ideas, yet the traditional newsroom creates barriers that keep them from contributing those ideas.

The next ring of the idea-group circle extends to those working at the newspaper but not in the newsroom, such as staff members in circulation, production and the pressroom. Some may have lived in the community far longer than the average reporter or assignment editor. The traditional thinking about advertising salespeople is that they have too much conflict of interest to suggest story ideas for the paper; the walls between advertising and the newsroom have been built tall in many places. At the same time, advertising sales representatives spend much time in the community because of their work and their home life. They may be able to offer story ideas that have nothing to do with the newspaper's clients or possible conflicts of interests. Idea-group meetings allow circulation, production, pressroom and even advertising staff members to contribute ideas that may end up as high-profile stories, if the newsroom's top decision makers see fit.

The outer ring of the idea-group circle reaches to readers who may be one-time contributors or who are part of regular reader advisory groups. For a high school or college publication, these groups might involve teachers or professors and parents as well as fellow students with unique insight or expertise. For a major metropolitan newspaper, a reader advisory group might be organized around a coverage topic, such as education, crime, economic development, the environment, and health and medicine. The advisory groups evaluate coverage, provide background information on trends and brainstorm on story ideas.

When to Hold Meetings

Idea-group meetings are held at times that allow as many people as possible to contribute easily. Depending on the size of the publication, the number of meetings may range from once a week to several happening at different times throughout a week or month. Daily newspapers that have adopted idea-group meetings tend to start with a short meeting Friday afternoon when the largest number of staff members are at work. The challenge in a meeting swiftly changes from generating good story ideas to logging them, then prioritizing and assigning the ideas afterward. Keeping up can become so difficult that the idea-group meetings often move from once a week to every two weeks and even once a month. That is what can happen when the pent-up creativity in a traditional newsroom is unleashed. Success amounts to no one ever again saying, "There's nothing good for page one." Take a moment to think about how idea groups could work at your publication.

2. MAESTROS COACHING WRITERS

Let's say a reporter is doing a story on the Maestro Concept for a media trade magazine, such as *Presstime* or *Editor & Publisher*. The idea popped out of an idea-group meeting after a senior editor attended a presentation on the concept at the World Association of Newspapers convention in Kobe, Japan. The editor was most intrigued by the idea that the Maestro Concept can make reporters' lives easier.

How can that be so? The answer lies in maestro-style coaching.

The Pre-maestro Test

In our example, the magazine's editor or assistant editor acts as the "maestro." The maestro applies a three-part "test," then works with the reporter to identify key reader questions. The three-part test and the brainstorming on readers' questions involve what is called the "pre-maestro check." The maestro assesses whether or not to move forward with a maestro session, which in this case would involve a copy editor, a photographer, an illustrator and a page designer. Let's listen in as the maestro talks to the reporter, who is walking by her desk.

Maestro: "How are you doing with that Maestro Concept story?"

Reporter: "You mean that trend story you assigned last week?"

Maestro: "That's the one."

Reporter: "Well, I've done some preliminary reporting, but I'm going to need more time."

Maestro: "Let's talk about it for a minute now. What is the story about? Can you summarize it in 30 words or less?"

Reporter: "Thirty words, huh. Maybe something like, 'The Maestro Concept has changed the way newspaper editors think and talk about story planning and newsroom organization here and abroad.' "

Maestro: "Good. Now I'm a busy reader, why should I care about this story? What's most interesting? What would make me stop and read this story?"

Reporter: "Well, the Maestro Concept has been talked about in English, Spanish, Portuguese, Hebrew, French, Japanese, Korean, Dutch, Polish, Turkish and Danish. The creator of the concept has tracked its use to 48 states and Washington, D.C., in the United States and to 12 other countries."

Maestro: "I think we've got something here. What might you see as the headline for your story?"

Reporter: "A headline? That's a copy editor's job. Isn't it a little early for that? After all, I haven't done all my reporting and I haven't even begun writing yet."

Maestro: "Well, your 30-words-or-less summary is really just the first draft of a headline. How about, "Maestro Concept changes newspapers here and abroad"?

Reporter: "That says it, but how about something like, 'Maestros have newsrooms singing a different tune'?"

Maestro: "I love it. Let's hold that thought for a copy editor to fine-tune. Now what about your lead? How might you start the story?"

Reporter: "Well, I really haven't thought about it yet."

Maestro: "Don't forget what you found most interesting. Can you see playing off the different languages some way?"

Reporter: "Maybe so. Something like:

'Concepto de Maestro.

'O Conceito de Maestro.

'No matter how you pronounce it—in English or in 10 other languages— the Maestro Concept has changed the way newspaper editors think and talk about story planning and newsroom organization here and abroad.' "

Maestro: "A good start. Keep working on it. I like the way you turned your 30-word summary into a nut graph. Now don't waste your answer to my question about what was most interesting. Listing the different languages and hitting the U.S. impact were strong stuff. You can work those into your next two sentences, and you'll have a very strong lead."

The maestro is almost ready to call a maestro session. She and the reporter successfully completed the first part of the "pre-maestro check": a 30-word summary, a preliminary headline and an early lead. Next, they will isolate readers' top questions about the story.

Maestro: "What questions do you think would immediately come to a reader's mind about the Maestro Concept?"

Reporter: "First, what is it? Then, how does it work? You know, when would you use it—or not use it? How many and what people are needed? Who oversees it all?

"What are the results?

"Where did the idea come from? Who created it and why?"

Maestro: "Sounds good. How much more reporting time will you need to answer those questions and any others?"

Reporter: "Another few days. I talked to the creator of the concept, and he sent me some materials and told me how to get other things, such as videotapes and reports from the American Society of Newspaper Editors."

Maestro: "Have you interviewed him yet?"

Reporter: "No, I wanted to do this background work first."

Maestro: "Good. Let's try to line up a photographer to go with you for the interview. Now let's picture the story on a page. We need a strong visual to stop readers. Any ideas?"

Reporter: "Can we get an artist to do an illustration?"

Maestro: "I'll see what I can do. I think we're ready for a maestro session."

Let's step back from this scene for a moment and debrief. Notice how the maestro nudges the reporter toward efficiency and makes sure he sees the big picture of how the story may end up on the page. It is a lesson in interdependence for many a reporter who prefers to be a lone wolf. Also notice how the maestro leads through questioning. The traditional assignment editor is more accustomed to telling reporters what to do than asking them questions.

Managing Time

In the maestro process, readers' questions serve several purposes: First, they represent a checklist for additional reporting. Second, they create a framework for photo and illustration requests, page design and display type, such as headlines, captions, graphics headers and labels. Third, they provide the basis for a critique of the finished package. In a few minutes, the maestro and the reporter have focused the story, set the stage for other journalists' work, provided a framework for presenting the story on a page and created the basis on which the success of the story package will be judged after publication. This is what effective time management is all about.

Fundamentally, the Maestro Concept is a time-management technique designed to maximize the amount of time for quality for everyone involved in a story: reporter, assignment editor, copy editor, photographer, designer and graphics artist. Remember what happened when the reporter requested more time for reporting the story? The maestro realized that this was a critical juncture in managing time for quality. A few things could have been true at that point:

- The reporter, in fact, needed more time for reporting, and trying to plan the story's presentation would have been a waste of time because no one was quite sure what the story was about yet.
- The reporter had done so much reporting that he had lost perspective.
- The reporter had done enough preliminary reporting to understand the essence of the story, though there may have been loose ends left to tie up.

The last possibility turned out to be true. How did the maestro determine that? She applied a simple three-part test: See if the reporter can (1) summarize the story in 30 words or less, (2) draft a headline with confidence and (3) sketch out an acceptable lead for the story.

If a maestro can work comfortably with a reporter to do these three things, without forcing the story or operating with contingencies, then enough preliminary reporting probably has been completed. The focus on preliminary reporting is important on two counts: First, the reporter has not started writing and has more time to do all the reporting necessary. Second, the sooner a copy editor, a photographer, a designer, a graphics artist—anyone else who will be involved in the story—can begin thinking about the story's presentation on a page, the more time they will have to do quality work.

If the essence of a story can be summarized before it is written, then these other journalists can begin their work while the reporter finishes reporting and begins writing. For a photographer, the essence gives a focal point in planning a shoot. For a copy editor, writing a headline is all about reflecting the essence of the story. With the summary of a story, a designer can begin thinking how a story might be segmented for ease of reading and understanding, and a graphics artist might be employed to turn one of those segments into a chart or graph. Without the intervention of the maestro, the reporter would have spent more time on reporting at the expense of quality thinking time for his partners in this story package.

Maestros create more time for quality by managing the preliminary reporting stage. The maestro monitors the progress of the reporting until both the maestro and the reporter feel confident that a good story is in hand, though maybe not fully developed. The maestro then can launch others involved in the storytelling on their parallel tracks creating more time for them to do quality work. In this way, the Maestro Concept is a balancing act of time and talent.

Preventing Blowups

The difference between a story idea and a story is vast. A reporter commonly will begin researching a story idea and realize that the best story is quite different from the original idea. That is why maestro sessions are convened not around story ideas but reported stories. Occasionally a story idea will lead to what the reporter believes is a good story, only to see that story change after further reporting. In maestroing jargon, the expression is that the story "blew up" after a maestro session. This will inevitably happen as new maestros get a feel for balancing when it is time to plan and when it is time to continue the reporting. Let's take a closer look at the maestro's three-part test. To ensure that stories do not blow up on them, maestros use these three techniques to understand—and to help reporters understand—when sufficient preliminary reporting has been done.

The 30-word Test

The first technique is the 30-word test. If a reporter responds to this challenge with a question, such as "What is the Maestro Concept and how does it work?" then the maestro should send the reporter back for more reporting. As we will see, the role for questions like this come later in the maestro process. If all the reporter can do in a 30-word summary is form a question about a story, then he or she is still at the story-idea stage. Talking about headlines or leads would be a waste of time.

Preliminary reporting can range from minutes on a telephone to months of investigation. The amount of time depends on the reporter's skill and the story's complexity. Not all reporters and not all stories are equally deep; the good maestro understands and manages those variables.

The first paper to adopt the Maestro Concept was the *Pharos-Tribune*, a 15,000-circulation newspaper in Logansport, Ind. In a year and a half of daily maestro sessions, the paper was transformed. It won double the awards it had ever won before. The first attempt at a maestro session there, however, was never completed; it lasted 30 minutes until the reporter left crying. This is all more difficult than it looks.

Two examples from the early days in Logansport were useful to the staff in helping everyone understand how preliminary reporting and time management fit with the Maestro Concept. The first involved a reporter interested in doing a story about the effect of a drought on milk prices. She called for a maestro session, but when she was asked to summarize the story in 30 words or less, she replied, "What is the effect of the drought on milk prices?" The maestro wisely directed her back to reporting, knowing that it may take her days to get to the point where her answer would be something more like: "The drought is expected to add 10 cents to a gallon of milk for Logansport residents." On another story, the reporter spent two minutes on the phone doing preliminary reporting and was ready for a maestro session. She told the maestro, who at this paper was the managing editor, that she had just gotten off the phone with the county's economic development director. He told her that he was resigning and that he would make his announcement the next day. The reporter called for a maestro session, and the maestro asked her to summarize the story in 30 words or less. This time she was able to reply something along the lines of, "The county's economic development director, who has been responsible for attracting new jobs to the community over his four years, is resigning to take a better job in Indianapolis." This time, the timing was right to begin thinking about a maestro session. In contrast with the drought-milk story, this was simple. The reporter's courtesy to the source over the years was returned by his courtesy call. The story's nature and the reporter's skill collapsed the time in the maestro process between story idea and maestro session.

In the first year of the Logansport Project, in which one to three maestro sessions might have occurred daily, the editor estimated that only three or four stories blew up after maestro sessions. In each case, not enough preliminary reporting had been done. Although the blowups were learning experiences, they felt more like wasted time and frustration. To avoid this, maestros must be adept at administering the 30-word test.

The Headline Test

A second technique that maestros use to assess whether there has been sufficient preliminary reporting is the headline test. Asking traditionally trained reporters to think of writing headlines, let alone consider a headline before a story is written, is a real stretch. Yet it is an important check to see how confident writers are about their reporting and an excellent way to focus stories. If writers feel uncomfortable about headline ideas because they have not done enough reporting, maestros send them back to the streets or the phones. If, as in our case, the reporter is at first reluctant to think of a headline but then joins in the fun, it is a good sign that we have the essence of a story, one that is very unlikely to blow up through more reporting. This is a key point that spells the difference between wasting time and effective story planning that allows time for quality for all involved.

The Lead Test

A third technique is the lead test. Like the headline test, the request for a lead idea forces the reporter to focus on the story's essence and inherent interest to readers. That focus will help with follow-up reporting and with getting others involved early in the process. In our case, the maestro asks about the lead by playing off an earlier question regarding what the reporter finds most interesting about the story. The answer to this question may find a home on the page in several possible ways: part of the headline or subhead, a pull-quote or display type summary, a caption, a sidebar story, or the lead. A decision about which device to use will be made in the context of other decisions.

The pre-maestro check combines techniques that good assignment editors have used for years into a simple method for coaching writers. The difference between a technique and a method is consistency. Following the maestro method has led to consistent quality. Maestro-style coaching of writers, especially ones steeped in tradition, is not always easy.

3. HURDLING TRADITION

Introducing the Maestro Concept involves redesigning mind-sets, not publications, though when minds change so will the look and feel of the publication. In our example, we were dealing with a traditionally trained reporter who had been instilled with notions such as these:

- You need to do all your reporting before you can begin thinking about writing.
- You write the story, then talk with your assignment editor about leads.
- Copy editors write headlines, not reporters.

These notions make sense in an assembly-line approach to publication production: A writer builds the chassis by reporting and writing a story, then the story gets passed down to an editor who edits it and makes a photo assignment, then the story gets laid out on a page and a headline is written, and so on. This method often works for many stories published in newspapers, magazines, newsletters and other publications, whether they be in high schools and colleges, in small towns or in major cities. When this same approach is applied to high-profile stories, such as cover stories for magazines or front-page or section-front stories for newspapers, the results often can be disappointing. These major stories usually have multiple elements, such as photos or illustrations and sidebar stories or graphics, and demand special design presentations. The traditional assembly-line approach provides time for quality reporting and writing, but relatively little time for quality copy editing, photography, design or graphics. This can be as true for front-page breaking news stories as for months-long special projects.

Effective time management and teamwork are two important keys to quality. Traditional approaches to story planning reinforce an assembly-line mentality that works against having time for quality in all areas and keeps people and departments working in isolation. The Maestro Concept challenges these traditional approaches and asks journalists to think about how they might be more successful and have more fun if they go about their work in new ways.

Making the Best Decisions

A hallmark of the Maestro Concept is putting decision making in the hands of those with the most expertise. Typically, the reporter has the most expertise about what a story is and is not, and in those cases the reporter sits in the driver's seat as the maestro process moves along. Typically, copy editors with a flair for words are the best ones to be writing headlines and captions. Typically, photojournalists will have the best sense of how to tell a story visually, whether a compelling photograph or an illustration will make a larger impact. Typically, a designer is the best judge of what typography depicts a story's mood or how a story might be best segmented to attract readers.

Part of the magic of a maestro session, however, is seeing a reporter come up with the best headline idea, or a designer identify a key reader question that everyone else missed, or a photographer come up with a source that the reporter did not know existed, or a copy editor suggest a great photo or illustration idea. This is the advantage of teamwork.

The typical newspaper newsroom has these key players working different shifts in different places. Their schedules have far more to do with the assembly-line production system than teamwork and face-to-face communication. On the assembly line, reporters typically work during the day when their sources are readily available, and copy editors and news-page designers typically work nights. That makes sense if newsroom leaders believe editing and page design cannot possibly begin until all stories are reported and written. Meanwhile, the precious few photographers are scattered across day and night, and, of course, on the street rather than in the building. This approach to newsroom organization and staffing, which makes experimenting with the Maestro Concept difficult, may make sense for the vast majority of stories published in a newspaper. But for the high-profile stories that would benefit from maestro sessions, a new approach becomes necessary.

Setting Meeting Schedules

Newspapers that regularly use the Maestro Concept have set regular times for maestro sessions, such as 10:30 a.m., 1:30 p.m. and 5:30 p.m. for a morning paper, and have created a space for the sessions to take place. This makes it easier for maestros to book reporters, assignment editors (when they are not maestros), photographers, copy editors, designers and others for maestro sessions. These sessions may occur on the same day a story package is published or weeks before a publication date, depending on the nature of the story. The smaller the newsroom and the more accustomed staff members are to teamwork, the easier it is to adopt the Maestro Concept. The high school newspaper is often a comfortable setting for the concept. College newspapers, whose editors are intent on mimicking the pros, generally run into more difficulties than their high school counterparts.

Before and after a maestro session, a maestro increases communication by navigating around walls set up in newsrooms that separate all the players involved in a story package. Maestros take good notes and lots of them; otherwise good ideas disappear, fall through cracks or get misconstrued through word of mouth. The maestros then share those notes with others who will be involved with the story.

The Copy Editor's Role

Some editors have expressed concern that the traditional detachment of copy editors, acting as surrogate readers, is lost through the maestro process. They see an advantage in copy editors seeing stories cold. The major difference between copy editors reading stories after they have been written and contributing in maestro sessions is that their questions and concerns are more likely to be addressed because of the maestro session. When copy editors read stories on deadline, many times the reporter and assignment editor are not available to deal with those questions. In the maestro session, the copy editor is face to face with the reporter and the assignment editor in a collaborative setting. In the traditional newsroom, when the copy editor is face to face with the reporter or the assignment editor, it is often because there is a problem with a story. Most often, they are not working together, and this detachment tends to lead to the most common mistake copy editors make: changing something that is unclear in a story to make the story clearly wrong.

With the maestro process, picturing a story's presentation on a page begins early, as does discussion of possible sidebars. Reporters know as early as possible about whether they are writing one story; or one story, plus one or two sidebars; or one story and one sidebar, plus information for a graphic. This saves a copy editor's time, especially if the person is expected to break one long story into these same parts.

Finding the Best Team

The maestro tries to take the story as far as possible in the pre-maestro check, then looks to assemble the best team—or the best team available—with particular editing, photojournalism, design and graphics expertise tailored to the nature of the story. Whether they be reporters, copy editors, photographers, designers or graphics artists, each staff member has strengths and weaknesses, preferences and dislikes, booked or open schedules. This team building is great for quality story presentation and fun for staff members, but because it is so foreign to the traditional newspaper newsroom operation, it takes diplomatic skill to be a maestro.

4. MAESTRO SESSION IN ACTION

To illustrate a maestro session, let's turn to one of the early examples at the afternoon newspaper in Logansport, Ind. At a small paper like this one, the managing editor, assignment editor and maestro are the same person. A maestro typically has the authority to make decisions on story placement, space, use of color and other such practical considerations. In other words, decisions made in a maestro session are not overruled by higher authorities. Either those senior editors participate or they delegate their authority to the maestro or another maestro session participant. In some cases, senior decision makers prefer to sit back and allow designers or photo editors to talk the team through the maestro session. They are there, however, to deal with big questions: Will this be a front-page Sunday paper centerpiece? Can we get color positions on the press for photos or illustrations? Can we have a "double-truck" (two-page) treatment inside the paper? Maestro sessions would be exercises in frustration and waste without having someone with this kind of authority involved.

Another safeguard is that only the best and most important stories are maestroed. Their high-profile nature makes it unlikely that other events bump or crunch them on a page. Reality being what it is, maestroed packages have been moved down newspaper front pages or section covers to accommodate big, late-breaking stories. If possible, they sometimes have been held a day to ensure proper play. Such is life in an unpredictable news business. Whereas some editors throw up their hands and feel planning is a waste of time, maestros realize that by putting a premium on planning, it is far easier not only to deal with surprises but also to improve quality.

In this example, a reporter on the education beat has heard about plans for a world-class music director from Indiana University to come to a local high school to work with choral students. The event will occur this afternoon and the story is scheduled for tomorrow's front page. The reporter has done preliminary reporting, and the maestro has completed the pre-maestro check. She decides it is time to convene a photographer and a copy editor/page designer for a maestro session with her and the reporter. To make the Maestro Concept routine, she holds regular maestro sessions after the main edition has closed in the late morning but before lunch.

The four journalists gather around a table next to the managing editor's desk (fig. 8.1). Here is a re-creation of the maestro session dialogue and actions. The maestro gets down to business quickly.

Maestro to reporter: "What's the story's slug?"

Reporter: "SING."

The maestro writes the word in the upper-left-hand corner of the "Pharos-Tribune Story Plan," a form used in maestro sessions for story planning and later for critique sessions to assess whether the team has accomplished what it set out to do (fig. 8.2).

Maestro to team: "The story is being planned to run tomorrow on the front page."

The maestro writes "Thursday" on the line for "Projected Run Date" and fills in the names of the writer, Nancy; the photographer, Andy; and the copy editor/designer, Royce.

Royce's name is listed on the line marked "Display," referring to a "display editor," a new job title suggested in the first article written about the Maestro Concept, entitled, "Goodbye, Copy Desk; Hello, Display Desk." The article called for dividing traditional copy desks so that some copy editors would work closely with reporters on "source desks" and focus on text while other copy editors would work on "display desks," where they would focus on layout and design, headlines, captions and production. Today at some newspapers, copy editors have been assigned to reporting or topic teams in keeping with the source desk idea, and others have joined a presentation team or desk in keeping with the display desk notion. See Chapter 12 for more on this team approach.

Fig. 8.1

Maestro sessions were held routinely around a table next to the managing editor's desk at the Logansport (Ind.) *Pharos-Tribune*. Maestro Diane Robinson (left) worked with the same designer but a different reporter and photographer on the SING story. (Photo by Tony Kelly)

Pharos-Tribune Story Plan

Fig. 8.2

The "Pharos-Tribune Story Plan" was a form used in maestro sessions for story planning and later for critique sessions. This is for the story slugged SING.

Story Slug _SING_   Projected Run Date _Thursday_

Special Deadlines _____

Story Idea _director of Singing Hoosiers critiques local choirs_

Writer _Nancy_   Display _Rose_   Photographer _Andy_

I. Reader's Viewpoint

Think Like A Reader

1. Questions readers would like to have answered:

1. Why is he here?

A 2. Does he do this a lot?

3. What suggestions does he offer?

B

4. What did the kids think?

C

5. Who's paying?

D

2. What is the single most important thing about the story? _the cooperative effort to get this organized_

3. What else do we need to find out? _____

II. Picture It On The Page

(Use back of form to sketch presentation with answers to reader's questions using high visibility points and graphic devices)

Communication Devices
❶ Q&A Box ....☐
❷ Sidebar Box ....☐
❸ Pull Quotes ....☐
❹ Lists ....☐
❺ Maps ....☐
❻ Graphics ....☐

III. Photo, Graphics, Writing

Writing Request	Photo Request	Graphics Requests
Proposed head _Noteworthy Suggestions_	1 _____	
Proposed subhead _Choir gets Crash course in professionalism_	2 _____	1 _____
Lead/Text/Sidebar _____	3 _____	
_____	4 _____	2 _____
Other _____	5. _____	

Reader Action: _____

Thinking Like a Reader

Maestro to reporter: "OK, can you summarize the story in 30 words or less?"

Reporter: "Yes, the director of the Singing Hoosiers at Indiana University will critique local high school choirs and offer advice on how to improve."

Under "Story Idea" on the maestro planning form, the maestro writes, "director of Singing Hoosiers critiques local choirs." These preliminary steps help the copy editor/designer and photographer get up to speed quickly on a story they are hearing about for the first time. The maestro and the reporter already have discussed it.

> Maestro to team: "What questions would immediately come to a reader's mind about this story?"

> Reporter: "Why is he here?"

> Copy editor/designer: "Does he do this a lot?"

> Reporter: "What suggestions does he offer?"

> Photographer: "What did the kids think?"

> Maestro: "Who's paying for all this?"

The maestro lists these questions on the story planning form. They serve as a double-check for the reporter who has time to get any unanswered questions answered. The questions will define how the story package will be designed and what content will be covered in photos, headlines, captions and other display type. The questions also will help determine how the lead of the story will be written. If you ask writers and editors if they focus on readers' questions in developing stories, they will likely answer, "Of course." If you asked them how they arrive at those questions and how they then focus on those questions, the response will be less definite.

The Maestro Concept provides a systematic way of doing what most reporters will tell you they are doing anyway. The reality is that because many reporters will rely on themselves to generate questions to be answered in a story, they inevitably will forget one or two and have to go back to sources after having their story read by their assignment editors. The maestro process helps to eliminate this rework. Also, the team approach takes some pressure off the reporter and usually provides a richer collection of questions to round out a story. At the same time, the traditional approach keeps these questions clear to the reporter and the assignment editor but unclear or unstated to the copy editor, photographer and others involved in making the story succeed on a page.

The maestro session provides a way those questions can be answered quickly for readers by having them addressed not only in the lead of the story but also in photos, headlines, captions, information graphics and other display elements. The concept frees the writer from relying on "inverted pyramid," or summary, leads and provides the license to start the story at any interesting point. By working as a team member on the story's presentation, the writer can act confidently knowing that the traditional answers to the who, what, when, where, why and how questions have been handled in headlines, subheads or summary dropouts; photos and captions; information graphics; or other elements on the page. By listing the key questions to be answered by a story, the maestro also has created a short checklist for a critique of the story package after publication.

Fig. 8.3

On the back of the story plan, the copy editor/ designer has sketched possible layouts. The goal is to provide high-visibility places on the page to answer key readers' questions.

Maestro to reporter: "I'm a busy reader; why should I care about this story? What would make me stop and read the story?"

Reporter: "The cooperative efforts by four high schools to get this organized— that's what's most impressive to me."

Photographer: "A lot of high school students will be involved in this, and their parents and grandparents are our readers."

Copy editor/designer: "We're dealing with a world-class music director here. Indiana University's music school has a tremendous reputation."

The maestro agrees on all counts and makes a short notation on the story planning form under the line, "What is the single most important thing about the story?"

Seeing It on the Page

Meanwhile, the copy editor/designer has been sketching possible layouts on the back of the form (fig. 8.3). The goal here is to provide high-visibility places on the page to answer the key readers' questions. The maestro asks the copy editor/designer to show everyone his ideas.

Notice that the first sketch, the one to the left, offers a traditional treatment of a dominant overview photo, a secondary close-up photo, and a headline over the text. An arrow is drawn from that sketch to one on the right, which offers more design avenues to answer the questions. Compare the readers' questions with the layout:

Questions No. 1 and 2: "Why is he here?" and "Does he do this a lot?"

Layout connection: Do you see four small photos sketched across the top of the dominant photo? The one in the upper-left is marked with a line and "The guy" written above it. To the right of the photo are lines representing space for a quote from the music director that answers these first two questions. The designer's sketch links the work of reporter and photographer: It directs the reporter to ask these questions for what everyone hopes will be a good quote, and it acts as a photo request for the photographer.

Question No. 3: "What suggestions does he offer?"

Layout connection: The writer will choose to answer this question at the top of her story. Here is her lead:

"Never let an audience see you thinking."

"Don't ever say, 'Aw, shucks.' That tells the world you made a mistake. We call it the darn-it syndrome. You make a mistake and say, 'Darn it,' and then you've made two."

"Pick a person in the audience and sing to that person."

The speaker is Robert Stoll of Indiana University, director of the renowned Singing Hoosiers. And he is giving mini-lessons in stage presence to members of the swing choirs from Cass County's four high schools.

Question No. 4: "What did the kids think?"

Layout connection: To the right of "the guy's" picture are sketches of three photos of high school students and spaces for their comments. This time the layout prompts the photographer to say to the reporter, "I will be on the lookout for students with great expressions, and then I will take them aside for you to interview." This exchange exemplifies how the maestro session integrates the work of reporters, photographers and designers, so that text, photos and design can work together on a page to help readers understand at a glance the key elements of a story.

Question No. 5: "Who's paying?"

Layout connection: This information could be added to the caption for either the dominant overview photo or the secondary close-up photo. The layout sketch includes a box to highlight information at the top of the second column of type under the headline and next to the secondary photo. The answer to question no. 5 could fit easily there as well. The maestro session now turns to display type.

Maestro to team: "What are we thinking for headlines?"

Reporter: "Noteworthy suggestions."

Maestro: "I like it. What about a subhead?"

Copy editor/designer: "How about, "Choir gets crash course in professionalism."

Maestro: "Good. That's it."

Getting to Work

The maestro session ends as quickly as it began. For this simple story a maestro session should last no more than 10 minutes. The reporter and photographer compare notes on whether they will travel separately or together this afternoon for the event. The copy editor/designer begins thinking about how his sketches will translate to an electronic page template. The maestro/assignment editor will be first to edit the story once it is written, and the copy editor/designer will edit it next, fine-tune the headline, write the captions, lay out the photos and paginate the page on a computer production system. If all goes well when the package is published, readers will see the essence of the story and its value immediately. Their questions will be answered at a glance, and they will be enticed to read the entire story. Figures 8.4 and 8.5 show the final product.

5. CONSTRUCTIVE CRITIQUES

To help train the newsroom staff to work quickly and efficiently as a team, the maestro routinely does brief "audits" of maestroed packages, comparing the story planning form with the published package in the paper. In these constructive critique sessions, the maestro solicits ideas from maestro session participants about how the process could be improved next time. The focus is on continuous improvement of newsroom processes to increase the newspaper's quality over time.

The next day the "Sing" team is reconvened for a quick critique of the package. As you can see in figures 8.4 and 8.5, the layout drawn in the maestro session was only a sketch. Just as a reporter writes a lead and then rewrites it to focus a story or to provide more punch, the designer in the maestro session is creating the first draft of the overall presentation of the story package. As circumstances change and reality sets in, the layout is fine-tuned. Anytime something is changed, everyone hopes it is for the better.

The critique of this package starts on a positive note: strong photos, an improved subhead (Indiana University choral director critiques county choirs) and risk taking with the lead. In discussing the photos, the critique leader notes there is no portrait of "the guy." The photographer suggests that the secondary close-up photo of the choral director provides a sufficient portrait.

The Acid Test

Now comes the heart of the critique, revisiting each reader question and identifying where it was answered. The goal is to answer the questions in the "high-visibility" spots on a page: in the photos, headlines, captions and display type quotes from the students. The five readers' questions create a "reader-friendliness index." If all five questions are answered in high-visibility posi-

235

tions, the story package receives the highest rating on the index. Let's see how the team scored.

Question No. 1: "Why is he here?"

The revised subhead and captions answer this one.

Question No. 2: "Does he do this a lot?"

There is no answer to this question in the photos, headlines, captions and display type quotes from the students. The critique turns to this consideration: Was this a big mistake in presentation, or upon reflection did this question not hold up as an important one for readers? Conclusion: This was a mistake, a missed opportunity that the team hopes not to have happen again.

Question No. 3: "What suggestions did he offer?"

The lead begins to answer this question.

Question No. 4: "What did the kids think?"

The two display type quotes from students begin to answer this question.

Question No. 5: "Who's paying?"

Like question no. 2, this one isn't answered in any high-visibility spot on the page—another missed opportunity. As a side note, neither question no. 2 nor no. 5 is answered anywhere in the front-page text. The Maestro Concept critique draws a distinction between answering questions in text and answering them in the high-visibility points on a page. The attempt is to align what is considered top-priority reader questions with the "tops" of the page. Even if the two questions had been answered in the fifth paragraph of the story, that would have

Fig. 8.4

This page uses the finished SING story as its centerpiece. (Courtesy of the *Logansport Pharos-Tribune*/ reprinted by permission)

been viewed as a mistake. The questions are hooks to pull in readers, and these hooks need to be set where readers are likely to look first. If they do not get hooked by the photos, headlines, captions and other display type, they are unlikely to make it to the first paragraph of the text, let alone the fifth.

The critique tally: The team set out to answer five top reader questions on the tops of the page and ended up answering only three, a 60 percent efficiency rate. With a little more attention to reporting details and sharper caption writing, the team could have easily gone five-for-five on the reader-friendliness index. The value of this style of critiquing is threefold:

- The approach shifts the emphasis away from personal opinions and finger pointing toward a team evaluation of how well everyone accomplished what they set out to do. "I don't like this," is replaced by, "We had a good idea here and didn't follow through. Why? What can we do next time to keep it from happening again?"
- The story-planning form allows for a quick, objective review. Everything important is written down, so there is little head-scratching or, worse, second guessing that tends to limit the value of traditional critiques.
- It is easy to keep score and plot different teams' effectiveness in meeting goals the team members set for themselves. The goal is continuous improvement, whether that be in identifying readers' questions or in answering them through page design and writing approaches.

The Challenge of Measurement

How effective are journalists at meeting the needs of readers for information most important to them? Many newspaper critique leaders may think they have the answer, and their loud voices and bold statements give them an aura of confidence. The complexity of trying to measure this effectiveness, however, can be overwhelming. Are circulation figures a good gauge? Certainly rising or falling circulation numbers get plenty of attention, but much of that variance may have more to do with time to read, population trends, pricing, availability and on-time household delivery than the paper's content. One of the most common questions about the Maestro Concept, usually asked by publishers, is whether it increases a newspaper's circulation. The answer is some newspapers have adopted the concept and their circulation has risen. But who can say for sure that those increases were related to the concept? Anyone who has been involved in reader research knows its limitations.

The Maestro Concept takes a different tack in evaluating a journalist's effectiveness at meeting the needs of readers for information most important to them. The concept respects the ability of journalists, especially those working in groups, to accurately list the questions that might be first in the mind of a typical reader, or at least one most likely to be interested in a particular story. Once that short list is generated, it provides the framework for the reporting, writing, editing, photojournalism, design and graphics involved in telling the story. Just as important, it provides the framework for a constructive critique of the finished story package that includes easily measured indicators.

The Maestro Concept has been called common sense. Yet putting common sense into common practice is difficult and complex. Both your staff members and your readers can win with the Maestro Concept. If you would like to try it at your publication, good luck and let us know how it works.

MAESTRO CONCEPT Q & A

1. What is it?

The Maestro Concept is not listed in the dictionary. If it were, the entry would look something like this:

> **Maestro Concept** (n.)—1. A time-management technique designed to provide the maximum time for quality work to everyone—reporters, assignment editors, photographers, copy editors, designers, artists, researchers—involved with a story package.
>
> 2. A project-based, teamwork-intensive approach to storytelling that requires a rethinking of who does what when in a newsroom.
>
> 3. A new approach to newsroom management, organization and operation that applies W. Edwards Deming's management principles used in manufacturing to the creative process.
>
> 4. A story-planning process that brings together all the principal participants in a story package as early as possible to picture how the story will be presented to answer readers' most pressing questions quickly.
>
> 5. A method designed to help make staff members more efficient, to make their jobs more enjoyable and to improve the overall quality of their publication for readers.
>
> **maestro** (n.)—A senior editor, section editor or facilitator who orchestrates the creative energy and talents in a newsroom or a publication office, who leads a maestro session and who handles the follow-up critique, or "audit."
>
> **maestro session** (n.)—1. A 10- to 15-minute work session for the key players involved in a story package to focus the story, to clarify its relevance to readers and to ensure that questions on the top of a reader's mind are answered quickly on the page. 2. A story-planning session that occurs after preliminary reporting but before writing. It involves drafting headlines, making photo or illustration assignments, sketching layouts, judging story lengths and setting deadlines for copy.

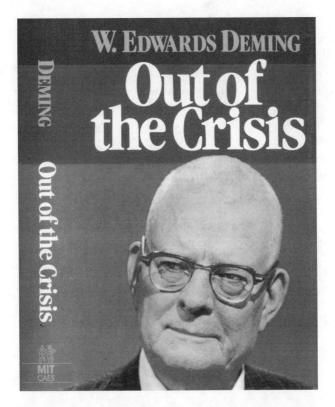

Fig. 8.6

The theories and philosophies of W. Edwards Deming, father of the quality movement, provide a framework for understanding the success of the Maestro Concept. (Courtesy of MIT Press/ reprinted by permission)

pre-maestro check (n.)—1. A coaching process in which a maestro checks if a reporter has done sufficient preliminary reporting. The maestro finds out if the reporter can summarize the story in 30 words or less and can draft a headline and lead. The maestro also asks the reporter to list key reader questions.

2. What are the results?

Early Adopters

The first newspaper to formally adopt the Maestro Concept, in 1991, was the *Pharos-Tribune,* a 15,000-circulation daily newspaper in Logansport, Ind., with 15 members in the newsroom. The managing editor served as maestro for news, features, business and special issues. The sports editor was the paper's other maestro. In the first year and a half after adopting the Maestro Concept, every staff member and two former staff members won awards from the state Associated Press or the state press association. That was double what the paper had ever won before. A few years later, similar results were achieved at another 15,000-circulation paper, the *News-Enterprise,* in Elizabethtown, Ky. A year after adopting the concept, staff members won 11 of 16 awards in the Landmark Community Newspapers annual competition.

3. How does it work?

Theoretical Underpinning

The theories and philosophies of W. Edwards Deming (fig. 8.6), father of the quality movement, provide a framework for understanding the success of the Maestro Concept. Deming's principles, such as to eliminate rework, create opportunities for teamwork, build in quality at the beginning rather than rely on inspection at the end, apply to the creative environment of newsrooms, though they were designed for the manufacturing setting.

A variation of the "Sing" story in Logansport, Ind., has been presented as a challenge in Maestro Concept workshops for professional journalists from Portland, Ore., to Madrid; from Copenhagen to Curitiba, Brazil; from San Jose, Calif., to Kobe, Japan. Their papers ranged from small weeklies to metropolitan dailies. The same exercise has been put to the test by dozens of high school journalism students and teachers gathered at conventions in Chicago and Kansas City, Mo., and by college journalism students in Evanston, Ill., and Lexington, Ky.

Regardless of age, experience, size or circulation, or language and cultural differences, essentially the same five reader questions tend to be raised in mock maestro sessions. The maestro method has hit on an important commonality in how journalists and journalism students think like readers. The difference in these mock maestro sessions tends to lie in individualized maestro forms and design ideas.

Question Connections

If a similar version of the "Sing" story had been maestroed at the *Oregonian*, the story planning form might look like figure 8.7.

Fig. 8.7

The *Oregonian* in Portland uses this expanded maestro form designed by Tim Harrower. Here's how the SING story form might look at that paper.

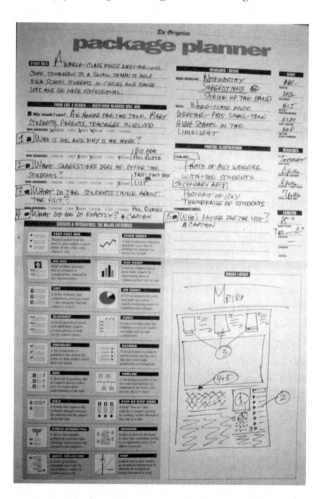

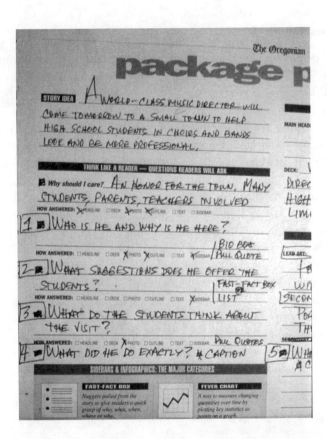

Notice how the original Logansport form has been adapted for answering readers' questions (fig. 8.8). After a story summary, the maestro asks for the most important or, if different, most interesting angle ("Why should I care?"). To ensure a connection between a key reader question and a high-visibility spot on the page, the form has boxes to check indicating where the question will be answered. The choices are headline; deck, or subhead; photo; cutline, or caption; text, meaning the lead; and sidebar, examples of which are included elsewhere on the form. Credit for this creative adaptation of the Logansport form goes to Tim Harrower, author of *The Newspaper Designer's Handbook*.

Down to Details

The upper-right quadrant (fig. 8.9) creates space to focus the story with headline suggestions and to outline what traditionally would be requests to the photo desk. Spaces for staggered deadlines and story lengths breathe clarity and reality into maestro sessions. Notice that in the list of staff members involved in a maestro session, the title "editor/head worrier" replaces "maestro." The *Oregonian*'s chief librarian asked that a line for researcher be added.

Graphics Tickler

In traditional story-planning sessions, where thinking visually is not always at a premium, it is easy to forget the many ways storytelling can be done. The *Oregonian*'s package planner provides a constant prompting to think beyond just writing text with its examples of sidebars and infographics (fig. 8.10).

Questions Drive Design

To emphasize the connections between readers' questions and the layout, the number of a question is aligned with where it will be answered on the page (fig. 8.11).

For question no. 1, the answer to "Who is he?" and "Why is he here?" could be in a quote from the music director in display type next to a photo of him that includes a caption. For example, the quote might be, "I graduated from this high school 40 years ago and it's wonderful to be back helping those who helped me get started." The caption would list his name and explain his world-class credentials. A "Bio Box" sidebar might be used instead of the caption.

For question no.2, his suggestions to students could be in a "Fast-Facts Box," "List" or "Step-by-Step Guide" indicating his top recommendations. Perhaps this same information could be turned into a "quiz" sidebar or presented in a "Q & A" format.

For question no. 3, students' reactions could be displayed in small photos of three students with quotations from them, or the photos may have been arrayed with a "Quote Collection" sidebar.

For questions no. 4 and no. 5, information about exactly what he did and who was paying for the event could be explained in the caption for a photo of him working with the students.

Fig. 8.9

The upper-right quadrant creates space to focus the story with headline suggestions and to outline what traditionally would be requests to the photo desk. On this form the title "editor/head worrier" replaces "maestro" in the list of staff team members.

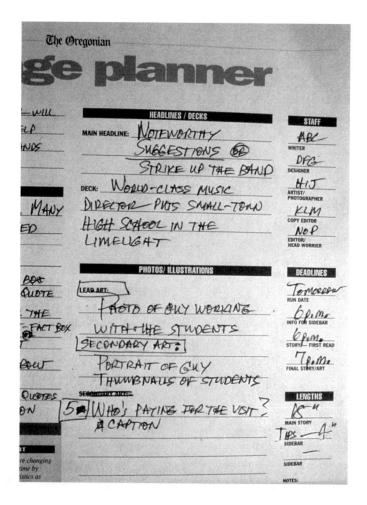

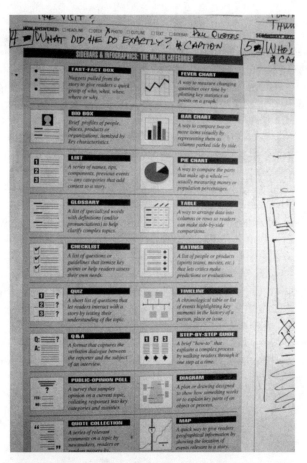

Fig. 8.10

The *Oregonian*'s package planner provides a constant prompting to think beyond just writing text with its examples of sidebars and infographics.

Fig. 8.11

To emphasize the connections between readers' questions and the layout, the number of a question is aligned with where it will be answered on the page.

Evolution of the Form

The maestro planning form has lived many lives. Figure 8.12 presents the first draft of one in the Logansport, Ind., newsroom. It followed a discussion of whether a form was needed at all. The notion of a form seemed too bureaucratic at first, but the advantages of having ideas written down in one place carried the day. The draft also followed a discussion about having an electronic form rather than a paper one. The paper form allowed everyone to take a break from their computers and talk in a more natural face-to-face setting.

Only by using the form did it become clear where more or less space was needed and how questions were best phrased. It took several versions to come up with a workable form (fig. 8.13).

The second daily newspaper to adopt the Maestro Concept was *The News-Leader,* a 60,000-circulation paper in Springfield, Mo., in 1993. Its form (fig. 8.14) derives from the one used in Logansport. Springfield Executive Editor Andy McMills hired Logansport's two maestros to jump-start the project at his paper. Once they were no longer part of a critical mass for innovation, they were pulled back into traditional newsroom roles. When the winds of tradition are strong, the flame of innovation flickers.

One important innovation in the Springfield experiment was tailoring the maestro form to ensure that key elements of the News 2000 program, such

Fig 8.12

The maestro planning form has lived many lives. Here was the first draft of one in the Logansport newsroom.

Pharos-Tribune Routing Plan

Story Slug:_____Run Date____ Photographer_____

Writer: _____ Display Editor:_____

Topic: _____ **Main Display Points**

Most Compelling Part: _____ ❶ _____

Interesting Facts: _____ ❷ _____

Potential Head_____ ❸ _____

Potential Deck_____

Potential Subhead_____ **Photo Possibilities**

❶ _____

Readers' Questions:

❶ _____ ❷ _____

❷ _____ ❸ _____

❸ _____

Communication Devices	Notes
❶ Q&A Box	

How Are Questions Displayed?

❶ _____ | ❷ Sidebar Box |
                               | ❸ Pull Quotes |
❷ _____ | ❹ Lists |
                               | ❺ Maps |
❸ _____ | ❻ Graphics |
                               | ❼ Common Sense |

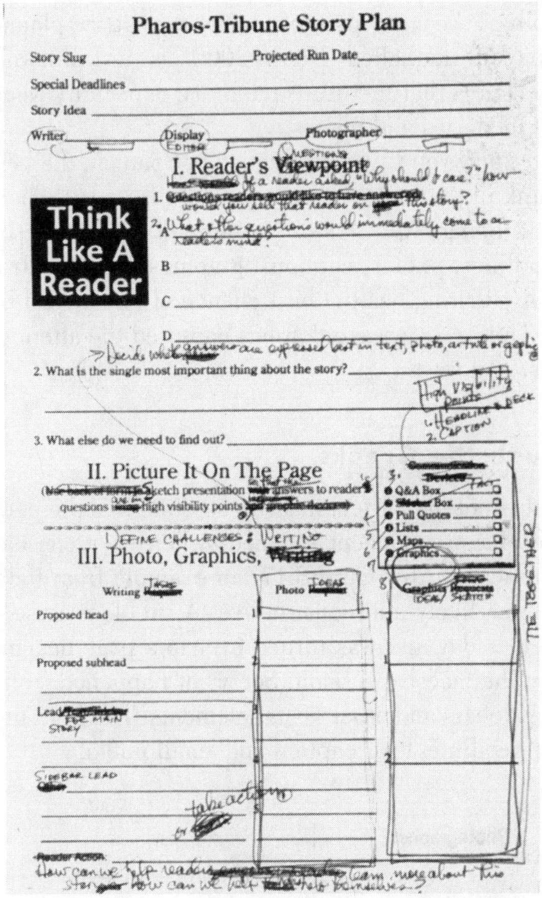

Pharos-Tribune Story Plan

Story Slug _____ Projected Run Date _____

Special Deadlines _____

Story Idea _____

Writer _____ Display Editor _____ Photographer _____

I. Reader's Viewpoint

Think Like A Reader

1. _____
   2. What other questions would immediately come to a reader's mind?

   B. _____
   C. _____
   D. _____

2. What is the single most important thing about the story? _____

3. What else do we need to find out? _____

II. Picture It On The Page

Sketch presentation, answers to reader questions, high visibility points and graphic devices.

Communication Devices
- Q&A Box
- Box
- Pull Quotes
- Lists
- Maps
- Graphics

III. Photo, Graphics, Writing

Writing | Photo | Graphics

Proposed head _____

Proposed subhead _____

Lead _____ FOR MAIN STORY

SIDEBAR LEAD _____

Reader Action _____
How can we help readers...

Fig. 8.13

Only by using the form did it become clear where more or less space was needed and how questions were best phrased. It took several versions to come up with a workable form.

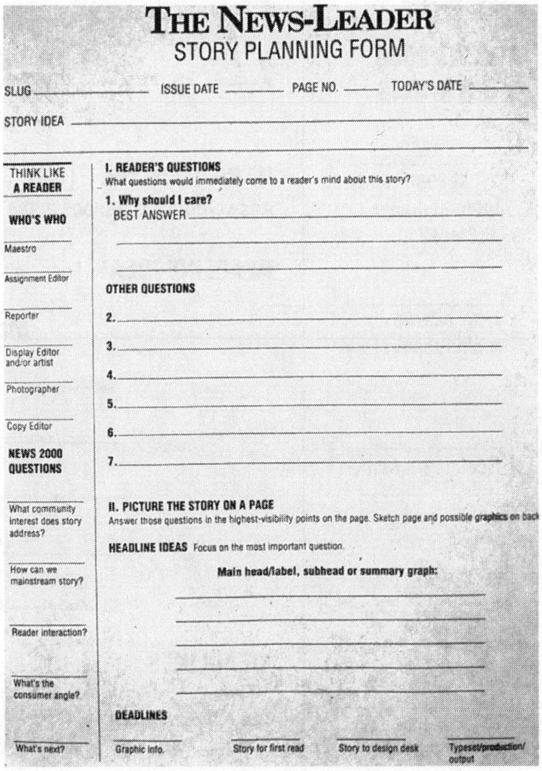

THE NEWS-LEADER
STORY PLANNING FORM

SLUG _____ ISSUE DATE _____ PAGE NO. _____ TODAY'S DATE _____

STORY IDEA _____

THINK LIKE A READER

WHO'S WHO

Maestro

Assignment Editor

Reporter

Display Editor and/or artist

Photographer

Copy Editor

NEWS 2000 QUESTIONS

What community interest does story address?

How can we mainstream story?

Reader interaction?

What's the consumer angle?

What's next?

I. READER'S QUESTIONS
What questions would immediately come to a reader's mind about this story?

1. Why should I care?
BEST ANSWER _____

OTHER QUESTIONS
2. _____
3. _____
4. _____
5. _____
6. _____
7. _____

II. PICTURE THE STORY ON A PAGE
Answer those questions in the highest-visibility points on the page. Sketch page and possible graphics on back.

HEADLINE IDEAS Focus on the most important question.

Main head/label, subhead or summary graph:

_____

DEADLINES

Graphic info. | Story for first read | Story to design desk | Typeset/production/output

Fig. 8.14

The Springfield (Mo.) *News-Leader* hired Logansport's two maestros to jump-start the concept at that paper and to develop this form.

as "mainstreaming," became part of day-to-day story planning (fig. 8.15). Gannett Newspapers launched News 2000 as a framework for change. Mainstreaming ensures that the full community, especially women and minorities, is reflected in stories and photos.

No matter how you say it, in English or Spanish, the key to the Maestro Concept is to think like a reader not a journalist (fig. 8.16). The emphasis is not on writing but on being read. A story is defined not as text but as all that a reader sees: headlines, photos, captions, graphics and text. It takes a team to ensure that quality writing has the best chance of being read by as many people as possible. This is a message that has captured the attention of journalists north, south, east and west.

Falling through the Cracks

The goal is not the perfect maestro session; it is the perfect publication for readers. The Maestro Concept succeeds when everyone can see improvements in the publication. In figure 8.17, an example from the *Oregonian*, the maestro session was lively and constructive. A problem arose, however, when the story was held a day and was turned over to a page designer who had not been involved in the maestro session. See what happened in figure 8.18. Lost are two graphic sidebars and other visual elements. The final product is a mundane package of headline, text, caption and small photo.

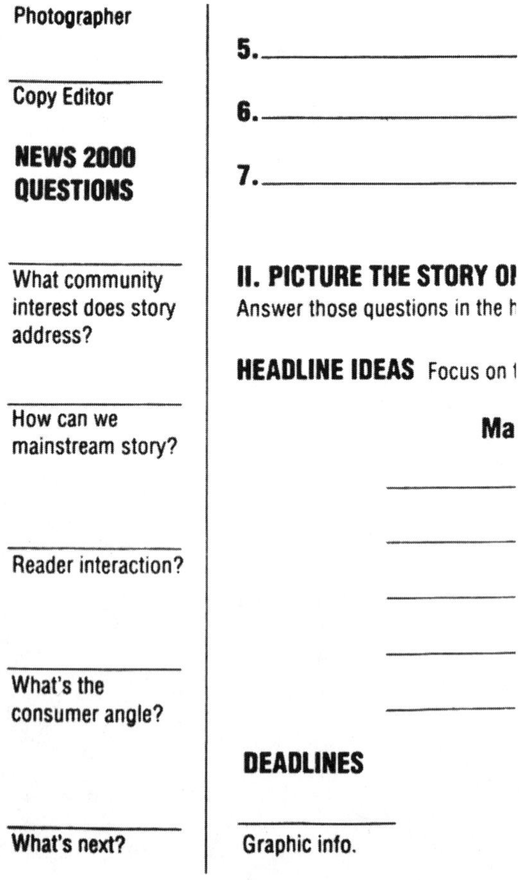

Fig. 8.15

One important innovation in Springfield was tailoring the maestro form to ensure that key elements of Gannett's News 2000 program became part of day-to-day story planning.

Plan del artículo del *Pharos-Tribune*

Palabra guía _____ Fecha prevista de publicación_____

La idea del artículo

_____

Reportero _____

Diseñador _____ Fotógrafo _____

Piensen como un lector

I. Preguntas que puede plantearse el lector

1. ¿Por qué debería yo interesarme en este tema? ¿De qué manera me puede afectar?
2. La respuesta a estas preguntas:

_____

Otras interrogantes que puede tener el lector:

1. _____

Fig. 8.16

The success of the Logansport project inspired journalists in Latin America. In English or Spanish, the key to the Maestro Concept is to think like a reader.

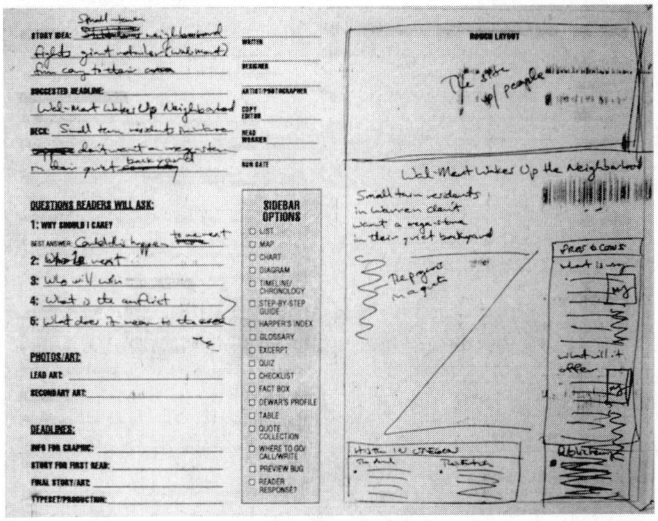

Fig. 8.17

Here is an example of a maestro form from the *Oregonian*. The maestro session was lively and constructive.

Fig. 8.18

When the story was held a day and was turned over to a page designer who had not been involved in the maestro session, all the planning evident in figure 8.17 was wasted. (Courtesy of the *Oregonian*/reprinted by permission)

247

When this package appeared in the paper, the reporter who had followed the maestro plan in figure 8.17 asked the painfully obvious question, "What happened?" A mistake like this offers three important lessons: (1) Maestroing can be a big help or a big waste of time, depending on the participants' attention to detail and willingness to follow through on a maestro plan. The maestro needs to be a vigilant shepherd. (2) Managing change is difficult enough without mistakes like these that demoralize participants and lead to a loss of confidence in the system. (3) Look at the difference between how this story package might have looked to readers and the way it ended up on the page. See how much more effort is involved in trying to engage readers through headlines, photos and sidebar graphics in the maestro process.

2. What are the results?

When newspapers adopt the Maestro Concept, they are encouraged to set up "Bravo! Boards" to display maestro forms and tear sheets of successful story packages (fig. 8.19). This not only celebrates success but also aids in training. This board was posted in the newsroom of the *News-Enterprise* in Elizabethtown, Ky.

3. How does it work?

Examples

Here are examples from two of the larger daily newspapers that have adopted the concept, the *Oregonian* in Portland, Ore., and the *Virginian-Pilot* in Norfolk, Va. With more than 300 newsroom staff members, the *Oregonian* is the largest paper routinely using the concept. The *Virginian-Pilot* is two-thirds the *Oregonian*'s size.

The essence of the business story in figure 8.20, from an early edition of the *Oregonian*, is essentially the same as the one in figure 8.21. The editor asked that the story be maestroed for the next edition. The maestro session was done on the fly. The maestro first asked the reporter, "What's the story about?"

Fig. 8.19

"Bravo! Boards" celebrate success and help with training. (Photo courtesy of the *News-Enterprise,* Elizabethtown, Ky.)

Fig. 8.20

After the Intel story on the business page appeared in an early edition of the *Oregonian*, the editor asked that the story be maestroed for the next edition. The maestro session was done on the fly.

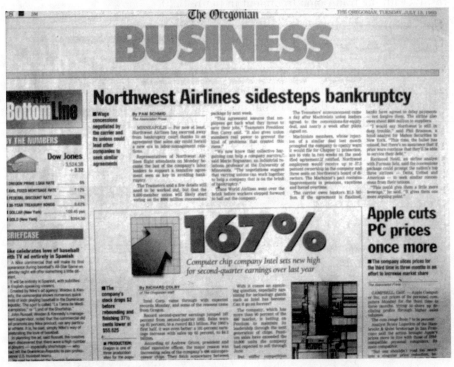

Fig. 8.21

This was the result of the quick, between-editions maestroing of the Intel story. (Courtesy of the *Oregonian*/reprinted by permission)

The reporter responded in a raised voice, "167 percent; Intel's profits are up 167 percent in the second quarter." The goal became clear: Reflect the enthusiasm in the reporter's voice on the page.

The business editor had assigned a photo to be taken of the computer chip at the center of Intel's sales success for the quarter. This was the kind of assignment that drives photo directors to early retirement. The maestro looked at the photo assignment and quickly realized that it would be next to impossible for a photographer to be permitted in the high-security world of this computer company, let alone to take a photo for a black-and-white page that is going to tell this story with impact. The maestro turned the photo assignment over and sketched the lead visual for the package (fig. 8.22). He then gave the sketch to a graphics artist. One of the Maestro Concept's principles is to put decision making in the hands of staff members with the most expertise. Photographers and photo editors know best what a photo can or cannot do to tell a story. Graphics artists know how to pick up where photos fall flat. Having these specialists in a maestro session, rather than putting section editors in charge of making photo and graphics assignments, saves time and improves quality.

The maestro's second question to the reporter was, "What are the three or four most important points in this story?" The maestro then jotted down the reporter's answers. Those ideas are reflected in the headline, the caption under a file photo of the computer chip and the bulleted items in the margin (fig. 8.23). The maestro took the words of the person with the most expertise and projected them onto the page with a designer's help, mostly word for word. The traditional approach of asking a copy editor to see this story cold and to pull out those items for display wastes time, and because the copy editor's expertise in this case is no match for the reporter's, the results might be misleading. The fact that the maestro process did not follow the smooth guidelines explained in this chapter does not matter. The story presentation works for readers. Compare the results with the traditional treatment in figure 8.20.

Planning for Sunday

Unlike the business story maestroed on deadline, this example from the *Oregonian* involves planning for the Sunday paper. A maestro session may occur anywhere from the day of publication to weeks beforehand. This story focuses on how cool weather has chilled the farm economy in Oregon. In the maestro session the suggested headline inspires a graphics artist to carry the image of "cooling off" to the page (fig. 8.24). Notice how the modest page sketch

Fig 8.22

For the Intel story, the maestro turned the photo assignment over and sketched the lead visual for the package and then gave the sketch to a graphics artist.

Fig. 8.23

The maestro asked the reporter, "What are the three or four most important points in this story?" Those ideas are reflected in the headline, the caption under a file photo of the computer chip and the bulleted items in the margin. (Courtesy of the *Oregonian*/reprinted by permission)

by the maestro, obviously not an artist, gets translated into a vivid package (fig. 8.25). The Maestro Concept puts design and graphics decisions in the hands of staff members with the most expertise.

Readers can see at a glance what the story is about. One of the goals set in the maestro session was to focus the lead on a single farmer and to begin telling the larger story from her perspective. Notice in figure 8.26 that the farmer highlighted in the lead is pictured along with a quote from her to help tie the storytelling together into a coherent package. This is the execution of an idea from the maestro session. It seems so simple, yet start counting the times you see someone highlighted in a lead and someone else featured in a picture with the story. Often this results because the reporter and the photographer, even though they may be working at the same place and at the same time, are not joined by a common vision of the story.

A Modified Maestro Session

This example (fig. 8.27) from the *Virginian-Pilot* in Norfolk, Va., presents another variation of the maestro process. At the morning news meeting, editors hear that Virginia's state police will roll out their latest crime fighter, Robocop, at a news conference later that day. The story quickly gains heavy support as a front-page centerpiece package for the next day's paper. After the morning meeting, senior editors, the page one designer and the maestro huddle for a quick maestro session. The reporter is in the field and a photographer is yet to be assigned.

One of the first reader questions to emerge from the brainstorming is, "How does it work?" A decision is made quickly that this question would be answered in an information graphic (fig. 8.28).

A second reader question generated in the maestro session, "How much does it cost?" gets answered in the headline (fig. 8.29). A third question, "Does it look anything like the movie version?" is answered by teaming the information graphic with a Hollywood still photograph. Whether a maestro session is done in classic style or, like this, on the fly, reader questions drive the design and display type elements.

Having Fun with the Lead

After completing his reporting in the late afternoon, but before writing, the reporter sits down with one of the senior editors involved in the morning maestro session. The senior editor shows the reporter the maestro sketch and list of key reader questions. He explains that the classic summary lead, answering who, what, when, where, why and how, has already been written in the information graphic, the headline and other display type. He challenges the reporter to pick up the storytelling from there in his lead. The result is a winner (fig. 8.30).

Figs. 8.24 and 8.25

Here is another maestro form from the *Oregonian*. Notice how the modest page sketch in figure 8.24 by the maestro, obviously not an artist, gets translated into a vivid package in figure 8.25 (opposite page). (Courtesy of the *Oregonian*/ reprinted by permission)

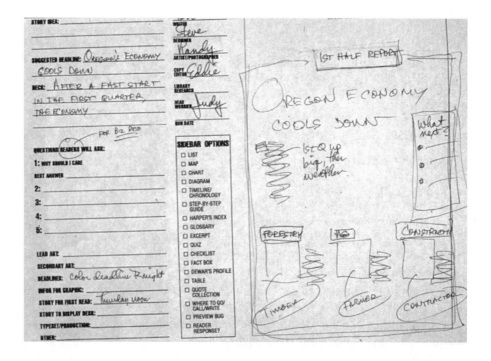

Fig. 8.25

Fig. 8.26

In the "cooling off" package, the farmer highlighted in the lead is pictured along with a quote from her to help tie the storytelling together into a coherent package. (Courtesy of the *Oregonian*/reprinted by permission)

By KEN HAMBURG
of The Oregonian staff

Sauvie Island farmer Nancy Grande knows exactly what happened to Oregon's economy in the second quarter of the year — it cooled off with the weather.

Sales at Grande's Sauvie Island Market are off about 15 percent compared with normal years, and down closer to 40 percent from last year — when the weather was unusually warm and dry, and fruits and vegetables ripened earlier than normal.

But this year, persistent spring rains dropped too much moisture on her 180 acres of crops. Now, beans, berries and tomatoes are spoiling on the vines.

Grande wasn't the only one who felt the pinch during the second quarter.

Jeff Hannum, the state's labor economist, said food processing, construction and a variety of other outdoor-related business activities also suffered from the unusually cool and damp spring.

And the slowdown was reflected throughout most sectors of the state's economy.

Although total employment actually edged up across the state in April, May and June, the numbers failed to match seasonal expectations.

In fact, Bill Conerly, chief economist and senior vice president of First Interstate Bancorp — who does his own crunching of state employment numbers — calculates Oregon actually lost 7,300 jobs from the first quarter to the second quarter on a seasonal basis.

"That's disappointing. Nationally, the economy is inching up. Oregon is sagging," Conerly said.

"It was essentially a no-growth second quarter, a pause after a strong first quarter," agreed John Mitchell, senior vice president and chief economist at U.S. Bancorp.

Oregon's unemployment rate also told the story: It soared to 7.6 percent in April before settling down to 7.2 percent in June. But it remained stubbornly higher than the national rate of 7.0 percent.

In the Portland metropolitan area — which accounts for about half the state's total employment — the unemployment rate was a more reasonable 5.8 percent by the end of the quarter.

But rural Oregon didn't fare as well. Eight counties still had rates above 10 percent in June, with Hood River County pegging in at 13.1 percent. Columbia County was close

> Things just aren't growing that well. All the things that thrive in heat are not thriving.

Nancy Grande
Sauvie Island farmer

Breaking the Tradition

The traditional approach to newspaper newsroom operations resembles the assembly line in manufacturing made famous by Henry Ford in the early days of the American automobile industry. The Maestro Concept, on the other hand, applies Deming's management principles from the manufacturing world to the creative processes in the newsroom. Here is a summary of how the two management approaches are different:

Traditional

Henry Ford's assembly-line approach to newsroom operations:

	Photo→			
Story→	**Layout/Design→**	**Headline→**	**Copy editing→**	**Production**
Chassis→	Body work→	Detailing→	Inspection→	Automobile

Fig. 8.27

The Robocop package from the *Virginian-Pilot* in Norfolk, Va., presents another variation of the maestro process. (Courtesy of the *Virginian-Pilot*/reprinted by permission)

Fig. 8.28

One of the first reader questions to emerge from brainstorming on the Robocop story was, "How does it work?" The question is answered in an information graphic. (Courtesy of the *Virginian-Pilot*/reprinted by permission)

Fig. 8.29

Here's how the *Virginian-Pilot* dealt with other reader questions: "How much does it cost?" gets answered in the headline. "Does it look anything like the movie version?" is answered by teaming the information graphic with a Hollywood still photograph. (Courtesy of the *Virginian-Pilot* /reprinted by permission)

Fig. 8.30

With many basic questions already answered on the page, the writer is challenged to advance the storytelling in the lead. (Courtesy of the *Virginian-Pilot*/reprinted by permission)

BY JON FRANK
STAFF WRITER

RICHMOND — He weighs 275 pounds, with zero percent body fat. His grip can crush a man's hand with ease. He's so flexible that his arm can rotate 360 degrees. He has eyes with the zoom capability of an expensive camera.

If that sounds like the movie "Robocop," there's good reason. Virginia law enforcement is catching up to Hollywood. State police have purchased a $80,000 Andros robot, which is about to strap on a specially designed shotgun and take its place alongside other troopers.

"This is a way to take care of a dangerous situation without putting an individual into it," said Frank A. Williams, deputy assistant director for the state police, moments before the Andros trooper was unveiled Thursday at the State Police Training Academy in Richmond.

For about 30 minutes, Andros showed off in front of troopers who may lead less hazardous lives because of what Virginia's version of Robocop can do.

At the remote-controlled direction of bomb squad expert

enforcement
FBI.

If the And
like its Hol
because he s
he's slow: To
a baby's craw

Adams, on
ists who hav
said doors t
minutes for t

But his va
numerous tir
and in a vari

Many were
sian Gulf wa
land mines.
years ago, a
negotiations
shot four pe
pieces, the m

Other susp

255

Maestro

W. Edwards Deming's management principles applied to the creative (not manufacturing) process:

Idea Group→ Story idea

Preliminary reporting

Pre-maestro check
▼
Maestro session

Writing, editing, photography, design
▼
Fine-tuning the maestro plan

Story package published in paper
▼
Ideas imprinted on reader's mind

Reconvene for audit

2. What are the results?

The Benefits

There are at least five benefits to the maestro approach:

1. *Fewer rewrites.* Writers and editors see less need to rewrite stories because of missing information or organization problems.

2. *Fewer unpublished photos.* Photographers and photo editors see less need to reshoot photos, and clearer assignments reduce wasted time and effort.

3. *Cost-cutting.* Mileage reimbursement checks dropped to $300 a month from $350 for photographers at the first paper to adopt the Maestro Concept.

4. *More camaraderie.* Teamwork across sections and departments raises the respect for each other's contributions to the paper.

5. *Increase in awards.* Typically, results can be seen from one year to the next where maestro sessions become daily events. The opposite also is true: As the number of maestro sessions decline, so do the awards.

4. Where did the idea come from?

The Maestro Concept's story begins with a mugging. At newspapers that introduced pagination in the late 1980s, copy editors were being mugged by mismanagement. Pagination technology was radically different, but newsroom

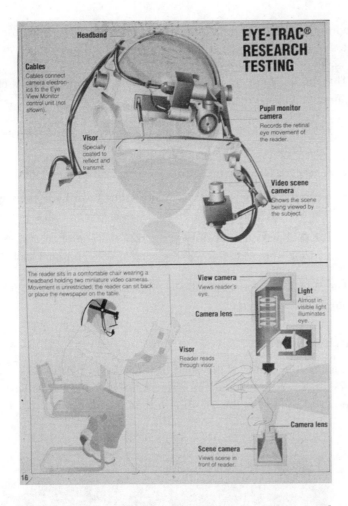

Within the figure:

Headband

Cables
Cables connect camera electronics to the Eye View Monitor control unit (not shown).

EYE-TRAC® RESEARCH TESTING

Pupil monitor camera
Records the retinal eye movement of the reader.

Visor
Specially coated to reflect and transmit.

Video scene camera
Shows the scene being viewed by the subject.

The reader sits in a comfortable chair wearing a headband holding two miniature video cameras. Movement is unrestricted; the reader can sit back or place the newspaper on the table.

View camera
Views reader's eye.

Camera lens

Light
Almost invisible light illuminates eye.

Visor
Reader reads through visor.

Camera lens

Scene camera
Views scene in front of reader.

16

Fig. 8.31

The EYE-TRAC® device followed the eyes of readers in three cities as they read mockups of their hometown newspapers for the Poynter Institute's *Eyes on the News* study. (Courtesy of the Poynter Institute for Media Studies/reprinted by permission)

organization and operation stayed essentially the same. As a result, copy editors were robbed of quality time to edit with precision. There had to be a better way to mesh human beings and technology to improve quality. The Maestro Concept was developed to answer that need.

The Maestro Concept's battle cry is, "Think like a reader." This relates to anticipating readers' questions, then answering them quickly on a page. But where and how? An early inspiration for the Maestro Concept was a 1991 study by Dr. Mario Garcia and Dr. Pegie Stark at the Poynter Institute for Media Studies entitled *Eyes on the News*. The study was based on EYE-TRAC® research. The EYE-TRAC® device (fig. 8.31) followed the eyes of readers in three cities as they read mockups of their hometown newspapers.

The cover to *Eyes on the News* was designed by Nuri Ducassi to be disturbing (fig. 8.32). After all, EYE-TRAC® research revealed that loyal Baby Boom readers, aged 25 to 43 at that time, did not always read newspapers the way many journalists thought they did. For example, color photos had less impact than expected in attracting attention to news stories; small visuals significantly increased the likelihood that a related headline would be read; and readers preferred brightly colored pages that designers considered troubling.

EYE-TRAC® research identified a typical reading pattern: Readers tend to look at photos or illustrations first, headlines second, captions and other display type third, and text fourth. When designers and editors put a premium on connecting the meaning of a visual with a headline, they present a powerful

1-2 punch to capture readers' attention, as in this example from *The News* in Boca Raton, Fla. (fig. 8.33). Just because readers tend to look last at the lead does not mean text is least important.

The Maestro Concept was designed to meet the challenge of creating a 1-2-3-4 punch to engage readers.

1. A photo or an illustration begins the storytelling by answering the question, "Who?"

2. A headline amplifies the visual's meaning by explaining "What?"

3. A caption or a graphic adds an interesting point by answering "When?" or "Where?"

4. The lead picks up the storytelling from there in place of summarizing who-what-when-where in an inverted pyramid lead.

The Maestro Concept calls this a "four-graph approach" to writing, editing, photography and design.

What's the Lead?

Imagine the writer of the "bad taste" story in figure 8.34 sitting in a newsroom cubicle working on a lead. "Eureka! I've found it," he says. "I have found the best way to start this story." He then begins typing text. This is the

Fig. 8.32

The cover to *Eyes on the News* was designed by Nuri Ducassi to be disturbing. (Courtesy of the Poynter Institute for Media Studies/ reprinted by permission)

Fig. 8.33

When the meaning of a visual connects with a headline, together they present a powerful 1-2 punch to capture readers' attention, as in this example from *The News* in Boca Raton, Fla. (Courtesy of *The News* of Boca Raton, Fla./reprinted by permission)

Fig 8.34

What's the lead of this story from *Florida Today* of Melbourne, Fla.? Readers begin the story with the illustration, not the text. (Courtesy of *Florida Today*/ reprinted by permission)

newsroom culture that has influenced introductory newswriting classes and textbooks for high school and college students. *Eyes on the News* allows us to see how the reader culture turns this traditional approach on its head. Where are readers likely to start reading this story? They likely would look first at the illustration, then read the headline. The four-graph approach defines the illustration as the "lead" and the headline as the second paragraph of the story. With the Maestro Concept, the writer would participate in discussions on the contents of the illustration and the headline, then begin writing his lead in this context, not in isolation in the newsroom.

Ho-hum "Leads"

Before the *Oregonian* adopted the Maestro Concept, the lead art on its front page and section covers was often "wild," or unrelated to the main story or to a centerpiece story package. Wild art as lead art often indicates a lack of collaboration by verbal and visual journalists and often represents a lost opportunity for a 1-2 punch, if not a 1-2-3-4 punch, to stop busy readers and engage them in stories. When the lead art is weak, as with these ice skaters (fig. 8.35), readers may get the impression that nothing very exciting is happening in town.

Fig. 8.35

Before the *Oregonian* adopted the Maestro Concept, the lead art on its front page and section covers was often "wild," or unrelated to the main story or to a centerpiece story package. (Courtesy of the *Oregonian*/reprinted by permission)

Before the Maestro Concept experiment began in Logansport, Ind., the same wild-art-as-lead-art problem existed, as with this bland photo of a man cooking hot dogs (fig. 8.36). The staff's rationalization was that there were too few photographers on the 15-member newsroom staff. The same reason was given at the 300-plus-member newsroom of the *Oregonian*. The real issue in both cases was not how many photographers, but how they were deployed. In both newsrooms, the linchpins to the Maestro Concept's success were photo directors who began to assign photographers to maestro sessions rather than to photo shoots.

Something like Maestroing

The greatest challenge in introducing the Maestro Concept at the *Oregonian* was getting staff members beyond their belief that they were "already doing something like maestroing." Photographers accompanied reporters on assignment, as with this story in Mexico (fig. 8.37), and designers were consulted on story play. But the difference between this approach and maestroing is clear in the results. The reporter's lead for this story focuses on two Oregon students; there are no photos of those students on this page or the jump page. Journalists can work together and still not collaborate. The missing link to successful collaboration was a method found in the Maestro Concept.

Fig. 8.37

At the *Oregonian,* photographers accompanied reporters on assignment, as with this story in Mexico. The lead focuses on two Oregon students; neither is in any photos accompanying the story. (Courtesy of the *Oregonian*/reprinted by permission)

9

Headlines

The language of truth is unadorned and always simple.
—Marcellinus Ammianus

Brevity is the soul of wit.
—William Shakespeare

Newspapers and magazines have had headlines since the days of Ben Franklin, and the ability to write clever, accurate headlines has long been admired in newsrooms. So why have most headlines been written as an afterthought?

In Chapter 8, we urged you to attempt a headline early in the editing process. That's not the way most editors do it. Instead, they finish everything else before they tackle the headline, sometimes leaving themselves short of time. We know because we've done it ourselves.

But headlines are too important to leave until the last minute. In the Poynter Institute study *Eyes on the News,* subjects were asked to read a newspaper prototype while their eye movements were recorded (see Chapter 8). The study found that 85 percent of headlines were "processed" by the readers. "Processed" meant that the subject's eyes stopped on that headline. By contrast, only 25 percent of the story leads were processed and many fewer were read in depth.

The message from the Poynter Institute study is that headlines are an important tool for communicating with readers. Many newspapers have responded by putting more effort into headlines. Today, editors must be skilled in writing complex headline combinations that are clever, direct and informative. Gone are the days of using the headline to "tease" the reader into looking at the story. For most readers, the headline *is* the story.

HEADLINE MECHANICS

In ancient times, say 1975, headlines were written on paper and "counted," then sent to a typesetter, who keyed the headline into a photo-typesetting machine. Counting the letters and spaces of a headline was a way of ensuring that the headline would fit on the column measure. In the days of photo and mechanical typesetting, a headline that was even a half-count too long had to be redone.

Appendix C describes how to count a headline. Even though headline counting is all but dead, we include it for two reasons: Learning to count headlines helps you understand type, and headline counting still can be a handy skill when the computer editing system goes down.

In today's newsrooms, headlines are written and fitted on computers. Computer editing systems are of two types: text based and WYSIWYG (what you see is what you get).

Older editing systems were text based; that is, the computer terminal was capable of displaying only text, only of one size and only of one style. On these systems, editors coded the headline according to what the makeup editor ordered. After writing a trial headline, the editor applied the "hyphenate and justify" (H&J) command. If the headline was too long, it "broke" to a second line. Through trial and error, the editor came up with a headline that fit. One trick for sizing up headline length on a text-based system was to add nonsense syllables to the headline until it broke. The headline then could be added to until it fit.

Many newer editing systems, based on desktop computers with graphic capabilities, allow the editor to see how headlines will look on the page. On some of these systems, when the editor applies the H&J command, a WYSIWYG window opens with a view of the story-headline combination as it will be laid out. The editor then can return to the easier-to-read text window to adjust the headline, or it can be adjusted in the WYSIWYG window.

Newspapers and magazines today are moving quickly toward pagination, a system in which entire pages are laid out by computer and sent to an image setter as a complete, or composite, page. In these systems, the editor may be asked to write a headline with broad specifications so that final adjustments can be made by the makeup editor on the electronic page. In one system, editors write headline combinations in "templates" that can be applied and adjusted to fit on the electronic page.

TYPES OF HEADLINES

The headline combinations being used in today's news environment are almost limitless. Today's publication designers seek out innovative ways to mingle headline type with pictures and graphics to create a layered, integrated look. Even so, we can break headline combinations down into several broad categories.

Keep in mind as you read about headline combinations and look at our examples that one headline still has to do the main job of answering the reader's number-one question: What's this story about? In the examples that follow, recreated from headlines that appeared in the *Star Tribune* of Minneapolis, note where that question is answered.

Headline Orders

When pages are laid out on paper dummies, headline orders don't have to be in a precise form as long as the basic information is all there. The makeup editor might use this common form: *2-36R-2.* Reading across, it means a two-column headline of 36-point roman type and with two lines. Roman, bold and italic are variations of the publication's standard headline typeface.

Many publications use two entirely different typefaces for headlines, so the headline order may have to elaborate on the basic information: *2-36CBR-2.* This means a two-column head of 36-point Century bold roman with two lines. Another order might read: *6-42FGB-1,* meaning a six-column head of 42-point

Weird science

High school inventions lean toward the wacky

Clinton
ACQUITTED

Perjury, obstruction charges defeated

Kickers

Kickers are small headlines of two to four words, usually about half the size of the main head. The role of the kicker is to provide contrast, introduce white space above the story and give the reader a quick, clever take on the story.

In figure 9.1, the kicker, *Weird science,* is in Franklin Gothic bold. The main headline, *High school inventions lean toward the wacky,* is in New Baskerville Roman.

Kickers usually are in a typeface that contrasts with the main headline. Kickers do not need a separate headline order; the editor usually is told simply to write a kicker. Kickers do not need to be a complete sentence. For the kicker, focus on a secondary element in the story or something that emphasizes the main thrust of the story.

Don't use a kicker for an attribution, as in *Mayor announces* (kicker), *City clerk stole funds* (main head). If the story is too long, the kicker may be cut and the headline becomes unfair or even libelous.

Hammers

The hammer is sometimes called the *reverse kicker.* Instead of two to four words set in small type, the hammer is at least twice as big as the main headline and often much bigger (fig. 9.2). The hammer grabs reader attention; it hits the reader over the head. A well-written hammer leads the reader to read the main head, where the theme of the story is found. But sometimes, as in figure 9.2, a simple statement of fact is called for.

Hammers are bold. Sometimes special heavy-faced fonts are used. Hammers introduce white space and provide contrast. Hammers sum up a story in a word or in a phrase.

Fig. 9.1

The kicker, *Weird science,* is in Franklin gothic bold. The main headline, *High school inventions lean toward the wacky,* is in New Baskerville roman.

Fig. 9.2

The hammer grabs reader attention; it hits the reader over the head.

(*continued*) Franklin gothic bold with one line.

When headline orders are entered in a computer editing system, the information changes. The second headline order above might be entered on the computer as *CBR36,25.4.* This tells the computer to use 36-point Century bold roman set on 25 picas 4 points, the width of two columns. We leave out the number of lines because the editor controls that. On computer editing systems, the coding must be exact, or the computer won't recognize it.

Note that headline-order conventions change from publication to publication, often according to what computer system they use. Also, special headlines such as kickers and hammers often are specified only by typeface and size; the editor simply writes two or three words.

Readouts

Readouts, sometimes called *drop heads* or *decks,* are smaller than the main headline, usually about half as big. Headlines are in a contrasting type, usually a lighter face or in italics. The type of readout in figure 9.3 is called an *underline.* It extends the full width of the main headline. But readouts often are set narrower than the main headline (fig. 9.4).

In writing a readout, look for a secondary element or theme that provides elaboration on the main head. Readouts get a separate headline order and must fit the column width. Readouts provide a visual transition; they take the reader from the big type of a main head to body type. Readouts direct the eye, serve as a buffer and provide contrast.

Jump Headlines

You'll notice in figure 9.4 that we've included a *jump line,* a line of type that tells the reader where the story continues on an inside page. Where the story continues, you'll find the *jump head* (fig. 9.5). Jump heads help the reader find the rest of the story inside.

At some publications, the jump heads cast another hook for those who didn't start on page one; figure 9.5 is an example. At other papers, such as the *New York Times,* the jump head simply echoes the main headline on page one. At many newspapers and magazines, the jump head is simply one or two words in a standard style.

Jump heads usually are smaller than the page one headline. If possible, the jump head should not be the lead headline on the page.

Sidebar Headlines

Sidebars are related stories that run with a main story and take a separate headline order. Sometimes sidebars are set in a box, so the headline is on an odd measure.

Fig. 9.3

The type of readout in figure 9.3 is called an *underline.* It extends the full width of the main headline.

Fig. 9.4

Readouts often are set narrower than the main headline. Notice that we've included a *jump line* that tells the reader where the story continues on an inside page.

Olympic bid may be probed
Gift violation may reopen Atlanta case

Wolves beat tired Grizzlies
Marbury's
23 points
key victory

WOLVES continues on C8:

WOLVES from C1

Regular-season home win streak reaches 10 with 19-point victory

An apologetic Clinton urges reconciliation

Sidebar headlines usually are set in a typeface that contrasts with the main head, through size, weight, or typeface. Figure 9.6 is a sidebar headline written to go on the same page as figure 9.2.

In writing sidebar heads, look for elements in the story that do not echo the main story. Try not to repeat words in the main head or other heads on the same page. Of course, some repetition is unavoidable, as in our examples.

Tripod Heads

The *tripod* headline is a variation of the hammer–main headline combination. Dr. Mario Garcia of the Poynter Institute gave the tripod its name. Like the three-legged stool, the tripod head rests on three elements: a main headline, a hammer and a special treatment given to a key word or phrase of the hammer. In figure 9.7, the third element is obvious.

Headlines that make use of special typefaces in varying sizes or colors are called *display heads*. Artists once laid them up by hand, so they had to be planned well in advance. Today, tripod heads show up on breaking-news stories, made possible by computer programs that allow easy and quick manipulation of type. The challenge for the designer is that the headline manipulation be meaningful. As Garcia writes, "As long as the design is functional and allows for easy reading, it is worth trying."

Summary Paragraphs

As *Eyes on the News* demonstrated, many readers rely on headlines to get their news. Readers "scan" the newspaper or magazine, looking for stories that interest them. To satisfy these "scanners," many publications use *summary paragraphs*.

Summary graphs, called *blurbs* by some papers, are set in moderately large type, 18 to 24 points, sometimes with "bullets" to attract the eye. Summary graphs usually appear at the top of the story on the same column width as the story (figs. 9.8 and 9.9). But a summary graph can be used with a hammer in place of a main headline (fig. 9.10).

Summary graphs are written as complete sentences with articles and all other words in place, unlike the truncated form regular headlines often take. The key to writing summary graphs is to understand the story completely and to reveal the depth of that story. The mortal sin in writing summary graphs is to repeat what appears in the main headline or the lead.

Fig. 9.5

Jump heads help the reader find the rest of the story inside.

Fig. 9.6

Sidebar headlines usually are set in a typeface that contrasts with the main head, through size, weight or typeface. This sidebar headline was written to go on the same page as figure 9.2.

HEADLINE SPLITS

When a headline has two or more lines, try to keep a strong subject and strong verb on the top line. You'll also want to avoid splitting up words that belong together, such as a preposition and its object, an adjective and its noun, or a verb and its helping verb.

These "splits" sometimes are necessary to keep key words in the headline on a tight count. But use an unorthodox split as a last resort, not first choice.

It's OK to use a split head that says something in place of an unsplit head that says nothing. Use a split head when it flows better than a hard-to-read or wooden unsplit head.

The evidence is inconclusive as to whether readers are affected by split heads. Some copy desks ban them but sometimes at a loss of quality.

Look at these two headlines:

**Car rams food
line; 1 killed**

or

**1 killed as car
rams food line**

Which is better? The first has a top line that sounds a bit silly until you pick up on the second line, but overall, it flows better than the second one. We

Fig. 9.7

The *tripod* headline is a variation of the hammer–main headline combination with a special treatment given to a key word or phrase of the hammer.

All fired
up

*Expansion project
will cut pollution,
increase efficiency*

Rebel leader's capture shrouded in mystery

Greece's attempt to
find asylum for the
Kurdish fugitive
backfired. Who's to
blame is in question

Figs. 9.8, 9.9, 9.10

Summary graphs usually
appear at the top of the
story on the same column
width as the story (figs. 9.8
and 9.9). But a summary
graph can be used with a
hammer in place of a main
headline (fig. 9.10).

Milosevic gets warning from talks on Kosovo

A U.S. envoy was sent
from France to tell the
Yugoslav leader to
accept the peace deal
or face NATO strikes.

Gov. Jesse Ventura blended his new job with an old one,
filling in for a day as a talk-show host on KSTP Radio

Broadcast muse

like the second one better just because it prevents a reader with an odd sense
of humor from laughing at a serious story.

Splits are a mistake when they cause the reader to do a double take,
when they might confuse the reader, or when they might be unappealing visually. Here's an example:

Clinton replaces Gore
aide in staff shake-up

This is a *modifier split*, the type that is most easily misunderstood.
Avoid these, and avoid splitting names in general. You could make it:

Gore aide replaced
as Clinton shuffles staff

269

Another kind of split is the prepositional split, between the preposition and its object. These are generally accepted on the second line of a three-line head with a tight count:

Starr heads to
San Francisco
for deposition

Look at this head and ask if you could avoid this split. If each line was at the maximum count, the split would be tough to avoid. You could write:

San Francisco
a Starr stop
for deposition

But this head doesn't read nearly as well as the first.
A third type of split is the verb split:

Mayor will
get award

The helping verb and the main verb are split. This is not as serious as other types of splits, but it's often avoidable as in:

Award going
to mayor

The fourth and final type of split is an infinitive split, between *to* and the verb. Here's an example:

Walker
tries to
kill self

This type of split, like the prepositional split, should be avoided but is acceptable on a tight count. With a maximum of six counts, this headline would be OK. Could you do better? Here are some possibilities, not all successful:

Walker
suicide
try told

or

Walker
attempts
suicide

or

**Walker
suicide
attempt**

The first headline has a split, and you wonder if it really is better than the original. The verb *told* used like this is headlinese. But *Walker attempts suicide* won't work because *attempts* is too long. The third head, *Walker suicide attempt*, fits, but has no verb. It's what we call a label head.

You rarely should resort to label heads for news stories. They can be used for graphics and some sidebars, such as one that is mostly a list: *President's top aides.*

Also avoid *verb heads,* ones that have no subject. They are amateurish and hard to read:

**Kills wife, then self
in fight over money**

Better to say:

**Argument over money
ends in murder, suicide**

HOW TO WRITE A HEADLINE

Take another look at the subheading above. You may have read articles with similar titles. The problem is that those articles were about something else: What to say or not to say in a headline.

This section outlines something different: a step-by-step approach on how to write various types of newspaper headlines. What follows is not only how-to but also hands-on, so before you read further, reach for a pencil.

The Skeleton Approach

What headline would you write for a story with the following lead? You have just four short words to do the job. Take a moment to think it through and jot down your headline.

> *The city's school board president was re-elected Monday in a
> close race that focused more on a textbook controversy than on
> the usual funding issues.*

The first step to writing a headline is to check the lead. If it is wrong, chances are the headline will be wrong. If its phrasing is weak, the headline probably will be weak. You must sweat every word of the lead to make sure it's the best summary for the story.

Headline writers often err by reaching for ideas that don't relate to the lead. Remember that the lead may be the first sentence or the first several paragraphs of a story. Any time you write a headline that doesn't relate in some way to the lead, either the headline is bad or the lead is bad. For our example, let's assume that this lead is fine.

The second step is to look for the lead's skeleton. You identify the simplest form of the subject, verb and object in the main clause and keep them in the same order as they are in the lead. You aren't picking out just key words; you're trying to write a scaled-down sentence that makes sense. By doing this, you are using the lead's structure to write the first draft. This first draft may be something you write out or just think through.

The full skeleton for this lead would be something like:

School board president re-elected in close race focusing on textbooks.

Now match the skeleton against the headline specifications. With a tight count, like the one you face here, only the skeleton's subject and verb may fit. In this case, your headline could read:

School board president re-elected

The last step is to ask whether your headline is really the best one for the story. A better idea may occur to you. In this example, can you do better than *School board president re-elected?* Probably not.

Some will argue that you should never repeat words in a headline that are also in the lead. But we repeat words from leads in headlines all the time. Think of how often you have seen "Yeltsin" or "Clinton" in a lead and in the story's headline. There's nothing wrong with that. But sometimes repeating words is a mistake. Two factors are involved in deciding when to avoid repetition. One is time management for headline writers and the other is whether the reader will notice the repetition.

Good headline writers know how to manage their time. They know when reworking a headline is worth it and when it's not. That school board headline is a "gimme"; it writes itself using the skeleton approach. Trying to fine-tune it by looking for another way to say *school board* or *president* or *re-elected* is wasting time that could be better spent on a more difficult headline.

Invariably during a shift, copy editors wish they had more time to spend on headlines, especially for those stories that have a special touch. Being able to size up a "gimme" and be done with it as quickly as possible buys time to handle the "toughie" that's just around the corner. The other factor in deciding when to avoid repetition takes a little more explaining.

Repeat after Me

Compare the challenge of writing the school board headline with this one. You have two lines, and each line can hold only three or four short words. Remember to use the skeleton approach. Here's the lead, which you can assume is correct:

When it comes to securing a mortgage these days, home buyers are facing a double whammy: Interest rates are high and lenders are scarce.

Applying the skeleton approach, you would focus on the main clause. The subject and verb would form the top line of the headline: *Home buyers facing.* The object would form the second line: *a double whammy.*

Now is that the best headline for this story? No, because readers will notice the repetition of the unusual words *double whammy.* Compare the use of that expression in this headline with the use of *school board, president* and *re-elected* in our first headline. Even though the same words are repeated in the school board headline and lead, readers aren't going to notice or even care. But in the second headline, those same readers might be intrigued by the term *double whammy* in the headline and then raise an eyebrow at the sight of it in the lead. You'll err anytime you distract readers like that.

Not to be ignored is the effect on the writer of such headlines. Stealing their unusual words—their thunder—will annoy them. Your job as a headline writer is to complement clever leads with clever headlines that make the same point but in a different way.

So what would be a good headline for this story? Well, if your top line reads *Home buyers facing* or *Home buyers face,* we think that's fine. How you finish the thought reflects your headline writing philosophy. You may be a person who just tells the story. Notice how this straightforward headline resulted from the skeleton approach but with a slight twist:

**Home buyers face
high rates, few lenders**

Or you may be the type who is concerned about reflecting the tone of the lead, which has a lighter touch than *high rates, few lenders* suggests. You might write:

**Home buyers face
1-2 punch on loans**

Both headlines have their merits, and both arose from using a combination of the skeleton approach and another method, the condense-and-patch approach.

Condense-and-Patch Approach

To illustrate this approach, let's work through another example. What headline would you write for a story with the following lead? You have just five short words to do the job. As always, we'll start with the skeleton approach and see how far it can take us. Think it through and jot down your idea above the lead.

> *Three area residents were killed Monday when their car hit a telephone pole, skidded 50 feet and flipped over, police said.*

First let's assume that in fact three people were killed and that the lead is fine. Now we look for the skeleton, which would go something like this: *Three killed when car hits pole, skids and flips over.* The first five words of the skeleton will not work for us as a headline, so we turn to the condense-and-patch approach.

Weigh each idea to see if it absolutely must be in the headline. This is not always as easy as it seems. It requires good news judgment, and all good headline writers have that. Remember, every idea in a lead is good or it wouldn't be in the lead. You have to decide what ideas must be represented and which would be nice to represent if you have room.

At the same time you're weighing each word's value, you should be looking for ways to shorten ideas without losing meaning. Let's take the ideas one at a time.

Three killed is a must, and it can become *3 killed* or *3 die* if you have to condense the idea. *Car* is a must, and you can't get any shorter than that. *Hits pole* and *flips over* are stronger than *skids* because just about all car wrecks involve skidding.

Now comes the moment of truth. You could liken this part to playing the parlor game "Lifeboat" in which you have to decide who in the boat deserves to live and who should be cast overboard for the betterment of the group. *Hits pole* seems more worthy than *flips over* because a car flipping over in a wreck is more common than a car hitting a pole.

Because of our five-word limit, we must deviate from the lead's structure, and condense and patch the headline together with a semicolon, like so:

Car hits pole; 3 killed

Before we move on, let's critique some other headline possibilities. What about *3 die as car flips*? The biggest problem is the word *as*. Did these people die as the car flipped, or as it hit the pole, or as it was skidding? Or did they die of heart attacks just before the car crashed? You don't know. You're better off going with the semicolon method or hedging with the word *in*, as with *3 killed in car crash*.

Now let's talk about the difference between *die*, in the present tense, and *killed*, apparently in past tense. Actually, both are present tense. *Die* is present tense, active voice. *Killed* translates to *are killed*, which is present tense, passive voice. We usually drop *is* and *are* in such constructions, and that confuses some people.

Is it better to have active voice verbs in headlines? Yes, most of the time. Then is *die* better here? Well, no. *Killed* is the stronger word. There isn't much action in dying; the idea of being killed, however, is more vivid. With a tighter count, you could go with *Car crash kills 3*.

Tightening the Noose

Sometimes the lead tends to defy headline writing. Take this example. What headline would you write for a story with this lead? You have only four words.

> *BUENOS AIRES, Argentina—The deadly rioting over economic austerity in Venezuela last week has sparked fears of similar social explosions across Latin America and has lent*

new urgency to calls for relief from the region's staggering foreign debt.

Assuming that the lead is accurate, we start with the skeleton approach and see how far it can take us. One obvious problem is that we're facing a *double-barreled lead*; it introduces two different but complementary themes. The first skeleton would be this: *Rioting in Venezuela sparks fears across Latin America.* The second skeleton would go something like this: *Rioting in Venezuela lends urgency to debt relief.*

Now which do you pare down using the condense-and-patch approach? With a double-barreled lead, the first statement is usually the most important one and the other provides a secondary idea. Sometimes the main idea goes in the main headline and the secondary idea goes in a deck, readout, underline or kicker. Because we have just four words, we'll concentrate on condensing the first skeleton.

Rioting in Venezuela can become *Venezuelan riots*. We get a kick out of *sparked fears* because it's the classic case of a writer using headlinese, those short words or expressions that headline writers must use because of tight counts but which writers should never use to replace simple, common language. Can you imagine flying in a plane, being jolted by turbulence and saying to the person next to you, "That sparked fear in me"? Never! You would say "scared me," or "frightened me," or "worried me," or something like that. So for the headline, let's say *worry.*

Now this headline-writing task has come down to one challenge: How do you say *across Latin America* in one word? Here's where many headline writers stumble. They conclude it's impossible, begin tearing up what they've done and inevitably end up with a bad headline. Sticking to the skeleton focuses the challenge. Headline writers succeed or fail based on their ability to condense ideas fairly and accurately. How do you say *across Latin America* in one word? How about *region* or *neighbors?*

Our headline for this story would be this:

Venezuelan riots worry neighbors

Now compare this with your idea. If you went with *Latin riots,* you need to be more specific. If you tried to work in the debt angle, you probably didn't do either skeleton idea justice. There just wasn't enough room.

Sizing Up Stories

Headline writers face basically three types of stories: ones that demand straight, serious headlines; ones that demand bright, clever headlines; and ones that can go either way. The school board and car crash stories fall into the straight, serious category.

The same goes for the Venezuelan riots story. The home buyers story falls into the last category. Some copy editors would be inclined to write just the straight headline and others would try to spend more time with it.

The middle category presents the "toughies." Although headline writers will struggle with tight counts, particularly those one-column, three-line dandies, they have a ready excuse for falling short of what needs to be said: There's just not enough room.

The stories that demand bright, clever headlines, however, offer no easy out. They also tend to render the skeleton approach and the condense-and-patch approach useless, so we'll need another strategy for them.

The Seed Approach

What headline would you write for a story with this lead? This is a toughie; you have eight to 10 words.

> *Sally Johnson learned the hard way that love can hurt. This Valentine's Day, she sent her beau a card expressing her affection, but the man's mother intercepted it. Now Sally, beaten and bruised, lies in a hospital bed, and the man's mother is facing battery charges.*

Remember, the first step in headline writing is to check the lead. Occasionally, when presented with this example, someone will object to the tack such a lead takes and will suggest rewriting it. The point can't be overlooked. If you work at a newspaper where the editor in charge feels that such a lead is inappropriate, that also will affect your headline writing. Headlines must reflect the tone and mood of the story.

Consider how different the headline challenge would be if you faced a lead like this:

> *A 53-year-old mother was charged Monday with battery in connection with the Valentine's Day attack on a woman who sent a message of affection to the older woman's son.*

It's true that stories dealing with injury most often will demand a straight, serious headline and will be written in a formal tone, but that's not always the case. Sometimes, odd as it might sound, there can be something amusing about the circumstances of injury, such as those in this case. Clearly, we would have to take an entirely different approach if the woman was killed. But that's not true, so let's go with the original lead.

Applying the skeleton approach, you would end up with a headline something like:

Woman learns the hard way that love can hurt

That's exactly the point, but it's a bad idea because you would be stealing the writer's thunder. The skeleton approach fails us here, so let's turn to the seed approach.

The first step is to identify a word or idea that must be represented in the headline. A good place to look for a clue is the story's slug, the name that distinguishes it from other stories. How would this story have been slugged? Probably *Valentine.* There's a seed.

The second step is to think of expressions that grow out of the seed and then focus on ones that can be used to tell the story. So think of valentine, and what ideas come to mind? Well, valentines are red and seeing red is an expression for being angry, which the mother was. You have a start on a headline: *Son's valentine makes mother see red.* But you also have to represent the injury angle. So maybe your headline is:

Woman sees stars after valentine makes mother see red

What else can you do with red? What about the Valentine's Day rhyme, "Roses are red, violets are blue"?

With a twist, you could write this headline:

Roses are red, valentine sender black and blue

Maybe you saw Cupid grow out of the valentine seed. What expression comes to mind about Cupid? Maybe something about his arrow? Apply it to this headline, and you may come up with:

Cupid's arrow ricochets: Valentine suffers broken heart—and more

No doubt you came up with other ideas for good headlines. The possibilities are endless. What if you find a seed but get stuck thinking of expressions? Turn to a good dictionary and look up *valentine* or *red* or *Cupid,* then check for ideas from the definition. Or better yet, look for idioms listed at the end of the entries.

The secret to success with the seed approach is to keep in mind that you need just one good idea to make a good headline and to realize that most of the expressions that come to mind will be bad ideas and should be discarded quickly. Don't waste time trying to force an expression into your headline. Look for another idea that will fit naturally.

Wrapping Up

Let's work through one more. Here's a summary of the step-by-step approach we've been using:

- Check the lead for accuracy and proper phrasing.
- Size up the headline: Is it a gimme or a toughie? If it's a gimme, the skeleton approach will write the headline for you. Don't worry about fine-tuning it; save that time for when you have to handle a toughie. If it's a toughie, see how far the skeleton approach will take you. You may have to use the condense-and-patch approach or seed approach.
- Size up the story: Does it demand a straight, serious headline, or a bright, clever headline, or can the headline go either way? Be sure to reflect the proper tone.
- Just before you let the story go, ask: Is this the best possible headline? A better idea may come to you.

Let's see how all this applies to the following case. You have five words to tell the story. Jot down your headline, assuming the lead is fine.

The city's mayor, facing charges of carrying two handguns without permits, denounced his arrest last week as a political ploy and insisted today that a mayor, like any citizen, had the right to bear arms.

Well, is this headline a gimme or a toughie? Because of the story's sensitive nature, you will want to spend more time than usual on it. Also, because this is a second-day story, a follow-up on the arrest story and headline of last week, it's more complicated than the crash story, a first-day account. So we would consider this a toughie.

How far will the skeleton approach take you? Again, this is a double-barreled lead, so there are two skeletons. The first would go something like this: *Mayor denounces gun arrest as political ploy.* That could translate into these five-word headlines:

Mayor: Gun arrest was ploy
Mayor calls arrest political ploy

The second skeleton would go something like this: *Mayor insists on right to bear arms.* That might end up in a newspaper headline looking like this:

Mayor defends right to guns

Now does this story demand a straight, serious headline? Well, it sure doesn't demand a bright, clever one. But it could go either way depending on your news organization's philosophy. A newspaper or magazine's personality can be defined by what headline would show up for this story, no doubt on page one. The same could be said for "teasers" used by different radio and television stations.

Informal polls of editors rarely produce agreement on what type of headline is appropriate for such stories and what type of headline would end up in their publication. At one headline-writing seminar, the managing editor voted one way and the executive editor the other. When such things happen, it's no wonder the poor copy editors are confused about what's expected of them. The managers who are clear about their product's personality are more consistent about evaluating headlines. And they make it easier for editors to write headlines.

Some more conservative news organizations would consider running only the headlines listed earlier; others would insist on something more. That would mean using the seed approach. The key word or idea here would be *gun.* You might see headlines like these:

Mayor takes shot at arrest
Mayor blasts arrest as ploy

The best approach for a copy editor, especially with page-one headlines, is to offer more than one idea expressing different tones and angles, and then to let the higher-ups decide. No list of possible headlines for this story would be complete without this one:

Mayor sticks to his guns

Headline writing is one of the most difficult jobs any journalist will do. This step-by-step approach should make life easier for those who have to do it every day.

WORKOUT: HEADLINES

Read each lead below and write a headline as directed. Then see how we would do it.

TIBET

A. Write a one-line headline of six or seven words
B. Write a hammer (two to four words) and a six-word main head.

BEIJING—Police and Tibetan protesters traded gunfire in Lhasa Sunday after an illegal Buddhist parade turned into a riot, leaving 11 dead and more than 100 injured, the New China news agency reported.

Hundreds of Tibetans demanding freedom from Chinese rule smashed windows, looted shops, restaurants and hotels, and vandalized police cars in Lhasa, the capital of the disputed region, the state-run news agency said.

Answer:
A. *Tibetan parade turns into riot; 11 dead*
B. *Tibetan shootout*
   Parade turns into riot; 11 killed
Comments: Play this straight. Would you say *demonstration* instead of *parade*? This is one time when you should repeat what's in the lead. The writer calls it a parade; don't read anything more into it.

RAIL

A. Write a one-line headline of eight or nine words.
B. Write a three-line headline with two words per line.

LONDON—At least five people were killed and more than 80 injured when two passenger trains collided Saturday in London's second big rail crash since December, police said.

Witnesses said the two trains smashed into each other at crossing points in Purley on the southern outskirts of the capital, sending six cars crashing over an embankment into suburban back gardens. One car stopped only a few feet from a house.

Answer:

A. *2nd London rail crash since December kills 5*

B. *5 killed*
   in London
   rail crash

OR

B. *Rail crash*
   in London
   kills 5

Comment: The difficult angle to work into the headline is that this was the second big rail crash since December. Note that you can't say only *2nd crash*, as in *2nd London rail crash kills 5, injures 80*. It has to have the qualifier *since December*. Avoid calling it a trend, as in *Fatal London rail crash continues trend*. You need considerably more than two incidents to have a trend.

SMASH

A. Write a one-line headline of five words.
B. Write a two-line headline with three or four words for each line.

JERUSALEM—Twenty-one Israeli paratroopers have been jailed for up to two weeks each for smashing cars and windows in a Sunday rampage at a Palestinian refugee camp, the army said Friday.

Lt. Gen. Dan Shomron, army chief of staff, said there was no excuse for the rampage, in which at least four cars and 20 houses were damaged when the paratroopers attacked the Kaiandia refugee camp north of Jerusalem after their bus was stoned.

Answer:

A. *Israeli paratroopers jailed after rampage*

B. *Israel jails paratroopers*
   after refugee camp rampage

Comment: Remember that headline A really is in the present tense: *Israeli paratroopers (are) jailed after rampage*. You can see how a lot gets left out with these short headlines. Here are some words that you might have tried and thrown overboard: *Palestinian, smashing cars and windows, bus stoned*. A news headline like this must concentrate on the who and what, and less on the why and how. By the way, don't call them *Israel paratroopers*. The adjective is *Israeli*.

IRAN

A. Write a one-line headline of six or seven words
B. Write a three-line headline with two or three words on each line.

NICOSIA, Cyprus—Iran renewed an offer Friday to work for the release of nine American hostages in Lebanon if the United States would make the same efforts on behalf of Iranian hostages there.

Parliament Speaker Hashemi Rafsanjani made the offer in a Friday prayer sermon broadcast on official Tehran radio. Other Iranian officials have made the same suggestion, but Rafsanjani also condemned former U.S. President Jimmy Carter for trying to link resumption of U.S.-Iranian ties to the hostage issue.

Answer:

A. *Iran offer on hostage release renewed*

B. *Iran renews*
   offer to assist
   with hostages

Comment: This is a complex story that can't be fully told in seven words. How do you decide what to emphasize? Look at the lead. The first words are what the writer considers most important; don't snag yourself on secondary elements.

CRASH

A. Write a one-line head of seven or eight words.

B. Write a three-line headline with two or three words on each line.

DRYDEN, Ontario—An Air Ontario jet with 69 aboard crashed into trees and burst into flames shortly after takeoff during a snowstorm Friday, killing up to 23 people, police said.

Forty-six people survived the crash of the Winnipeg-bound Fokker F-28, said provincial police Constable Bill Brayshaw. One person was confirmed dead and 22 others were unaccounted for and presumed dead after several hours of searching in deep snow and rough terrain.

Answer:

A. *23 feared dead in Canadian air crash*

B. *46 survive*
   fiery crash
   of Canadian jet

Comment: Why do we say *(are) feared dead* instead of *(are) killed*? Notice that the lead says *up to 23 people* were killed. The writer knows that 69 were aboard and 46 have definitely survived. But until the other 23 bodies are identified, you have to hedge on the number killed. It's not totally unlikely that one survivor wandered off.

Do you emphasize the number killed or the number who survived? You can go either way, but we think it's remarkable when more people survive an air crash than are killed.

JUDGE

A. Write a one-line headline of six or seven words.

B. Write a two-line headline with four to six words on each line.

LOS ANGELES—A Superior Court judge Friday ignored a recommendation that Sheryl Lynn Massip be confined to a state mental hospital and ordered her to undergo at least a year of outpatient therapy to determine whether she has recovered from a psychosis that led her to kill her infant son two years ago.

Judge Robert R. Fitzgerald appeared to have based his unexpected ruling on an 11th-hour disclosure that a Los Angeles County man in circumstances similar to Massip's had been allowed to undergo outpatient therapy at a clinic in Fullerton, contrary to what was described as established procedure in Orange County.

Answer:

A. *Judge orders outpatient therapy for killer*

B. *Judge orders outpatient therapy*
for woman who killed infant son

Comment: Another complex story. The headline can be written with the skeleton and condense-and-patch approaches. Can we call her a killer? If she's been convicted, sure.

TORNADO

A. Write a one-line headline of five or six words.

B. Write a three-line headline with two or three words on each line.

ALBANY, N.Y.—An eighth child injured when a tornado slammed into a school cafeteria died Wednesday, a hospital spokesman said. Jennifer Homan, 8, died in Albany Medical Center, where she had been in critical condition with multiple injuries since the tornado last Thursday struck East Coldenham Elementary School near Newburgh, said spokesman Elmer Streeter.

Answer:

A. *Killer tornado claims 8th victim*

B. *Killer storm*
claims life
of 8th child

Comment: Once you come up with the seed *killer tornado,* the headline almost writes itself.

BOOTS

A. Write a hammer and a main headline of seven or eight words.

B. Write a main headline of six or seven words and a summary graph of 20 to 25 words. Remember to write the summary graph as a complete sentence.

WASHINGTON—If unusually big orders for combat boots are a tip-off to imminent hostilities, then America must be hurtling headlong toward war.

The 1992 defense spending bill given final passage by Congress Friday includes a provision requiring the Defense Department to buy $70 million worth of combat boots, even though the department already has 2 million pairs in stock.

The provision was added to the bill at the last minute after executives of the Pentagon's four combat boot suppliers met with representatives of several senators and congressmen with influence over defense spending.

The $70 million will buy roughly 1.5 million pairs of boots—half again as many as the Pentagon had been buying in the years before it started cutting the size of the armed forces. Next year the military is scheduled to shrink by 106,000 people.

Answer:
 A. *Congressional foot soldiers*
    Combat-boot purchase ordered despite peacetime cutbacks
 B. *Lobbyists win battle over combat-boot order*
    The defense spending bill passed by Congress requires the Pentagon to buy 1.5 million pairs at a time when the military is shrinking.

Comment: How clever can you get with the hammer? News organizations can be accused of bias based on the headline alone. Is this hammer fair? It fits the main thrust of a story that can't help but cast Congress in an unfavorable light.

With headline B, we're depending on the summary graph to fill in gaps in the headline. Note how we refer to *pairs* in the summary graph, relying on the headline to tell the reader what that means. When a story uses a summary graph, the headline should make the two elements work together.

10

Photos and Captions

—

I would willingly exchange every single painting of Christ for one snapshot.
—George Bernard Shaw

Photographs have never been more important in presenting the news. Technology enables newspapers and magazines to transmit and process pictures almost instantly. Modern presses provide better reproduction of photos than ever before, more and more often in color. But the foremost reason photos have gained in importance is that editors and reporters have developed a new appreciation for the storytelling power of photographs.

At larger news organizations, the task of selecting photos and preparing them for publication falls to specialists, the photo editors. They are involved in the photo process from making the assignment to archiving the finished product. At smaller publications, news editors or page designers often will double as their own photo editors.

All editors need to know how photos get on the page, if for no other reason than to foster an appreciation for what the photographer and photo editor do. What follows is a simplified approach to photo editing.

Photo editing involves five decisions:

- Should we run it and where?
- How big do we run it?
- How do we crop it?
- Should we retouch it?
- What does the caption say?

SELECTION PROCESS

Should we run it? The answer to this question usually comes in two parts. First, the photo editor usually has more than one photo to choose from. Second, the editor must make a broad decision about the newsworthiness of the photo chosen.

Good photos make the reader stop and think. Look for photos with emotion, ones that make the reader feel different, and impact, ones that make the reader understand.

Pictures should be informative. Harold Evans, in his book *Pictures on a Page*, writes that news photos must have "relevant context," details that put the reader at the scene. Angus McDougall, professor emeritus at the University of Missouri, adds that a good news photo makes a "clear statement." Its message is easily understood. McDougall also advises the photo editor to ask if the photo is suitable for the audience, and if it is fair to those who appear in it.

Other factors that a news editor should consider are: Is the photo well-composed? Will its technical quality allow for adequate reproduction? Is one picture enough, or are two needed?

Photo editors must be sensitive to charges of sensationalism. Somewhere photo editors must draw the line between using powerful images and turning readers off completely. But they can't be afraid to disturb people. Readers shouldn't be shielded from reality. Newspapers and magazines can soften the blow of controversial images by not running them on page one or on the cover.

Photo editors should know when not to run photos. They should try to avoid staged shots, check-passing shots or group shots. A group shot of a choir is better if the people are singing. At least it has some action. The choice between two pictures can be critical. The photo editor also has to make sure the image fits the story.

SIZE

Several factors go into how big a photo should run. Most important is the picture's newsworthiness. The first cloudy picture of Neil Armstrong on the moon, taken off a television monitor, covered the entire front of some newspapers in 1969. Despite a lack of quality, that picture was big news.

Beyond newsworthiness, the photo editor must consider space, size and sensationalism.

- How much space is available? A large, dominant photo will get a reader into a page like nothing else. In dividing up scarce real estate on a page, editors and writers should be willing to balance text with good photo play. The photo editor also should be willing to make the sometimes tough decision as to what photo will dominate the page. The other photos must run smaller, no more than half as big.
- Will the photo "read" if it runs small? An image like a face that fills up the frame can run small and still be recognizable. But pictures with a lot of small details must run larger, or readers won't be able to recognize what's in them.

Fig. 10.1

The original photo of former astronaut James Lovell. It's a vertical photo, but note that the bottom half is "negative space." It adds almost nothing to the meaning of the picture. (Photo by Michael O'Donnell)

- Will the photo be too sensational if it runs big? When photo editors have great shots, they want to run them as large as possible. But that zeal must be tempered with good taste. If the photo is gruesome but newsworthy, running it smaller will reduce its impact.

CROPPING

A good crop can help focus a photo and enhance its size. Photojournalism professor Ken Kobré of San Francisco State University advises the photo editor to "crop ruthlessly" while preserving the information in the photo. First, size up the photo and determine how many columns wide you want to run it. Most photos fall naturally into a vertical or horizontal shape.

How would you crop figure 10.1, a picture of astronaut James Lovell?

The original photo is full frame, how the photographer shot it. But because Lovell's hands and face are the focus of the photo, a better crop would make the photo into a horizontal (fig. 10.2). Note that this crop eliminates negative space, the part of the picture below Lovell's waist that adds nothing to the message. But you should avoid cutting off people exactly at the waist; note how we crop this photo slightly above the waist.

Most pictures are cropped to fit a standard column width. Once you've determined how many columns you want it to cover, convert to picas (see Chapter 11 for more on column widths). Because the image of James Lovell is large, filling the frame, the photo could run as small as two columns wide (about four inches), or it could be used as large as four columns wide (about eight inches) depending on the importance of the story.

Cropping and resizing are done on a computer using photo-editing software. The picture is digitized using a scanner and stored in a database. The photo editor opens the photo using editing software such as the Associated Press Leafdesk system (fig. 10.3) or Adobe Photoshop. The photo editor enters the width and draws the desired crop on the screen. The computer does the rest.

Electronic photo handling makes the task of cropping and sizing photos simpler in that less math is required. But mastering the computer equipment and the software takes practice. This is one reason photo editing has become a specialized task in many news rooms.

The key to getting a good crop is to let the photo play you; don't force a horizontal photo into a vertical shape or vice versa. Figure 10.4 shows a photo of a football team running on the field for its first practice. How would you crop it?

Fig. 10.2

This crop focuses on the subject and eliminates negative space.

Fig. 10.3

The Associated Press Leafdesk photo editing system. Photos stream into the system from a satellite feed, or an editor can scan in pictures locally. (Photo by Tony Kelly)

Fig. 10.4

The swarm of football players presents a horizontal shape. Note that the bleachers above their heads represent negative space: it doesn't add anything to the content of the picture. (Photo by Michael O'Donnell)

The original photo is a strong horizontal. Figure 10.5 shows a crop that forces the photo into a weak vertical shape. Besides changing the shape, and not for the better, this crop changes the information in the photo from a swarm of football players rushing on the field to a few stragglers. This crop isn't honest.

In figure 10.6, the photo is used full width, with some of the dead space cropped off the top. This crop strengthens the horizontal shape and focuses the photo on the players without losing information.

Mug Shots

A mug shot is a picture of a person's face. These small photos are regular items in most publications and are worth a little extra attention. Mug shots often are cropped to a standard width and height. The photo editor enters both dimensions into the computer rather than just the width. This means that sometimes a mugshot doesn't get the ideal crop.

Here are some tips on making the most of mug shots.

Fill the Frame

Often photo editors give in to the temptation to squeeze or stretch a mugshot to save or take up space. The result is a mug that looks too loose or too tight. Follow these three guidelines:

1. A small amount of space should be left above the head and on each side of the ears. Generally, the space will be about a half-pica for a 1-column mug.

2. The bottom crop should be near the knot of a tie or just below the Adam's apple.

3. Mug shots must be in balance. In other words, if several photos appear on the same page, all faces must be of the same relative size.

Fig. 10.5

This crop forces the horizontal picture into a vertical shape. It is a dishonest crop because it changes the content of the photo from a swarm of players to a small group.

A Bit of History

Before the computer, the photographer had to produce a print using an enlarger, a time-consuming process for black and white and a real deadline buster for color.

The print was cropped and sized using a grease pencil and a sizing wheel. Some editors used sizing scrolls instead of the wheel, and a few had begun using calculators about the

Fig. 10.6

This crop retains the original information of the picture but focuses our attention on the players by eliminating negative space above them.

Fig. 10.7

A halftone pattern enlarged. By varying the size of the dots, the halftone gives the illusion of many shades of gray. Today, computers produce halftones.

Figure 10.10 shows three crops. The crop on the right is most desirable. The one on the left is too tight, and the one in the middle is too loose.

SIZING WHEEL

Here's how to use a sizing wheel to do what is done on a computer.

1. First, decide the ideal crop. Mark it on the photo using a grease pencil by making eight marks in all, two on each side of the photo. Don't mark the part of the photo you want to use (fig. 10.8).

2. Measure your original width (OW) and your original depth (OD). The original width (OW) is the number of picas between the crop marks determining the width of the photo. The original depth (OD) is the number of picas between the crop marks determining the depth of the photo.

3. You'll record the original width and original depth, and three other figures:

   • The final width (FW): The number of picas equal to the number of columns wide the photo will be printed.

   • The final depth (FD): The number of picas equal to how tall, or "deep," the photo will be printed.

   • The size of reproduction (SOR): The percentage of difference between the original size of the cropped photo and the final size of the published photo.

(continued)
time that the first desktop computer picture editing systems came along. The marked-up photo then went to the camera room, where it was reduced or enlarged and made into a halftone, a pattern of dots that gives the illusion of gray using black ink and white paper (fig. 10.7).

SLUG: _____Bassey_____

OW: _12p_____ FW: _6p0_____

OD: _15p0_____ FD: _7p6____

SOR: _50%_____

Fig. 10.8

When cropping and sizing a photo for camera reproduction, the markup must include the picture slug, eight crop marks (two on each side of the photo) and five numbers: original width (OW), original depth (OD), final width (FW), final depth (FD) and size of reproduction (SOR). (Photo by Michael O'Donnell)

Some publications used special routing slips that were pasted on the photo and contained this information. At many smaller papers, the information was written on the back of the photo.

You'll determine three of these figures. By cropping, you determine the original width and depth, and by using news judgment, you determine the final width when you decide how many columns wide to run the photo.

4. You use the wheel to determine the final depth and the size of reproduction. You may have to do some translating of figures:

- First translate columns into picas after you've determined your final width.

- Some publications may require that you describe picture depth in inches. If so, reconvert your final width from picas to columns and translate your final depth from picas to inches. Many newspapers and magazines today describe picture depth in lines of type; this may require a more complicated calculation when you transfer the dimensions to the page dummy.

- Remember, when using the wheel, you must use the same unit of measurement for the width and the depth, whether that is inches or picas. We'll use picas.

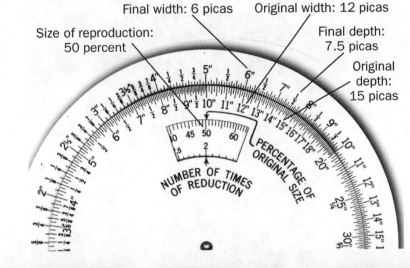

Final width: 6 picas   Original width: 12 picas

Size of reproduction:
50 percent

Final depth:
7.5 picas

Original
depth:
15 picas

Fig. 10.9

Use the sizing wheel to determine the final depth and
the size of reproduction.
Remember to use the
same unit of measurement
for the width and the
depth, whether that is
inches or picas.

Fig. 10.10

Three crops of a mug shot:
The one on the right is
most desirable; the one on
the left is too tight; the
middle one is too loose.
(Photo by Michael
O'Donnell)

5. Your original figures always are on the inside wheel. The final figures are always on the outside. Line up your original width with
   your final width. In our example (fig. 10.9), we started with an
   original width of 12 picas. Find that on the inside wheel and line
   it up with the final width of six picas.

6. Look on the inside wheel for the original depth, in this case 15
   picas. Now look at the corresponding figure on the outside: 7$\frac{1}{2}$
   picas, or 7 picas 6 points.

7. Your SOR is found in the little window as a percentage; 100 percent means the OW equals the FW and OD equals the FD. If
   the original photo is smaller than the final published photo, it
   must be blown up and the SOR will be more than 100 percent.
   If the original photo is larger than what will appear in the paper,
   the SOR will be less than 100 percent.

Profile Shots

Mug shots often have to be made from photos of people in profile. The
secret is to avoid crowding the subject's face. In other words, give the person
somewhere to look.

Figure 10.11 is an original with crop marks to show how a mug shot was
carved out of a regular photo; no special portrait was taken. Notice also how the
crop marks are arranged to "straighten" the mug shot.

Fig. 10.11

Notice how the mug shot is carved out of a regular photo. The mug is straightened during the cropping process. The crop on the left is most desirable. (Photo by Michael O'Donnell)

The crop on the right is too tight on the face. The one on the left is better. To make a profile mug shot work, you may have to crop out some of the back of the head.

Intruding Objects

What do you do when an object intrudes into the frame? Figure 10.12 shows an original of a hockey player and two possible crops. You can:

- crop out the subject's hand altogether (right).
- include the object in the mug shot (left). When you do this, make sure that just enough of the object is in the frame to be recognizable.

Fig. 10.12

Intruding objects can be cropped out or left in, but notice how the size of the subject's face is much smaller when room is made for the intruding hand. (Photo by Michael O'Donnell)

If the object is a hand, as in this example, the reader should be able to tell whose hand it is.

The danger is that to make room for the object, you'll reduce the size of the face too much. The crop with the hand in it will work better on a bigger mug shot, say one column instead of a half-column.

RETOUCHING PHOTOS

In the early part of the 20th century, virtually every photo had to be retouched. This was because the technology for running photos was new and crude, and photography itself was less exact. As reproduction and photography improved, retouching became less necessary. But today the retouching of photos is a hot topic because of digital photo handling. Sophisticated computer programs make exotic alterations simple and easy.

Figure 10.13 shows a photo digitized on a desktop film scanner and altered using Adobe Photoshop. The alterations were made with equipment that costs about $2,500.

Professional photographers and photo editors are concerned that readers will begin to doubt the truthfulness of all photos if they suspect some have been altered. As a result, many professionals advocate no electronic retouching beyond clarifying a picture: removing dust and scratches, correcting color and tone, and restoring sharpness lost in the scanning process. Anything that might mislead readers should not be done; the credibility of the publication is at stake.

THE CAPTION

A photo may be worth a thousand words, but usually a few words more are needed to explain the photo and expand on its content. That is the function of a caption, sometimes called a *cutline*.

A photo caption briefly answers the who, what, where, why, when and how questions brought up by a picture. All the journalistic canons about brevity and precision apply with particular force to caption writing.

In its most basic form, the caption identifies people or objects. Simple captions also can include the where and when. But many photos need explanation and background. In such cases, a caption will place the event or action shown in context and sum up its significance.

Fig. 10.13

One John Hancock building becomes many thanks to digital retouching. (Photo illustration by Michael O'Donnell)

A photo should be analyzed to determine why it has been selected and what caption elements are needed. One way to determine what the caption needs to say is to look at the photo without any caption to see if the photo communicates on its own. If it does, the caption can be brief; if not, the caption must start out with the salient facts.

Each caption requires the writer to edit a mountain of facts down to those that apply to the photo. This may take a careful reading of the story that goes with the photo. Here are three tips:

1. Avoid the obvious.

2. When in doubt, let the picture do the talking. The caption is a selective writing job that demands clarity to help the reader understand the photo quickly.

3. The first sentence often is cast in the present tense. The writer can shift to past tense in following sentences. This use of the "historical present" is a long-standing practice. Some editors believe using past tense is more honest. In any case, don't hesitate to drop the present tense if it would give a false impression that something happened more recently than it did. Writing in the present tense works with action photos but should not be done with file photos. Verbs are preferred but a caption can be written without one if the action is obvious or the photo is an illustrator that works best with a label caption.

Common Types of Photos and Captions

News photos, feature photos, filers and illustrators are common types of photos with unique caption requirements. Photos that go with feature stories require a lighter treatment than news photos. A picture retrieved from the archives to go with a story—what we call a "filer"—needs special handling. Stand-alone photos require different caption information than those running with a story and headline.

News Photos

News photos need captions that contain facts and as many identities as feasible. When a photo stands alone, without an accompanying story, a small headline called a *catchline* can state the facts or try to act as a bridge from image to caption. Tread on the side of caution when considering levity for a news catchline. Figure 10.14 shows a news photo and caption.

Features

Features can be light or serious. Light features need a special writing touch with a witty catchline. Often these photos have at least a partial weather relationship, which spurs caption writers to repeat almost verbatim a forecast that is available in at least two other places in the paper. Generalities are fine, such as "Spring doesn't officially begin until Saturday," but repeating forecasts

AP WORLDWIDE PHOTOS; USED BY PERMISSION

Somber members of the House Judiciary Committee talk with reporters Friday after the Senate acquitted President Clinton on the articles of impeachment. From left: Lindsey Graham, R-S.C., Asa Hutchinson, R-Ark., Henry Hyde, R-Ill.

Fig. 10.14

A news photo with caption. Note that this style of caption writing uses present tense. (AP/Wide World Photos; used by permission)

should be avoided. Serious features, such as the street department figuring out what to do about a pavement collapse, often work best with a witty catchline and a certain amount of flair in the writing, but don't let levity lead to a lawsuit. Figure 10.15 shows a feature photo and caption.

Filers

For many stories, photos are retrieved from the reference library or another source. These require special care so that the reader is not misled into thinking the photo is current.

The object of the caption should be to tie the photo tightly to the story. The caption should alert the reader that the photo is not current in as unobtrusive a manner as possible. One method is to handle the opening sentence as an explanation of the story's crux and not address the specific action of the photo. Caution is advised in using noncurrent photos as generic illustrators, especially those containing identifiable people. And be careful of dead giveaways: In that file photo of tennis star Andre Agassi, is he wearing his 1994 hairdo?

Often only a name line is necessary for a file photo unless the photo is old and needs to be dated in the caption, or if obscure or secondary subjects in a story need to be identified. This happens often with mug shots on the business page, where a caption can add clarity by giving an executive's title.

Illustrators

These often are environmental portraits of people, taken in their own surroundings. Many times, illustrators are set up for the camera. Don't lead readers into thinking otherwise. Illustrators include publicity shots provided by

PHOTO BY MICHAEL O'DONNELL

Chill out, man

Sub-zero temperatures and two feet of snow Thursday could not force this Waldorf College student into donning long pants. Saturday's forecast promises temperatures that might get the job done. For more on the weather, see Page 12.

Fig. 10.15

A stand-alone feature photo with a "kicker." It refers to the weather story elsewhere in the paper. (Photo by Michael O'Donnell)

an ad agency, such as those received from a record company when a music group is scheduled to perform.

The easiest method of writing a caption for an illustrator is to identify the person and use a quote after a colon. Strive for something more, either a mention of the surroundings or a contextual quote that contains no more than a phrase in direct quotes (fig. 10.16).

Combination Captions

When more than one photo is used, the best approach is to give each picture its own caption. An exception is when the photos are closely related, such as in chronological order. Writing "combo" captions for several photos requires care in guiding the reader around the page.

The Right Words

Caption writing, like headline writing, has its own language. But the much-used language of captions is riddled with clichés and weak verbs. Here's some advice:

FILE PHOTO BY MICHAEL O'DONNELL

Bill Veeck: He'll forever be remembered as the man who sent a midget up to bat in a major-league baseball game.

Fig. 10.16

When a file photo is used, a good approach is to borrow a quote or line from the story while letting the photo speak for itself. (Photo by Michael O'Donnell)

- An empty verb tells the obvious and takes up precious space. Empty verbs, such as the following, should be used only as a last resort: *poses, stands, waves, sits, points, shares a laugh* and *looks on.* These verbs call attention to the weaknesses of a photo. It may lack action, look posed or come up short on context. If the caption can't be reworded, go without a verb: *Mel Gibson and his wife, Robyn, at the Golden Globe Awards.* Not *Mel Gibson and his wife, Robyn, pose at the Golden Globe Awards.*
- Most adjectives and adverbs can be cut to make a caption fit.
- If you must use the verb *stand,* make sure the subject is standing with his or her feet visible.
- Describe the photo without stating the obvious, but note that the *when* and *where* of a photo often are not apparent. Make sure to clarify this for the reader.
- A good caption tells what happened before and after the action shown in the picture. If the action is obvious, telling the before and after is often a way out of stating the obvious.
- *Who* is important even when it is obvious.
- *What* and *how* should be obvious, visually or verbally.
- Use only good quotes and only when they help tie the photo to the story.
- Don't assume and don't try to describe emotions or what a subject might be thinking. For example, a person at a funeral is rubbing his eye. Don't guess at what is going on and write, *Joe Johnson fights back tears.*
- Photographers are responsible for caption information but often deadlines or other problems intervene, leaving many of the facts in question until the caption writer is involved. Similar situations arise with wire photos. A call to the wire service, assignment desk or staff photographer may clear up the problem. If not, alert the picture editor. Sometimes a different photo can be used.

Identity Clues

Identity clues can be enclosed in parentheses or set off with commas. Use as few as necessary. Often (from left) is all you need. More and more news organizations are using the convention of giving readers a starting point then advising them to move clockwise or counterclockwise. The identity clue can be placed after a verb introducing a string of people or after the first name in the group. Go back to figure 10.14 for an example of how to use identity clues.

When more than one photo is used with a combination caption, the situation becomes more complicated. The preferred method is to introduce each photo's part of the caption with its location and a colon, as in *TOP: President Clinton boards Air Force One.* But some news organizations incorporate the location into the sentence: *At top, President Clinton boards Air Force One.*

Start the caption by referring to the photo directly above the caption. Use the word *above* as a last resort.

11

The Page

—

The proportions of a page are like an interval in music. In a given context, some are consonant, others dissonant. Some are familiar; some are also inescapable because of their presence in the structures of the natural as well as the man-made world.
—Robert Bringhurst

The design of a page is a valuable tool for communicating with the reader. It tells the reader what's important and what things are related. It organizes information so it's easy to navigate.

Page design is easier if the editor understands the hierarchy of the news. When we establish a hierarchy on the page, we signal to the reader what we think is important; we set an agenda for reading the publication.

Hierarchy is established through the following:

- Space: A lot of space devoted to a story signals its importance.
- Type size: A big headline signals an important story.
- Placement: Placing one story above another signals which is most important.
- Artwork: The use of a big picture or illustration signals that this story is the one to read first.

If a page is budgeted thoroughly and if the editor is fully informed of the hierarchy that budget establishes, then obvious strategies for page design should present themselves. The Maestro Concept, discussed in Chapter 8, was developed to give the page designer the important elements of a story in a predictable way. From there the keys to good design are a knowledge about type and an understanding of the page grid.

TYPE

The most powerful tool a designer commands is type. Pictures can be made bigger or smaller, and stories can be arranged according to an agenda, but type sets the tone for the story and for the whole page. Look at this page from the *Star Tribune* (fig 11.1). As important as the picture may be, the type delivers the message loud and clear in a way that says, "This is important, this is serious."

Typefaces for general use come in two broad categories: *serif* and *sans serif*. A serif is the finishing stroke across the bottom or top of a letter. Sans serif type does not have these finishing strokes (fig. 11.3).

Newspapers and magazines work with a limited number of typefaces. In general, a publication will have a body type, a headline dress and a "special effects" typeface. These will be organized into type "style sheets," with

Fig. 11.1

The front page of the *Star Tribune* for Sunday, Dec. 20, shows how type can be used creatively to make a statement. Notice how the message is pared down, using enlarged body type and large headlines.
(© *The Star Tribune;* used by permission)

Basic Measurements

Type is measured in points. For the record, 72 points equals one inch, 6 picas equals one inch and 12 points equals one pica.

Column widths are stated in picas and points. A column 12.2 picas wide would measure 12 picas and 2 points, not 2/10 of a pica. Thus, a column marked 14.10 (14 picas 10 points) is not the same as one marked 14.1 (14 picas 1

Serif

72 pt. = 1 inch

Serif

SERIF

SANS SERIF

Fig. 11.2

Type size is measured from the top of the ascender to the bottom of the descender. Note that the actual type may be slightly smaller than the nominal size, in this case 72 points.

Fig. 11.3

Typefaces for general use come in two broad categories: *serif* and *sans serif*.

dozens of combinations of type size, weight, leading and alignment. The style sheets are set up to provide the right type for the subject matter (news, features, sports) and for the tone desired (serious or light). For instance, the basic body text may be justified across the column for news stories, set flush left (or "ragged right") for features and enlarged slightly for editorials. The special-effects typeface may be used in boldface capitals for bylines, boldface and uppercase and lowercase for captions, and lightface and all capitals for photo credits (fig. 11.4).

Most publications maintain a *graphics style sheet.* This is a list of type styles with the type specifications, examples of appropriate use and list of special codes that need to be used with the computer system.

Body Type

Body type is used for the main text in a publication. By definition, body type is 12 points or smaller. Leading is the space between lines of type. Leading is measured from the top of one line of type to the top of the next line. A typical newspaper body type might be a 9-point serif face such as Times Roman set on 9.5-point leading.

Headline Dress

Years ago, newspapers and magazines used one headline typeface. To introduce contrast, the publications would vary weight from light to bold and mix roman and italic. Today, italic headlines are used less, and many publications now mix serif and sans serif typefaces to gain contrast in headlines. *USA Today* was the pioneer in mixing serif and sans serif typefaces. Most publica-

(continued)

point). With some computer systems, these measures are expressed as 12p2, 14p10 or 14p1.

A measure of 13.5 picas is not 13½ picas; it's 13 picas 5 points. A measure of 13½ picas would be 13.6 because 6 points equals half a pica.

A headline of 72 points would measure one inch from the top of the tallest letter to the lowest descender (fig. 11.2).

Type often is specified by size and by leading, pronounced *ledding*, the space between lines of type. Body type might be specified as 10 point on 11 leading, or 10 on 11. That means the distance from the top of one line of type to the top of the next line is 11 points.

tions avoid using too many typefaces. Typefaces are like voices in a choir; they must sing in harmony.

Chapter 9 showed examples of several headline combinations. The skilled designer uses the available combinations of typefaces, type weights (bold or light) and type sizes to index the news. A large, bold headline tells the reader that this story is important. Small, lightfaced headlines are used for briefs and short items.

Special Effects

In addition to body type and headline dresses, newspapers and magazines use a typeface for special effects and accessories, such as teasers, captions, subheads and credit lines. A special effects typeface is chosen to contrast with body type; it signals the reader that this type is something different from a normal story.

Display Type

Some designers consider any type bigger than 12 points to be display type. The term also is used to mean special type designs such as the tripod headline discussed in Chapter 9.

Display type headlines, a staple of features sections, are finding their way onto the news pages for stories that deserve special treatment. With computer typesetting and composition, designers have hundreds of typefaces at their fingertips.

Fig. 11.4

Most newspapers and magazines define how they use type with a *graphics style sheet*.

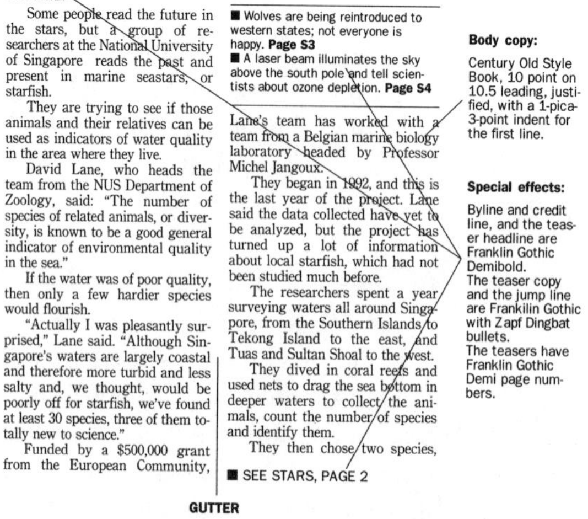

FIGURE 11.4

Headline dress:

Hammer headline is Franklin Gothic Condensed Heavy. Main head is Century Book Condensed.

Body copy:

Century Old Style Book, 10 point on 10.5 leading, justified, with a 1-pica-3-point indent for the first line.

Special effects:

Byline and credit line, and the teaser headline are Franklin Gothic Demibold. The teaser copy and the jump line are Franklin Gothic with Zapf Dingbat bullets. The teasers have Franklin Gothic Demi page numbers.

Star search

Sea creatures give clues to ocean's pollution levels

BY HEIDI YEO
STAFF WRITER

Some people read the future in the stars, but a group of researchers at the National University of Singapore reads the past and present in marine seastars, or starfish.

They are trying to see if those animals and their relatives can be used as indicators of water quality in the area where they live.

David Lane, who heads the team from the NUS Department of Zoology, said: "The number of species of related animals, or diversity, is known to be a good general indicator of environmental quality in the sea."

If the water was of poor quality, then only a few hardier species would flourish.

"Actually I was pleasantly surprised," Lane said. "Although Singapore's waters are largely coastal and therefore more turbid and less salty and, we thought, would be poorly off for starfish, we've found at least 30 species, three of them totally new to science."

Funded by a $500,000 grant from the European Community,

Inside

■ Wolves are being reintroduced to western states; not everyone is happy. **Page S3**
■ A laser beam illuminates the sky above the south pole and tell scientists about ozone depletion. **Page S4**

Lane's team has worked with a team from a Belgian marine biology laboratory headed by Professor Michel Jangoux.

They began in 1992, and this is the last year of the project. Lane said the data collected have yet to be analyzed, but the project has turned up a lot of information about local starfish, which had not been studied much before.

The researchers spent a year surveying waters all around Singapore, from the Southern Islands to Tekong Island to the east, and Tuas and Sultan Shoal to the west.

They dived in coral reefs and used nets to drag the sea bottom in deeper waters to collect the animals, count the number of species and identify them.

They then chose two species,

■ SEE STARS, PAGE 2

ALLEY

GUTTER

Agate

The term *agate* refers to the small type used for stock market tables, sports statistics and election results. At larger newspapers and magazines, agate clerks may be responsible for arranging most of this type, but at medium and small publications, editors may be responsible for coding this type. Sometimes agate is in the same typeface as the body type, but more often agate is set in its own simple, easy-to-read typeface. Special typefaces, such as Bell Centennial and Spartan Classified, are available, designed to be used small in tight places.

THE PAGE

Newspapers come in two sizes: broadsheet and tabloid. The broadsheet page is 14 inches wide and 22 inches tall. Allowing for a half-inch margin, the printable part of the page is 13 inches wide (78 picas) and 21 inches tall (126 picas). The tabloid newspaper page is half the size of the broadsheet: 11 inches wide and 14 inches tall with a printable area of about 10 inches (60 picas) by 13 inches (78 picas).

The differences between the two formats go beyond page size. The broadsheet is "quarterfolded": It's folded into sections, then folded over again. This allows separate sections to be inserted into each other. The tabloid comes as one big section. It isn't as easy to pull apart as a broadsheet is.

Magazine formats vary widely, but all share one thing in common: The page size is governed by the content. *Reader's Digest,* for instance, is a compact 5.25 inches wide and 7.25 inches tall. It's perfect for fitting in a pocket. Because it emphasizes text, it doesn't need the larger display space of a news magazine such as *Time,* about 8.5 inches by 11 inches. Meanwhile, *ESPN: The Magazine* goes with an even bigger 10 inches by 12 inches to accommodate its huge color pictures that often extend across two full pages.

Gutters and Alleys

Gutters are the vertical spaces between columns of type. Alleys are strips of horizontal space that separate stories, pictures and headlines from those above and below. In newspaper use, gutters and alleys commonly are 1 pica wide. Magazines commonly use wider gutters, 1 pica 6 points for the *Atlantic Monthly,* for instance.

Don't underestimate the effect of uniform gutters and alleys, with text and artwork lined up precisely. These areas of white space define the shape and often the direction of the page; they serve as lines of organization. When gutters and alleys are not straight or are irregular in width, the page will look disorganized.

Some publications define their alleys in lines of type. For example, if the standard body type is 9 point on 9.5-point leading, the minimum alley between related items might be 9.5 points, or one line of type; the minimum alley between unrelated items might be 19 points, or two lines of type. Often publications using this scheme make all vertical measurements in lines of type, including picture height.

Many publications will use much wider gutters and alleys for special designs, as much as 6 picas. This white space sets off stories and pictures, making them stand out from other elements.

Column Measures

Most newspapers have a standard column width, or standard measure, of about 12 picas (2 inches) wide. This width fits the requirements of national advertisers, who need a standard column width to run the same ads in many newspapers at once.

For a full-size broadsheet newspaper, the standard measure usually is 12.2 (12 picas 2 points). On the broadsheet's 78-pica-wide page, this 12.2 measure produces six columns with five 1-pica gutters.

For a tabloid newspaper, the standard measure might be slightly different. A standard measure of 11.6 (11 picas 6 points) would produce five columns with 1-pica gutters on a page 61.6 picas wide.

Some tabloid newspapers are laid out on five columns of 12.2 picas for a total width of 64 picas 10 points. The page is then reduced during the plate-making process, ads and all, to fit on the regular tabloid page.

Odd measures, typeset on something other than the standard measure, should be no narrower than 9 picas and no wider than 19 picas for standard body type. Type set too narrow produces eye fatigue with the constant shifting from line to line. Type set too wide becomes difficult to follow from the end of one line to the start of another. If for some reason you want to set type on an extra-wide measure, consider increasing the leading. Odd measures are used primarily for stories in boxes, such as sidebars or opinion columns, or for stand-alone photos (fig. 11.5).

Always allow for internal space when you lay out elements in a box or tint block (fig. 11.6). Leaving too little internal space is one common error beginners make. Text has shape, and that shape is defined by white space. Providing white space around type in a box gives the type definition, makes it more attractive and adds to readability.

In laying out stories, remember that column widths have meaning for the reader. Something set wider than usual, for instance, signals the reader that

Fig. 11.5

Leaving too little internal space is one common error beginners make. Text has shape, and that shape is defined by white space. Providing white space around type in a box gives the type definition, makes it more attractive and adds to readability.

HERE'S THE SPECS FOR A PHOTO IN A BOX:

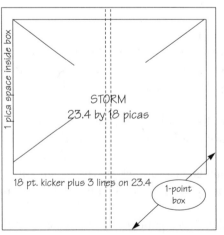

HERE'S HOW IT LOOKS (REDUCED IN SIZE):

PHOTO BY MICHAEL O'DONNELL

Fernando fanatics
Dodgers rookie sensation Fernando Valenzuela signs autographs at Wrigley Field before his first start against the Cubs. Valenzuela has won his first six outings.

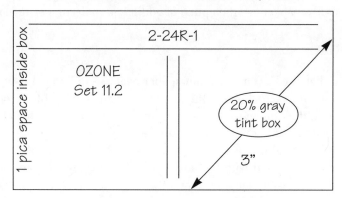

TINT BOXES NEED INTERNAL SPACE, TOO:

1 pica space inside box

2-24R-1

OZONE
Set 11.2

20% gray
tint box

3"

HERE'S HOW IT LOOKS (REDUCED IN SIZE):

Laser beam measures ozone

A laser beam is stabbing the sky above the South Pole, and scientists expect that it will illuminate vital details about the depletion of the ozone layer.

A team of scientists from the University of Illinois will operate the beam during the Antarctic winter, when darkness prevails 24 hours a day.

The ozone layer in the upper atmosphere contains a small amount of ozone gas, a compound containing three atoms of oxygen. Ozone blocks harmful ultraviolet rays.

Laser probing is expected to show how stratospheric ice crystals change as the ozone hole is created.

Fig. 11.6

Always allow for internal space when you lay out elements in a tint block, too.

this story is special. The disciplined publication will reserve certain measures for special uses. Also be aware that smaller type can be set on a narrower measure. Agate type of 5 or 6 points can be set on a measure as narrow as 7 picas.

The Flag

The streamer across the top of page one carrying the name of the newspaper is called the flag or nameplate. Each section such as sports, feature or business may have its own flag, too.

Some flags, like that used by *USA Today*, are elaborate graphic devices. *USA Today*'s flag has boxes on each side, called ears, that contain pictures and teasers. Most newspapers choose a simpler design for the flag, commonly about 2 inches deep at the top of page one.

Headline Sizes

Make sure that your headlines carry the proper weight; that is, that they are large enough or small enough for the length of the story running under them.

The person who lays out a page should make sure the headline writer has a long enough headline to tell the story without it being so long as to require padding. As a rough guide, give the headline writer at least 25 counts but no more than 50.

Remember, you can add counts by making the headline smaller or by adding lines. You also have the option of adding an underline or readout.

THE GRID

Until about 15 years ago, newspaper pages were laid out using dummy sheets, simple representations of the newspaper page reduced to fit on a sheet of paper. Often the dummy sheets weren't in the same proportion as the newspaper page itself, making it difficult for the news editor to get an accurate mental picture of the final product.

All that changed with the advent of computer page layout, or pagination, and other forms of computer typesetting such as block composition. With pagination, the entire page is laid out on the computer screen, then set all at once as a composite page (fig. 11.7). Desktop publishing programs such as QuarkXpress and Adobe PageMaker are really pagination programs. Many magazines and newspapers use those same programs with special modifications to produce their pages. Often the paginator is the same person who designs the page, and sometimes he or she is called the page designer. A paginator often does not use a paper dummy at all.

Block composition involves coding type on the computer so that it comes out in its final shape, with headlines and space for pictures and cutlines in place. The block then can be pasted down as a unit. With block composition, a paper dummy still is used, but it must be extremely accurate if all the pieces are to fit on the page. Coding of type may be complex and may be done by specialists. Block composition is still used by many large newspapers.

With pagination and block composition, the old, simple page dummy sheet has been replaced by a grid. The grid is a detailed diagram that allows accurate representation of vertical and horizontal space. Some grids, such as the Swiss grid, use line of type as the basic unit of vertical measurement. The

Fig. 11.7

An editor at the *Times* of Munster, Ind., lays out a page on an electronic grid. The *Times'* system was one of the first in the country to use desktop computers and programs as a pagination system. (Photo by Tony Kelly)

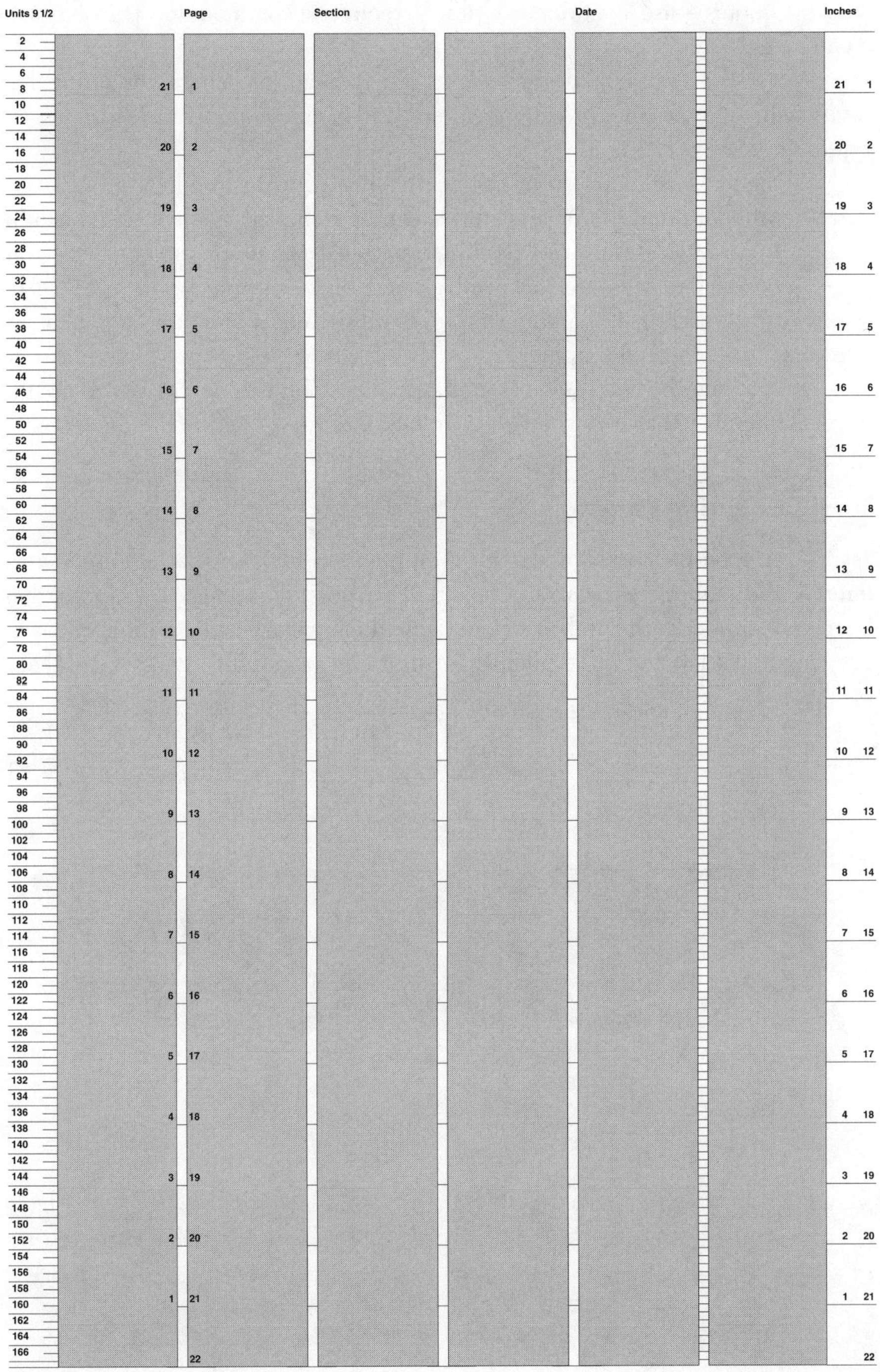

Fig. 11.8

A modified Swiss grid. The units down the left side are lines of type, 9-point body text on 9.5-point leading. The units down the right are inches to accommodate advertising.

columns also may be divided in half to increase flexibility of design (fig. 11.8). Page grids for magazines take in a smaller space, with the emphasis on flexibility (fig. 11.9).

Modular Layout

Most newspapers and magazines use modular layout. With modular layout, all the elements that go with a story—headlines, photos, captions, teasers, quotes—are contained within a rectangle, or module. This has two advantages.

First, it forces the designer to treat text, headlines and art as a unit. The relationships in the final product are clear, and each component adds to the storytelling power of the text.

Second, modular layout has many advantages for production. Modules can be shifted around easily, and stories can be replaced by clearing a module.

Figure 11.10 shows six thumbnail pages divided into modules. On each page, secondary stories are arranged around the centerpiece story (CP). The secondary modules may contain only a headline and a story, or they may include other photos and graphics.

Modular layout provides unlimited possibilities for dividing up the page. Remember that how you use your space will help define the news.

Designing the Page

A good page design starts with a detailed budget, with accurate story lengths and realistic estimates of how much will fit on a page. If planning has been done properly, the budget will indicate the top story and secondary stories, the length of each story, the photos, illustrations or graphics that go with each

Fig. 11.9

A six-column magazine grid that is commonly used with a page size of about 8 inches by 10 inches. It can accommodate a variety of type sizes and formats: three column, two column or six column—or any combination.

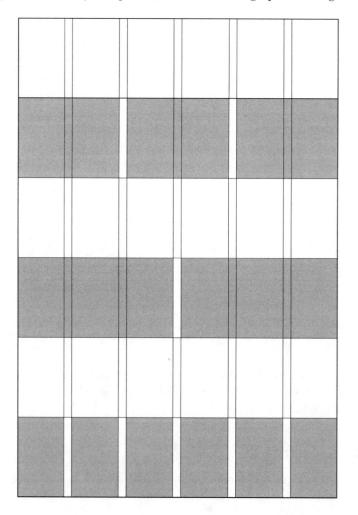

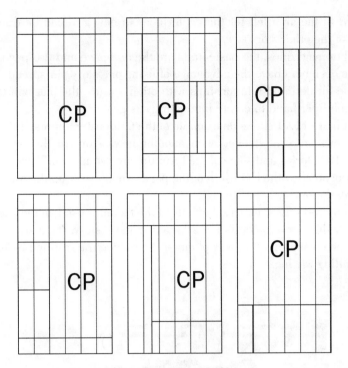

Fig. 11.10

Modular layout provides almost unlimited possibilities for design, but with clearly defined relationships and a refined sense of organization.

story and the "furniture." The furniture includes items that must run on the page, such as standing features, teasers or indices.

The number of stories and pieces of art used on page one will affect how many stories are jumped, or continued to an inside page. Some papers jump all the page-one stories; others use fewer stories and try to contain entire stories on the front page. Because page-one stories tend to be the longest in the paper, you will no doubt have to jump some stories despite studies showing that readers don't like jumps.

From the budget, determine your centerpiece story. Often the centerpiece is also the top news story of the day, but sometimes it's a secondary story that has the best possibilities for combining art and text. The Maestro Concept described in Chapter 8 is an effective way to produce these centerpiece stories.

Determine what will be the dominant element of your centerpiece, most often the largest photo. Occasionally, type may serve as your dominant element; that often means a big, bold headline or special display type.

Size up the shape of the dominant element and consider how type might be arranged around it. Will you need a horizontal module, one that's wide rather than tall? Or will you need a vertical module, one that's tall rather than wide?

Now, here's the trick to laying out a page with a centerpiece: Figure out roughly the space you'll need, horizontal or vertical, for your centerpiece, then arrange the other stories, leaving that space clear. Sometimes the designer will lay a story across the top of the page and another down the side and another across the bottom, leaving a letter-size space, about 8 inches by 10 inches. Often, with broadsheet pages, the designer will confine the other stories to narrow strips down the side and across the bottom, leaving a tabloid-size space of about 10 inches by 13 inches. Sometimes the designer will arrange the other stories across the bottom to leave a centerpiece across the full width of the page. Some designers refer to designing around a centerpiece as the *miniposter* approach. In the area left for the centerpiece, a new grid can be drawn independent of the other stories.

For magazines, the basic units are the one-page and two-page spreads. Magazine designers have the advantage of using one story per spread. With the need gone for defining relationships with other stories, the magazine designer has a much freer hand to create interesting designs.

Figure 11.11 shows an example of the miniposter approach. Notice that the top news story is stacked with another news story in the two left-most columns. Two stories and some of the furniture are "squared off" across the bottom to form an alley the full width of the page. An alley set up this way is sometimes called a brace.

Figure 11.12 shows a schematic of the modules used on the page. You'll notice that this centerpiece is not a breaking news story. It's a story about an issue in the community that was planned to produce interesting photos as well as compelling writing.

Fig. 11.11

The centerpiece approach as executed by the *Star Tribune* of Minneapolis. (© *The Star Tribune;* used by permission)

Fig. 11.12

Notice how stories are arranged in modules around the centerpiece. (© *The Star Tribune;* used by permission)

The Dominant Element

The dominant element is another way of saying where the reader will look first on the page. Research has shown that readers almost always enter a page through the largest photo, whether it's in black and white or color. When a designer puts a strong dominant element on the page, it tells the reader where to start. Then other visual cues—headlines, graphics, other photos—move the reader around the page.

For years, the rule at newspapers has been that the dominant photo must be at least twice as big as any other photo on the page. If you look over the pages of well-designed newspapers, however, you'll find that the dominant photo often is even bigger proportionally than that.

A large photo and a much smaller photo create contrast. The same can be done with very large type and much smaller type. Contrast creates eye movement and visual excitement.

Showing Relationships within the Module

How you arrange elements within the module often depends on the shape of the photo, the headline style used and what else is on the page. The goal is to integrate the text, photo and headline and show their relationship.

An umbrella headline covers all elements and provides a clear line of organization within the module. Underneath the umbrella head, the text can be arranged in an L-shaped wrap around the photo (fig. 11.13) or in a U-shaped wrap (Figure 11.14). The L-shaped wrap works well when you need to separate the dominant photo from an unrelated photo on the left. The U-shaped wrap provides less separation but tighter integration of text and photo. Notice that the L-shaped wrap leaves a large area of gray type to the left of the photo.

To make this gray type look less imposing, we use several breakers: a large initial at the start of the story called a drop cap, a quotation set in special type called a pull quote or drop quote, and small headlines within the story called subheads.

The umbrella head creates a strong horizontal element that can give the module a solid, calm feel. To increase the visual tension, headlines can be stacked in a vertical arrangement with the picture to the side and the text forming the L-shaped wrap. (fig. 11.15). With this arrangement, you can use the picture to separate the headline from another headline to the right.

Switching from a horizontal approach to a vertical one will change the personality of the module. You should try to fit that personality to the content. Strong, exciting vertical packages are good for hard news, while calmer horizontal packages can be used for features and softer news.

Fig. 11.13

This module uses an umbrella headline and an L-shaped type wrap to integrate the picture and text into a tight package. Note the use of "breakers" such as a drop cap, a drop quote and subheads. These break up the mass of gray type. (Photo © J. Carl Ganter; used by permission)

Battle down below

$3.8-billion Deep Tunnel joins fight against pollution

By J. Carl Ganter
STAFF WRITER

Three hundred feet under Chicago, groundhogs coax the giant mole along inch by inch, every foot a painstaking effort. Together they move forward a hundred feet a day, eating through dolomite limestone and leaving a worm's world of subterranean tunnels behind.

Downunder has its own climate. In showers of rain and mists of drizzle, the tunnel's subtle turns stretch into miles lit by the yellow glow of sodium lights 30 feet overhead. Above - 30 stories above - the day is hot and sunny. Here, it is always 50 degrees and gloomy.

But the dank labyrinths underground, where workers are called groundhogs and the mole

'It took us years and years to screw up the environment. Here with Deep Tunnel we have a chance to clean it up.'
— engineer Ray Rimbus

is a giant digging machine, are helping to brighten Chicago's water and environmental picture. That is what officials of the Metropolitan Water Reclamation District say when they show off Deep Tunnel, the largest municipal water project in America and one that is designed to keep pollutants out of the Chicago waterways. It is part of a multi-front war waged in Chicago for clean water, of which sewage control is just one battle.

Clean water comeback

Most scientists and environmentalists agree that Chicago area water quality is on the rebound from decades of polluted squalor and that projects like Deep Tunnel have improved water quality.

But the threats and realities of invisible toxins in the water and the toxic chemicals that still linger on the bed of Lake Michigan, on river bottoms and in underground aquifers have for the

most part been untouched and perhaps pose the most deadly legacy of the future.

"We've gotten better in some respects, but we still have a lot to worry about," says Cameron Davis, a water pollution specialist of the Lake Michigan Federation.

"The problems have not decreased, they've just changed," he says. "We won't be seeing people drop dead overnight from polluted water anymore, but we are beginning to see subtle toxicological effects. It's not an acute, but a chronic problem."

In 1854, the consequences of polluted water were more immediate and clearly defined. In that year, almost 4,000 people died in Chicago from diseases carried by dirty water. The same Lake Michigan where the city drew its water supply for more than 750,000 people was the dumping ground of the growing population's sewage.

A river runs backward

The Chicago River became a plume of filth and disease reaching at times up to three miles into the lake. Instead of choking the discharge pipes of a burgeoning city, city fathers in 1890 moved water intakes farther from shore. Ten years later, in an historic feat of civil engineering, the river was reversed, sending its befouled waters to the Mississippi.

Since the late 1800s, sewage has been treated more carefully and levels of disease-causing bacteria have declined. Deep Tunnel is the latest engineering effort to address the continuing problem of keeping water clean in the midst of five million people.

The 33-foot-diameter tunnels, more than 50 miles of them in operation and another 59 miles under construction, collect rainstorm overflows from regional sewer systems that would otherwise be dumped into the Des Plaines and Chicago rivers.

"We catch the first flush," says Ray Rimbus, assistant chief engineer of the project. Rimbus says the tunnels act as a billion-

PHOTO BY J. CARL GANTER

"Groundhogs" inspect Deep Tunnel 300 feet below the surface of Chicago. The tunnel is designed to catch overflow from rainfall and keep pollution out of the water system.

gallon reservoir when area sewage treatment plants become overloaded by rainstorm runoff mixed with sewage. Although the incomplete tunnel system provides relief from the onslaught of summer storms, engi-

neers say the system still overflows up to half a billion gallons of untreated water to the Chicago River after the year's worst rainfalls.

Before Deep Tunnel, billions of gallons of a smelly, pea-gray

soup of sewage and rainwater overflowed directly into the Chicago Sanitary and Ship Canal system after every storm. From there, the untreated sewage made its way down the canal to-

See TUNNEL, page 2

Battle down below

$3.8-billion Deep Tunnel joins fight against pollution

By J. Carl Ganter
STAFF WRITER

Three hundred feet under Chicago, groundhogs coax the giant mole along inch by inch, every foot a painstaking effort. Together they move forward a hundred feet a day, eating through dolomite limestone and leaving a worm's world of subterranean tunnels behind.

Downunder has its own climate. In showers of rain and mists of drizzle, the tunnel's subtle turns stretch into miles lit by the yellow glow of sodium lights 30 feet overhead. Above - 30 stories above - the day is hot and sunny. Here, it is always 50 degrees and gloomy.

But the dank labyrinths underground, where workers are called groundhogs and the mole

'It took us years and years to screw up the environment. Here with Deep Tunnel we have a chance to clean it up.'
— engineer Ray Rimbus

is a giant digging machine, are helping to brighten Chicago's water and environmental picture. That is what officials of the Metropolitan Water Reclamation District say when they show off Deep Tunnel, the largest municipal water project in America and one that is designed to keep pollutants out of the Chicago waterways. It is part of a multi-front war waged in Chicago for clean water, of which sewage control is just one battle.

Clean water comeback

Most scientists and environmentalists agree that Chicago area water quality is on the rebound from decades of polluted squalor and that projects like Deep Tunnel have improved water quality.

But the threats and realities of invisible toxins in the water and the toxic chemicals that still linger on the bed of Lake Michigan, on river bottoms and in underground aquifers have for the

"Groundhogs" inspect Deep Tunnel 300 feet below the surface of Chicago. The tunnel is designed to catch overflow from rainfall and keep pollution out of the water system.
PHOTO BY J. CARL GANTER

most part been untouched and perhaps pose the most deadly legacy of the future.

"The problems have not decreased, they've just changed," he says. "We won't be seeing people drop dead overnight from polluted water anymore, but we

ist of the Lake Michigan Federation.

"We've gotten better in some respects, but we still have a lot to worry about," says Cameron Davis, a water pollution specialist of the Lake Michigan Federation.

are beginning to see subtle toxilogical effects. It's not an acute, but a chronic problem."

In 1854, the consequences of polluted water were more immediate and clearly defined. In that year, almost 4,000 people died in

Chicago from diseases carried by dirty water. The same Lake Michigan where the city drew its water supply for more than 750,000 people was the dumping ground of the growing population's sewage.

A river runs backward

The Chicago River became a plume of filth and disease reaching at times up to three miles into the lake. Instead of choking the discharge pipes of a burgeoning city, city fathers in 1890 moved water intakes farther from shore. Ten years later, in an historic feat of civil engineering, the river was reversed, sending its befouled waters to the Mississippi.

Since the late 1800s, sewage has been treated more carefully and levels of disease-causing bacteria have declined. Deep Tunnel is the latest engineering effort to address the continuing problem of keeping water clean in the midst of five million people.

The 33-foot-diameter tunnels, more than 50 miles of them in operation and another 59 miles under construction, collect rainstorm overflows from regional sewer systems that would otherwise be dumped into the Des Plaines and Chicago rivers.

"We catch the first flush," says Ray Rimbus, assistant chief engineer of the project. Rimbus says the tunnels act as a billion-gallon reservoir when area sewage treatment plants become overloaded by rainstorm runoff mixed with sewage. Although the incomplete tunnel system provides relief from the onslaught of summer storms, engineers say the system still overflows up to half a billion gallons of untreated water to the Chicago River after the year's worst rainfalls.

Before Deep Tunnel, billions of gallons of a smelly, pea-gray soup of sewage and rainwater overflowed directly into the Chicago Sanitary and Ship Canal system after every storm. From there, the untreated sewage made its way down the canal to-

See TUNNEL, page 2

Antipollution underground

$3.8-billion Deep Tunnel joins fight for cleaner water

By J. Carl Ganter
STAFF WRITER

Three hundred feet under Chicago, groundhogs coax the giant mole along inch by inch, every foot a painstaking effort. Together they move forward a hundred feet a day, eating through dolomite limestone and leaving a worm's world of subterranean tunnels behind.

Downunder has its own climate. In showers of rain and mists of drizzle, the tunnel's subtle turns stretch into miles lit by

'It took us years and years to screw up the environment. Here with Deep Tunnel we have a chance to clean it up.'
— engineer Ray Rimbus

the yellow glow of sodium lights 30 feet overhead. Above - 30 stories above - the day is hot and sunny. Here, it is always 50 degrees and gloomy.

But the dank labyrinths underground, where workers are called groundhogs and the mole is a giant digging machine, are helping to brighten Chicago's water and environmental picture. That is what officials of the Metropolitan Water Reclamation District say when they show off Deep Tunnel, the largest municipal water project in America and one that is designed to keep pollutants out of the Chicago waterways. It is part of a multi-front war waged in Chicago for clean water, of which sewage control

is just one battle.

Most scientists and environmentalists agree that Chicago area water quality is on the rebound from decades of polluted squalor and that projects like Deep Tunnel have improved water quality.

But the threats and realities of invisible toxins in the water and the toxic chemicals that still linger on the bed of Lake Michigan, on river bottoms and in underground aquifers have for the most part been untouched and perhaps pose the most deadly legacy of the future.

"We've gotten better in some respects, but we still have a lot to worry about," says Cameron Davis, a water pollution specialist of the Lake Michigan Federation.

"The problems have not decreased, they've just changed," he says. "We won't be seeing people drop dead overnight from polluted water anymore, but we are beginning to see subtle toxilogical effects. It's not an acute, but a chronic problem."

History of problems

In 1854, the consequences of polluted water were more immediate and clearly defined. In that year, almost 4,000 people died in Chicago from diseases carried by dirty water. The same Lake Michigan where the city drew its water supply for more than 750,000 people was the dumping ground of the growing population's sewage.

The Chicago River became a plume of filth and disease reaching at times up to three miles

"Groundhogs" inspect Deep Tunnel 300 feet below the surface of Chicago. The tunnel is designed to catch overflow from rainfall and keep pollution out of the water system.
PHOTO BY J. CARL GANTER

into the lake. Instead of choking the discharge pipes of a burgeoning city, city fathers in 1890 moved water intakes farther from shore. Ten years later, in an historic feat of civil engineering, the river was reversed, sending its befouled waters to the Mississippi.

Since the late 1800s, sewage has been treated more carefully and levels of disease-causing bacteria have declined. Deep Tunnel is the latest engineering effort to address the continuing problem of keeping water clean in the midst of five million peo-

ple.

The 33-foot-diameter tunnels, more than 50 miles of them in operation and another 59 miles under construction, collect rainstorm overflows from regional sewer systems that would otherwise be dumped into the Des Plaines and Chicago rivers.

"We catch the first flush," says Ray Rimbus, assistant chief engineer of the project. Rimbus says the tunnels act as a billion-gallon reservoir when area sewage treatment plants become overloaded by rainstorm runoff mixed with sewage. Although

the incomplete tunnel system provides relief from the onslaught of summer storms, engineers say the system still overflows up to half a billion gallons of untreated water to the Chicago River after the year's worst rainfalls.

Before Deep Tunnel, billions of gallons of a smelly, pea-gray soup of sewage and rainwater overflowed directly into the Chicago Sanitary and Ship Canal system after every storm. From there, the untreated sewage made its way down the canal to-

See TUNNEL, page 2

You can turn the same elements into an even more vertical presentation by stacking them with the photo on top (fig. 11.16). With the picture on top, the module can go next to another without bumping headlines.

Some newspapers and many magazines allow the use of the Dutch wrap (fig. 11.17). With this approach, the photo and headline are stacked with the copy then wrapping underneath in a reverse L shape. This is sometimes called a raw wrap. This approach works well with magazines, especially those that may have different stories on facing pages, such as news magazines. The Dutch-wrapped column separates the photo and headline from ones to the right.

The biggest difference in magazine and newspaper layout is that magazines usually have one story on a page. This allows for more freedom in design because the danger of confusing the reader is so much less.

When space dictates that the text and photo can't be integrated, you can use a closed package—one enclosed in a box—to strengthen relationships (fig. 11.18). The closed package often is used with the miniposter approach because it allows freer arrangements of elements within the module.

Fig. 11.16

An even stronger vertical approach. This top-to-bottom arrangement has a natural feel and visual excitement, but it's limited in size by the depth of the page. (Photo © J. Carl Ganter; used by permission)

PHOTO BY J. CARL GANTER

"Groundhogs" inspect Deep Tunnel 300 feet below the surface of Chicago. The tunnel is designed to catch overflow from rainfall and keep pollution out of the water system.

Antipollution underground
Deep Tunnel joins fight for clean water

By J. Carl Ganter
STAFF WRITER

Three hundred feet under Chicago, groundhogs coax the giant mole along inch by inch, every foot a painstaking effort. Together they move forward a hundred feet a day, eating through dolomite limestone and leaving a worm's world of subterranean tunnels behind.

Downunder has its own climate. In showers of rain and mists of drizzle, the tunnel's subtle turns stretch into miles lit by the yellow glow of sodium lights 30 feet overhead. Above - 30 stories above - the day is hot and sunny. Here, it is always 50 degrees and gloomy.

But the dank labyrinths underground, where workers are called groundhogs and the mole is a giant digging machine, are helping to brighten Chicago's water and environmental picture. That is what officials of the Metropolitan Water Reclamation

'It took us years and years to screw up the environment. Here with Deep Tunnel we have a chance to clean it up.'
— engineer Ray Rimbus

District say when they show off Deep Tunnel, the largest municipal water project in America and one that is designed to keep pollutants out of the Chicago waterways. It is part of a multi-front war waged in Chicago for clean water, of which sewage control is just one battle.

Most scientists and environmentalists agree that Chicago area water quality is on the rebound from decades of polluted squalor and that projects like Deep Tunnel have improved water quality.

But the threats and realities

See TUNNEL, page 2

"Groundhogs" inspect Deep Tunnel 300 feet below the surface of Chicago. The tunnel is designed to catch overflow from rainfall and keep pollution out of the water system.

PHOTO BY J. CARL GANTER

Battle down below
Deep Tunnel fights pollution

By J. Carl Ganter
STAFF WRITER

Three hundred feet under Chicago, groundhogs coax the giant mole along inch by inch, every foot a painstaking effort. Together they move forward a hundred feet a day, eating through dolomite limestone and leaving a worm's world of subterranean tunnels behind.

Downunder has its own climate. In showers of rain and mists of drizzle, the tunnel's subtle turns stretch into miles lit by the yellow glow of sodium lights 30 feet overhead. Above - 30 stories above - the day is hot and sunny. Here, it is always 50 degrees and gloomy.

But the dank labyrinths underground, where workers are called groundhogs and the mole is a giant digging machine, are helping to brighten Chicago's water and environmental picture. That is what officials of the Metropolitan Water Reclamation District say when they show off Deep Tunnel, the largest municipal water project in America and one that is designed to keep pollutants out of the Chicago waterways. It is part of a multi-front war waged in Chicago for clean water, of which sewage control is just one battle.

Clean water comeback

Most scientists and environmentalists agree that Chicago area water quality is on the rebound from decades of polluted squalor and that projects like Deep Tunnel have improved water quality.

But the threats and realities of invisible toxins in the water and the toxic chemicals that still linger on the bed of Lake Michigan, on river bottoms and in underground aquifers have for the most part been untouched and perhaps pose the most deadly legacy of the future.

"We've gotten better in some respects, but we still have a lot to worry about," says Cameron Davis, a water pollution specialist of the Lake Michigan Federation.

"The problems have not decreased, they've just changed," he says. "We won't be seeing people drop dead overnight from polluted water anymore, but we are beginning to see subtle toxilogical effects. It's not an accute, but a chronic problem."

In 1854, the consequences of polluted water were more immediate and clearly defined. In that year, almost 4,000 people died in Chicago from diseases carried by dirty water. The same Lake Michigan where the city drew its water supply for more than 750,000 people was the dumping ground of the growing population's sewage.

A river runs backward

The Chicago River became a plume of filth and disease reaching at times up to three miles into the lake. Instead of choking the discharge pipes of a burgeoning city, city fathers in 1890 moved water intakes farther from shore. Ten years later, in an historic feat of civil engineering, the river was reversed, sending its befouled waters to the Mississippi.

Since the late 1800s, sewage has been treated more carefully and levels of disease-causing

> 'It took us years and years to screw up the environment. Here with Deep Tunnel we have a chance to clean it up.'
> — engineer Ray Rimbus

bacteria have declined. Deep Tunnel is the latest engineering effort to address the continuing problem of keeping water clean in the midst of five million people.

The 33-foot-diameter tunnels, more than 50 miles of them in operation and another 59 miles under construction, collect rain-storm overflows from regional sewer systems that would otherwise be dumped into the Des Plaines and Chicago rivers.

"We catch the first flush," says Ray Rimbus, assistant chief engineer of the project. Rimbus says the tunnels act as a billion-gallon reservoir when area sewage treatment plants become overloaded with rainstorm runoff mixed with sewage. Although the incomplete tunnel system provides relief from the onslaught of summer storms, engineers say the system still overflows up to half a billion gallons of untreated water to the Chicago River after the year's worst rainfalls.

Before Deep Tunnel, billions of gallons of a smelly, pea-gray soup of sewage and rainwater overflowed directly into the Chicago Sanitary and Ship Canal system after every storm. From there, the untreated sewage made its way down the canal toward the Mississippi or into Lake Michigan, killing fish and other aquatic life along the way.

"It took us years and years to screw up the environment," Rimbus says. "Here with Deep Tunnel we have a chance to

See TUNNEL, page 2

Antipollution underground
Deep Tunnel joins fight for clean water

By J. Carl Ganter
STAFF WRITER

Three hundred feet under Chicago, ground-hogs coax the giant mole along inch by inch, every foot a painstaking effort. Together they move forward a hundred feet a day, eating through dolomite limestone and leaving a worm's world of subterranean tunnels behind.

Downunder has its own climate. In showers of rain and mists of drizzle, the tunnel's subtle turns stretch into miles lit by the yellow glow of sodium lights 30 feet overhead. Above - 30 stories above - the day is hot and sunny. Here, it is always 50 degrees and gloomy.

But the dank labyrinths underground, where workers are called groundhogs and the mole is a giant digging machine, are helping to brighten Chicago's water and environmental picture. That is what officials of the Metropolitan Water Reclamation District say when they show off Deep Tunnel, the largest municipal water project in America and one that is designed to keep pollutants out of the Chicago waterways. It is part of a multi-front war

> 'It took us years and years to screw up the environment. Here with Deep Tunnel we have a chance to clean it up.'
> — engineer Ray Rimbus

waged in Chicago for clean water, of which sewage control is just one battle.

Clean water comeback

Most scientists and environmentalists agree that Chicago area water quality is on the rebound from decades of polluted squalor and that projects like Deep Tunnel have improved water quality.

But the threats and realities of invisible toxins in the water and the toxic chemicals that still linger on the bed of Lake Michigan, on river bottoms and in underground aquifers have for the most part been untouched and perhaps pose the most deadly legacy of the future.

"We've gotten better in some respects, but we still have a lot to worry about," says Cameron Davis, a water pollution specialist of the See TUNNEL, page 2

"Groundhogs" inspect Deep Tunnel 300 feet below the surface of Chicago. The tunnel is designed to catch overflow from rainfall and keep pollution out of the water system.

PHOTO BY J. CARL GANTER

Fig. 11.17

A "Dutch wrap" or raw wrap. Magazines make use of this arrangement more than newspapers. (Photo © J. Carl Ganter; used by permission)

Fig. 11.18

With a side-by-side layout, integration of picture and text is achieved by boxing the elements into a closed package. Note the use of white space within the box. (Photo © J. Carl Ganter; used by permission)

Note that figure 11.18 uses a rule, or line, around the package to create the box. Some newspapers use extra white space with narrow rules to define the box.

Whatever approach you use, remember that it all starts with thorough planning. We saw in Chapter 8 how the Maestro Concept can be used to ensure that the designer has elements that work together. When this is not the case, page design becomes merely "layout," where ill-fitting photos, graphics and headlines are wrestled into place with the text. The results are disappointing and all too predictable.

CHAPTER

12

Your Career in Editing

——

You can never plan the future by the past.
—Edmund Burke

The future ain't what it used to be.
—Yogi Berra

What is the future of editing? In 1997, Wendy Navratil of the *Chicago Tribune* attempted to answer that question by peering 10 years into the future, to 2007. In the ASNE special report "A Return to Quality Editing," she followed a mythical copy editor on the night Frank Sinatra died.

Navratil described how the future copy editor prepared material for television first, accessing a database of video clips with the same computer she used to edit stories and pictures for the newspaper. Next the editor put together a package of stories and images for the internet, and finally she adapted the same stories for the print version.

The future really isn't what it used to be. Frank Sinatra died in May 1998, about nine years too soon for Navratil's scenario. We'll have to wait to find out if her specific predictions come true. But Wendy Navratil really wasn't predicting the details of life in the 21st century; instead, she was concerned with a broad concept, that technology will profoundly affect how news is handled and how editors will do their jobs.

The effect will be twofold: The instant nature of internet publishing will require editors to have a strong sense of news judgment that will allow them to make correct decisions quickly; and the melding of print, video and cyberspace will require editors to develop skills to work across many media.

Owen Youngman, the *Chicago Tribune*'s director of interactive media, told Navratil that the editor's role in the future will be critical "not just for catching mistakes but for helping reporters and source editors have the maximum amount of impact." Randall Weissman, the *Tribune*'s associate managing editor for news editing, added: "That is where the great editors of the future will be made. They will be those who can determine which medium this event should be pointed toward and how to adapt it for other media."

Navratil based her predictions on things that were happening around her in the *Tribune*'s newsroom. A small video pod had been installed a few years earlier to create a symbiosis between the *Tribune*'s newspaper resources and its Chicagoland Television cable outlet. In another part of the newsroom, "online editors" had taken over a cubicle. Their task was to prepare copy for the Chicago Online, a part of America Online. The *Tribune* had been an early investor in AOL and had produced one of the nation's first online versions of a daily newspaper.

Since she wrote her article, the *Tribune* has done over its newsroom to foster "synergy" between the newspaper, WGN radio, WGN-TV, cable outlet CLTV and Tribune Online. In an article written for the *American Journalism Review* that was published on its website, AJR Newslink, Ken Auletta described how *Tribune* executives "and editors, too" talk about "synergy and brand extension, about how their individual companies are not mere newspapers, broadcast stations or websites, but partners and information providers." Auletta writes that the *Chicago Tribune* has embraced "the new media that many newspaper executives still regard with fear and bewilderment." He notes that an exclusive story on the Chicago police superintendent's friendship with a felon ran first in the *Tribune*'s online edition, then on the front page.

For editors at the *Chicago Tribune*, the future is now. Other newspapers, magazines and broadcast outlets aren't far behind.

THE PROFESSIONAL EDITOR

One prediction seems certain: The demand for good editors will increase. For the young journalist, an editing job offers more stable hours than reporting and often a premium in pay, at least for entry-level jobs. Editors work in an environment charged with the excitement of handling news stories from around the world. And they associate with a literate group of coworkers with wide-ranging interests.

A new professionalism is growing among copy editors. In September 1995, January 1996 and October 1996, the American Society of Newspaper Editors Human Resources Committee held a three-part National Newspaper Copy Editors Conference. Out of that grew the American Copy Editors Society (ACES), with the goal of improving copy editors' professional lives. It held a "flying short course" for editors early in 1998 that covered subjects such as grammar, headline writing and editing in the age of cyberspace. ACES held its first national conference in September 1998 at Portland, Ore. It has a quarterly newsletter and a website.

With traditional copy desks being broken apart (see sidebar), editors more than ever need to maintain contact with each other. Professional organizations such as ACES help do that. Editors need to build networks through newsletters, online services, chat rooms and workshops.

Taking One for the Team

The traditional structure of the copy desk—a "slot" editor surrounded by copy editors who serve a section of the paper—is changing. Newspapers are trying to deal with the demands of new media and with the realities of smaller staffs by building new structures. A few of these efforts based on news teams were described in April 1997 in the ASNE's special report *A Return to Quality Editing.*

St. Paul Pioneer Press

The St. Paul paper "blew up" its copy desks and placed the editors on various teams with reporters. As described in an article by Dick Thien, a University of Nebraska lecturer and former Gannett executive, the change has been good and bad. Copy editors believe

To become a member of ACES, visit its website at www.copydesk.org. It includes a job board and links to other sites.

Other resources for editors include newsletters and magazines, websites, professional groups. media institutes, and colleges and universities.

Newsletters and Magazines

The *Copy Editor* is a bimonthly newsletter that offers "Language News for the Publishing Profession." A subscription costs $69 for one year. To subscribe, call 212-995-0112, or write P.O. Box 230604 Ansonia Station, New York, N.Y. 10023-0604. The *Copy Editor* has a website at www.copyeditor.com that includes a job board and links to other sites.

Many professional magazines contain items of interest to editors, including the *American Journalism Review*, the *Columbia Journalism Review*, *Editor & Publisher* and *Presstime*.

Websites

As mentioned above, ACES has a website at www.copydesk.org. As those familiar with the internet know, one website can list links with dozens of other sites worth exploring. For your job search, the classified pages of websites operated by professional magazines offer databases of ads that you can search by specialty, region and publication size. Two of the best are the *American Journalism Review*'s job page at ajr.newslink.org/joblink, and *Editor & Publisher* at epclassifieds.com.

Virtually every professional organization or publication has a website. Getting to know them is one of the best ways you have of staying connected with other editors.

Professional Groups

The American Society of Newspaper Editors has taken an increased interest in editors through its Human Resources Committee. You can write the ASNE at 11690B Sunrise Valley Drive, Reston, Va. 20191-1409, or call 703-453-1122. Its website address is www.asne.org.

Society of Professional Journalists is one of the oldest professional organizations for journalists. Write to its headquarters at 3909 N. Meridian St., Indianapolis, Ind. 46208 or call 765-653-3333 extension 220. The group's website address is spj.org; it includes excellent resources for those seeking internships.

Many editors find themselves edging into page design, and one of the best places to go for help, moral support and networking is the Society of News Design. It's an international organization that prints a newsletter, a magazine and an annual "best of" contest for newspapers, magazines and graphics. Contest winners are published in a glossy annual that's worth the price of membership by itself. Write to SND at 129 Dyer Street, Providence, R.I., 02903-3904 or call 401-276-2100. The society has an excellent website at www.snd.org.

The Canadian Association of Journalists provides a rich website for all journalists, including a job board. Its internet address is www.eagle.ca/caj.

(continued)

they have gained respect from reporters by working with them face to face. They believe content has improved because they enter the story process earlier and get answers to questions about stories. The move to teams has caused copy editors to feel isolated at times, and they miss the camaraderie of the desk. The editors at St. Paul also said workloads were uneven and style errors had increased, but they were unwilling to go back to the days of old. Nation/world Editor Martha Malan told Thien, "Overall, copy editors are happier, but we don't have the same crisp editing and overall headline writing that we did before."

The Wichita Eagle

The *Eagle* was a pioneer in *public journalism*, a move away from institutional reporting to broad areas of coverage more in tune with readers. Malcolm Gibson, an assistant professor at the University of Kansas and a former newspaper editor, wrote in the ASNE report that leaders at the *Eagle* had planned a gradual reorganization into reporter-editor teams based around areas of coverage such as learning (public schools, colleges and universities), public life (city, county and state government) and Kansas roots (agriculture, environment, history, tourism and the like). The team members, including copy editors, would be responsible for formulating coverage. Assistant managing editor Gary

Media Institutes

For the working journalist, media institutes offer an opportunity for professional growth through short courses and publications. Often a person is sponsored by his or her news organization to attend classes.

The Poynter Institute for Media Studies in St. Petersburg, Fla., mixes editors with managers, photographers and artists, and it engages its students in all types of media. It offers seminars on writing, design, newsroom leadership and ethics. You can call the Poynter Institute at 727-821-9494 or 1-888-POYNTER, or visit its website at www.poynter.org.

The American Press Institute in Reston, Va., offers one-week seminars for copy desk chiefs and news editors. API also invites news editors and copy editors to attend its desk-specific seminars, for business, city and metro, design and graphics, editorial pages, lifestyle and sports. For information, call 703-620-3611.

The Maynard Institute in Oakland, Calif., offers an eight-week Editing Program for Minority Journalists each summer at the University of Arizona. The seminar is open to those with at least a year of experience. While the Maynard Institute emphasizes non-white representation, it is open to all journalists. Call 510-891-9202 for information.

Colleges and Universities

Many journalism schools have worked to strengthen their editing programs and at least one, at North Carolina, has a sabbatical program for copy editors. But perhaps the most overlooked avenue for growth is through teaching. Experienced editors often find they learn as much as their students.

WHAT IT TAKES TO SUCCEED

When editors met for a national conference in April 1996 at the University of Kentucky, they held lively discussions about the place of editors in newsrooms where they haven't always found respect. Pat Embry, managing editor of the *Nashville Banner*, summarized "the 3 P's" of gaining respect and recognition for the editing task:

Passion

Embry suggests that passion for the job should translate into editors reading as many newspapers as possible, but first their own, to gain ideas and offer suggestions or intelligent and useful critiques. Too many editors adopt a passive attitude instead of actively involving themselves in the publishing process.

Personnel

Copy desks are loaded with people of varied talents and interests. Desk chiefs must know their people and match their expertise with stories in the works. For example, a plane-crash story could be assigned to an editor who had

---

(continued)

Graham told Gibson, "We tried it with a few teams, but none of the copy editors wanted to stay with the core news desk."

Graham and his associates eliminated the copy desk at the end of January 1995. Today the *Eagle* officially has no copy editors; they are listed as team members or team leaders. The experience at the *Eagle* has been similar to that at St. Paul. Opportunities have increased for copy editors, who have found new respect from their team members and have enjoyed a greater hand in shaping copy. But staff members at the *Eagle* also believe that a lack of mentoring has caused an increase in routine typos and editing errors.

The Oregonian

John Russial, a journalism teacher at the University of

---

a pilot's license. Desk chiefs also should let upper management know about the talents that exist on the desk. Copy editors could be added to reporters' source lists. Beginning editors can do their part by letting their superiors know about their backgrounds and interests.

Prudence

Copy editors face a negative stereotype as nitpickers, or as frustrated writers trying to leave their fingerprints on someone else's story. Editors must show prudence in applying "rules" to the stories in front of them. We know of editors who believe no paragraph can be longer than two sentences, and they make every story fit this rule. Instead, the editor must try to understand what the writer is attempting and help that cause, even if it means breaking the rules. The editor also must accept the role of supporting cast, not star of the show.

The copy desk doesn't have to be an enclave of sourpusses with an "us or them" mentality. Another discussion group, led by *Dallas Morning News* publisher Bob Mong, suggested that instead of a "siege mentality," the copy desk must sell itself to the rest of the paper by explaining to others why editing is important, by recognizing good work on the desk, and by cooperating with others, either through asking for their help when you need it or through pitching in with coaching and teamwork. The copy desk needs to encourage new ideas and, most of all, set an upbeat tone for itself.

ARROWS IN THE QUIVER

After all these years, we are still amazed by young people who apply for editing jobs but forget to edit their application materials. Before we discuss what should go into the job package, we want you to understand the seriousness of grammar, spelling or punctuation errors in a job application. Many news people use such errors as an excuse for instant rejection. So adopt the editing attitude and proceed.

To apply for that dream job you'll need a résumé, a cover letter and clips.

A Résumé

Here are the key elements of a résumé:

- *Who you are and how you can be reached.* Start with your name, address (local and permanent, if different), phone number (local and permanent, if different) and e-mail address. Add your fax number if you have one.
- *Relevant work experience.* Provide clear information on where you worked (name and location), the position you held and job responsibilities (title and description), and when you worked there (months and years). Please note that you do not have to present your experience in chronological order. You can put your most relevant experience, including internships, first under a heading such as "media experience."

(continued)
Oregon and a former editor at the *Philadelphia Inquirer,* described in the ASNE report how the Portland, Ore., newspaper was gradually moving to a team-based system. In a reorganization begun in 1993, the *Oregonian* created a dozen topic teams in a 320-member "newsroom without walls." A few of the teams, such as sports and business, were much like the old departments. Others drew together unrelated beats and new coverage areas, such as "Living in the '90s" (culture, relationships, religion and other areas), "New Northwest" (the environment) and "Health, Science and Medicine." Inside this nontraditional newsroom are five traditional copy desks: a main desk, features, sports, zones and national/international. Rim editors edit copy and write headlines, captions and other display type to specs designed by a presentation team. Copy moves through slots before it is typeset. The goal, as with other team-based newsrooms, is to have closer involvement of editors in the story process and less editing at the last minute. Copy Chief Jerry Sass said a good team copy editor is self-motivated, flexible, assertive but not aggressive, gregarious, an advocate of reader interests and an advocate of the editing process.

Then put your other jobs under another heading such as "general experience" or "non-media experience." Put your best qualification first. You can list your job on the college newspaper, magazine or radio station here, especially any leadership job.

- *Education.* If you don't have any media work experience, put your media-related education first, ahead of work. List your college, your major and your expected date of graduation. A listing of relevant courses may be impressive. You also can list your high school, location and date of graduation, too, especially if you were involved in the school paper, yearbook or other media organization.
- *Honors and affiliations.* These include awards, scholarships and organizations you are or have been involved in. List the media-related activities and awards first.
- *References.* List three people—former employers, supervisors or teachers—who can recommend you. Be sure to list their titles, addresses and phone numbers. You may have been advised to put "references available on request" on your résumé, but why add to a prospective employer's work load? List your references on the résumé.

Do not fabricate, exaggerate or project yourself into the future with knowledge and experience you expect to have by graduation. It will come back to haunt you.

Cover Letter

The cover letter is your big chance to sell yourself to a prospective employer with everything you have to offer. If you feel insecure about the amount of practical experience you have, get some more—immediately!

Here are the key elements of a cover letter:

- Date
- Opening. Address the letter by name, title and address of the appropriate person to ask for a job or internship. If you don't know who this person is, call and find out. Let's say you want to address your letter to the managing editor. Call information and ask for the paper's general number, then ask the first person who answers, "Who is your managing editor?" They'll know. Be sure to ask how to spell the name, first and last. This information also may be listed at the paper's website.
- Appropriate greeting, followed by a colon, such as, *Dear Mr. Ryan:*
- Body of the letter

    The first paragraph summarizes who you are and what position you are seeking. The second paragraph summarizes your qualifications for the position. The third paragraph includes an interesting fact or two about the prospective employer to show that you have done your homework and you know something about the company or institution, but don't try to flatter. The fourth paragraph explains when you will be available for an interview, if possible, and that you will be following up with a phone call to confirm a possible interview time.
- Closing. Express your thanks for the person's time and consideration.

- Sign-off. Use an appropriate sign-off, followed by a comma, such as *Sincerely,*
- Your signature above your typewritten name.

Even if you lack professional experience, you can display your professionalism in introducing yourself to a prospective employer. Make your best pitch, and don't be afraid to hear no.

Clips

Even if you are applying for an editor's job, include your clips. These can be from your school paper or from internships. Pick your best five or six, arrange them on letter-size sheet of paper and photocopy them. Include the name of the publication, the page number and the date.

If you have had design experience, include tear sheets with a brief note describing your role in producing the page.

Another approach is to get a copy of the publication you are applying to and produce a thoughtful critique of it. Give the date, section and page number, and describe briefly what you see, then offer up your thoughts.

This isn't the place to rip up the publication; you won't help your cause with comments such as, "It's stupid for the *Klaxon-Gazette* to devote so much space to World Cup soccer." Instead, look for positives that show your knowledge, such as, "The extensive amount of World Cup coverage tells me that the *Klaxon-Gazette* understands its local sports scene, with its 31 soccer leagues and a state-tournament high school team."

Negative comments should be formulated in terms of how you want to help. Don't say, "Somebody at the *Klaxon-Gazette* needs a grammar teacher, and I fill the bill." Instead say, "Grammar and other language skills are important to me, and I believe I can help the *Klaxon-Gazette* improve in this area."

Finally, if you have a web page in your background, something you did in college or even a page you've maintained since high school, include its address. If it's not online, you can send a disk with samples. Be sure to include the necessary images with the HTML document itself.

GOOD LUCK!

Although you may be unsure of your abilities, remember that experience is still the best teacher. The professional copy editor at a daily newspaper handles more tasks in a week than a student sees in a semester-long editing class. A newspaper designer might put together 80 pages in a month while a student in a college design class might be lucky to see 15 assignments in a semester.

Here is one final thought that comes from our years of observing reporters, editors, photographers, artists and designers at papers ranging from the smallest dailies on earth to the nation's largest: The only thing separating you from the top rung of the ladder is how much you care.

Good luck and happy editing!

Commonly Misspelled Words

Part of being a good editor is recognizing problem words, then looking them up. The following words are often misspelled by writers and editors alike.

A
accelerate
accessible
accommodate
accordion
acoustical
acquitted
accumulate
admissible
advantageous
adviser
affidavit
African-American
afterward
alleged
allegiance
allotment
allotted
all right
a lot
anoint
antidote
antiquated
appall

apparatus
argument
asinine
asphalt
assassinate
assistant
ax
B
backward
bailiff
battalion
beige
bellwether
benefiting
berserk
bettor
black (referring to a
person's race)
bureaucracies
buses (vehicles),
busses (kisses)
bourgeois
C
caffeine

camaraderie
camouflage
canceled
cannot
carburetor
caress
cello
cemetery
changeable
chaperon
chastise
chauffeur
chieftain
Cincinnati
coconut
Colombia (South
American nation)
colossal
commemorate
commitment
complement (add to),
compliment (praise)
conscientious
consensus

consistent
consul
counsel
counterproposal
contemptuous
corroborate
connoisseur
copy editing
copy editor

D

defendant
definitely
delicatessen
demagogue
dependent
descendant
desirable
desperate
despondent
detrimental
dietitian
dilettante
diphtheria
disastrous
disc
discipline
dismantle
dissension
divisive
Doberman pinscher
drudgery
dumbbell
dumbfounded
drunkenness
drought

E

ecstasy
eked
embarrass
emphysema
enforceable
entrepreneur
exaggeration
evidently
exhilarate
excerpt
excusable
existence
exonerate

exorbitant
exuberant

F

Fahrenheit
familiar
feasible
fictitious
fidget
flaunt (show off)
flout (disregard)
flounder (struggle in the water)
fluorescent
founder (helplessly at sea)
forego, forgo
fraudulent
fraught
fulfill

G

gaiety
gauge
gelatin
genealogy
goodbye
grammar
guarantee
gubernatorial
guerrilla
guttural

H

hangar (planes), hanger (clothes)
harangue
harass
hemorrhage
hierarchy
hitchhiker
homicide
hygiene

I

icicle
idiosyncrasy
illegible
impostor
incidentally
impresario
indispensable
inconceivable

incredible
indestructible
innocuous
inoculate
insurer
interfered
interrogate
iridescent
irresistible
independence

J-K

jeopardize
judgment
jukebox
kamikazes
kidnapped
kimono

L

lascivious
Legionnaires' disease
liaison
lieutenant
lightning
liquefy
logjam
longtime

M

maintenance
manageable
maneuver
mantel (shelf), mantle (cloak)
marijuana
marriageable
marshal, martial
mayonnaise
medieval
memento
miniature
minuscule
mischievous
miscellaneous
missile
misspell
moccasin
Muhammed
monocle
movable
Muslim

N-O
naphtha
necessary
negotiable
nerve-racking
nickel
noticeable
nutritious
obsolescence
occasionally
occurred
occurrence
OK
omission
ophthalmologist
ordinance (city law)
ordnance (artillery
shells)
oscillate
P
pageant
paid
panicked
pantomime
papier-mâché
parallel
paraphernalia
parasol
parliament
pastime
pavilion
penicillin
penitentiary
peremptory
permanence
permissible
perseverance
persistent
personnel
Ph.D.
Philippines
phony
pre-emptive*
picnicking
playwright
politicking
pompon
possessive
potpourri

precede
preceding
preferable
preferred
prerogative
presumptuous
principal (first),
principle (rule)
privilege
procedure
proceed
pronunciation
propeller
prostrate (lying face down)
prostate (the gland)
protester
publicly
Q-R
quandary
questionnaire
queue
racketeering
rarefy
Realtor
recommend
reconnaissance
re-create (to create anew)
recreate
referring
regardless
reminiscent
renaissance
resistance
responsibility
restaurateur
resuscitation
rhythm
rock 'n' roll*
rococo
receive
rock 'n' roll
S
sapphire
sacrilegious
schizophrenic
schoolteacher
seize
saloon
Scotch whisky

screech
secede
separate
sheriff
siege
silhouette
sizable
skillful
smoky
soothe
souvenir
specimen
stationary (set),
stationery (paper)
straitjacket
strait-laced (see AP)
succeed
superintendent
supersede
summonses
surprise
susceptible
swastika
subpoenaed
T-U
tariff
teen-age*
terrific
titillate
tortoise
toward
traffic
traveling
tumultuous
twelfth
undoubtedly
unmistakable
usable
V
vaccine
vacuum
vaudeville
vengeance
vermilion
Veterans Day
veterinarian
vice versa
vichyssoise
vigilance

vilify
villain
volunteerism (now in
common usage)
voluntarism (preferred)

W-X-Y-Z
weird
whiskey
wield
wondrous

X-ray
yacht
yield

* AP style disagrees with the dictionary.

B

AP Stylebook Study Guide

Editors are responsible for making copy conform to their news organization's style. The *Associated Press Stylebook* is the industry standard; additions and exceptions for a news organization fall under the heading of local style. Editors and reporters don't need to memorize the AP stylebook, but they must be familiar with it.

The list below begins with the most often cited entries from the stylebook, ones a reporter or editor needs to know by heart because those points come up so often. The list continues through other important groups of entries. The more of these you know, the faster you will be able to edit. The rest of the stylebook is there for you to consult as questions arise. The stylebook is a dictionary, an almanac and an encyclopedia as well as a stylebook. This guide breaks it down for you.

MUST-KNOW ENTRIES

abbreviations and acronyms	people, persons
addresses	plurals
capitalization	possessives
courtesy titles	quotation marks
datelines	spelling
dictionaries	state names
dimensions	that
directions and regions	time element
essential, nonessential clauses	times
essential, nonessential phrases	titles
numerals	United States
organizations and institutions	verbs

OFTEN-USED PUNCTUATION RULES

apostrophe
colon
comma
dash
ellipsis

hyphen
periods
question mark
semicolon

MORE SPELLING HELP: HYPHEN AND COMPOUND WORD ENTRIES

all-
abti-
bi-
by-
co-
counter-
down-
-down
ex-
full-
half-
in-
-in
inter-
intra-
-less
like-
-like
-ly
mid-
mini-
multi-
non-
off-

-off
one-
out-
-out
over-
-over
-persons
post-
pre-
pro-
re-
self-
semi-
sub-
super-
trans-
ultra-
un-
under-
up-
-up
wide-
-wide
-wise

ENTRIES THAT OFTEN APPEAR IN COPY

academic degrees (departments, titles)
ages
burglary, larceny, robbery, theft
church
city (city council)
collective nouns
committee
company, companies
compared to, with
compose, comprise, constitute
composition titles

convince, persuade
corporation
damage, damages
department of
doctor
downstate
drowned, was drowned
drunk, drunken
fewer, less
flaunt, flout
flounder, founder
following

334

forego, forgo
foreign legislative
bodies
full time, full-time
fund raising,
fund-raising,
fund-raiser
gamut, gantlet, gauntlet
governmental bodies
grade, grader
her
homicide, murder,
manslaughter
hopefully
imply, infer
include
innocent
jury
last
late
lay, lie
legislative titles
legislature
majority, plurality
mass
middle initials
military titles
mishap
months
National Weather Service
nicknames

No.
on
over
parentheses
part time, part-time
party affiliations
percentages
police department
political parties philosophies
prison, jail
pupil, student
race
religious references
religious titles
Rev.
Russia, Soviet Union
secretary-general
sentences
speeds
subcommittees
subjunctive mood
Teamsters union
union names
United Nations
U.S. Postal Service
vice-
weapons
women
word selection
years
youth

APPENDIX

C

Counting Headlines

___

Counting headlines may seem like a page out of journalism history, and frankly it is. Thirty years ago, editors scrawled headlines on a piece of paper, then counted them according to the formula you see below. When they found a combination that fit, they would type it up and send it to the composition room, where a printer would set it in headline type.

One thing headline counting gave us was the ability to gauge the width of a word by its mix of letters. We became adept at finding those "skinny" words, ones with lots of t's, i's, and l's. We hope you'll enjoy trying to count a few headlines.

LETTER WIDTHS

Capital Letters

All = $1\frac{1}{2}$ counts except M and W = 2 counts
I = $\frac{1}{2}$ count

lowercase Letters

All = 1 count except
m, w = $1\frac{1}{2}$ counts
f l i t j = $\frac{1}{2}$ counts
Numerals
All = 1 count
Spaces and symbols
Spaces = $\frac{1}{2}$ count
- , . : ; ! ' ( ) = $\frac{1}{2}$ count
$ % & ? = 1 count
—(fat dash) = 2 counts

How to Count Headlines

Follow these steps for counting headlines:

1. Look up the correct count from the headline schedule. For a headline call of 4-48R-1 (4 columns, 48 Roman, 1 line), the count would be 28. Your headline may fall short of this by three counts, four at the most, but cannot be more than a half-count longer. With computer typesetting, headlines can be "squeezed" by about that much.

2. Assign each letter its correct value according to the "Headline Counts" chart. An easy way to do this is to use plus marks for each half-count:
   1+11111111+1111+1+1111111++1+11
   Gorbachev asks European talks

3. Count the ones and note the total. This headline has 24 one-counts.

4. Count the pluses and divide by two. This headline has seven pluses for $3\frac{1}{2}$ full counts.

5. Add the full counts and half-counts together. The total of $27\frac{1}{2}$ is just right for this head order.

A Shortcut

You'll have certain key words that, in your judgment, must go in the headline. To save time, count those words and make a note of them:

1+11111111
Gorbachev = $9\frac{1}{2}$

1+1111111
European = $8\frac{1}{2}$

+1+11
talks = 4

Now, as you shift words around, searching for the one or two counts you need to make the headline fit, you can just plug in the total counts for these words, remembering to add half counts for the spaces.

HEADLINE SCHEDULE

Times Roman or Times Light Headline	Max	Times Italic Headline	Max
1-14	.23	1-14	.22½
1-18	.18	1-18	.18
1-24	.13	1-24	.13
2-14	.47½	2-14	.47
2-18	.36	2-18	.35
2-24	.27	2-24	.26½
1-30	.10½	1–10	.10½
2-30	.21½	2-30	.21
3-30	.32½	3-30	.32
4-30	.43	4-30	.42
1-36	.9	1-36	.9
2-36	.18½	2-36	.18
3-36	.27	3-36	.26½
4-36	.37	4-36	.36
1-42	.7½	1-42	.7½
2-42	.15½	2-42	.15½
3-42	.23½	3-42	.23
4-42	.31	4-42	.31
5-42	.39	5-42	.38
6-42	.47	6-42	.46½
1-48	.6½	1-48	.6½
2-48	.14	2-48	.13
3-48	.21	3-48	.20½
4-48	.28	4-48	.27
5-48	.36	5-48	.33½
6-48	.44	6-48	.41
1-60	.5½	1-60	.5½
2-60	.11	2-60	.11
3-60	.17	3-60	.16½
4-60	.23	4-60	.22
5-60	.29	5-60	.27½
6-60	.36	6-60	.33
1-72	.4½	1-72	.4½
2-72	.9	2-72	.9
3-72	.15	3-72	.13
4-72	.20	4-72	.18
5-72	.24½	5-72	.22½
6-72	.30	6-72	.27

APPENDIX

D

Brevity and Simplicity

BREVITY

Every unneeded word you kill gives life to the rest of the copy. Redundant expressions and superfluous words in copy are like weeds in a garden, obscuring vision and choking vitality. In the following examples, the wordy constructions are in parentheses followed by a briefer, better replacement:

A

(adequate enough) enough
(and moreover) moreover
(angry clash) clash
(a number of) several
(absolutely complete) complete
(advance planning) planning
(as a matter of fact) in fact
(ask the question) ask
(at the present time) now
(assembled together) together
(along the lines of) like
(as of this date) today
(as to) about
(awkward predicament) predicament
(appear to be) appear
(appointed to the post of) appointed
(as to whether) whether
(as yet) yet
(atop of) atop
(at some time to come) to come

(and so as a result) so
(any and all) any
(ahead of schedule) early
(a large proportion of) many
(am in possession of) have
(a percentage of) some
(present in greater abundance) more
(at an early date) soon
(as far as he is concerned) as for him
(are currently or are now) are

B

(be in a position to) can
(by means of) by or with
(but nevertheless) nevertheless
(both of them) they
(big in size) big
(biography of his life) biography
(blue in color) blue
(best of health) well or healthy
(by the name of) named

C

(completely destroy) destroy
(continue on) continue
(cooperate together) cooperate
(consensus of opinion) consensus
(close proximity) proximity
(collaborate together) collaborate
(christened as) christened
(connect together) connect
(Capitol building) Capitol
(commute to and from) commute to
(classified into groups) classified
(call a halt to) stop
(caused injuries to) injured

D

(dates back from) dates from
(descend down) descend
(depreciate or appreciate in value)
    drop in value or rise in value
(destroyed by fire) burned
(doctorate degree) doctorate
(draw the attention of him) show,
    point out
(during the time that) while

E

(each and every) each
(enclosed herein) enclosed
(exactly identical) identical
(end result) result
(eliminate altogether) eliminate
(entirely complete) complete
(every now and then) now and then
(environment of surroundings) sur-
    roundings

F

(fellow colleagues) colleagues
(final completion) completion
(follow after) after
(for the purpose of) for
(for the reason that) because
(frown on his face) frown; same for
    smile
(few in number) few
(filled to capacity) filled
(from a commercial standpoint)
commercially

G-H-I

(give due consideration to) consider
(general public) public
(good benefit) benefit
(gather up) gather
(graceful in appearance) graceful
(give rise to) cause
(hurry up) hurry
(had occasion to be) was
(in order to) to
(in the event that) if
(in the matter of) in
(in possession of) have
(in order that) so
(in the case of) about
(in the near future) soon
(in view of) because
(in the nature of) like
(in connection with) in, on, of, about
(in relation to) to, about, toward
(in the amount of) for
(in a number of cases) some
(invited guest) guest
(in advance of) before
(in the vicinity of) near
(in this day and age) today
(in the case of workers who are late)
for late workers
(in some instances these books)
some of these books
(in spite of the fact that) although
(in view of the fact that) as
(is located on) on

J-K-L-M-N

(joint cooperation) cooperation
(join up) join
(knots per hour) knots, meaning nau-
    tical miles per hour
(little duckling) duckling
(last of all) last
(major breakthrough) breakthrough
(more superior) superior
(mutual cooperation) cooperation
(made out of) made of
(made a statement saying) stated,
    said
(made good an escape) escaped
(new innovation) innovation

(new beginning) beginning
(never at any time) never

O

(on the basis of) by
(on the grounds that) because
(owing to the fact that) because
(on the part of) for, by, among
(on the subject of) about
(on behalf of) for
(on a few occasions) occasionally
(old adage) adage
(original source) source
(on the occasion whenever) whenever
(over and done with) over
(one and the same) the same
(of a similar nature) similar

P

(prior to) before
(passing phase, passing fad) phase,
fad
(past history) history
(present incumbent) incumbent
(proposed plan) plan
(penetrate into) penetrate
(persist still) persist
(prejudge in advance) prejudge
(pair of twins) twins
(place under arrest) arrest
(put in an appearance) appear

Q-R

(quite unique) unique
(repeat again) repeat
(root cause) cause
(recoil back) recoil
(revert back) revert
(remand back) remand
(results so far achieved) results
(render assistance to) help
(retain position as) remain

S

(subsequent to) after
(self-confessed) confessed

(separate entities) entities
(serious danger) danger
(surrounding circumstances)
circumstances
(sink down) sink
(swoop down) swoop
(skirt around) skirt
(shuttle back and forth) shuttle
(strangle to death) strangle
(surgeon by occupation) surgeon
(separate and distinct) separate
(sparsely scattered) sparse
(suburban area) suburbs
(succumbed to injuries) died

T-U-V

(total annihilation) annihilation
(total destruction) destruction
(total extinction) extinction
(true facts) facts
(termed as) termed
(today's modern woman) today's
woman
(take action on the matter) act
(take into consideration) consider
(tender his resignation) resign
(the reason why) the reason
(under the circumstances) because
(usual customs) customs
(undergraduate student) undergraduate

W-X-Y-Z

(with regard to) about
(with the result that) so that
(with a view to) to
(with reference to) about
(weather conditions) weather
(when and if) if
(was of the opinion that) said,
thought
(was witness to) saw
(young infant) infant

SIMPLICITY

Ernest Hemingway said good dialogue is good conversation only better. Newsroom copy editors should reduce stilted writing to simple, straightforward, conversational language and in that way make copy more understandable.

We should write the way we talk but, as Hemingway said, only better. That is, keep the simple tones but clear up any ambiguity that may arise in imperfect speech. In the spirit of simplicity, here is a list of words whose ideas can be expressed with fewer syllables. The list is inspired by Rudolf Flesch and Robert Gunning, who suggested that the more syllables a word has, the more obscure its meaning. The overly complex words are in parentheses.

A
(accumulate) gather
(acquaint with) talk about
(additional) added
(advise) tell
(aggregate) total
(ameliorate) improve
(apparent) clear
(approximately) about
(ascertain) find out
(assist) help
(assistance) aid

C
(cognizance) knowledge
(commence) start
(commitment) promise, vow
(compensation) pay
(construct) build
(contribute) give
(cooperate) help

D
(deceased) dead
(demonstrate) show
(desire) want
(determine) find out, figure
(disclose) show

E
(encounter) meet
(equivalent) equal
(expedite) hasten
(explicit) plain

F-G-H
(facilitate) make easy
(failed to) didn't

(forward) send

I-J-K
(inconvenience) trouble
(indicate) show
(initial, inaugural) first

L-M-N
(locality) place
(materialize) appear
(modification) change

O
(objective) aim, goal
(obligation) debt
(optimum) best

P-Q-R
(participate) take part
(proceed) go
(procure) get
(purchase) buy
(reimburse) pay back

S
(submit) give, send
(subsequent) later, next
(substantial) big
(sufficient) enough

T-U-V-W-X-Y-Z
(terminate) end, stop, fire
(transmit) send
(transpire) happen
(utilize) use
(vehicle) car, truck
(visualize) picture
(youth) boy, girl

E

Copy Editing Symbols

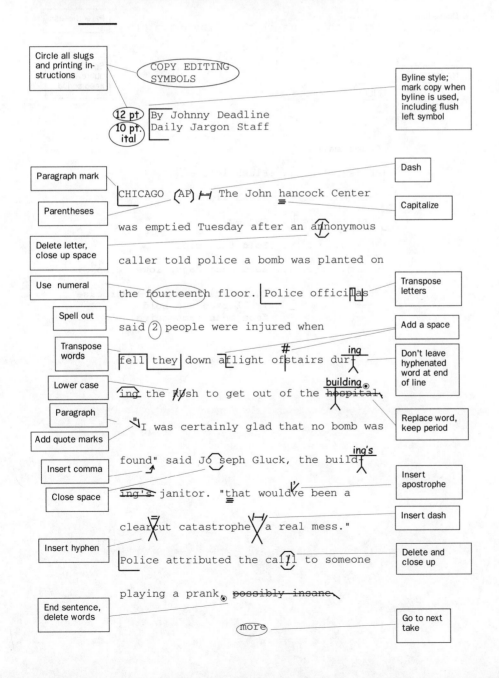

Circle all slugs and printing instructions

COPY EDITING SYMBOLS

Byline style; mark copy when byline is used, including flush left symbol

12 pt.
10 pt. ital

By Johnny Deadline
Daily Jargon Staff

Paragraph mark

Parentheses

Dash

Capitalize

CHICAGO (AP) ⊢ The John hancock Center

was emptied Tuesday after an annonymous

Delete letter, close up space

caller told police a bomb was planted on

Use numeral

the fourteenth floor. Police officilas

Transpose letters

Spell out

said ② people were injured when

Add a space

Transpose words

fell they down a flight of stairs dur #ing

Don't leave hyphenated word at end of line

Lower case

ing the Rush to get out of the hospital building.

Replace word, keep period

Paragraph

Add quote marks

"I was certainly glad that no bomb was

Insert comma

found" said Jo seph Gluck, the build ing's

Insert apostrophe

Close space

ing's janitor. "that would've been a

Insert dash

clear cut catastrophe a real mess."

Insert hyphen

Police attributed the call to someone

Delete and close up

End sentence, delete words

playing a prank. possibly insane

more

Go to next take

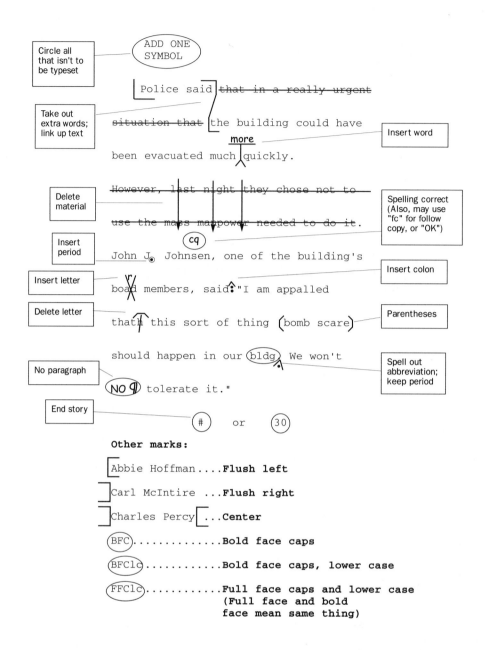

__Bibliography

GENERAL REFERENCES AND STYLEBOOKS

Associated Press Stylebook and Libel Manual, ed. Norm Goldstein. Reading, Mass.: Perseus Books, 1998.

Bernstein, Theodore M. *The Careful Writer: A Modern Guide to English Usage.* New York: Atheneum, 1977.

Chicago Manual of Style. 14th ed. Chicago: University of Chicago Press, 1993.

Follett, Wilson. *Modern American Usage: A Guide* New York: Hill and Wang, 1966.

Fowler, H. W. *A Dictionary of Modern English Usage, Second Revised Edition.* London: Oxford University Press, 1987.

Legasse, Paul. *The Concise Columbia Encyclopedia.* 3d ed. New York: Columbia University Press, 1994.

Lewis, Norman. *The New Roget's Thesaurus of the English Language in Dictionary Form.* New York: Putnam, 1981.

McFarlane, J. A., and Warren Clements. *The Globe and Mail Style Book.* Toronto: Penguin Books, 1994.

Merriam-Webster's Biographical Dictionary, Springfield, Mass., 1995.

Merriam-Webster's Geographical Dictionary, Springfield, Mass., 1997. *National Geographic Atlas of the World,* 1995.

New Fowler's Modern English Usage, ed. R. W. Burchfield. 1996.

Strunk, William Jr., and E. B. White. *The Elements of Style.* 3d ed. New York: Macmillan, 1979.

Webster's New World College Dictionary, Fourth Edition. New York: Macmillan, 1999.

Webster's Third New International Dictionary of the English Language. Springfield, Mass.: Merriam-Webster, 1986.

BOOKS

Argyris, Chris. *Behind the Front Page: Organizational Self-Renewal at a Metropolitan Newspaper.* San Francisco: Jossey-Bass, 1974.

Barnhurst, Kevin G. *Seeing the Newspaper.* New York: St. Martin's Press, 1994.

Bohle, Robert H. *Publication Design for Editors.* Englewood Cliffs, N.J.: Prentice Hall, 1990.

Cohn, Victor. *News & Numbers: A Guide to Reporting Statistical Claims and Controversies.* Ames: Iowa State University Press, 1989.

Deming, W. Edwards. *Out of the Crisis.* Cambridge, Mass.: Advanced Engineering Study, 1986.

Emery, Edwin. *The Press and America: An Interpretive History of Journalism.* Englewood Cliffs N.J.: Prentice-Hall, 1962.

Evans, Harold. *Pictures on a Page: Photojournalism and Picture Editing.* Belmont, Calif.: Wadsworth, 1978.

Flesch, Rudolf. *How to be Brief: An Index to Simple Writing*. New York: Harper & Row, 1962.

Garcia, Mario. *Contemporary Newspaper Design*. 3d ed. Englewood Cliffs, N.J.: Prentice Hall, 1993.

Giles, Robert H. *Newsroom Management*. Detroit: Media Management Books, 1991.

Gunning, Robert. *The Technique of Clear Writing*. New York: McGraw Hill, 1968.

Harrower, Tim. *The Newspaper Designer's Handbook*. Portland, Ore.: 4th ed. New York: Macmillan, 1999.

Holmes, Nigel. *Designer's Guide to Creating Charts and Diagrams*. New York: Watson-Guptill, 1984.

Kobré, Ken. *Photojournalism: The Professionals' Approach*. 3d ed. Boston: Focal Press, 1995.

McDougall, Angus, and Veita Jo Hampton. *Picture Editing and Layout: A Guide to Better Visual Communication*. Columbia, Mo.: Viscom Press, 1993.

Meyer, Philip. *Precision Journalism: A Reporter's Introduction to Social Science Methods*. Bloomington: Indiana University Press, 1973.

Moen, Daryl R. *Newspaper Layout and Design*. 2d ed. Ames: Iowa State University Press, 1989.

Monmonier, Mark. *Maps with the News: The Development of American Journalistic Cartography*. Chicago: University of Chicago Press, 1989.

Nelson, Roy Paul. *Publication Design*. 4th ed. Dubuque, Ia.: Wm. C. Brown, 1987.

Newspaper Design 2000 and Beyond. Reston, Va.: American Press Institute, 1988.

Smith, Michael P., and Steve Rhodes, eds. *The Local News Idea Book*. Evanston, Ill: Knight Ridder, 1993.

Tufte, Edward R. *The Visual Display of Quantitative Information*. Chester, Conn.: Graphics Press, 1983.

PERIODICALS AND REPORTS

Anderson, N. Christian. "What exactly are they trying at the Orange County Register?" *ASNE Bulletin*, April 1991,13–14.

ASNE. *How We Can Help Each Other*. Report to the Annual Convention of the American Society of Newspaper Editors from the Human Resources Committee, April 1996. Reston, Va.: ASNE Foundation, 1996.

ASNE. *Maestro Concept: A New Approach to Writing and Editing for the Newspaper of the Future*. Video and report presented at the annual convention of the American Society of Newspaper Editors, Baltimore, Md., 1993.

ASNE. *Multicultural Newsroom: How to Get the Best from Everybody*. Manager's Guide on Leading a Diverse Work Force. Reston, Va.: ASNE Foundation, 1994.

ASNE. Return to Quality Editing. Reston, Va.: ASNE Foundation, 1997.

ASNE. Timeless Values: Staying True to Journalistic Principles in the Age of New Media. Reston, Va.: ASNE Foundation, 1995.

ASNE. Why and How Newsrooms Are Changing. Reston, Va.: ASNE
　　　Foundation, 1995.

ASNE/SND Technology Survey '96. Reston, Va.: ASNE Foundation, 1996.

Atwood, L. Erwin, and Gerald L. Grotta. "Socialization of News Values in
　　　Beginning Reporters." *Journalism Quarterly* 50:4 (Winter 1973):
　　　759–761.

Auman, Ann. "Design Desks: Why Are More and More Newspapers Adopting
　　　Them?" *Newspaper Research Journal* 15, no. 2 (Spring 1994):128–42.

———. "Seeing the Big Picture: The integrated editor of the 1990s."
　　　Newspaper Research Journal 16, no. 1 (Winter 1995):35–47.

Bowers, David R. "A Report on Activity by Publishers in Directing Newsroom
　　　Decisions." *Journalism Quarterly* 44:1 (Spring 1967):43–52.

Breed, Warren. "Newspaper 'Opinion Leaders' and Processes of
　　　Standardization." *Journalism Quarterly* 32:3 (Summer
　　　1955):277–284.

———. "Social Control in the Newsroom: A Functional Approach." *Social
　　　Forces* 33 (May 1955):326–335.

Cook, Betsy B., and Steven R. Banks. "Predictors of Job Burnout in
　　　Newspaper Reporters and Copy Editors." *Journalism Quarterly* 70,
　　　no. 1-10 (Spring 1993): 108–117.

Cook, Betsy B., Steven R. Banks, and Ralph J. Turner. "The Effects of Work
　　　Environment on Job Burnout in the Newsroom." *Newspaper Research
　　　Journal* 14 (Summer-Fall 1993):123–36.

de Sola Pool, Ithiel, and Irwin Shulman. "Newsmen's Fantasies, Audiences
　　　and News Writing." *Public Opinion Quarterly* 23 (1959):145–58.

of Journalism. Englewood Cliffs, N.J.: Prentice-Hall, 1962.

Flegel, Ruth C., and Steven H. Chaffee. "Influences of Editors, Readers and
　　　Personal Opinions on Reporters." *Journalism Quarterly* 48:4 (Winter
　　　1971): 645–651.

Fowler, Gilbert, and John Marlin Shipman. "Pagination and Job Satisfaction
　　　in American Newsrooms." Paper presented at the Association for
　　　Education in Journalism and Mass Communication Convention,
　　　Washington, D.C., August 1989.

Geiber, Walter. "How the 'Gatekeepers' View Local Civil Liberties News."
　　　Journalism Quarterly 37:1 (Spring 1960): 199–205.

Grey, David L. "Decision Making by a Reporter under Deadline Pressure."
　　　Journalism Quarterly 43:3 (Fall 1966): 419–428.

Jarris, Pam. "News 2000 Lays Foundation for Success." *Gannetteer,*
　　　September 1991: 4–5.

Rosen, Jay. "Public Journalism: First Principles." Monograph published by
　　　the Kettering Foundation, Dayton, Ohio (1994).

Russial, John. "Pagination and the Newsroom: A Question of Time."
　　　Newspaper Research Journal 15 (Winter 1994): 91–99.

———. "What Content Shows about Topic-Team Performance." Paper pre-
　　　sented at the Association for Education in Journalism and Mass
　　　Communication Convention, Anaheim, Calif., August 1996.

Slater, Michael D., Donna Rouner, and Martha Tharp. "Impact of VDTs on
　　　Structural and Mechanical Editing." *Journalism Educator* 45, no. 4
　　　(Winter 1991):44–48.

Solomon, William S. "The Process of Technology: Newspaper Copy Editors Adapt to the VDT." *Journal of Mediated Communication* 9 (3): 85–102.1993.

Underwood, Doug C., Anthony Giffard, and Keith Stamm. "Computers and Editing: Pagination's Impact on the Newsroom." *Newspaper Research Journal* 15, no. 2 (Spring 1994):116–27.

———. "How Pagination Affects Job Satisfaction of Editors." *Journalism and Mass Communication Quarterly* 72, no. 4 (Winter 1995): 851–862.

Websites

Auletta, Ken. "On the Road to Synergy City." In *The State of the American Newspaper, American Journalism Review* Newslink. ajr.newslink.org/special/part1.html, 1998.

Downie, J. Stephen. "LIS Session 12." www.lis.uiuc.edu/~jdownie/sample/survey.html

Drudge, Matt. "The Drudge Report." www.drudgereport.com.

Lynch, Patrick J., *The Yale Style Manual*. www.info.med.yale.edu/caim/manual/contents.html.

McAdams, Melinda, "Mindy McAdams' Home Page." www.well.com/user/mmcadams/index.html.

Index

Note: Italicized page locators denote photographs/illustrations.